W9-BGG-487

School-based Decision-making and Management

School-based Decision-making and Management

Edited by
Judith D. Chapman

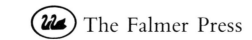 The Falmer Press

(A member of the Taylor & Francis Group)
London · New York · Philadelphia

UK The Falmer Press, Rankine Road, Basingstoke, Hampshire, RG24 0PR

USA The Falmer Press, Taylor & Francis Inc., 1900 Frost Road, Suite 101, Bristol, PA 19007

© Selection and editorial material copyright Judith D. Chapman 1990

All rights reserved. No part of this publication may be reproduced, stored in a retrieval system, or transmitted in any form or by any means, electronic, mechanical, photocopying, recording or otherwise, without permission in writing from the Publisher.

First published 1990

British Library Cataloguing in Publication Data

Chapman, Judith D.
  School-based decision-making and management.
  1. Schools. Management
  I. Title
  371.2
  ISBN 1-85000-780-2
  ISBN 1-85000-781-0 (pbk.)

Library of Congress Cataloging-in-Publication Data

School-based decision-making and management/edited by Judith
  D. Chapman.
    p. cm.
  Includes bibliographical references.
  ISBN 1-85000-780-2 ISBN 1-85000-781-0 (pbk.)
  1. School management and organization—Decision making.
  2. Teacher participation in administration. I. Chapman,
  Judith D.
LB2806.S3415 1990
371.2′07—dc20   90-31781
                                                    CIP

Jacket design by Benedict Evans

Set in 10½/13 Bembo by
Graphicraft Typesetters Ltd, Hong Kong

Printed in Great Britain by Burgess Science Press, Basingstoke on paper which has a specified pH value on final paper manufacture of not less than 7.5 and is therefore 'acid free'.

371.207
Sch65

Contents

Contents

Part 3 Perspectives on Practice

Part 4 Research Findings

Part 5 Summation

Lists of Tables and Figures

Tables

Figures

Lists of Tables and Figures

Foreword

'Local school management' has been claimed as a panacea, proposed as a solution or implemented as a policy in many countries' school systems. Its virtues are maintained to be many but chief among them must surely be those of the relocation of the focus of decision-making away from a central bureaucracy into the hands of the local community and, with that, of ensuring the availability of a more immediately sensitive process of accountability. At the same time, it is claimed, the local institution of school-based decision-making will relieve central authority of much of the tedium of detailed management and budgetary control. It cannot be entirely fortuitous that this approach has coincided with the arrival and adoption of policies of economic rationalism and political minimalism that have been widely promulgated and taken up in many countries.

It was high time that these claims, proposals or actual implementations of policy in the administration of educational institutions should be subjected to critical appraisal and review. First, it is not self-evident that delivering control and management of such institutions into local hands will automatically bring about all or indeed any of the advantages widely claimed for them. Experience in the UK, for example, might tend to suggest that, while an increase in autonomy will confer some benefits, a parallel increase in financial obligations and burdens can lead to outcomes that militate directly against some of the educational goals for which local communities are also concerned and for which they are also suddenly responsible.

Dr Chapman has assembled contributions from an impressive array of leading international experts in the field of educational studies, who have subjected the claims of this most recent feature of educational administration policies, its theory, meta-theory, principles and practice to rigorous scrutiny. Writing from a wide range of perspectives — from the standpoints of the so-called educational disciplines right through to organizational application — the writers working together in this volume mount a powerful weight of argument to demonstrate that the implementation of local school management policies is by no means so simple or so easy as its proponents believe. Their analyses show that the adoption of such policies is a matter requiring much greater theoretical sophistication than has hitherto appeared in the pronouncements of its defenders, while its institutional implementation at the local and systemic levels will be in any case an enterprise fraught with contentiousness, and considerable practical difficulty, that may also bid fair to compromise other goals to which its supporters at local and system levels are committed.

In this way the volume is a model of the best kind of research now being undertaken in leading educational institutions: policy-related, subtle and informed, and drawing upon the insights provided by a range of disciplinary perspectives and practical experience, it provides sober yet responsible comment and caution upon those avenues of supposed advance in the organization and administration of educational institutions down which less well-informed politicians, bureaucrats and local interest groups often seek to lead us. The contributions of all the scholars in this volume demonstrate how illusory the prospects of reform such parties hold out to us might well prove to be. In this way they provide citizens who have ultimately the task and indeed the social responsibility of evaluating and finally judging these and other such ideas with a touchstone against which their theoretical value and practical realizability may with value be measured.

Dr Chapman's editing of all these varied contributions into a clear and consequentially argued whole is a valuable and insightful presentation of their combined point and force. It is also a manifestation of and a tribute to the quality of the work produced as a result of the research effort of the School Decision Making and Management Centre in the Faculty of Education at Monash University, of which she is Director. I have been stimulated and encouraged by reading this volume and I commend it to policy-makers, administrators, teachers, community leaders and parents — in fact, to all those in any way involved in the education service: it offers for the consideration of the former and the improvement of the latter a closely argued, experience-based and academically integrated set of critical comments, conclusions and suggestions that demand the most serious and careful attention of both.

D.N. Aspin
Monash University

Preface

School-based management refers to a form of educational administration in which the school becomes the primary unit for decision-making. It differs from more traditional forms of educational administration in which a central bureaucracy dominated the decision-making process. In recent years many school systems have moved towards a school-based approach. This has resulted in a wide range of decisions relevant to such areas as curriculum, personnel and budgeting being made by members of the school community at the school site. In this book school-based decision-making and management is examined.

The book is structured into five parts. In Part 1 international developments in school-based decision-making and management are documented and analyzed. In Part 2 theoretical perspectives are offered and in Part 3 these are complemented by perspectives on practice. Part 4 contains the findings of research conducted in school systems that have moved towards school-based decision-making and management and Part 5 contains an analysis of school-based decision-making and management based on the contents of this book and a discussion of future prospects in the field.

In Chapter 1 Brian Caldwell describes developments in selected countries, namely Australia, Canada, France, New Zealand, the United Kingdom and the United States, where changes in the organization of education have taken place. Attention is given to the concepts which seem appropriate to describe the shift in responsibility to the school level, with the concept 'self-management' being considered most appropriate. An analysis of issues associated with self-management is then provided. The chapter concludes with a discussion of the approaches which in certain countries are proving to be effective in coping with change at both the school and system levels.

Chapter 2 begins Part 2 on theoretical perspectives. In this chapter

Terri Seddon, Lawrie Angus and Millicent Poole examine the broad economic and political dynamics that have contributed to the rise of school-based decision-making and management as an administrative strategy. The authors argue that conventional literature has presented an overly optimistic view of school-based decision-making and management as a significant democratic reform. Such literature, they argue, fails to analyze school-based decision-making and management within an historical context or in relation to social and political spheres; it therefore neglects institutional social power relationships which are unlikely to be interrupted by administrative rearrangements. Analysis of educational administration, they argue, should see education as an integral part of the contemporary social order. Further research into school decision-making and management would therefore treat it as an historically specific form of educational governance that is linked to particular patterns of social conflict and to ways of politically managing conflict. This chapter adds to an emerging theory of context in examining school-based decision-making and management from the perspective of the relationship between education and society.

In Chapter 3 Colin Evers employs arguments from the theory of knowledge, control theory and economics to challenge the claim that a hierarchical, centralized decision structure is the mode of organization most likely to promote efficient decision-making. His central argument is that hierarchical organizations, at best, promote the reliable transmission and diffusion of directives. Against this he points to a Popperian theory of knowledge and its stress on the fallibility of directives and its emphasis on error correction. The growth of knowledge in general proceeds by a process of conjecture and refutation, Evers argues. Thus at the organizational level he suggests that decision-making can be improved by the provision of structures for promoting organizational learning. For educational organizations these structures need to involve the participation, at all levels, of those most likely to be aware of the consequences of decision-making. In this way a very broad range of consequences can be detected. Evers concludes that, given suitable organizational arrangements, participation and efficiency in decision-making go hand in hand.

However, in the following chapter, 'What Price Democracy?', some of the costs of participation are highlighted. Whilst acknowledging that participative, collaborative decision-making at the school level may be an ideal, Gabriele Lakomski argues that its realization raises problems which are largely unrecognized in the educational community. The problems which she highlights are of a technical nature. Informed by Arrow's Impossibility Theorem she argues that there is no procedure for voting or making formal choices that is simultaneously rational, decisive and egalitarian. Such generally accepted and desired criteria, Arrow revealed, are incompatible. Lakomski claims it therefore follows that if we want egalitarian decision procedures, then we have to give up the idea that the decisions made will be rational and decisive. If we adopt a consensus procedure, it is at the cost of being able to make decisive choices; if we want decisive choices, we ought to opt for dictatorship.

In the final two chapters of this section perspectives are offered on broader system-wide concerns relevant to school decision-making and management. In Chapter 5 Jim Walker argues that the issue should be understood in the context of the debate over centralization versus decentralization. This debate, he claims, has been conducted almost completely in terms of geographical criteria. He proposes an alternative pattern of school organization based on functional decentralization. Schools performing particular functions, he argues, should be accountable to those with legitimate interests in those functions. There is an argument, Walker claims, for reconstructing functionally the role of the local school in terms of the meeting of local needs.

Also addressing school decision-making and management in the context of centralization versus decentralization, John Hattie, in Chapter 6, takes up the issue of accountability. He points out that when a school system devolves responsibility, typically it needs to ensure that its dollars are appropriately and well spent, that quality education is provided, that the school syllabus is followed and that schools are minimally efficient. Whilst some critics have maintained that to do this while saying that schools are primarily responsible is paradoxical, Hattie argues that it is not necessarily the case that there is a conflict between an emphasis on accountability of performance, on one hand, and local autonomy on the other. Accordingly, he proposes a model of decision-making which enables people at the school level to have a critical role in the accountability process. Let us involve participants at the school level, says Hattie, to formulate evaluation plans, to determine processes, and beyond this to conduct evaluations and assess their methods, but in addition, let metaevaluators assess the quality of evaluation received from many schools. Accountability, Hattie argues, is relative. Parents and students at the school level need real options and much information about the relative effectiveness of different teachers and different schools. People at the school level have a prime role in evaluation; the system has a prime role in ensuring accountability.

Other responsibilities of people at the school level are taken up in Part 3 of the book, 'Perspectives on Practice'. The first chapter describes ways in which schools can develop their self-management capabilities. The author, Jim Spinks, indicates the ways in which need identification and goal-setting, policy-making, priority-setting, strategic planning, curriculum planning, resource allocation, program implementation and evaluation can be linked together to form an annual cycle of school planning aimed at school effectiveness and improvement. This approach is now being widely used in the United Kingdom, New Zealand and Australia as a basis for schools to develop their management capabilities.

The theme of managing for school improvement is expanded in Chapter 8 in which Colin Marsh reviews the literature on school improvement and coalesces the ideas into general approaches or 'models'. These approaches are offered as conceptual maps for school-based personnel to apply and vary to suit the needs of their particular schools. Included in the approaches are the situational analysis model, the collaborative school management model, the concerns-based adoption model, the people-centred model, the organization development model and the action research model.

The development of school-based personnel is the focus of Chapter 9, in which Lawrence Ingvarson discusses the conditions which will stimulate and enable professional development policy-making and planning to become an integral part of schools. Ingvarson argues that the professional culture within a school is a major determinant of the effectiveness of any professional development activity, and the authority to exercise responsibility for staff development in schools actually restructures staff relationships so that the 'steady work' of maintaining and enhancing the quality of education can occur. To be effective, Ingvarson suggests that the purposes of professional development must be conceived as much in terms of enhancing professional relationships and mutual responsibilities as they are in terms of individual teacher development.

From personnel needs, the next chapter moves to a consideration of the information needs of a school. If schools are allocated new responsibilities, Phillip McKenzie says in Chapter 10, it is critical that they have access to the information necessary to perform those tasks in an effective manner. Four major types of necessary information are identified: information that monitors the institutional health of the schools, work and learning environment; analytical frameworks that permit schools to explore the implications of alternative strategies; means of clarifying the value positions that underpin school decision-making; and tools that facilitate institutional self-evaluation. The discussion concludes that policies to encourage a greater degree of school level decision-making need not unleash a massive new round of information collection, collation and analysis. In most instances the necessary raw material is seen already to be held either at school or central level as a by-product of routine administrative functions. Therefore, McKenzie argues that the emphasis should be on assisting schools to transform that material into a more usable and relevant shape. In this regard McKenzie sees that action is needed on four fronts: schools have to become convinced that an investment of time and resources in local decision-making is likely to be worthwhile; existing forms of data held within schools and central administration need to be catalogued, integrated and key indicators of school operations extracted; summary information on other schools and their programs needs to be provided by central administration so that individual schools have a broader context for understanding their own operations; and analytical frameworks need to be developed that enable schools to explore alternative ways of using school resources.

In Chapter 11 Brian Spicer addresses this issue of effective utilization of resources. Arguing for the adoption of 'strategic management' as the key approach to school management, he outlines the elements of resource management and curriculum management decision-making. While his emphasis in this chapter is on program budgeting strategies, Spicer makes it clear that he is arguing most strongly for an integration of decision-making. Ultimately resource management decisions are integral to, not separate from, decisions about educational goals, curriculum and student evaluations, he argues. If we recognize the significance of this integration, he concludes, then we shall avoid the danger that any movement towards the business model in educational management may create in placing more stress on money rather than on people and learning.

Part 3 of the book contains four chapters which report on experiences in school systems which have moved towards a school-based approach to decision-making and management. In Chapter 12 developments in Australian schools are outlined and research findings that have revealed the implications for school-based personnel are discussed. Attention is focused on the redistribution of influence, alteration in the relationships among people, and the necessity for school-based personnel to adopt new roles.

In Chapter 13 emphasis is placed on school-based decision-making and teacher unions. Theories of corporatism and the state are used by Jill Blackmore to elaborate upon the theme of how the democratic theory of decision-making and management in Australia was incorporated and eventually modified within a new administrative framework of corporate management. Although school-based decision-making and management was the focus of this new form of reorganization, it is argued that the participative character of school-based decision-making and management has been subsumed into the rhetoric of efficiency and effectiveness. Blackmore argues that teachers see many of the more progressive elements of the reforms gained through teacher action at the school level submerged, negated or absorbed by system level negotiations between bureaucracies and educational organizations. School decision-making and management, she concludes, has become focused more on market than democratic principles and this has implications for teacher professionalism and autonomy.

Chapter 14 changes the focus from personnel issues to the curriculum. In this chapter Andrew Sturman reports on the findings of research designed to examine the effects upon the curriculum of the decentralization of decision-making. In studying the relationship between changes in the control of curriculum decision-making and the nature of the curriculum, Sturman uses the concept of 'frames', arguing that the freedom of teachers to make decisions about curriculum is constrained by four frames: the system frame, the school frame, the community frame and the individual frame. These four frames relate in turn to different types of decentralization. Emerging from this research is the development of a framework for analyzing curriculum decision-making at the school level.

In the final chapter of this section Fazal Rizvi examines the available data on experiments which have been used by those who have sought to carve out a practical balance between the need for public audit regarding the efficient use of resources in education and the goal of school-based decision-making. In considering the attempts to resolve the tensions posed by these seemingly competing requirements, he seeks to describe the practical politics of reform committed to school-based decision-making. Drawing on extensive evaluation material, he suggests that the requirements of public accountability and school-based decision-making and management are not as irreconcilable as many educational writers have suggested.

Part 4 of the book contains a summation of its contents, presented by Patrick Duignan, and a discussion of future prospects of school-based decision-making and management.

This ends a collection of writing which, it is hoped, will provide insights to scholars, practitioners and students of educational administration. The collection has been made possible through the contributions of a wide range of individuals and organizations. In offering my appreciation I should like to highlight my gratitude to Professor Mal Logan, Vice-Chancellor of Monash University, who, in his support for the creation of the School-Based Decision-Making and Management Centre, provided an organizational base for dialogue, research and writing in the field. I should also like to pay tribute to the scholars and practitioners who contributed chapters to this volume and to those who attended the invited conference on School-Based Decision-Making and Management at Woodend. For the organization of this conference I would like to express my appreciation to Ms Helen Modra and in the review of papers of a philosophical kind I should like to thank Dr Colin Evers. With this book, as with all efforts associated with the School Decision Making and Management Centre, I am especially grateful to the Reference Group of the Centre and to Lawrie Angus, Vern Wilkinson and especially to Julie Gray.

Judith Chapman

Part 1
Developments

Chapter 1

School-based Decision-making and Management: International Developments

Brian Caldwell

If an international perspective among many Western nations is adopted, there has, in recent years, been an assumption of greater responsibility for decision-making at the school level. But to consider this trend or the concept of 'school-based decision-making' in isolation can be misleading since these developments have occurred at the same time as there has been a significant assumption or regaining of power at the system level. In other words, trends of a decentralizing and centralizing nature have occurred at roughly the same time. Thus any comprehensive examination of school-based decision-making in the international context is incomplete unless the underlying causes, issues and tensions associated with both trends are considered together.

The first part of this chapter is devoted to a description of trends in Australia, Canada, France, New Zealand, United Kingdom (England and Wales) and the United States. Attention is then given to concepts which seem appropriate to describe the shift of responsibility to the school level in the broader context outlined above, with the concept of 'self-management' considered the more appropriate. The second part of the chapter is devoted to an analysis of issues associated with self-management. Seven issues are identified: factors underlying shifts in patterns of management, tensions in centralization and decentralization, the extent of the focus on teaching and learning rather than a narrow concern for management, equity in resource allocation among schools, system support for schools, time and the apparent importance of an evolutionary approach to the institutionalization of change, and evaluation and testing. The chapter concludes on an optimistic note, with brief reference to approaches which are proving effective in coping with change at school and system levels.

Trends in Centralization and Decentralization

Australia

Education is a state responsibility in Australia and, for more than 100 years until the early 1970s, public education at primary and secondary levels was administered in each state through highly centralized state government departments of education. Curriculum was for the most part determined centrally, with tight control exercised through an inspectorial system and state-wide external examinations at the end of secondary schooling. Most funds for education came from state sources, with centralized allocation of resources which provided little money for discretionary use by schools other than that raised by voluntary contributions from parents and the local community. The federal government provided very limited support until the 1960s when aid for libraries and science facilities in both public and private schools was introduced.

There have been dramatic changes to this pattern of governance since the early 1970s. In a major change of a centralizing nature the federal government became involved in a very significant way through the Australian Commonwealth Schools Commission established in 1973. A comprehensive grants scheme administered by the Commission for both public and private schools was designed to achieve greater equity among schools and equality of opportunity for students. The task of administration in state departments of education became immediately more complex, with several states, notably Tasmania, decentralizing to the school level decisions related to a substantial portion of recurrent grants received from the Commission. The early 1970s were also marked by administrative decentralization of education departments through the formation of regional units in several states. South Australia and the Australian Capital Territory led the way in providing greater freedom and autonomy for schools, with provision in both instances for school councils or boards having advisory and limited decision-making powers.

The trend to a decentralized system of school governance continued most markedly in Victoria. Administrative decentralization to regional units proceeded throughout the 1970s and 1980s. In 1975 the state government required all public schools to establish school councils of teachers, parents and other members of the school community. Several models were offered as a guide, with most providing powers of advice only to the principal and staff. These initiatives in regionalization and decentralization to the school level were taken by a relatively conservative Liberal government. In 1983, however, the election to government of the

Australian Labor Party saw a dramatic change, with substantial commitment to further decentralization and devolution.

The government in Victoria gave consideration in late 1986 to recommendations of its Ministry Structures Project Team which would allow public schools meeting certain criteria to become 'self-governing'. Such schools would be fully funded by the state but, apart from operating a program consistent with the general policies and priorities of the government, would be governed independently by their councils. While ultimately rejecting the concept of 'self-governing schools', the government agreed to decentralize further in the areas of curriculum, special programs, finance and facilities and, at the same time, provide stronger direction and support to schools through reorganized and expanded operations at the regional level.

While the most extensive change of a decentralizing nature has come in Victoria, there are similar changes under way in other states, notably Western Australia (Western Australia, Ministry of Education, 1987), where 'self-determining schools' with 'school-based decision-making groups' describe what is proposed, and the Northern Territory (Northern Territory, Department of Education, 1987), where the term 'devolution' is preferred. Trial or pilot schemes for substantial decentralization of decisions related to the allocation of resources, including staff, are under consideration in Tasmania and Queensland.

There is evidence, however, of centralization or recentralization in the areas of curriculum and testing. In 1988 the Minister of Education, Employment and Training (Commonwealth) indicated that the Commonwealth Government desired a national curriculum framework and provision for a national testing program. Despite initial scepticism (since powers with respect to education lie with the states) it was apparent at the time of writing that states will cooperate, a response shaped in large measure by state reliance on financial support from the Commonwealth. At the state level, too, governments are now formulating strategic plans and specifying priorities which must be addressed by schools.

Canada

Education is a provincial responsibility in Canada, with the school district being the unit for local policy-making and administration. Leithwood and Begley (1986, p. 92) report 'increased centralization of decision-making in most provinces and in many school systems', especially in the areas of curriculum and testing. They also noted a trend to school-based planning and participative decision-making, with principals now expected to 'give more than token instructional leadership' (Leithwood and Begley, 1986, p. 72).

As far as decentralization to the school level is concerned, practice in one school system is attracting national and international attention. Indeed, it is now becoming in some respects a model for what is happening elsewhere. In the Edmonton Public School District in Alberta the change as far as schools are concerned is described as an initiative in 'school-site decision-making'. A comprehensive account of decentralization in Canada is offered by Sackney and Dibski (1989) and Brown (1987).

Edmonton is an urban system with about 60,000 students. Over a period of ten years decisions related to the allocation of resources for teaching and ancillary staff, equipment, supplies and services have been decentralized to schools. This means that the principal and staff of a large high school must plan for the allocation of several million dollars each year. Staff are hired centrally but are selected by principals. Salaries and working conditions are established for the system as a whole in collective bargaining between the organization representing the interests of teachers and the school board. Average salaries are used as the unit cost of a teacher in planning at the school level. The school board (the governing body for schools in the district) has determined broad goals for the system and annually sets priorities for all schools. Schools are free to determine their own pattern of resource allocation, with the only constraints being that they must address system as well as local goals and priorities and must take account of conditions which are specified in collective agreements. District-wide standardized tests in language, social studies, mathematics and science are conducted in Grades 3, 6 and 9. Annual system-wide and school-based surveys of all principals, teachers, parents and students seek opinion on the quality of education and educational services.

Of special interest in Edmonton is a trial of school-level planning for the use of centralized curriculum and student services. These services have traditionally been available to schools upon request and are not usually considered in a school's annual educational plan. Fourteen schools reflecting diversity in the district were selected for a trial in 1986–87. These schools had their lump-sum budget allocations supplemented by amounts which reflected the historical use of these services according to type of school and level of student need. Standard costs for various types of service were then determined, on a per hour or per incident basis, with costs charged to the school as service was provided. Participating schools were free to acquire these services from any source: from the central office, from other schools or from outside the system. It is noteworthy that the level of utilization of central services declined in the first year of the trial, with schools opting in many instances to acquire services from other sources to solve their problems. For example, additional teachers were acquired or expertise was obtained ('purchased') from other schools.

France

France has traditionally been considered highly centralized as far as the organization of education is concerned, with legislation in the 1980s serving to introduce a measure of decentralization. A closer examination reveals, however, that the traditional stereotype and recent intentions are an oversimplification.

Secondary schools in France have always been corporate institutions, with a board of governors having control over their budgets and legal responsibility for what transpires. This framework for autonomy has prevailed since pre-revolutionary times, but much freedom for action was subsequently lost when boards of governors became the subjects of control in a hierarchy of centralized administration in government. Decentralization in modern times began in 1969 as a response to the turmoil of 1968. In this respect, then, secondary schooling might be regarded as traditionally 'school-centred', with centralization over a long period of time followed by decentralization, or a return to 'school-centredness', as central controls have been released.

The reforms of 1969 resulted in wide participation in the governing body of a secondary school, with representatives of the immediate school community (staff, parents, students), personalities from the local community such as the mayor or a councillor, representatives of employer or employee unions, and nominees of the principal. The principal, who is centrally appointed, serves as chairperson of this body which has the power of decision on the budget and on regulations pertaining to the life of the school but is advisory only in all other matters. The budget does not include personnel; staff are employed, selected and placed by the state.

Substantial progress for all schools was made in 1982–84, with local authorities rather than the state becoming responsible for financial support, and with powers of secondary boards extended in some areas. While the selection and placement of teachers remain highly centralized, each school now receives a lump-allocation of teaching hours, with the principal determining the mix of staff needed for the particular program offered by the school. An attempt to decentralize decisions related to curriculum and instruction came in 1984 when a five-year plan of limited scope for the college level (for students 11–15 years of age) was launched, but little has been achieved to date.

Traditionally, French primary schools have been directed by the inspectorate in both administrative and pedagogical roles. Principals were teachers (released from teaching tasks according to the size of the school) with special responsibilities for functions such as coordination, organization, relations with parents and security. They are the link between the local (state) inspector and the teachers. The Chirac Government attempted by decree to increase the powers of principals, especially in areas of staffing and curriculum, but was only partly successful following union opposition. It seems that teachers prefer to keep authority afar rather than near. A compromise resulted in an increase in salary for primary principals.

There has been a change in 1988 as far as the appointment of principals is concerned. A process of local selection from the ranks of teachers has been replaced by selection on the basis of written and oral examination. In several ways, then, there are some inconsistencies in the pattern of decentralization.

In general, what has emerged in France is at least a partial return to 'school-centredness' which, to some extent, is a result of a loss of power at the centre in a national system of such size that it is difficult if not impossible for a minister to ensure implementation with fidelity. But changes are not occurring easily, with tensions which are similar to those encountered in other nations.

New Zealand

Perhaps the most dramatic change is unfolding in New Zealand where the government has accepted (Lange, 1988) the major recommendations of the Picot Report (Picot, 1988) which called for a virtual transfer of decision-making from the system to the school level. From late 1989 each school will have a school board, the majority of which will be parents, with a charter which, once approved by the Minister, will provide a framework for operations. More than 90 per cent of the costs of running each school will be decentralized to the school level in a school-based budget. Staff will be selected and employed by the school board.

There will be a national curriculum framework in New Zealand but the number of staff employed at the system level will be relatively few, serving mainly to monitor (or audit) operations at the school level and to provide limited support to schools, especially in the area of special education services. In general, however, the support of schools will be secured in a quasi-free market arrangement in which schools will plan and acquire the services they need from whatever source they feel appropriate and using their own funds.

The Picot Report concluded that 'the present administrative structure is overcentralized and made overly complex by having too many decision points' and believed that an 'effective administrative system must be as simple as possible and decisions should be made as close as possible to where they are carried out' (Picot, 1988, p. xi). Yet it should be noted that New Zealand schools will start from a point which is relatively decentralized in the centralization–decentralization continuum compared to that which prevailed before recent initiatives in countries such as Australia, France and to some extent Canada and the United States. Writing in 1981, Barrington stated, 'What is certain ... is that formal provisions for parental or lay participation in school government is at least as extensive in New Zealand as in any other Western country' (p. 157).

Currently in New Zealand each primary school has a school committee of local householders elected every two years. Provincial education boards are formed from representatives of school committees, with boards having responsibility for a range of tasks including the appointment of teachers and the allocation of grants. Most secondary schools are controlled and managed by a board of governors with strong representation from parents and other members of the community. Interest in an even larger amount of community involvement was apparent throughout the 1970s with a broadly conceived Educational Development Conference, for example, involving about 60,000 people in some 4000 discussion groups. It seems that existing structures did not allow the degree of influence that many desired and that powers formerly held had been lost to school boards and the central department. Barrington (1981) described the situation in the following terms:

> The seventies witnessed a strong expression of opinion by some parents, chiefly expressed through the Educational Development Conference, for the balance to tip back in their favour, giving them a greater and more effective say in how schools are governed. Historical evolution left School Committees, in particular, with only very minor responsibilities, their rights being largely limited to participating in the election of the Education Board, deciding in consultation with the Principal whether or not thirty minutes of religious instruction a week should be allowed in the school, maintaining school premises and undertaking minor

financial administration including the payment of the care-
taker. . . .

Secondary school Boards of Governors have, over the years, also
lost much ground to the central Department and in terms of their
remaining authority bear little resemblance to their nineteenth
century forebears. (pp. 164, 166)

Interest throughout the 1970s in a greater degree of community
involvement in New Zealand, in education and in other fields of public
endeavour, clearly paralleled that in Australia and many other Western
countries. It is interesting that in some ways it paralleled the return to
'school-centredness' which was noted in the French context. The government response to the Picot Report in 1988 ensures that this return will
now take place.

United Kingdom (England and Wales)

The policies of the Thatcher Government provide the most graphic
evidence to date that 'the traditional balance of autonomy, power and
accountability in education is being redefined' in Britain (Ranson and
Tomlinson, 1986, p. 3). The following initiatives, which apply to England and Wales only, are embodied in the 1988 Education Act:

a national core curriculum and provision for national testing and
reporting;

control over school budgets to be given to governing bodies and
principals of all secondary schools and many primary schools within
five years;

increasing parental choice by fostering diversity and increasing
access;

allowing state schools to opt out of local education authority (LEA)
control on a majority vote of parents, with grants from the national
government being made directly to the school.

The significance of these developments is evident, given that there
has never been a national curriculum. There will be a national testing
program at two points in primary education and two points in secondary
education, with results made public on a school-by-school basis. These
intentions are essentially centralizing in nature and are consistent with the
general pattern which is emerging in many Western countries. As for
intentions which are essentially decentralizing, there is great significance

in making provision for schools to opt out of LEA control. This will allow schools to leave when, for example, a majority of parents do not support contentious aspects of the curriculum which have been proposed by a local authority. In some instances it may be an opportunity for schools which were formerly selective grammar schools to leave after a number of years as comprehensive schools. In the case of budget control being devolved to schools, generally described as local financial management (LFM) or local management of schools (LMS), the initiative follows successful trials by a number of authorities. A catalyst for greater responsiveness by schools and school systems comes through the fostering of greater choice and diversity and removal of restrictions on school attendance.

The net effect of these changes for England and Wales is a loss of power of the local authority which is essentially the educational arm of county or borough government. The national government has clearly taken a more powerful role in curriculum areas where decisions have traditionally been taken at the local or school levels. Local authority has also been weakened with the shift in budget responsibility, including wider powers with respect to staff, to the school level. It appears that the national government is 'trading' on public dissatisfaction with the quality of education and, by association, with local education authorities, effectively to curtail the role of the latter. In this respect what has transpired in England may be viewed as a 'consumer-led' reform shaped by the interests and concerns of parents, in contrast to earlier changes which might be regarded as 'producer-led' reforms shaped by the interests and concerns of teachers and other professionals. It is interesting to note, however, that direct parent involvement in school governance is relatively low, partly it might seem as a result of earlier reforms which were influenced so heavily by professionals.

United States of America

As in Canada, education in the United States is constitutionally a state responsibility, with the school district the unit of local policy-making and administration. The federal government has a limited and, recently, diminishing role which is restricted mainly to particular areas of financial support.

There have been recommendations from influential individuals and organizations in the United States for the adoption of school-site or school-based management. For example, the National Governors' Association has called for 'incentives and technical assistance to districts to promote school-site management and improvement', reflecting a belief that 'providing discretionary resources to schools gives them a major incentive to improve. Where this has been tried, it has unleashed creative energies and helped schools develop a diversity of approaches and strategies to meet particular goals' (National Governors' Association, 1986, p. 59). The National Education Association, the largest union of teachers in the United States, and the National Association of Secondary School Principals issued a joint report which stated that 'the NASSP and NEA remain committed to the principle that substantial decision-making authority at the school site is the essential pre-requisite for quality education' (NEA–NASSP, 1986, p. 13).

While interest in school-site management is to some extent a revival of interest in a practice which was adopted in a few school districts in the 1970s, what is now occurring in the United States is best seen as part of the so-called second wave of educational reform, with the first wave being the many state commissions and regulations and the diminution of federal involvement which followed the report of the National Commission on Excellence in Education (1983). The first wave of reform saw centralization at the state level of some functions, including curriculum and tests; the second wave involves decentralization of other functions, with the focus being the school and the support of schools.

It should be noted, however, that support for school-site management is not yet widely based, despite the recommendations of influential groups and advocacy by union leaders such as Albert Shanker, President of the American Federation of Teachers. Despite earlier interest in the 1970s and recent recommendations, relatively few school districts have taken the initiative. It seems that there are tensions between the nature and purpose of the first and second waves of reform.

A Cautionary Note

Not all Western countries are experiencing changes of the kind under consideration in this chapter and not all intentions regarding decentralization are coming to reality. In Germany, for example, concepts like decentralization and school-based decision-making have little meaning: schools are very much part of a system and when change occurs it is intended to be system-wide. Even within this pattern of stability in Germany, with a system rather than school focus when it comes to change, it is worth noting that there is no centralization of assessment: it is difficult to make comparison between schools. But public knowledge of assessment at the school level is relatively high and in some ways similar to what is sought in other countries. Parents are informed about the range of marks in each class for every test and where in this range the marks of their children are located. But practice in Germany warns against 'mind sets' as far as centralization and decentralization are concerned.

In a further contrast, plans for a substantial shift in responsibility to the school level have not come to fruition in Italy where important changes have been underway since 1974 when boards of education at the school, district, provincial and national levels (*organi collegiali*) were established:

> They were set up in an attempt to delegate certain tasks or decisions to local, elected boards with representation of all social groups concerned. They acknowledge the principle that within a common framework local characteristics require context-focused considerations and a wider base of representation and involvement in decision-making. The intention is that this new structure should encourage decentralised initiative focused on local needs while maintaining a centralised approach to overall policy decision-making. (Ricatti, 1986, p. 186)

It seems, however, that many of these changes have not yet had the impact implied in the intentions.

In general, then, what has emerged in this review of trends is a shift to the school level of authority and responsibility to make certain decisions which were formerly made at the system or central level. Significant powers in others areas have been retained or regained at the centre.

Conceptualizing the Change from the School Perspective

The concept of 'school-based decision-making' is perhaps too broad to capture what is happening on the international scene. There has always been 'school-based decision-making', but shifts in patterns of management call for a more narrowly constrained concept. Some difficulties arise here since efforts to increase the autonomy of schools have differed in scope and nomenclature. In Britain, where the focus in decentralization has been largely on decisions related to the allocation of financial resources, the initiative has been described by pioneering authorities as Local Financial Management (Cambridgeshire) and the School Financial Autonomy Scheme (Solihull), although the more general term Local Management of Schools (LMS) is now preferred. In Canada the initial focus in Edmonton, Alberta was also on the school budget, with the practice described as school-based budgeting. With the introduction of teacher effectiveness programs and school-by-school approaches to program evaluation, school-site decision-making became the preferred descriptor. In Victoria, Australia the general term 'devolution' has been used to describe the quite sweeping change to the pattern of school governance which began with the enactment of legislation giving policy powers to school councils. The term 'self-governing school' was used in a proposal to give a very high measure of autonomy to state schools meeting certain requirements. 'Self-determining' school and 'school-based decision-making groups' have been used in Western Australia. In the small number of districts in the United States where changes along these lines have been made a financial focus was known as school-site or school-based budgeting, with a more comprehensive approach, especially where teacher and community involvement was sought, being described as school-site or school-based management.

The term 'self-management' seems a more appropriate concept to describe what is emerging at the school level. A self-managing school may be defined as one for which there has been significant and consistent decentralization of authority to make decisions related to the operation of the school. This decentralization is administrative rather than political, with decisions at the school level made within a framework of local, state or national policies and guidelines. The school remains accountable to a central authority as well as to its community.

A capacity for self-management is required at the school level when a central authority such as a nation, a state or a school system, for all schools in the system, sets goals, establishes priorities, defines outcomes, supplies resources (in the narrow sense of buildings, staff and money), and then provides each school, operating within this framework, with the responsibility and authority to make all of the decisions about how the particular needs and interests of each student will be addressed.

Some Issues in New Patterns of Management in Education

A number of issues have emerged in countries where there have been developments of the kind under consideration in this chapter. Seven are identified: factors underlying shifts in patterns of management, tensions in centralization and decentralization, the extent of the focus on teaching and learning rather than a narrow concern for management, equity in resource allocation among schools, system support for schools, time and the apparent importance of an evolutionary approach to the institutionalization of change, and evaluation and testing. Some promising approaches to resolving these issues are identified.

Underlying Factors

An examination of factors underlying the adoption of new patterns of management is interesting in light of the fact that initiatives have come from different ends of the political spectrum. Seven factors are identified here which, together, readily account for the broad appeal of these patterns. Particular attention is given to factors which seem to account for the decentralizing trend.

First, it seems that many of the initiatives as far as decentralization is concerned are a government response to complexity. In a contribution to a conceptual guide on school improvement van Velzen and Robin (1985) offered an account of the recent and emerging environment for education. They describe a transition from an industrial society to an information society, with the latter characterized by ready access to information, multiple options, a reduction in common interest, continual change in the nature of industrial life and international interdependence. Tensions have arisen — pluralism, individuality, a redefinition of the family, the development of networks and volatility — so that change, including turbulence, is a 'permanent condition' (van Velzen and Robin, 1985, p. 21). The challenge for schools lies in a number of areas: helping students cope with changes in the way of life, developing competence through a constantly changing curriculum, preparing students for effective use of an increasing amount of leisure time, developing high levels of talent among all students, meeting manpower requirements and developing social competence, all to be accomplished in a period of demographic and economic contraction. The dilemmas, according to these writers, are conservation versus change, equity versus excellence and the debate is about quality in education.

In this environment a substantial amount of decentralization is an appropriate response. A recent OECD report notes that: 'the recent experience of ... OECD countries shows that it is increasingly difficult, if not impossible, to control complex modern education systems from a single centre' (OECD, 1986, p. 23). Yet, almost paradoxically, schools must more than ever before respond to the changing needs of their society, necessitating a framework of policies and priorities determined at the system level. An implication here is that decentralization is to some extent a reaction rather than the outcome of policy-making in an active or rational mode. Expressed more bluntly, a case might be made that 'the state can't govern anymore' in some circumstances. A shift in power may really be a state of powerlessness.

Second, on the other hand, interest in a state or national curriculum along with standardized testing — a centralizing trend — seems to reflect the view that a system of education must also make a contribution to the well-being of the nation. This reason has been offered quite explicitly in several of the countries considered in this chapter. In each instance there has been concern that the nation has been 'falling behind' in an economic sense and that a major factor in improving the situation is education. A state or national curriculum, with a testing program to monitor progress, has been the response.

Third, returning to factors which seem to account for the decentralizing trend, another explanation seems to lie in a new view of equity (this analysis is based on Murphy and Hallinger, 1986). The major value driving public policy over the last 100 years has been equity. In the later nineteenth century, at the time when governments took the initiative in providing education which was 'free, compulsory and secular', equity was conceived largely in terms of access to a school for all children. Concern then shifted to ensuring that all children had access to the same general set of resources, with money being the major resource in most instances. Governments at the national or state level became more extensively involved through a series of special grants to redress various kinds of personal or social disadvantage. In the United States and Canada the 1960s and 1970s were marked by a shift from reliance on a local property tax to major support from the state or provincial governments, in response to public dissatisfaction with the inequities of the tax base in different communities. In one national initiative in the United Kingdom the resource under consideration was the school itself: the rise of the comprehensive school and the decline of the selective grammar school was a drive for equity in terms of access to the range of backgrounds and aptitudes of other students and to a broad curriculum. The establishment of the Australian Schools Commission, and grants which steadily increased in number and complexity, reflected a concern that all schools had access to resources which were needed for a quality education.

The most recent shift in the way equity is viewed seems to place emphasis on ensuring that each individual student has access to the particular rather than aggregated mix of resources in order to meet the needs and interests of that student, with resources in this mix being considered broadly to include school, curriculum, learning experience, teachers, supplies, equipment and services. Greater weight is now placed on regarding each student as an individual, a value reinforced by advances in knowledge about developmental and learning processes. Advances in technology have also made possible a variety of highly individualized approaches. Garms, Guthrie and Pierce (1978) argued the case for school-site management along these lines, asserting that the approach would also contribute to the achievement of other key values. In addition to equality (or equity) they contended that decentralization would also contribute to liberty, efficiency and choice.

In terms of management processes to support learning and teaching, it seems that determining what the particular mix of resources should be for each student is a decision which is best made in most, if not all, instances at the level of the school rather than in a central location.

Fourth, findings from studies of school effectiveness and school improvement have been mentioned as justification of decentralization in the United States (National Governors Association, 1986; NEA–NASSP, 1986). The model for creating an effective school offered by Purkey and Smith (1985) and the case for 'strategic independence' argued by Finn (1984) are examples of literature which is influencing developments. The essence of these recommendations and findings is that highly effective schools or schools that have shown outstanding improvement have been given a high level of responsibility and authority to make decisions about staffing and the allocation of resources and, within these schools, teachers have been empowered in a variety of ways to make a contribution to planning and decision-making processes. Recent research by Miles and his colleagues on improvement in urban secondary schools (Miles, 1987) provides further evidence of the link between improvement and a relatively high degree of school autonomy and empowerment. This empowerment of school and teacher does not occur in a vacuum. Schools operate within a framework of broad goals and priorities for the system as a whole and are given the necessary support.

Fifth, increased autonomy for teachers and fewer bureaucratic controls have invariably been included as elements in the case for the enhancement of teaching as a profession. In the United States, for example, the reports of the Carnegie Forum on Education and the Economy (1986) and the Holmes Group (1986) advocated this course, with the latter setting a goal of making schools better places for teachers to work and to learn: 'This will require less bureaucracy, more professional autonomy, and more leadership for teachers' (Holmes Group, 1986, p. 4).

Sixth, the general public in countries under consideration is now showing much greater interest in the exercise of choice as far as perceptions of quality in education are concerned. The metaphor of 'market' is widely used, especially in the United Kingdom, with parents and students seen as clients or consumers and schools and school systems being called upon to provide a quality product or service to satisfy the market. The language of 'deregulation' and 'privatization' has made its appearance in education as in other fields where governments have, traditionally provided a public service.

Seventh, while not explicitly offered as reasons for change, theories and perspectives from fields other than education have been offered in support or explanation of an appropriate balance of centralization and decentralization. An example is contained in the work of Peters and Waterman whose studies of excellent companies led them to the identification of 'simultaneous loose-tight properties'. They found that excellent companies are both centralized and decentralized, pushing autonomy down to the shop floor or production team for some functions but being 'fanatical centralists about the core values they hold dear' (Peters and Waterman, 1982, p. 14). The parallel in education is thus centralized determination of broad goals and purposes of education accompanied by decentralized decision-making about the means by which these goals and purposes will be achieved, with those people who are decentralized being accountable to those centralized for the achievement of outcomes.

A review of all seven factors readily reveals why the concept of self-management has had wide appeal across the political spectrum, with parties of the left being comfortable with initiatives which address the issues of equity and empowerment while those of the right are attracted in particular by the issues of choice and the economy.

Tensions in Centralization and Decentralization

A cluster of issues is associated with tensions which are experienced in simultaneous shifts of a centralizing and decentralizing nature. After describing the kind of leadership found in studies of school improvement in urban high schools and then noting a number of centrally determined constraints on leadership, Farrar (1987, p. 8) described a major source of tension in the following terms:

> I think there is a paradox in this situation, one that has serious implications for the prospect of improving urban high schools through school-based planning models. These approaches aim to decentralize authority, to shift responsibility for improvement needs, plans and strategies from the district to the school, where ownership and collegiality foster faculty commitment to improvement. Yet groups outside the school make a number of education decisions that seriously hamper the school's efforts. Some decisions ... have the effect of maintaining or recentralising responsibility to the district or state over critical school functions and policies. This leaves building administrators and faculties with decision-making responsibility only along the periphery of school affairs.

With research on school effectiveness and school improvement so consistently supportive of a capacity for self-management at the school level, the management of conflict such as that illustrated by Farrar seems dependent on minimizing the number of constraining rules and regulations, including many that may be part of collective agreements. A strong central role is important but should be limited to establishing a vision for the system as a whole, setting expectations and standards for student learning, and providing strong support for schools.

The position of Al Shanker, President of the American Federation of Teachers, is interesting in regard to this issue. While Purkey and Smith (1985) anticipated union resistance to school-site management, Shanker has thrown his weight behind decentralization and believes that unity can be better attained through commitment to a shared vision than through extensive rules and regulations:

> How would the school reform movement have developed if these principles of management [decentralization] had been followed? For one thing, we would have looked for ways to encourage more decision-making by teachers in classrooms and principals in schools, rather than bind them by rules and regulations set down by legislatures and state education departments.... And perhaps most important of all ... our education leadership would have risen above the petty squabbles about merit pay, the length of the school day and school year, and created a vision of our public school system, what it has meant to our country, why it succeeded in the past and what challenges lie ahead, and shared that vision with (teachers, board members and parents) without whom our goals will not be accomplished. (Shanker, 1987)

Shanker's stance, along with the support for school-site management from the National Education Association (NEA-NASSP, 1986), holds promise for resolving some of these tensions. There are other implications for those employed at levels above the school and these will be addressed separately in this analysis.

A related issue in this tension of centralization and decentralization is the extent to which there should be central control of curriculum. This issue lies at centre stage in the United Kingdom at this time as the government implements legislation which will achieve a high degree of centralization as far as curriculum and testing are concerned but also a high degree of decentralization through the local management of schools. Participants in public and legislative debates fiercely contested the issue of curriculum control, with the government's initial rather detailed and prescriptive approach (Department of Education and Science, 1987) coming under heavy fire. Those advocating that the values of choice should prevail called for the government to drop this aspect of policy altogether (O'Keeffe, 1987; Sexton, 1987, 1988).

A third area of tension considered here arises from efforts to reorganize systems of education to bring about new patterns of management along the lines discussed in this chapter. A comprehensive account of the issues has been provided for developments in Australia and the United States, especially as they concern the changing roles of chief education officers (Harman, Wirt and Beare, 1987) and different roles at all levels, especially the principalship (Boyd and Chapman, 1987). Issues related to reorganization have appeared intractable at times and their resolution remains a matter of concern.

Focus on Learning and Teaching

There has been concern that the shifting of management responsibilities to the school level is in some way a distraction from the central processes of schooling, namely, learning and teaching, and that principals and teachers will become accountants. These fears have been expressed in most settings where decentralization of budgeting has been a major feature of change. In the United Kingdom, for example, the General Secretary of the National Union of Teachers commented on government plans for local financial management by asserting that 'headteachers [principals] should be educational leaders not accountants struggling to balance books ...' (Clare, 1987, p. 2). Writing more generally, Hughes (1987, p. 307) noted with concern that developments in Australia and the United States had not yet had the impact desired: 'It seems that the reforms so far put in place may not yet have reached the real focus for improvement — teacher, student and classroom, together with factors that directly affect performance and response in that setting.'

These concerns are especially justified if the focus of change is money. A broader perspective must be adopted so that budgeting is seen as an important phase of the educational planning process wherein goals are set, needs are identified, policies are formulated, priorities are established and resources are allocated so that, as far as possible, the learning needs of every student can be addressed. The purpose of these new patterns of management must be expressed unmistakably in terms of their contribution to an end, that is quality of schooling, rather than simply as a means of ensuring greater efficiency in the utilization of resources conceived narrowly in financial terms. The sharing of findings from studies of school effectiveness and school improvement can help alleviate this concern, especially those by Miles and his colleagues (Miles, 1987; Farrar, 1987), which reveal that high levels of school autonomy as far as allocation of resources is concerned are associated with success in school improvement. Moreover, models for management at the school level must focus on learning and teaching. Such a model emerged from an Australian study of school effectiveness (see Caldwell and Spinks, 1988, for a detailed account). It has proved helpful in several states in Australia, with utility in New Zealand and the United Kingdom (England and Wales) now emerging.

Equity in Resource Allocation

Another concern is related to equity in the allocation of resources among schools. If schools are to have the responsibility and authority to formulate educational plans, can there be assurance that each school, regardless of geographic location and socio-economic setting, will receive an equitable allocation within which school level planning can take place? School systems in Canada and the United States with a decade or more of experience have developed approaches to allocating resources so that each school receives an aggregate according to the precise mix of student needs. Edmonton, for example, uses eleven levels of per-pupil allocation to meet forty-seven categories of student need when determining the aggregate for a school. Extensive experience with program accounting and budgeting, together with improved computer-based cost-accounting and management information systems, have aided the effort. So too has the setting by state and local authorities of policies and priorities for meeting the needs of all students, with appropriate means of ensuring accountability. But these developments take time, with five years or more required to trial, plan and refine the procedures. Acquiring information along these lines about experience elsewhere can guide implementation efforts in other places.

Central Support for Schools

A crucial issue is support for schools. Can schools be 'self-managing' in the sense implied in this examination of new patterns of management? What is the role of those currently employed in central and regional offices? Roles and responsibilities have changed in systems with extensive experience. Governing bodies at national, state or local levels now devote more time to setting policies, priorities and standards for the system as a whole, with extensive use of information obtained in system-wide tests and other approaches to program evaluation. Senior educators provide information to assist in the setting of policies, priorities and standards and then work to ensure that these are achieved. Curriculum and student services become highly responsive to the needs of schools. The trial of decentralized planning for curriculum and student services in Edmonton is evidence that an even higher level of responsiveness was sought after almost ten years' experience in the new pattern of management.

Time and the Importance of an Evolutionary Approach

Developments of the magnitude under consideration raise many implications concerning the human dimensions of change. New knowledge, skills and attitudes must be acquired and structures must be changed. It seems that change has not always been managed well in these respects. Time-lines have been unrealistically short, with experience to date suggesting five years or more are required. In Edmonton, for example, the approach is still evolving after ten years. Rarely have adequate time and resources been set aside prior to, or during, change for the necessary professional development of staff. Restructuring has been difficult in some settings, especially in Victoria, Australia, where three attempts were made before the government finally 'got it right', with each attempt involving a readvertising of virtually all non-school positions. Such difficulty may not be encountered if there is a common shared vision of what is intended and if adequate time and resources are provided.

The importance of an evolutionary approach at the school level is supported by findings in research by Miles and his colleagues on success in school improvement. They found that two kinds of shared vision are important for success: a vision of a preferred future for the school and a vision for the process of change, with the latter congruent with central expectations or 'buffered from external intervention' (Miles, 1987, p. 12).

Evaluation and Testing

Many educators are uncomfortable with the attention given to evaluation and testing, especially as far as the focus on basic skills is concerned. Surely, it is argued, this will distort the learning and teaching process to the detriment of 'higher order' outcomes. This distortion has occurred in some places but it is not a necessary outcome if a comprehensive range of approaches is adopted. In Edmonton, for example, standardized tests are conducted in language, social studies, mathematics and science. All certified and non-certified staff (teachers and support staff), principals, central and regional staff and students complete an opinion survey each year. In addition to breadth in the system-wide approach to evaluation, schools should be encouraged to develop a comprehensive approach to program evaluation. Most important, however, is that each school should have an ongoing cycle of goal-setting, policy-making, planning, implementing and evaluating to ensure that information from a variety of sources is used to enhance the quality of learning.

There is evidence in the United Kingdom that the initially strong and adverse reaction by teachers and principals to plans for national testing has been tempered with the release of a commissioned study which proposed an approach which satisfied the government's interest in system-wide testing, with publication of results, and professional concerns about inappropriate comparisons and competitiveness (Black, 1987).

Conclusion

That school-based decision-making, more narrowly conceived as school self-management, is an emerging phenomenon in a number of Western countries has been confirmed in the international review in the first part of the chapter. These developments were set in a broader context which revealed more or less simultaneous trends of a centralizing and decentralizing nature. In addition to an examination of underlying factors, the second part of the chapter identified and addressed issues which have emerged as systems have endeavoured to initiate and support the self-managing school.

Despite the many issues which have arisen, it is possible to conclude the chapter on a note of optimism. It is clear that a relatively high level of self-management can be achieved at the same time that a more powerful and focused role is adopted at the system level. The success of the Edmonton Public School District in Alberta, Canada was cited as an example (see Smilanich, 1989). There are models for management which can guide change at the school level, with an Australian example described by Spinks in another chapter providing support in several countries. Caldwell, Smilanich and Spinks (1988) furnish a more detailed account of how the Edmonton experience and the model for self-management developed in Australia can work together to support initiatives of this kind. It is evident, however, that new ways of thinking about centralization and decentralization are required but that associated changes can be successfully managed.

References

BARRINGTON, J. (1981) 'State Government in New Zealand: Balancing the Interests,' in BARON, G. (Ed.), *The Politics of School Government.* Oxford: Pergamon Press.

BLACK, P. (1987) 'Report of the Task Group on Assessment and Testing.' Professor Paul Black (Chair). London: Department of Education and Science.

BOYD, W.L. and CHAPMAN, J.D. (1987) 'State-wide Educational Reform and Administrative Reorganization: Australian Experience in American Perspective,' in BOYD, W.L. and SMART, D. (Eds), *Educational Policy in Australia and America.* Lewes: Falmer Press.

BOYD, W.L. and SMART, D. (Eds) (1987) *Educational Policy in Australia and America.* Lewes: Falmer Press.

BROWN, D.J. (1987) 'A Preliminary Inquiry into School-based Management,' Report to the Social Sciences and Humanities Council of Canada for Grant Number 410–83–1086.

CALDWELL, B.J. and SPINKS, J.M. (1988) *The Self-Managing School.* Lewes: Falmer Press.

CALDWELL, B.J., SMILANICH, R. and SPINKS, J.M. (1988) 'The Self-managing School,' *The Canadian Administrator,* 27, 8, May.

CARNEGIE FORUM ON EDUCATION AND THE ECONOMY (1986) *A Nation Prepared: Teachers for the 21st Century.* New York: Carnegie Forum.

CATHIE, I. (1986) *The Government Decision on the Report of the Ministry Structures Project Team.* Melbourne: Victorian Ministry of Education.

CLARE, J. (1987) 'Plans to Give Schools More Control Calm Council Fears,' *The Times,* 21 July, p. 2.

DEPARTMENT OF EDUCATION AND SCIENCE (1987) *The National Curriculum, 5–16: A Consultation Paper.* London: HMSO.

FARRAR, E. (1987) 'Improving the Urban High School: The Role of Leadership in the School, District and State,' Paper read at a symposium of Effective Schools Programs and the Urban High School at the Annual Meeting of the American Educational Research Association, Washington, D.C., 23 April.

FINN, C.E. (1984) 'Toward Strategic Independence: Nine Commandments for Enhancing School Effectiveness,' *Phi Delta Kappan,* February, 518–24.

FRAZER, M., DUNSTAN, J. and CREED, P. (1985) *Perspectives on Organizational Change.* Melbourne: Longman Cheshire.

GARMS, W.I., GUTHRIE, J.W. and PIERCE, L.C. (1978) *School Finance: The Economics and Politics of Public Education.* Englewood Cliffs, N.J.: Prentice-Hall.

GOODLAD, J.I. (1984) *A Place Called School.* New York: McGraw-Hill.

GUTHRIE, J.W. and REED, R.J. (1986) *Educational Administration and Policy: Effective Leadership for American Education.* Englewood Cliffs, N.J.: Prentice-Hall.

HARMAN, G., WIRT, F.M. and BEARE, H. (1987) 'Changing Roles of Australian Education Chief Executive Officers,' in BOYD, W.L. and SMART, D. (Eds), *Educational Policy in Australia and America*. Lewes: Falmer Press.

HOLMES GROUP (1986) *Tomorrow's Teachers: A Report of the Holmes Group*. East Lansing, Mich.: The Holmes Group.

HOPES, C. (Ed.) (1986) *The School Leader and School Improvement*. Technical Report No. 2 of the International School Improvement Project, Center for Educational Research and Innovation, OECD. Leuven: Acco.

HUGHES, P. (1987) 'Reorganization in Education in a Climate of Changing Social Expectations: A Commentary,' in BOYD, W.L. and SMART, D. (Eds), *Educational Policy in Australia and America*. Lewes: Falmer Press.

LANGE, D. (1988) *Tomorrow's Schools*. Wellington, New Zealand: Government Printer.

LEITHWOOD, K.A. and BEGLEY, P.T. (1986) 'Canada,' A case study in HOPES, C. (Ed.), *The School Leader and School Improvement*. Technical Report No. 2 of the International School Improvement Project, Center for Educational Research and Innovation, OECD. Leuven: Acco.

MILES, M.B. (1987) 'Practical Guidelines for School Administrators: How to Get There,' Paper presented at a symposium of Effective Schools Programs and the Urban High School at the Annual Meeting of the American Educational Research Association, Washington, D.C., 23 April.

MURPHY, J. and HALLINGER, P. (1986) 'Educational Equity and Differential Access to Knowledge: An Analysis,' Unpublished paper, University of Illinois at Urbana.

NATIONAL COMMISSION ON EXCELLENCE IN EDUCATION (1983) *A Nation at Risk*. Washington, D.C.: Government Printing Office.

NATIONAL EDUCATION ASSOCIATION–NATIONAL ASSOCIATION OF SECONDARY SCHOOL PRINCIPALS (1986) *Ventures in Good Schooling: A Joint Report*. Washington, D.C. and Reston, Va.: NEA-NASSP.

NATIONAL GOVERNORS' ASSOCIATION (1986) *Time for Results*. A report on education, Lamar Alexander (Chairman). Washington, D.C.: National Governors' Association.

NORTHERN TERRITORY. DEPARTMENT OF EDUCATION (1987) *Towards the 90s: Excellence, Accountability and Devolution in Education*. Darwin: Department of Education.

OECD (1986) *Spain: A Review of National Policies for Education*. Paris: OECD.

O'KEEFFE, D. (1987) 'Against a National Curriculum,' in *A National Curriculum?* Monograph No. 2/87 of the Institute of Economic Affairs Education Unit. London: IEA.

PETERS, T.J. and WATERMAN, R.H. (1982) *In Search of Excellence*. New York: Harper and Row.

PICOT, B. (1988) *Administering for Excellence*. Report of the Task Force to Review Education Administration, Brian Picot (Chairperson). Wellington, New Zealand: Government Printer.

POLICY AND PLANNING UNIT (1987) *Implementation of School-level Program Budgeting: Progress Report*. Melbourne: Ministry of Education, Victoria.

PURKEY, S.C. and SMITH, M.S. (1985) 'School Reform: The District Policy Implications of the Effective Schools Literature,' *The Elementary School Journal*, 85, 353–89.

RANSON, S. and TOMLINSON, J. (1986), 'Introduction,' in RANSON, S. and TOM-
LINSON, J. (Eds), *The Changing Government of Education.* London: Allen and
Unwin.

RICATTI, E. (1986) 'Italy,' A case study in HOPES, C. (Ed.), *The School Leader and
School Improvement.* Technical Report No. 2 of the International School
Improvement Project, Center for Educational Research and Innovation,
OECD. Leuven: Acco.

SACKNEY, L.E. and DIBSKI, D.J. (1989) 'Canadian Practice in Decentralized
Budgeting,' in CALDWELL, B.J. and COOPER, B.S. (Eds), *Schools at the Centre.*
Greenwich, Conn.: JAI (forthcoming).

SEXTON, S. (1987) *Response to Government Consultation on Education.* Monograph
No. 7/87 of the Institute of Economic Affairs Education Unit. London: IEA.

SEXTON, S. (1988) *A Guide to the Education Reform Bill.* Monograph No. 1/88 of
the Institute of Economic Affairs Education Unit. London: IEA.

SHANKER, A. (1987) 'Management Creates a Sense of Purpose,' *New York Times,*
18 January.

SIZER, T.R. (1984) *Horace's Compromise.* Boston, Mass.: Houghton Mifflin.

SMILANICH, R. (1989) 'The Edmonton Experience,' in CALDWELL, B.J. and
COOPER, B.S. (Eds), *Schools at the Centre.* Greenwich, Conn.: JAI (forthcoming).

VAN VELZEN, W.G. and ROBIN, D. (1985) 'The Need for School Improvement in
the Next Decade,' in VAN VELZEN, W.G., MILES, M.B., EKHOLM, M.,
HAMEYER, U. and ROBIN, D. (Eds), *Making School Improvement Work.* Book
No. 1 of the International School Improvement Project, Centre for Educational Research and Innovation, OECD. Leuven: Acco.

WESTERN AUSTRALIA. MINISTRY OF EDUCATION (1987) *Better Schools for Western
Australia: A Program for Improvement.* Perth: Ministry of Education.

Part 2
Theoretical Perspectives

Chapter 2

Pressures on the Move to School-based Decision-making and Management

Terri Seddon, Lawrence Angus, Millicent E. Poole

Forms of school-based decision-making and management have become largely accepted as a policy initiative in a number of Western nations including Australia (Angus *et al.*, 1983; Angus and Rizvi, forthcoming), Britain (Whitehead and Aggleton, 1986), Canada (Bryden, 1982; Coleman, 1987), Sweden (Lundgren, 1986) and the United States (Dunlap, 1985). Why has this come about? This chapter begins to examine the economic, political, social and cultural pressures which have contributed to the rise of school-based decision-making and management as an administrative strategy in education. However, this substantive task is made more complex by the diverse ways in which these contextual factors, and indeed educational administration itself, are being conceptualized in contemporary research. Over the past twenty years the theoretical perspective which has informed research in educational administration has become increasingly fluid, with different assumptions being made about the nature of the social world. As the theoretical perspective has changed, so too have the taken-for-granted notions of what counts as educational administration and the social phenomena seen to be significant in shaping administrative strategy in education.

Our review of the literature clearly indicates different views of the rise of school-based decision-making and management, premised upon different assumptions about schooling, society and change, as well as the role and nature of the administrator and management. The bulk of this research we have found to be informed generally, if not always explicitly, by broadly functionalist assumptions. From this perspective school-based decision-making and management appears to be a significant democratic reform — an evaluation which seems quite problematic in the light of other theoretical perspectives.

This view is confirmed by the chapters in Part 2 of this book, which consider, and evaluate, school-based decision-making and management from a variety of theoretical perspectives. The present chapter adopts a theoretical perspective informed by conflict theory and critical social science to examine its emergence. Specifically, we adopt a relational view which sees society being shaped by the large-scale structures of class and gender, the organization of the state and the national and international relationships between states and economies. These social relationships form a complex field of forces which bear on, and mould, social arrangements, practices and ideas. Over time the field of social forces changes, as do the social phenomena, which, being shaped by those social relationships, take distinctively different forms at specific points in history.

From this relational, and intensely historical, perspective school-based decision-making and management cannot be seen as an unproblematic democratic educational reform as implied in more functionalist analyses. Instead, we argue, that while it contains possibilities for more democratic administrative strategies in education, its potential is severely curtailed because it does not interrupt the largely institutionalized network of social power relationships which become evident when school-based decision-making and management is seen in broader social and historical circumstances.

The chapter is organized into four main sections and, while it deals with school-based decision-making and management as a general feature of educational governance in many Western nations, some specific points are illustrated by reference to the example of Victoria, Australia. The first section briefly indicates our working definition. Second, we present a focused and selective review of the literature with a view to indicating the nature of mainstream socio-political analyses of the rise of school-based decision-making and management. The third section explores the limitations of these analyses, drawing on the small body of critical literature on educational administration, on research in the social sciences more generally and on our own emerging critiques. Finally, we suggest directions which offer a more extensive perspective on the rise of school-based decision-making and management and which attempt to locate education in a historical and social context.

School-based Decision-making and Management: A Working Definition

Following the lead of Simpkins (1981), we focus our attention on school-based decision-making and management as participative decision-making. He notes in regard to the Australian situation:

Administrative change in Australian schools is taking a particular direction with many centralised agencies of government changing their participative arrangements to produce modifications of long established structures of administrative centralism. The new approaches to participation involve sometimes subordinates and sometimes outsiders, with participative adaptations taking some-what different directions across Australian States. (Simpkins, 1981, p. 3)

In a similar vein Conway (1984, p. 19) notes that participative decision-making entails the intersection of concepts of participation and decision-making, limiting attention to 'that participation by two or more actors in the process of reaching a choice'. This process occurs in a context which assumes relationships of subordination and domination between those actors.

The Rise of School-based Decision-making and Management: Proximal and Higher Order Frames

In the preparation of this chapter literature which examined the rise of school-based decision-making and management was identified through an extensive ERIC search of material published since 1984. A variety of descriptor combinations, including those used in Simpkins' (1981) re-view, was used to identify this material. The resulting body of literature was grouped according to its focus. One group of literature discussed the rise of school-based decision-making and management in terms of deci-sions made at the level of schools and classrooms. The second group focused on factors at the societal and school system level which have shaped school-based decision-making and management.

The rough division of literature was informed by Kallos and Lund-gren's (1979) notion of frame factors. The concept of 'frame' defines those tangible features within educational systems which constrain and direct the character of pedagogical and administrative activity. They are seen functionally in terms of their effects in limiting the available courses of action open to decision-makers. For example, both fiscal resources, decided at a broad social level, and timetabling, operating in the im-mediate local context, are frames which limit options in teaching and administration.

The example highlights a further point, that frames exist at different levels. Kallos and Lundgren (1979, pp. 29–30) elaborate on these levels, identifying 'higher order' and 'proximal' frames. The former are frames which are outside the control of actors in the local context of school and classroom, and indeed shape and constrain the more immediate proximal frames. Higher order frames derive from 'the decision making matrix within the educational bureaucracy and ultimately, from the political and economic structure of which the educational system is a part' (Smith, 1985, p. 146). 'Proximal' frames operate at the level adjacent to personnel in the immediate context of school and classroom. The proximal frames define an operational space for planning and action by teachers, students and school administrators. Decisions at the proximal level are circumscribed and directed by decisions at higher levels and in many circumstances school level decisions can be seen as allocations of resources which have been determined higher up in the bureaucracy.

With this notion of 'frame' clarified, three observations can be made about the literature which examined the rise of school-based decision-making and management. First, this body of literature was not extensive. Our overwhelming impression is that the emergence of school-based decision-making and management is a somewhat neglected research topic.

Second, the vast majority of the literature focused on the proximal frames which promote school-based decision-making and management as an administrative strategy in education. It examines, particularly, the way management, leadership and administrative style influence operational space. For example, there are numerous analyses of school-based decision-making and management as a management strategy for the production of excellence (e.g. Yin *et al.*, 1984; Bone and Ramsay, 1981; Wells, 1986); as a possible course of action for developing more effective processual negotiation which will assist decision-making (Savage, 1984; Artis, 1980; Burckel, 1984; Lezotte, 1986); and as a strategy for seeking greater community involvement and participation (Jakes, 1986; Pink and Wallace, 1984; Pink, 1986; Ornstein, 1983; Davies, 1985). More rarely, research presents school-based decision-making and management as a means of developing moral and democratic communities (Beyer, 1986; Herrick, 1985) or socially just ones (Keeley, 1984; Zerchykov, 1985).

The significance of 'principals' and their shifting and ambiguous operational space is a major focus in much of the literature (e.g. Macpherson, 1982; Greenfield, 1985; Thomas, 1986; Chapman and Boyd, 1986). With emphasis on devolution of authority, collaborative decision-making, and responsiveness to the needs of the immediate community, principals become key actors, offering leadership in, and solutions to, the problems of participative management (Thomas, 1986, p. 12).

Third, research on higher order frames is far less common. The sparse literature focuses on a small number of highly complex factors.

The political climate of the 1960s is seen as particularly important, as are the more recent economic concerns with individual and national survival.

The political climate of the 1960s in Western nations is presented as a key impetus to community involvement. One facet of this climate was the encouragement of resource and facility sharing; another was the demand for more radical restructuring of education leading to community involvement (even control) in school management and curriculum development. The concern was to institute a democratic order in schools which would both reflect and confirm the broader processes of democracy in the wider society (Beyer, 1986; Boyd, 1986).

This press for participation and reform in Western democracies has been explained in terms of the increasing demands of cultural minorities and women, of a highly educated citizenry concerned with human rights and the education of their children, and of more militant teachers pursuing economic and professional needs (Bakalis, 1983). Such demands appeared as extensive social critique and accompanied the growth of new advocacy groups (Ornstein, 1983). Education became more political in nature as regional pressure groups sought to transfer real power to the community level (Simpkins, 1981; Lindelow, 1981; Boyd, 1986; Davies, 1985). The rise of explicit pluralist politics and pressure for reform are seen to have played a part in forcing school authorities in many large school systems to restructure and increase community participation in schools (Lundgren, 1986; Ornstein, 1983). The result has been shifts to devolution, decentralization and deconcentration, so much so that there is now talk in several countries of a new 'partnership theory' (Boyd, 1986) of community advocacy leading to participation and representation (Simpkins, 1981).

A further impetus that is described in the literature on school-based decision-making and management is the state of the economy, which is argued to have led to government questioning of the nature and value of the contribution of educational services and provisions to society (Bakalis, 1983). Such disquiet has been linked to post-war demographic changes which have put increasing pressure on the provision of post-compulsory education and training (Shears, 1985; McCulloch, 1986). These pressures have become increasingly and insistently visible in the literature, appearing in terms of productivity, quality control, effectiveness, human resource development and worker satisfaction to enhance productivity. Such concerns are linked to more broadly based accountability and national productivity factors. For example, 'public systems of universal schooling are coming under criticism for not providing the workforce with the technical skills necessary to promote job opportunities and economic growth' (Simpkins, 1981, p. 24). These concerns place new demands on participative decision-making and are seen to require closer school-community relationships for 'accountability checks which guarantee economies through efficiency' (Simpkins, 1981, p. 24; Whitehead and Aggleton, 1986).

The language of crisis and mobilization in the face of threats to national survival, well illustrated in reports such as *A Nation at Risk* (National Commission on Excellence in Education, 1983) in the United States, the *QERC Report* (Quality of Education Review Committee, 1985) in Australia and the British Green Paper on *Better Schools* (DES, 1985), is another factor seen to contribute to its rise. School-based decision-making and management makes the school the unit of analysis for cost-efficiency analyses and for evaluation of outputs, whether in terms of retention rates, quality, accountability, standards evidenced in a number of reports addressing a perceived crisis in education, and in nation-states in terms of economic performance in comparative terms.

Narratives describing educational restructuring provide a further body of literature indicating higher order frames in the move to school-based decision-making and management. For instance, drawing on the literature which portrays restructuring in Victoria — the case with which we are most familiar — we find the factors identified in the more general literature reconfirmed. Dunstan (1986), for example, notes that in the early 1970s the movement towards a more decentralized system of organization in education was seen as a means to bring decision-making much closer to schools and communities.

In the Victorian case the increasing commitment to participation in decision-making led to restructuring — at the school, regional and central levels — to ensure that participative decision-making involved representatives of interest groups, rather than bureaucratic modes of decision-making (Dunstan, 1986, p. 24). Creed (1986, p. 1) notes the significance of 'the present climate of continuing change' in the press for school-based decision-making and management. He sees restructuring resulting from political pressure at the top as well as from grass roots advocacy: 'The successes for administrative reform in Victoria are more accurately attributed to "top-down" strategies for the implementation of Government policy in response to well orchestrated "bottom-up" pressures for change' (Creed, 1986, p. 25).

Additionally, new higher order frames are identified. The significance of the political party currently in government is frequently noted (e.g. Bates, 1985; Creed, 1986; Matthews, 1986). The level of parent and teacher activism is seen to be important (e.g. Kirner, 1985), as are changing demographic pressures on schools (Shears, 1985). An important higher order frame evident in these narratives is the structure of the educational bureaucracy. Dunstan (1986, pp. 7–8) comments that dysfunctions in Victoria's complex administrative structures of the late 1970s, in which administrative responsibility was based simultaneously on categories of students, administrative functions and geographical regions, were an important factor in further restructuring. Yesterday's present has become today's past and exerts a significant influence on both today's solutions and tomorrow's problems. But the relationship of past, present and future does not just concern the impact of an immediately prior restructuring but also the long-term historical pressures which shape the educational present. The significance of such a historical perspective is emphasized by Selleck (1985):

> Like other large organizations, an Education Department is an intricate system of personal relationships, of political, social and economic pressures, and of vested interests, customs and ideologies which, over the years, develop, support each other, conflict or fade. If Rome wasn't built in a day, neither were other empires. To twist a phrase slightly: time is of the Department's essence. Its history cannot be left in the past, because it is part of the present. Not to have a sense of this history is to be politically illiterate — you will be unable to read some quite clear messages. (Selleck, 1985, p. 107)

Higher order frames evident in the literature are usefully captured and elaborated on in two helpful reviews: Simpkins (1981) and Conway (1984). We turn now to these reviews to extend the analysis and to begin to structure a critique.

An Administrative Perspective on School-based Decision-making and Management

Simpkins' (1981) Australian review was written when there were already strong moves away from centralized administration of education toward more participative structures. Conway (1984), the second review, provides a chronological survey of reviews of participative decision-making, indicating a variety of rationales for it and the inconclusive evidence concerning its effectiveness in educational organizations. Interestingly, they both pre-date much of the literature we examined, yet they raise issues which remain pertinent and are often insufficiently addressed. They turn our attention to higher order frames which influence three facets of school-based decision-making and management: the nature of (1) participative decision-making as an administrative strategy of school-based decision-making and management; (2) the social context; and (3) the school's relationship with the social context. We address these in turn.

The Nature of School-based Decision-making and Management.   Our view of school-based decision-making and management as a form of participative decision-making has already been noted. This recognized that school-based decision-making and management occurred between subordinates and superiors, that is, in a context of power inequality. Simpkins elaborates this by noting that the move to participative decision-making entailed shifts in the pre-existing power relativities of a centralist administrative structure. Power inequalities, which had been accepted as legitimate, between those inside and outside education, as well as between superiors and subordinates within the education system, were changed. The move to school-based decision-making and management was like a stone cast into a pool. Its ramifications rippled throughout the practice of educational administration. The core problem was how to manage plural-ist demands in education while simultaneously maintaining the legitimacy of the system by attending to questions of representation, evaluation, resource management and accountability. Of the four rationales for parti-cipative decision-making identified by Conway — the management, humanistic psychology, democratic and participatory left or revolution-ary rationales — such management rested upon the first two. The strength of the managerial and humanistic psychology rationales in con-temporary educational administration, with emphasis upon efficiency, effectiveness and interpersonal harmony, is clearly illustrated in Con-way's paper as he first identifies, and then completely neglects, the democratic and participatory left rationales in his own discussion. Cole-man (1984, p. 1), too, noted the efficiency-oriented nature of school-based decision-making and management, identifying four common objectives: project diversity, cost effectiveness, staff involvement and accountability.

From this perspective administrators appear as neutral mediators, standing between internal and external pluralist demands. Their role is to 'manage' these spheres of politics in the interests of the educational system. To this end they appear to stand above, and dissociated from, politics. This image of the administrator is problematic, for it fails to locate the administrator within the power inequalities of both the school system and the broader social context. It asserts neutrality when, in fact, such neutrality has to be proven.

The key point to recognize about school-based decision-making and management, then, is the contradictory nature of participative decision-making. It is a feature of power inequality which has become increasingly widespread as power relativities have shifted and legitimacy has been eroded. Simultaneously, it is a managerial style concerned with both economic efficiency and human relationships.

The Social Context. Simpkins also directs our attention to the broader social and historical context with has shaped the rise and nature of school-based decision-making and management. While his social and historical perspective is limited, he is able to identify three stages in the development of participative administrative practice. He presents school-based decision-making and management as an emerging alternative to centralist administration. This poses new administrative problems, such as the nature of representation and participation, and of appropriate forms of evaluation and accountability. But these problems have been compounded by further changes in the context of schooling. Thus high unemployment, economic stringency, financial cutbacks, increased public disenchantment with education, increased demands for accountability, falling rolls: these symptoms of accelerating economic, political and social restructuring in Western society impose new administrative demands on the management of pluralism in education.

Simpkins' important contribution here is to indicate that participative decision-making does not occur against a constant social background. Rather, over time the context changes, giving rise to decentralization and participative decision-making in the earlier 1970s and school-based decision-making and management in the 1980s. School-based decision-making and management appears, then, as a historically specific feature of a more general dynamic to participative decision-making, being linked to the particular social circumstances of the late 1970s and 1980s. The effect is, first, to raise questions about our earlier working definition of school-based decision-making and management and, second, to place firmly on the research agenda the problem of conceptualizing context in a historically dynamic way.

The School's Relationship with the Social Context. Simpkins' further contribution to an understanding of school-based decision-making and management as an administrative strategy is to highlight schools as adaptive institutions.

> Administrative changes presently underway are adaptive in intent, initiated to help school systems sustain their service role and status position in a changing society. Thus administrative changes can be viewed as responses to the need for administrative systems to sustain their modes of operation under the varied pressures of

current social and economic circumstances. In times of change systems must adapt if they are to function well, or to appear to function well. (Simpkins, 1981, p. 3)

From this point of view schools adapt in order to maintain their utility as functional systems within a coherent society. Mitter, for example, sees adaptation by schools in Western societies as a necessary aspect of 'their effort for survival and modernization' (Mitter, 1987, p. 263). Such press for modernization springs, not just from economic development, but also from features such as 'reduction in class differences (social), development of democratic structures (political) and ethnic self-determination (cultural)' (Mitter, 1987, p. 264). In relation to employment, for instance, teachers and schools are expected to regard the current international economic crisis as merely one of the 'crucial trends' which they have to cope with and which, in this case, 'directly influence the conditions of education and schooling, and consequently the expectations of schools, as regards their function to provide the employment system with a workforce' (Mitter, 1987, p. 266). The onus is therefore upon individual schools, administrators and teachers to respond appropriately to broader social change.

The useful observation that schools adapt to broader social change is made problematic in Simpkins and Mitter by functionalist assumptions which regard schools and society as harmoniously integrated, functional systems. The problem is that this view of education and society has become increasingly difficult to reconcile with the experience of pluralism and politicization of education since the 1970s.

To summarize, the movement toward school-based decision-making and management is understood and explained in mainstream educational administration literature as a response to changed circumstances and demands in the broader public environment which schools unproblematically serve. Administration, management and, indeed, schools themselves appear neutral components in a well functioning, adaptive system.

Limits of the Administrative, Structural Functionalist Perspective

This structural functionalist view of school-based decision-making and management is confirmed in the educational administration literature. Management texts are replete with strategies and techniques for motivating organization members to cooperate and work together with management to achieve the prior, and generally uncontested, goals of the organization. Within the prevailing human relations approach administrators are urged to stimulate and motivate their subordinates by holding appropriate expectations of them (McGregor, 1966), paying attention to motivation factors such as responsibility and recognition (Herzberg, 1972) and involving them in forms of participatory management (Likert, 1976). We would not deny that this approach has led to a reduction in the extremes of impersonal, mechanical management previously associated with Taylorist scientific management (Taylor, 1947). But we must also note the limits of structural functionalist forms of management, both in practice and in theory.

The critics of such forms of management argue that they do little to give employees any substantial measure of control over workplaces (e.g. Braverman, 1974; Wood, 1985). Human relations management attends in a somewhat superficial way to the personally and psychologically alienating effects of impersonal workplaces, and so is able to reduce industrial and other forms of disruption and stimulate productivity. The human relations approach accurately recognizes the virtual impossibility of direct authoritarian control in which subordinates unquestioningly obey orders. It is limited, however, because it assumes both extremely limited autonomy on the part of organization members and a value consensus such that stability is the natural order of things and goals are shared and unproblematic. So, despite the rhetoric of democracy, worker involvement and satisfaction, a bureaucratic rationality pertains (Rizvi, 1986, p. 20). Participation is therefore of instrumental value as it will forward the supposedly agreed purposes of the institution.

If we turn from the practice of participative decision-making to the analyses of school-based decision-making and management which have been summarized through the reviews of Simpkins and Conway, four broad conceptual shortcomings emerge: (1) the structural functionalist assumptions which inform mainstream analyses of school-based decision-making and management; (2) the neglect of power in any elaborated sense; (3) the neglect of the ideological context in which school-based decision-making and management has arisen; and (4) the impoverished analysis of the social and historical context. Identifying these shortcomings is not merely academic nit-picking, for critiques also highlight further higher order frames not identified in structural functionalist notions of school-based decision-making and management. This difference is a consequence of the rather different assumptions made in structural functionalist, and more socially critical, analyses which shape researchers' views of the world and the elements of significance within it. Thus, for example, we see power inequalities noted in passing by Simpkins (1981), being central to our more critical analyses.

We would argue that both structural functionalist and more socially critical frameworks are legitimate intellectual approaches for analyzing the social world, including the rise of school-based decision-making and management. However, we would also argue that adjudicating between these different approaches is essential. Procedures for such adjudication exist (e.g. Keat and Urry, 1975; Benton, 1977; Walker, 1985), but the simplest basis for judging depends upon assessing each intellectual approach in terms of its adequacy in representing the empirical world. We must ask, is society a consensual functioning whole? Or is it better seen in terms of social conflict? The rise of conflict approaches since the 1970s attests to the perceived significance of the latter. With this in mind, we turn to the shortcomings of structural functionalist analyses of the rise of school-based decision-making and management.

The Rise of School-based Decision-making and Management: From Structural Functionalist to Conflict Theories

Perhaps the most startling weakness of human relations theories, and current approaches to controlled participation and purposeful leadership in education (Sergiovanni, 1986; Starratt, 1986), is that, in keeping with a functionalist perspective, they assume, rather than demonstrate, the harmony and functionality of education within the social system. Conversely, these theories underplay both instability and disorder (Tinker, 1986, p. 376), social features which, we would suggest, have been paramount. Conflict is generally regarded as dysfunctional and must be controlled or channelled towards creative ends. While the existence of conflict is at least recognized, such conflict 'may be intraindividual, intragroup; it is never social structural' (Tinker, 1986, p. 377). Thus, for Simpkins, power inequalities have little significance, except as indicator of dysfunction and hence inefficiency. By contrast, critics have tended to see society more in terms of conflict, emphasizing pluralist pressure groups pursuing particular interests or more structural class antagonisms. Within such frameworks power inequalities are highly significant because they help to explain social conflict and its outcome.

The neglect of power is the second major weakness of structural functionalist approaches. Power inequality in education tends to be disguised by the rhetoric of school-based decision-making and management for it assumes that equal participation is offered in an educational arrangement which is legitimate, neutral and free from power. That is, the moral legitimacy of education's formal structures is taken as given and participants are invited to contribute to educational governance within the accepted paradigm. In keeping with the distinction between power and authority, derived from a particular reading of Weber (1947), power is thought to be exerted only when officials or properly elected representatives attempt to exceed their legitimate authority. Maintaining the agreed rules and given structure is an exercise of proper authority. Forcing through changes involves power.

Clegg and Dunkerley (1980, p. 436) point out that this artificial distinction between legitimate authority and self-interested power has the important effect of taking for granted, as legitimate and appropriate, the prior and possibly inequitable arrangements into which new participants must fit. Power, therefore, only becomes visible when conflict arises within these arrangements. But as Lukes' perceptive analysis makes clear, an important aspect of power is the prevention of such conflict arising in the first place (Lukes, 1974, p. 23). Conflict is contained, as power is exercised through systematic biases that are 'not sustained simply by a series of individually chosen acts, but also, more importantly, by the socially structured and culturally determined patterned behaviour of groups and practices of institutions' (Lukes, 1974, pp. 21–2). Participants, therefore, may not be aware when their interests are not being served because, although their formal participation may give them the authority to intervene, the systematic biases mean that they accept their role in the existing order of things, either because they can see or imagine no alternative to it, or because they see it as natural and unchangeable.

This view of power, as institutionalized in existing relationships and organizational arrangements, regardless of anyone's actively choosing or directing them, helps us to understand power as a conserving force, maintaining established relationships despite increased participation (Burbules, 1986, p. 96). This institutionalized power is well illustrated in the notion of schools as 'loosely coupled systems' (Meyer and Rowan, 1978; Meyer, Scott and Deal, 1980). In the apparent absence of tightly coordinated hierarchical controls upon teachers, schools show a stability reminiscent of top-down control. A new form of leadership is demanded in 'loosely coupled systems' (Duignan and Macpherson, 1987; Sergiovanni, 1987; Starratt, 1986). Leaders are expected to inspire purposeful activity on the part of organization members and harness this within their own vision of what is possible. As Weick notes, '. . . you (the administrator) don't influence less, you influence differently. The administrator . . . has the difficult task of affecting perceptions and monitoring and reinforcing the language people use to create and coordinate what they are doing' (Weick, 1986, p. 10).

Leadership depends, not simply on coercion, but also on the construction of consent. But both, as a senior Australian education official perceptively notes, entail forms of power:

> Educational administrators are usually anxious to sponsor some sort of interpersonal transaction that will move others in some intended manner. They need some sort of power to do this. Some sort of change will hopefully take place as a result of interpersonal transactions. The hope is held that the reaction will be positive; that people will not only comply with the intended goals but will also be enthusiastic about achieving them. (Cullen, 1981, p. 3)

However, it would be a mistake to assume that institutionalized power entails just the development of an interpersonal consensus of ideas and values. These are important, but so too are the institutional arrangements, orthodoxies, procedures and practices which also shape people's activity. This is certainly true in the case of participative decision-making. In all realms of social life, including education, people have always participated in shaping the conditions, structures, organizations, rules and agreements that shape their lives (Giddens, 1984). But, because in many situations participants may have a limited awareness of, or limited opportunities to exert, their agency, participation may be of an utmost minimal kind. It may simply take the form of passive consent.

These general points about the significance of institutionalized power as a higher order frame can be illustrated with reference to the rise of school-based decision-making and management in Victoria, Australia.

Institutionalized Power in Victorian School-based Decision-making and Management

In Victorian education there has been a widespread endorsement of participation, devolution and collaboration. But this apparent consensus involves contradictory notions of the general principle of school-based decision-making and management. There is a tension between school-based decision-making and management as a form of community control and as corporate management (Bates, 1985; Watkins *et al*, 1987). This tension is not restricted to Victoria, as Whitehead and Aggleton's (1986) elaboration, building on British experience, indicates.

> Within this common discourse of 'participation', it is possible to identify two main clusters of ideologies: the first associating changes in the composition of school governing bodies with the

creation of more open and democratic forms of institutional management; the second equating more open and democratic forms
of school government with greater accountability and an increase
in overall 'effectiveness' and 'efficiency'. (Whitehead and Aggleton, 1986, p. 436)

In Britain, where the conservative potential of school-based decision-
making and management is ascendant, parents are encouraged 'under the
guise of involvement and partnership, ... to become agents in the
implementation of central government policies' (Whitehead and Aggleton, 1986, p. 444).

In Victoria, too, this conservative trajectory is becoming more evident. The recently published *The Structure and Organization of the Schools
Division* (Victorian Ministry of Education, 1987) indicates that participation is to be reduced in scope and 'encouraged' only within tighter central
guidelines. Within the complex and contradictory pressures for increased
autonomy and participation at various levels of educational governance,
and for improved efficiencies and corporate management, the current
Victorian government has opted for accountability and control.

With a notion of institutionalized power, we should not be surprised
at this development in Victoria (and elsewhere). According to Wallin
(1985, p. 344), '"reforms" entail a change in the goals and basic values
underlying school activities, *any structure of change which does not take these
goals and values into account has a fundamentally wrong approach.*' In the
absence of such a shift in values and its institutionalization in bureaucratic
and ideological structures, Victorian restructuring, including the shift to
school-based decision-making and management, can, like the Scandina-
vian, European and American cases examined by Wallin, be characterized
as 'dynamically conservative' rather than 'reformist'. Institutionalized
power confirms such conservatism in a number of ways, some of which
can be readily identified.

First, despite a rhetoric of reform, people's participation in education
rests upon institutionalized expectations about the nature of education and
educational administration, and the roles of education participants. These
are built upon widely shared, historical understandings. Participants in
educational governance therefore tend to shape themselves to fit this
pattern of established, neutrally defined role positions.

Second, school-based decision-making and management in Victoria
has been defined in terms of 'devolution' of formerly centralized authority. But devolution seems not to have been regarded dynamically as a
way of doing things that needed to be asserted and defended. Rather, it is
a policy delivered from the centre to be implemented in a bureaucratically

efficient and politically neutral manner. The sense of limited discretion granted from above, of limited participation according to approved formats within an overall government policy and framework, reinforces among education participants bureaucratic modes of thinking while partially disguising the bureaucratic structures within which participation occurs. These structures shape and channel participation in relatively safe directions, while leaving untouched entrenched educational understandings, practices and arrangements. As Dunstan, a very senior educational administrator in Victoria, disarmingly comments: 'The thrust towards regionalization was an effective means whereby lay participation in education could be at the one time valued, harnessed and controlled' (Dunstan, 1986, p. 6).

Third, the apparently neutral and legitimate authority structure within which participation occurs can present a universal discourse, speaking for all participants in education. Alternative initiatives, developing among particular groups, appear as opposition to current 'legitimate' educational structures and practices. Such oppositional notions may be assimilated into the universal discourse, as we see with the notions of access, equity and relevance promoted over the last two decade by teachers, teacher unions and parent groups. They may also be discredited as pessimistic, premature, cynical or even irrational criticism of the approved and 'appropriate' participatory process, and hence disregarded.

Fourth, the universal discourse emanating from bureaucratic structures has been a further conservative force because it has led to a concern with appropriate consultative processes as much as with the substance of, and the values inherent in, policy. The expectation is that school-based decision-making and management should follow processes that result in genuine consensus and 'good' decisions — ones that all parties can support. This emphasis on process can overshadow what participants are participating in, and why. Issues of genuine significance can become submerged in negotiated procedures that are to be correctly implemented. Such participation also seems innocuous because it is linked to a notion of equality in participation: '... equality is defined as an equality of process, an equality of entry into interaction. The process of interaction makes no distinctions between the parties to the interaction — parents, students, teachers, bureaucrats are, ideally, to enter equality' (White, 1985, p. 72). But while we certainly recognize this formal equality of parties to participation, the constitution of those parties and their representation entail further forms of institutionalized power, which are inherent in school-based decision-making and management based upon representative democracy.

Institutionalized Power in the Politics of Participation

The politics of participation, for this is what we are really now discussing, are deeply influenced by relationships within the broader society, as well as by those of family and school, adult and child. These relationships beyond school-based decision-making and management shape the nature of the parties to participation, and their activity within school-based decision-making and management.

First, the relationships define constituencies and their particular concerns. For example, educational participation takes two forms. Participation *within* schools primarily concerns teachers and students. Participation *over* schools generally excludes students or, at best, as in Victoria, expects students to enter into the formal adult framework in a way that isolates them from their constituency. 'Parents' is the constituency which represents parents and acts on behalf of students. Furthermore, the assumed relationship between parents and students, institutionalized in law, can take a variety of forms:

> Parents may be addressed ... as individuals responsible for *their children*. But they may also appear as a group with a larger social responsibility for '*our*' children, even for *all children*. In the 1940's for example, parents were addressed as active, participating citizens, contributing not just to their own child's welfare, but the shape and character of the system of schooling as whole. (Center for Contemporary Cultural Studies, 1981, pp. 26–7)

Second, defining constituencies also defines 'non-constituencies' exclusively. Those who do not form a recognizable constituency, who are disorganized, whose position and concerns are fragmented or poorly articulated, and who, for whatever other reason, fail to take a political stance are excluded from participation. They may develop 'games' (Burawoy, 1985), resist or rebel, but they have no legitimate means of indicating their consent, or opposition, to the current arrangements.

Third, the representative nature of participation in school-based decision-making and management implies that limited opportunities for some parents to sit on the educational governing bodies are equivalent to total community involvement and that community interests are relatively homogeneous such that common aspirations can become defined as 'needs'. But the assumption of common interest, evident in unspecific terms like 'parent involvement' and 'community involvement', presents a homogenized view of parents and community which overlooks major social and cultural differences, even antagonisms.

Fourth, despite the complexity of parent and community groups, it has been demonstrated (Deakin Institute for Studies in Education, 1984) that for a host of reasons active parent participants often come from the ranks of 'concerned citizens' — those articulate, relatively prominent and often privileged members of the community who are likely to be found also in other local bodies and service associations. Representation of the 'parent' constituency by such parents is likely to be in harmony with the values of school-based decision-making and management. It is therefore less likely to interrupt or challenge existing arrangements for participation or education.

Finally, the emphasis in school-based decision-making and management on participation means that 'non-participation' must be recognized as a form of participation (Srivastva and Cooperrider, 1986, p. 685). This applies to those excluded from active participation through the construction of constituencies and the nature of representation, and also to passive parties to participation. In any form non-participation is read conservatively as consent.

Education, 'Context' and the Rise of School-based Decision-making and Management

The discussion has now proceeded well beyond the boundaries of what is commonly seen as 'education'. This, we would argue, is proper, for an adequate analysis of the rise of school-based decision-making and management must address the higher order frames which have impinged from the social and historical context. The literature we have reviewed recognizes the impact of the social context to a limited degree. There is rather empty talk of economic and political factors, which the reader is expected to fill, and ad hoc instances, such as the Labor Party victory in Victoria. We would agree that these are higher order frames in the rise of school-based decision-making and management, but in the absence of a sustained analysis and coherent theory of context, we can only ask, what is their significance?

The lack of systematic analysis of the context of school-based decision-making and management inhibits explanation of its rise. Higher order frames are identified, but their impact and interacting effects are unclear. Other features of society which would appear to be significant from a perspective in conflict theory are neglected. A more comprehensive view of its rise must address, for example, the state, the particular character of economic development and the nature of public opinion and 'common sense'.

The literature on school-based decision-making and management assumes a facet of the state — the educational bureaucracy and its schools — but this is not analyzed in detail as a part of the state, nor considered in relation to the state more broadly as an institutional complex and arena of politics (Burawoy, 1985). Neglect of the state means that its relation to civil society is also ignored. Economic developments appear, for example, as amorphous, and uninformative, economic factors. The changing nature of the private sphere, of family and unpaid domestic labour is entirely ignored, despite the empirical and conceptual impact of such themes (e.g. Pateman, 1985; Connell, 1987). Further omissions which we have begun to discuss include the ideological context and institutionalized power relationships which construct consent to current educational arrangements (Angus and Rizvi, 1989). But these must be seen in broader terms, as elements of public opinion and 'common sense'; further higher order frames which have shaped the rise of school-based decision-making and management must be explored. But analysis must go beyond simply identifying further higher order frames. It must also begin to query the adequacy of a notion of context as a backdrop, comprising more or less discrete factors that act exogenously upon education. We would argue that the assumptions embedded in this 'atomist' notion of context limit the analysis of school-based decision-making and management, and of education more generally, because, for example, it is unable to conceptualize the relation between education and society in an integrated, dynamic and historically specific way (Seddon, 1986).

We would suggest that a more adequate analysis of the rise of school-based decision-making and management would not start by being preoccupied with education which is seen only secondarily or incidentally in a context, but would rather see education as an integral part of the contemporary social order. In other words, in analyzing its rise, we must take a historical 'slice of society' in the late 1970s and early 1980s, and examine the place of schooling and its form of administration in that 'slice'. A theory of 'context' is not a list of exogenous factors or higher order frames which act upon education, but a theory of the relationship between education and society in all its dynamic complexity.

Steps are being taken in this direction. The relationship between education and society has been a traditional concern in the sociology of education where Archer (1979), Musgrave (1979, 1987), Lawn and Ozga (1981), Connell, Ashenden, Kessler and Dowsett (1982), Apple (1982), Connell (1985) provide a variety of insights. The focus on the education-society relationship has been usefully elaborated on by including an analysis of the state (e.g. Althusser, 1971; Salter and Tapper, 1981; Dale, 1982; Shapiro, 1982; Carnoy and Levin, 1985). But such analyses do not always offer a very dynamic or historical picture.

Some of the most interesting research in education at present is beginning to grapple with this problem, conceptualizing the relationship of education, state and society in a historically dynamic way. This leads to an examination of education, state and society as social processes, rather than as static phenomena or as snapshots of their development. The focus, for example, is on 'state formation' rather than 'the state'. Lundgren (1985) offers one perspective, exploring education as a facet of the historically changing process of production and reproduction, effected through the dynamic relationship of state and society.

The notion of 'settlement' offers a further perspective which has proved powerful. A 'settlement' is a period of temporary relative stability in the social order. It appears as a framework of agreement between conflicting social forces, one which structures social conflict so there is agreement at least over what to disagree about, the forms of disagreement and the procedures of resolution. This temporary stability rests upon a historically specific pattern of social relationships, a kind of truce. The settlement endures until the truce breaks down. What follows is a period of instability, a 'transition' leading toward a new, and qualitatively different, settlement.

Bates (1985) has used the notion of settlement in relation to Victorian educational restructuring. He suggests the policy of the Liberal Hunt Ministry in Victoria marked the end of a settlement in education. The prior pattern of extensive bureaucratic control, existing within an ostensibly 'non-political' system of education, was shattered by Hunt's restructuring: 'Unwittingly, Hunt, by using the rhetoric of devolution and participation to legitimate an essentially conservative reform, ... stirred these ideals into new life' (Bates, 1985, p. 299). The effect was to stimulate debate which went beyond questions of efficiency and effectiveness of the existing corporate structure, to raise fundamental questions about the control, and political nature, of education.

Bates (1985) offers an interesting, but fairly cursory, analysis. 'Settlement' is being used somewhat more extensively in other branches of educational research. These focus on historically specific shifts in educational practice which suggest the emergence or collapse of a settlement (e.g. Centre for Contemporary Cultural Studies, 1981; Grace, 1985; Freeland, 1986; Lawn, 1987; Seddon, 1987) in a process of 'transition' (Seddon, 1988). The conceptual framework of these analyses would prove very powerful in explaining the rise of school-based decision-making and management for it would see the international movement towards participative decision-making as being related to the increasing political instability and the need to manage pluralist political demands in the later 1960s. This marked the end of the post-war Keynesian settlement (Freeland, 1986). But as social, political, economic and cultural restructuring accelerates, it is accompanied by financial stringency, and more conservative approaches to the management of pluralism emerge. In education these include corporate management and school-based decision-making and management.

School-based Decision-making and Management:
A Redefinition

From this perspective school-based decision-making and management appears, not simply as participative decision-making, as our earlier working definition suggested, but as a historically specific form of participative decision-making which could, logically, be linked to particular patterns of social conflict. School-based decision-making and management is a politically based way of managing conflict and a stage in an ongoing social process. It is not merely a strategy for managing schools, but is part of an attempt to sustain the legitimacy of public institutions and of the state.

References

ALTHUSSER, L. (1971) 'Ideology and Ideological State Apparatus,' in *Lenin and Philosophy and Other Essays.* London: New Left Books.

ANGUS, L. and RIZVI, F. (1989) 'Power and the Politics of Participation,' *Journal of Educational Administration and Foundations*, 4, 1, pp. 6–23.

ANGUS, L., PRUNTY, J. and BATES, R. (1983) *Restructuring Victorian Education: Regional Issues.* Geelong: Deakin University, School of Education.

APPLE, M.W. (1982) *Education and Power.* London: Routledge and Kegan Paul.

ARCHER, M.S. (1979) *Social Origins of Educational Systems.* London: Sage.

ARTIS, J.B. (1980) *An Ethnographic Case Study of the Administrative Organization, Processes, and Behaviour in a Selected Senior High School.* Madison, Wisc.: Wisconsin University Research and Development Centre for Individualized Schooling. (ED210787)

BAKALIS, M.J. (1983) 'Power and Purpose in American Education,' *Phi Delta Kappan*, 65, 1, pp. 7–13.

BATES, R.J. (1985) 'The Socio-political Context of Administrative Change,' in FRAZER, M., DUNSTAN, J. and CREED, P. (Eds), *Perspectives in Organizational Changes: Lessons from Education.* Melbourne: Longman Cheshire.

BENTON, T. (1977) *Philosophical Foundations of the Three Sociologies.* London: Routledge and Kegan Paul.

BEYER, L.F. (1986) 'Schooling for Moral and Democratic Communities,' *Issues in Education,* 4, 1, pp. 1–18.

BONE, T.R. and RAMSAY, H.A. (Eds) (1981) 'Quality Control in Education? The Proceedings of the Annual Conference of the British Educatio al Management and Administrative Society,' *Educational Administration,* 9, 2, pp. 1–122.

BOYD, R. (1986) 'Collaborative Decision Making in Local Developments of School Policy and Practices,' Paper presented to the symposium 'A State in Action: Working with Schools on Program Improvement' at the Annual Meeting of the American Educational Research Association, San Francisco, Calif., 16–20 April.

BRAVERMAN, H. (1974) *Labour and Monopoly Capital.* New York: Monthly Review Press.

BRYDEN, (1982) 'Public Input into Policy-making and Administration: The Present Situation and Some Requirements for the Future,' *Canadian Public Administration,* 25, 1, pp. 81–107.

BURAWOY, M. (1985) *The Politics of Production: Factory Regimes under Capitalism and Socialism.* London: Verso.

BURBULES, N. (1986) 'A Theory of Power in Education,' *Educational Theory,* 36, pp. 95–114.

BURCKEL, N.C. (1984) 'Participatory Management in Academic Libraries: A Review,' *College and Research Libraries,* 45, 1, pp. 25–34.

CARNOY, M. and LEVIN, H.M. (1985) *Schooling and Work in the Democratic State.* Stanford, Calif.: Stanford University Press.

CENTRE FOR CONTEMPORARY CULTURAL STUDIES (1981) *Unpopular Education.* London: Hunchinson.

CHAPMAN, J. and BOYD, W.L. (1986) 'Decentralization, Devolution, and the School Principal: Australian Lessons on Statewide Educational Reform,' *Educational Administration Quarterly,* 22, 4, pp. 28–58.

CLEGG, S. and DUNKERLEY, D. (1980) *Organization, Class and Control.* London: Routledge and Kegan Paul.

COLEMAN, P. (1987) 'Implementing School-based Decision-making,' *The Canadian Administrator,* 26, 7, pp. 1–6.

CONNELL, R.W. (1985) *Teachers' Work.* Sydney: Allen and Unwin.

CONNELL, R.W. (1987) *Gender and Power.* Sydney: Allen and Unwin.

CONNELL, R.W., ASHENDEN, D.J., KESSLER, S. and DOWSETT, G.W. (1982) *Making the Difference: Schools, Families and Social Division.* Sydney: Allen and Unwin.

CONWAY, J.A. (1984) 'The Myth, Mystery and Mastery of Participative Decision Making in Education,' *Educational Administration Quarterly,* 20, pp. 11–40.

CREED, P.J. (1986) 'Australian Perspectives on State-Wide Educational Reform: Restructuring the Victorian Education Department. Implementing Structural Change in a State Department of Education,' Paper given at Annual Meeting of American Educational Research Association, San Francisco.

CULLEN, P. (1981) 'Devolution of Power — The Political Reality', *ACER Bulletin,* 22, pp. 30–40.

DALE, R. (1982) 'Education and the Capitalist State: Contributions and Contradictions,' in APPLE, M.W. (Ed.), *Cultural and Economic Reproduction in Education: Essays on Class Ideology and the State.* London: Routledge and Kegan Paul.

DAVIES, D. (1985) 'Parent Involvement in the Public Schools in the 1980s: Proposals, Issues and Opportunities,' Paper presented at the Research for Better Schools Conference, Philadelphia, 9–10 May.

DEAKIN INSTITUTE FOR STUDIES IN EDUCATION (1984) *Restructuring Victorian Education: Current Issues.* Geelong: Deakin University.

DEPARTMENT OF EDUCATION AND SCIENCE (1985) *Better Schools*, White Paper. London: HMSO.

DUIGNAN, P. and MACPHERSON, R. (1987) 'The Educative Leadership Project,' *Educational Management and Administration*, 15, pp. 49–62.

DUNLAP, D. (1985) 'New Ideas for School Improvement', *OSSC Report*, 23, 3, pp. 1–4.

DUNSTAN, J.F. (1986) 'The Impact of Changing Values on Organizational Structures in Education,' Paper presented at the 67th Annual Meeting of the American Educational Research Association, San Francisco.

FREELAND, J. (1986) 'Australia: The Search for a New Educational Settlement,' in SHARP, R. (Ed.), *Capitalist Crisis and Schooling: Comparative Studies in the Politics of Education.* Melbourne: Macmillan.

GIDDENS, A. (1984) *The Constitution of Society.* Cambridge: Polity Press.

GRACE, G. (1985) 'Judging Teachers: The Social and Political Contexts of Teacher Evaluation,' *British Journal of Sociology of Education*, 6, 1, pp. 3–16.

GREENFIELD, W. (1985) 'Studies of the Assistant Principalship: Towards New Avenues of Inquiry,' *Education and Urban Society*, 18, 1, pp. 7–27.

HERRICK, N.Q. (1985) 'Is the Time Finally Ripe for Educational Democracy?' *Journal of Social Policy*, 16, 2, pp. 53–6.

HERZBERG, F. (1972) *Work and the Nature of Man.* London: Stapler Press.

JAKES, H.E. (1986) 'The Effect of Public Participation and the Utilization of Third Party Neutrals on the Reorganization of a Large Ontario School System,' Paper presented at the 14th Annual Meeting of the Canadian Society for the Study of Education, Winnipeg.

KALLOS, D. and LUNDGREN, U. (1979) 'The Study of Curriculum as a Pedagogical Problem,' in *Curriculum as a Pedagogical Problem.* Stockholm: GWK Gleerup.

KEAT, R. and URRY, J. (1975) *Social Theory as Science.* London: Routledge and Kegan Paul.

KEELEY, M. (1984) 'Impartiality and Participant Interest Theories of Organizational Effectiveness,' *Administrative Science Quarterly*, 29, 1, pp. 1–25.

KIRNER, J. (1985) 'Organizational Change in Education: The Parent Line,' in FRAZER, M., DUNSTAN, J. and CREED, P. (Eds), *Perspectives in Organizational Change.* Melbourne: Longman Cheshire.

LAWN, M. (1987) 'The Spur and the Bridle,' *Journal of Curriculum Studies*, 19, 3, pp. 227–36.

LAWN, M. and OZGA, J. (1981) 'The Educational Worker? A Re-assessment of Teachers,' in BARTON, L. and WALKER, S. (Eds), *Schools, Teachers and Teaching.* Lewes.: Falmer Press.

LAWN, M. and OZGA, J. (1986) 'Unequal Partners: Teachers under Indirect Rule,' *British Journal of Sociology of Education*, 7, 2, pp. 225–38.

LEZOTTE, L.W. (1986) 'School Effectiveness: Reflections and Future Directions,' Paper presented at the Annual Meeting of the American Educational Research Association, San Francisco, Calif., 16–20 April.

LIKERT, R. (1976) *The Human Organization*. New York: McGraw-Hill.

LINDELOW, J. (1981) 'School-based Management,' *ERIC Clearing House on Educational Management*. Eugene, Ore.

LUKES, S. (1974) *Power: A Radical View*. London: Macmillan.

LUNDGREN, U.P. (1985) 'Curriculum from a Global Perspective,' in *Current Thought on Curriculum: 1985 ASCD Yearbook*. Alexandria, Va.: Association for Supervision and Curriculum Development.

LUNDGREN, U.P. (1986) 'Education — Society, Curriculum Theory,' *Swedish National Board of Educational School Research Newsletter*, January/February.

McCULLOCH, G. (1986) 'Policy, Politics and Education: The Technical and Vocational Education Initiative,' *Journal of Educational Policy*, 1, 1, pp. 35–52.

McGREGOR, D. (1966) *Leadership and Motivation*. Cambridge, Mass.: MIT Press.

MATTHEWS, R. (1986) 'Education in Victoria: The Context,' in *A State in Action: Working with the Schools for Program Improvement*, Symposium presented at the 67th Annual Meeting of the American Educational Research Association, San Francisco.

MEYER, J. and ROWAN, B. (1978) 'Institutionalized Organizations: Formal Structure as Myth and Ceremony,' *American Journal of Sociology*, 83, 2, pp. 340–63.

MEYER, J., SCOTT, N. and DEAL, T. (1980) *Institutional and Technical Sources of Organizational Structure: Explaining the Structure of Educational Organizations*. Stanford, Calif.: Stanford University, School of Education.

MITTER, W. (1987) 'Expectations of Schools and Teachers in the Context of Social and Economic Changes,' *International Review of Education*, 33, 3, pp. 263–75.

MUSGRAVE, P.W. (1979) *Society and the Curriculum in Australia*. Sydney: Allen and Unwin.

MUSGRAVE, P.W. (1987) *Socialising Contexts*. Sydney: Allen and Unwin.

NATIONAL COMMISSION ON EXCELLENCE IN EDUCATION (1983) *A Nation at Risk*. Washington, D.C.: US Government Printing Office.

ORNSTEIN, A.C. (1983) 'Administrative Decentralization and Community Policy: Review and Outlook,' *Urban Review*, 15, 1, pp. 3–10.

PATEMAN, C. (1985) 'Introduction', in GOODNOW, J. and PATEMAN, C. (Eds), *Women, Social Science and Public Policy*. Sydney: Allen and Unwin.

PINK, W.T. (1986) 'Introduction: An Issue on School Reform,' *Urban Review*, 18, 1, pp. 3–5.

PINK, W.T. and WALLACE, D.K. (1984) 'Creating Effective Schools: Moving from Theory to Practice,' Paper presented at the Annual Meeting of the American Educational Research Association, New Orleans.

QUALITY OF EDUCATION REVIEW COMMITTEE (1985) *Quality of Education in Australia (QERC Report)*. Canberra: Australian Government Publishing Service.

RIZVI, F. (1986) *Administrative Leadership and the Democratic Community as a Social Ideal*. Geelong: Deakin University Press.

SALTER, B. and TAPPER, T. (1981) *Education, Politics and the State: The Theory and Practice of Educational Change*. London: Grant McIntrye.

SAVAGE, G.T. (1984) 'Decision Making as Negotiation: A Comparison of Two

Labor-Management Committees,' Paper presented at the 34th Annual Meeting of the International Communication Association, San Francisco.

SEDDON, T.L. (1986) 'Education and Social Changes: A Critique of Contextualism,' *Australian Journal of Education*, 30, 2, pp. 150–67.

SEDDON, T.L. (1987) Schooling, State and Society: The Federation Settlement in New South Wales, 1900 to the 1930's, Unpublished PhD thesis, Macquarie University, Sydney.

SEDDON, T.L. (1988) 'The Transition in New South Wales Schooling: From Federation to Keynesian Settlement,' *Education Research and Perspectives*, 15, 1, pp. 60–9.

SELLECK, R.J.W. (1985) 'The Restructuring: Some Historical Reflections,' in FRAZER, M., DUNSTAN, J. and CREED, P. (Eds), *Perspectives in Organizational Change: Lessons from Education*. Melbourne: Longman Cheshire.

SERGIOVANNI, T. (1987) 'Leadership for Quality Schooling: New Understandings and Practices,' Paper prepared for the Southwestern Bell Conference, 'Restructuring Schooling for Quality Education: A New Reform Agenda', Trinity University, Texas.

SHAPIRO, H.S. (1982) 'Education in Capitalist Society: Towards a Reconsideration of the State in Educational Policy,' *Teachers' College Record*, 83, 4, pp. 519–28.

SHEARS, L. (1985) 'The Fragmentation of Power,' in FRAZER, M., DUNSTAN, J. and CREED, P. (Eds) *Perspectives on Organizational Change: Lessons from Education*. Melbourne: Longman Cheshire.

SIMPKINS, W.S. (1981) 'The Australian Literature on School Administration: Power, Participation and School Management. A Select Bibliography,' *Journal of Educational Administration*, Occasional Paper 1.

SMITH, R. (1985) 'The Policy of Education Change by Changing Teachers: Comments on the "Democratic Curriculum",' *Australian Journal of Education*, 29, 2, pp. 141–9.

SRIVASTVA, S. and COOPERRIDER, D. (1986) 'The Emergence of the Egalitarian Organization,' *Human Relations*, 39, pp. 290–301.

STARRATT, R. (1986) *Excellence in Education and Quality of Leadership*, Occasional Paper No. 11. Geelong: Institute of Educational Administration.

TAYLOR, F. (1947) *Scientific Management*. London: Harper and Row.

THOMAS, A.R. (1986) 'Up and Over with the Principalship Down Under,' Paper presented at the Annual Meeting of the American Educational Research Association, San Francisco, Calif., 16–20 April.

TINKER, T. (1986) 'Metaphor or Reification: Are Radical Humanists Really Libertarian Anarchists?', *Journal of Management Studies*, 23, 4, pp. 363–83.

VICTORIAN MINISTRY OF EDUCATION (1987) *The Structure and Organization of the Schools Division*. Melbourne: Government Printer.

WALKER, J.C. (1985) 'Philosophy and the Study of Education: A Critique of the Common Sense Consensus,' *Australian Journal of Education*, 29, 2, pp. 101–14.

WALLIN, E. (1985) 'To Change a School: Experiences from Local Development Work,' *Journal of Curriculum Studies*, 17, 3, pp. 321–50.

WATKINS, P., RIZVI, F. and ANGUS, L. (1987) 'Regional Boards and Victorian State Education,' *Australian Journal of Education*, 31, 3, pp. 252–71.

WEBER, M. (1947) *The Theory of Social and Economic Organization*. Trans T.

PARSONS and A. HENDERSON, with an introduction by T. PARSONS. London: Routledge and Kegan Pual.

WEICK, K. (1986) 'The Concept of Loose Coupling: An Assessment,' *Organizational Theory Dialogue*, December, pp. 8–11.

WELLS, L.C. (1986) *Minnesota K-12 Education: A Catalogue of Reform Proposals. A Summary Version. A Report of the Cura/College of Educational Project on the Future of K-12 Education in Minnesota*. Minneapolis, Minn.: Minnesota University, Centre for Urban and Regional Affairs.

WHITE, D. (1985) 'Education: Controlling the Participants,' *Arena*, 72, pp. 63–79.

WHITEHEAD, J. and AGGLETON, P. (1986) 'Participation and Popular Control on School Governing Bodies: The Case of the Taylor Report and Its Aftermath,' *British Journal of Sociology of Education*, 7, 4, pp. 433–49.

WOOD, S. (1985) 'Work Organization,' in DEEM, R. and SALAMAN, G. (Eds), *Work, Culture and Society*. Milton Keynes: Open University Press.

YIN, R.K. *et al.* (1984) 'Excellence in Urban High Schools: An Emerging District/School Perspective,' *Cosmo Corp*, Washington D.C.

ZERCHYKOV, R. (1985) 'Why School Councils?' *Journal of Equity and Choice*, 2, 1, pp. 37–8.

Chapter 3

Schooling, Organizational Learning and Efficiency in the Growth of Knowledge

Colin W. Evers

It has sometimes been supposed that the mode of organization most likely to promote efficient decision-making is a hierarchical, centralized decision structure. In this chapter I shall employ some arguments from theory of knowledge, control theory and economics to suggest that this claim is, in general, untrue. In particular, I shall suggest that for a public good like education, where provided by government, there are good grounds for preferring less hierarchical and more decentralized decision structures. That is, under certain defensible conditions, efficiency in educational decision-making can be enhanced by reductions in the concentration of organizational control.

In summary, the main argument of the chapter runs as follows. Hierarchical organization, instantiated as a network of superordinate-subordinate authority relations, promotes consistency or uniformity in the implementation of centrally produced decisions. At its best it promotes the reliable transmission and diffusion of directives. Against this model, theory of knowledge nowadays stresses the fallibility of directives or decisions (Popper, 1963). As a result it urges that some attention be given to error correction, at the expense of attention to the prevention of error. This broadly Popperian view of the nature and growth of knowledge is, in general, isomorphic to the main structures of organizational control posited by control theory, which is concerned with the application of detected error to system management (Simon, 1952; Beer 1966; Strank, 1983). Combining these views of knowledge and control leads most naturally to an adaptive view of organizational learning (Argyris, 1982; Argyris and Schön, 1978). Where information about the outcomes of organizational decision-making can be produced and reliably transmitted to centrally located decision-makers, even hierarchical organizations can learn adaptively (from their mistakes, or better advice) to make better decisions. My claim is that if these organizations are educational systems, the information assumption is less likely to be true. Given an understanding of the measurement of efficiency for the control of public goods, and the epistemological advantages of adaptive learning strategies, I claim that educational organizations can make certain decisions more efficiently (and effectively) where some form of participation in a less centralized decision process exists, including participation at the school level.

Participative Decision-making in Education: Some Empirical Considerations

There are many arguments in the literature for participative decision-making, some more easily adjudicated empirically than others. One large survey of students, Conway (1984), usefully reflects on some of the methodological complexities here and the equivocal nature of much of the evidence. In assessing some of this evidence for the effects of participation, it is important to distinguish, for example, the external perspective: the involvement of parents and other lay citizens in the educational process; and the internal perspective: the involvement of teachers and students. In addition to the question of who participates, there is also the question of the qualities of the process. According to Conway (1984, p. 20), 'the set of qualities that appear to be most useful deal with the *degree* of participation, the *content* for decisions, and the *scope* of the participant powers or the stage of the decision process involved.' The degree of participation has to do with the amount of input a participant has in the decision process and the extent to which this input is heeded. Content concerns the type of decisions made: financial matters, curriculum content, personnel issues, the organization of the school, educational policy and so on. Finally, the scope of participation refers to the stage of decision-making or problem-solving at which participation occurs; that is, whether it occurs at all stages or only some.

Now if the justification of internal (teacher and student) participation in school-based decision-making depends on current evidence for the promotion of more effective change, satisfaction with job, or greater productivity, then for Conway (1984, pp. 23–9) the support is at best modest. On change, there appears to be little evidence of a difference in effect between change initiated in collaboration with rank-and-file and change without such participation. On the relationship between job satisfaction and participation, Conway (1984, p. 25) notes an increase in job satisfaction observed in studies, but cautions that 'the ratio still shows about one of three investigations not confirming the relationship.' This is slightly more favourable than the 40 per cent of studies not confirming the relationship reported in Locke and Schweiger's (1979) large survey of (mainly) non-educational organizations.

On the question of productivity, Locke and Schweiger (1979, p. 316) concluded 'that there is no evidence that participation in decision-making is superior to more directive methods in increasing productivity.' However, they made the important concession that a major contextual factor was knowledge possessed by participants. Although Conway (1984, p. 17) is cautious about making inferences from findings on non-educational organizations to educational organizations, as Chapman (1990) notes, what amounts to the knowledge factor appears sufficiently important to suggest 'that in the longer term, at least, there may be a direct positive relationship between increased school-based decision-making and improvement in educational outcomes.' Indeed, the relevance of participant knowledge may explain why, on even quite narrow productivity criteria of teacher teaching behaviours and student test scores, the cumulative evidence seems 'to indicate that mid-level participation is probably desirable for both effective teaching and student achievement' (Conway, 1984, p. 29).

With respect to the external perspective of lay participation, for comparable indicators much the same pattern of evidence exists. In what follows, therefore, I propose to examine more explicitly the kind of organizational structures that permit a more focused application of participants' knowledge and judgment to the decision process.

Knowledge, Complexity and Error

A one-way directive view of decision-making, with instructions for implementation propagating down an organizational hierarchy, places a great premium on the initial correctness of decisions. Given the magnitude of the complexities that invest educational policy and decision-making, this top-down approach to decision can be seriously affected by error. It is worth considering at least three types of error and possible associated hierarchical resources for prevention.

Perhaps the simplest is error of calculation. All the knowledge required for a decision may be at hand, but an error had occurred somewhere in, say, the calculation of consequences. The simplest organizational hedge against any malfunction is to build in redundancy of function. Where the cost of malfunction is high, and its stochastic properties known, reliable calculation, and hence the quality of decision-making, will invariably depend on maintaining a certain amount of functional redundancy. Indeed, von Neumann has proved that given enough redundancy, it is possible to construct systems of arbitrarily high reliability from unreliable parts. (The massively parallel architecture of the human brain is a design instance of how long-term reliability is maintained against the ongoing degradation of components.)

Strictly speaking, duplication of function is a horizontal extension of organizational structure, and so involves a measure of decentralization. However, to provide information, independent calculators need to be coupled somewhere by a match/mismatch feedback loop which in turn may involve supervision (though not always, as further calculation can continue to be initiated automatically until matching occurs).

Errors in knowledge which are not simply the result of malfunction call for more drastic prevention strategies. When it comes to cataloguing the limits of human knowledge in policy analysis and decision-making, the arguments of the incrementalists (e.g. Braybrooke and Lindblom, 1963) and the satisficers (Simon, 1976) are decisive (see Evers, 1988). For example, in knowing all the relevant details required in deciding on, say, a major reallocation of funding resources to schools, or even the introduction of local selection of school principals, it would be useful to know the relevant regularities or laws that govern the behaviour of the system. But our current knowledge of predictively useful law-like generalizations in social science is modest indeed, though a little better in some quantitative disciplines like economics, provided the drastic simplifying assumptions about human (economic) behaviour hold up.

It may be thought that this failing, occurring as it does in the most theoretical reaches of theory, can be quarantined from the descriptive taxonomies used to make observations and gather data. We now know, however, that there is no sharp theoretical/observational distinction to be drawn in accounting for the structure of empirical theories (see Quine, 1960, pp. 1–79). Since failure of generalization may reflect not so much a concession to real world complexity as a failure to carve the world in theoretically interesting ways, the infirmities of generalization can also be the infirmities of data gathering.

Theory, of course, also shapes perceptions of the relevance of information, including that which bears on the tracing of more attenuated causal chains. As an example of this, Herbert Simon (1976, p. 82) traces a devious causal link between the number of elderly English spinsters and the size of the clover crop in different English counties, inviting legislators on matters of marriage to beware! Knowledge for decision can thus fall short of what is required through weaknesses of theory, poverty of imagination when it comes to exploring and testing possible relevant information, and the limited resources of research. Since the consequences of decision alternatives can ramify in arbitrarily extensive ways without the simplifying assumptions and approximations of theory, the costs of research needed to minimize the occurrence of error will fairly quickly outrun the costs of detecting and correcting the consequences of error. It was partly for these reasons that Lindblom suggested a range of simplifying and approximating stratagems in the approach he called 'disjointed incrementalism': for example, limiting consideration to a few familiar alternatives; exploring only some of the (more important) possible consequences of an alternative; and, more controversially, dividing the work of analysis 'to many (partisan) participants in policy making' (Lindblom, 1979, p. 517).

However, this approach does not so much solve the problem of error prevention in knowledge as give up on it. The obvious efficiency trade-off against the costs of increased lapses in prevention due to savings and real time constraints on knowledge acquisition is the provision of a mechanism for error correction. Administratively, within a hierarchy, this amounts to the provision of a feedback loop between sampled outcomes (or perhaps localized expert knowledge) and centralized decision structures. Where knowledge is reckoned as fallible, there is nothing out of the ordinary in a design which confers, at its strongest, de facto veto over the outputs of centralized decision-making. As Popper (1968) has argued, this kind of design is ubiquitous in natural learning systems. For all learning, all growth in fallible knowledge, is really a matter of improving some pre-existing body of knowledge. There can be no learning without some prior (unlearned) knowledge or set of dispositions (see Popper, 1963, pp. 43–8; Watanabe, 1969, pp. 376–9; Evers, 1985, 1988). The principal mode of improvement is by resolving mismatches between prediction and theory-driven experience. One may expect, therefore, that organizations which instantiate in their structure a basic learning design would, over time, become more efficient decision-makers.

The last type of error to be considered, error of judgment, is really in my view just an extension of the knowledge category. This claim requires some argument, however, since I use the term 'judgment' to include values or very broad goals, and these are sometimes supposed to be either other than knowledge or immune from the usual forms of refutation. I have given this argument elsewhere (Evers, 1985, 1987, 1988) and I do not propose to add to it here. The central claims are as follows. Our learning of values appears to be contiguous with our learning of everything else. The epistemological failure of empirical content to distribute unevenly over the sentences of a theory, which leads to a blurring of the theoretical/observational distinction, also appears to blur the fact/value distinction and in the direction, I should add, of ethical naturalism. This suggests that the same apparatus and details of theory revision that apply to the more central elements of a theory also apply to value claims. A merit of this conclusion is that it posits a needed mechanism for explaining the adjustments experience counsels we make to the weightings we are willing to accord decision alternatives. In positing the same mechanism for the learning of purported means and ends, it permits the justification of trade-offs to be embedded in the same epistemological framework.

Inasmuch as values (and maybe other knowledge claims) tend to be sensitive to variations in a person's background, interests and experience, the administrative provision of communication feedback loops for the correction of errors of judgment may require a sampling of those most affected, or likely to be most affected, by decisions. I shall argue later that this provision will be crucial for efficient decision-making concerning the public good of education. Needless to say, arrangements in this direction will be towards decentralization and away from hierarchy, involving as they do a weakening of executive forms of decision control. For, as Strank (1983, p. 55) has argued, 'the normal hierarchical form of organizational structure puts great barriers in the way of such horizontal communication.'

A Note on Control Theory

The use of error feedback loops to regulate both the growth of knowledge and organizational decision-making is an application of designs that are part of the usual subject matter of control theory. For in general, control theory deals with the regulation of systems through the use of feedback (see Wonham, 1984; Schoderbek *et al.*, 1975, pp. 57–84). The most basic design for a feedback regulated control system can be expressed diagrammatically as follows:

In this model output from PLANT is regulated by the CONTROLLER matching SENSED output from PLANT against input.

This simple design is sufficient to describe the operation of a thermostatically controlled heating system. To see this let input be Ti, the required room temperature; let PLANT be the heater which is used to produce room temperature output To; finally, let CONTROLLER be an error detector that measures the difference between *Ti* and *To*. The total system would then be:

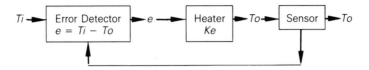

Although this model, as a first order feedback system, is only capable of goal attainment, it is not a trivial design. For example, if we make the (reasonable) assumption that energy consumed by the heater to raise room temperature is some multiple, K, of e, the model yields the equations

$$e = Ti - To$$
$$To = Ke$$

from which we can derive an expression for K $(= To/(Ti - To))$ to estimate the work done (and hence costs incurred) in heating the room to the required temperature (see Simon, 1952).

A first order design for decision–making would be slightly more complex and should contain at least the following features

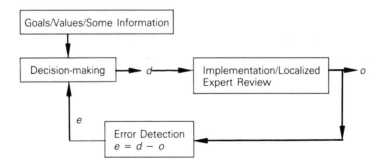

where *d* is decisions made, *o* is the outcomes of implementation or, perhaps, the results of localized expert review, and *e* the difference between the two. (I omit drawing in the sensors.) Note that I have drawn Goals/Values/Some Information (i) apart from the Decision-making box into which error feeds back, and (ii) connected by a one-way arrow. This is to indicate that these items have been removed from feedback driven critical scrutiny, a limitation that is a defining feature of first order systems.

In second order systems, however, goals, aims, objectives, values, in fact all knowledge that figures in the making of a decision, is subject to revision through error elimination. These systems are rather more complex to represent diagrammatically because goal evaluation will itself be a function of reviews of past successes and failures, thus implying additional feedback from a memory component. More extravagant reviews will keep track of the match/mismatch rate for whole decision strategies, a feature of third order systems which provides feedback on the outcomes of different learning designs. Powerful heuristic problem-solvers like the current best chess playing machines employ second and third order design features.

Some of these designs analyzed by control theorists, especially second order designs, have also been studied by organizational theorists interested in designing structures that promote organizational learning, and hence more efficient problem-solving and decision-making. In the next section I consider briefly the work of one such influential theorist who has studied both business and educational systems.

Organizational Learning

In a series of studies of a large range of organizations Chris Argyris and co-workers have distinguished two main categories of organizational learning. In single loop learning

> there is a single feedback loop which connects detected outcomes of action to organizational strategies and assumptions which are modified to keep organizational performance within the range set by organizational norms. The norms themselves — for produce quality, sales, or task performance — remain unchanged.... In order for *organizational* learning to occur, learning agents' discoveries, inventions and evaluations must be embedded in organizational memory. (Argyris and Schön, 1978, p. 19)

Organizational learning can occur by so structuring the possibility of individual learning that certain shared perceptions of the organization — the organization's theory-in-use — are changed.

Argyris regards single loop learning, which in design corresponds to our earlier first order systems, as being quite inadequate for the decisions and problems that most organizations face (for an extended analysis see Argyris, 1982, pp. 3–155.) For example, while such a design makes it possible for organizations to 'create continuity, consistency, and stability, and to maintain the status quo in order to achieve objectives within desired costs' (Argyris and Schön, 1978, p. 123), it contains no provision for the correction of its goals and values, or the basis of weightings used to structure decision alternatives. So while participation in decision-making is enhanced through the process of organized feedback, the scope for error elimination is somewhat restricted. Single loop organizational learning makes for 'dynamic conservatism', a condition inimical to long-term success or survival in a changing internal or external environment. It is a learning structure ill-suited to coping with discontinuity, instability and changes in the status quo.

The second type of learning, which Argyris regards as the most appropriate given the conditions under which most organizations exist, is called 'double loop learning'. This applies to 'those sorts of organizational inquiry which resolve incompatible organizational norms by setting new priorities and weightings of norms, or by restructuring the norms themselves together with associated strategies and assumptions' (Argyris and Schön, 1978, p. 24). This corresponds to our earlier second order systems, and should also be regarded as containing the possibility for third order learning — learning to learn more effectively — which Argyris calls 'deutero-learning' (Argyris and Schön, 1978, p. 26).

What effect does the implementation of double loop learning have on hierarchy in decision-making and how can it promote participation? One advantage of hierarchy, in addition to its top-down control capacity, is its facility for resolving complexity. Complex tasks, when decomposed into more manageable specialized subtasks coordinated as part of the execution of organizational goals, admit readily of a hierarchical control structure. Indeed, 'the pyramidal pattern, which is so invariant that people often define organizations as pyramidal structures, derives from the principles of specialization of work and of hierarchical control' (Argyris and Schön, 1978, p. 120). A fundamental design problem for this type of structure consists in maintaining knowledgeable control in the face of expertise decentralized in order to provide high level specialized function. Hierarchical control may be undermined for gains in efficient decision-making to the extent that decentralized error detection and corrective advice can be fed back to influence, perhaps decisively, all the relevant determinants of decision-making.

Whether or not these cybernetic participative designs do make for more efficient decision-making or problem-solving is finally an empirical matter. Argyris' evidence suggests that they do, and this is a reasonable result given what we know of the epistemic virtues of these designs. However, there are some complexities in the measurement of efficiency that call for a distinction between the (mainly) business organizations that Argyris deals with and educational organizations that produce (at least to some extent) public goods. This distinction is also worth making when considering the participative perspective. For almost all of the evidence for second loop organizational learning involves internal participation, whereas an important dimension in the argument over educational decision-making concerns external participation. Both of these distinctions have some bearing on the issue of efficiency.

Efficient Educational Organizations

'Efficiency' is well defined in engineering contexts where the term has standard uses. Consider, for example, the mechanical system of a car engine. It converts the chemical energy contained in the fuel into mechanical energy for propelling the car. From an engineering perspective the efficiency of the engine is the ratio of energy input, chemical energy, to desired or usable energy output, the mechanical energy available for the car. Conservation of energy thus sets a maximum level of engineering efficiency for any physical system at 100 per cent. (A good car engine is about 40 per cent efficient in this sense.) When we move to consider organizational efficiency, some disanalogies appear. For example, there is no equivalent conservation principle. So the costs sustained in having, say, a fire department, the inputs, may very well be less than the costs incurred in not having one, the output being the consequent losses from fire (Simon, 1976, p. 181).

In the case of the car and the fire department the construction of an input/output ratio is possible because input and output are measured in the same units: energy for the car and dollars for the department. The possibility of a similar calculation for, say, the efficiency of an art gallery seems to be thwarted for want of a suitable identity of units of input and output. One solution often adopted is to shift to a measurement of relative efficiency. Instead of saying that a gallery, *A*, is efficient, we say that it is more efficient than some other gallery, *B*. If inputs be dollars and outputs be reckoned as some quantity, say 'arts', relative efficiency compares, legitimately, ratios of arts per dollar. Turning to educational systems, we can now say that a participative system is relatively more efficient than a non-participative system if it delivers more educational outputs per, say, dollar cost.

An alleged advantage of relative efficiency is that comparisons can be made independently of an adjudication on goals or values: 'the efficiency criterion is completely neutral as to what goals are to be attained' (Simon, 1976, p. 14). This means that the efficiency formula can be stated in relation to any specified educational output regardless of the merits of that output. Goals are one things, about which there can be disagreement and debate; efficiency in realizing goals is something else again.

I want to note some qualifications on this conclusion which imply that the matter of efficiency as a policy objective cannot be separated so readily from the matter of educational goals when these are considered as further policy objectives. The key difficulty emerges when one considers what I would call the *equivalence of complementary efficiencies*. To give a simple example, suppose system *A* produces knowledge more efficiency than *B*. Then if the complement of knowledge is ignorance, we can say that *B* produces ignorance correspondingly more efficiently than *A*. Since a complement can formally be defined for any arbitrary performance measure, it follows that for unspecified outputs any system is as efficient as any other system. (This counter-intuitive result is related to the Popper/Quine/Watanabe claim, 'if *X*, *Y* and *Z* are distinct objects — say two swans and a duck — there are as many similarities between *X* and *Y* as there are between *Y* and *Z*', which provides the basis for an error elimination view of the growth of knowledge. The claim implies that logically, there is no such things as a class of similar objects.)

The equivalence of complementary efficiencies means that for unspecified educational outcomes efficiency cannot function in a normative way in educational decision-making. So efficiency can be used normatively only given some prior weighting or selection of outputs. Unfortunately, this condition for normativeness does not decide in general on the desirability of efficiency, since presumably we would prefer a little less efficiency in the production of ignorance from a school. To secure desirability, we appear to need reliable knowledge of the sorts of outputs appropriate for an educational system. But the defensibility of sources here will presumably reflect judgments of expertise, knowledge of educational theory, relevant experience and legitimate interests in the outputs of educational systems (on the last item see Walker, 1987). The belief that all of this can be provided without recourse to (i) second order feedback loops that permit the correction of educational aims and objectives, and (ii) the provision of an external perspective is, if not clearly false, at least worth testing against the inputs from (i) and (ii). This suggests that our most reliable knowledge of some particular level of efficiency as a desirable goal for an educational system depends on the existence of some form of internal and external participative contribution to the broader range of educational policy and decision-making.

Developing an argument from Goodin and Wilenski (1984), we can now propose a considerable extension of external participation in educational decision-making. For once the virtue of efficiency is admitted to be relative to the satisfaction of other desirability conditions, the importance of competing desirable desiderata needs to be adjudicated. To see the consequences of this, consider a set, W, of wants, including the (first order) want of efficiency. Let S be a system that satisfies these wants to such an extent that any other system always satisfies fewer wants. We can call S a Pareto optimal system. Now it is simply an open question whether optimal S implies a ranking of wants *within* S that places efficiency at the top. The (second order) efficiency of S does not guarantee first order efficiency *within* S. This is because first order efficiency determines a ranking of other wants that can run contrary to a ranking determined by some other element of W, say some first order want associated with a conception of justice. So if people have a very strong desire to live in a society governed by such a view of justice, increasing the second order efficiency of S, that is optimizing the global satisfaction of wants, will entail reducing efficiency within S. Similarly, systematic views of educational goals — perhaps equity, democratic participation and the growth of knowledge — imply preferred rankings of wants that can fail to coincide with a ranking that places the want of efficiency first. Of course, what people want in complex, continuously changing circumstances is not known a priori. But to ensure that education contributes to a more efficient satisfaction of global wants — the good of the community — participative feedback from a broader community spectrum seems reasonable, though by now the amount of relevant input resulting from feedback output would require a more piecemeal approach to decision-making, with perhaps more decentralization.

Some of these consequences may tempt second thoughts about the move to relative efficiency which was motivated by unequal units of inputs and outputs. A sterner approach would seek to place a dollar value on outputs as well as inputs. The issues here are quite complex and I do not propose to discuss any of them at length. Instead, I shall briefly indicate the directions of a particular efficiency strategy based on certain results. One approach to input-output unit equivalence is to consider the constraints imposed on an educational system producing for a perfectly competitive market in equilibrium. Consider, first, some industry under these conditions. To begin, we know that the market is Pareto efficient (for a proof, see Sugden, 1981, pp. 67–93.) So for the industry it is not possible to increase production of goods without decreasing production in some other industry; the industry is (Pareto) production efficient. It is not possible to reallocate the factors of production between industries to produce a different mix of goods without reducing consumers' utility, so it is product-mix efficient; and so on. So one might suppose that educational systems can be reorganized more efficiently by requiring them to operate under conditions of perfect competition.

The trouble with this idea is that education is also a public good, since to some extent everyone gains some benefit from an educated community, and we know that there is no Pareto efficient equilibrium for a market with public goods (see Sugden, 1981, pp. 89–92). The central problem, then, is to devise reasonable efficiency rules for systems operating in less than a perfect market. Unfortunately, a result known as the 'general theory of second best', due to Lipsey and Lancaster (1956), implies that there are no precise rules to be had here. In achieving second best, global gains can sometimes be made by further system violations of efficiency, say of product, or mix, or exchange. As Mishan (1981, p. 223) notes in a review of the economic doctrines of the Chicago School,

> the traditional goal of promoting competition through the economy suffered a severe blow from ... the general theory of second best.... Although it is not possible to infer from the theorem that, in the absence of a first-best solution for the economy, any allocation was as good or as bad as any other, it certainly took the wind out of the sails of many a competitive model notwithstanding some limited counterblasts.

It is possible to argue the merits of certain allocations of shares, say, within education or to education, under second best circumstances, but often more piecemeal strategies are required (see Ng, 1977, and McKee and West, 1984, for a discussion of the complexities).

One approach that coheres well with our broadly Popperian conditions for promoting the growth of knowledge is piecemeal welfare economics. In implementing this approach the strategy Sugden (1981, p. 111) suggests is for each (government) agency pursuing objectives other than the maximization of profit to work out independently 'its decisions in a framework of partial equilibrium, considering only those sectors of the economy that are most closely related to its own activities. This is the sense of the word "piecemeal": no [agency] is asked to take an overall view of the economy or to make overall judgements about social welfare.' Needless to say, efficiency decentralized to the agency level collapses back into judgments of the relative efficiency of achieving more worthwhile agency goals per unit cost; to which we may add: subject to the constraint of optimizing the realization of the set of first order agency goals including relative efficiency. Given the community-wide distribution of relevant knowledge required to make these sorts of judgments, especially in education, there is evidently no escaping, at least on the grounds of efficiency, the virtues of participation in educational decision-making.

Conclusion

Instead of summarizing, again, the main argument of this chapter, I want to note a number of limitations on the conclusion. First, despite some of the advantages of more decentralization and less hierarchy in decision-making, there are natural limits to the amount of feedback that can usefully be processed, and limits, too, to the number of participants who should be involved. For this reason I have spoken of sampling various sources for feedback. Some version of the Burnheim/Walker notion of statistical democracy seems helpful here (Burnheim, 1985; Walker, 1987, 1990). The feedback driven mechanism of error elimination and correction in decision-making does not really work as a perfectly competitive marketplace for the adjudication of all individual ideas. Moreover, even if it did, it would assume far too passive and idealistic an account of knowledge. For the growth of knowledge assumes some power over experimentation, a capacity to influence the organizational testing of hypotheses. A chief executive in a hierarchical organization enjoys this power in virtue of the organization's authority relations. However, another source of power can derive from being a representative of a large number of people (even when organized very loosely). For efficient decision-making well beyond the school level, representative participation seems more helpful.

These constraints set limits to the value of complete individual participation in all decisions and hence the amount of decentralization that is desirable in education. They do not undermine the efficiency of more valuable modes of participation in educational decision-making.

References

ARGYRIS, C. (1982) *Reasoning, Learning and Action*. San Francisco, Calif.: Jossey-Bass.

ARGYRIS, C. and SCHÖN, D. (1978) *Organizational Learning: A Theory of Action Perspective*. Menlo Park, Calif.: Addison-Wesley.

BEER, S. (1966) *Decision and Control*. New York: John Wiley.

BRAYBROOKE, D. and LINDBLOM, C.E. (1963) *A Strategy of Decision*. London: Collier-Macmillan.

BURNHEIM, J. (1985) *Is Democracy Possible? The Alternative to Electoral Politics*. Cambridge: Polity Press.

CHAPMAN, J.D. (1990) 'School-based Decision-making and Management: Implications for School Personnel,' in CHAPMAN, J.D. (Ed.), *School-based Decision-making and Management.* Lewes: Falmer Press.

CONWAY, J.A. (1984) 'The Myth, Mystery and Mastery of Participative Decision-Making in Education,' *Educational Administration Quarterly*, 20, 3, 11–40.

EVERS, C.W. (1985) 'Hodgkinson on Ethics and the Philosophy of Administration,' *Educational Administration Quarterly*, 21, 4, 27–50.

EVERS, C.W. (1987) 'Ethics and Ethical Theory in Educative Leadership,' in EVERS, C.W. (Ed.), *Moral Theory for Educative Leadership*, pp. 3–30. Melbourne: Ministry of Education.

EVERS, C.W. (1988) 'Policy Analysis, Values and Complexity,' *Journal of Education Policy*, 3, 3, 223–33.

GOODIN, R.E. and WILENSKI, P. (1984) 'Beyond Efficiency: The Logical Underpinnings of Administrative Principles,' *Public Administration Review*, 44, November/December, 512–17.

LINDBLOM, C.E. (1979) 'Still Muddling, Not Yet Through,' *Public Administration Review*, 39, November/December, 517–26.

LIPSEY, R.G. and LANCASTER, K. (1956) 'The General Theory of Second Best,' *Review of Economic Studies*, 24, 1, 11–32.

LOCKE, E. and SCHWEIGER, O. (1979) 'Participation in Decision-Making: One More Look,' in CUMMINGS, L.L. and STAW, B.M. (Eds), *Research in Organizational Behaviour*, Vol. I, pp. 265–339. London: JAI Press.

McKEE, M. and WEST, E.G. (1984) 'Do Second-Best Considerations Affect Policy Decisions,' *Public Finance/Finances Publiques*, 39, 2, 246–60.

MISHAN, E.J. (1981) *Economic Efficiency and Social Welfare.* London: Allen and Unwin.

NG, Y-K. (1977) 'Towards a Theory of Third Best.' *Public Finance/Finances Publiques*, 32, 1, 1–15.

POPPER, K.R. (1963) *Conjectures and Refutations.* London: Routledge and Kegan Paul.

POPPER, K.R. (1968) 'Epistemology without a Knowing Subject,' in Van ROOTSELAAR, B. and STAAL, J.F. (Eds), *Proceedings of the Third International Congress for Logic, Methodology and Philosophy of Science.* Amsterdam: North Holland Publishing.

QUINE, W.V. (1960) *Word and Object.* Cambridge, Mass.: MIT Press.

SCHODERBEK, P.P., KEFALAS, A.G. and SCHODERBEK, C.G. (1975) *Management Systems.* Dallas, Tex.: Business Publications.

SIMON, H.A. (1952) 'On the Application of Servomechanism Theory in the Study of Production,' *Econometrica*, 20, 247–68.

SIMON, H.A. (1976) *Administrative Behaviour*, 3rd ed., rev. London: Macmillan.

STRANK, R.H.D. (1983) *Management Principles and Practice.* London: Gordon and Breach Science Publishers.

SUGDEN, R. (1981) *The Political Economy of Public Choice.* Oxford: Martin Robertson.

WALKER, J.C. (1987) 'Democracy and Pragmatism in Curriculum Development,' *Educational Philosophy and Theory*, 19, 2, 1–10.

WALKER, J.C. (1990) 'Functional Decentralization and Democratic Control,' in CHAPMAN, J.D. (Ed.), *School-based Decision-making and Management*, Lewes, Falmer Press.

WATANABE, S. (1969) *Knowing and Guessing*. New York: John Wiley.
WONHAM, W.M. (1984) 'Regulation, Feedback and Internal Models,' in SELF-RIDGE, O.G., RISSLAND, E.L. and ARBIB, M.A. (Eds), *Adaptive Control of Ill-Defined Systems*. New York: Plenum Press.

Chapter 4

What Price Democracy? An Examination of Arrow's Impossibility Theorem in Educational Decision-making

Gabriele Lakomski

> While purity is an uncomplicated virtue for olive oil, sea air, and heroines of folk tales, it is not so for systems of collective choice. (Amartya Sen)

The current rhetoric in education places much emphasis on decentralization of decision-making and increasing participatory decision-making at the school level. Although I believe that a case for school-based decision-making in democratic fashion can be made, such a case must incorporate, and have an answer to, some fundamental problems of actual decision procedures by means of which lofty ideals of participative democracy would have to be put into practice. With few exceptions, actual voting or other decision procedures have either been left unspecified or, where mentioned, have not been examined in terms of their inherent technical properties.

In this chapter I want to raise some dilemmas which result from inherent, technical features of egalitarian decision procedures. These have been brought to light by the economist Kenneth J. Arrow in the form of his so-called 'Impossibility Theorem'. The result of this theorem states that if we do want egalitarian decision procedures, then we have to give up the idea that the decisions made are rational or decisive. If we want to maintain a degree of rationality, we may adopt a consensus procedure — at the cost of being able to make decisive choices. If, on the other hand, we want to have decisive choices, we ought to opt for dictatorship. According to Arrow, such generally shared objectives as equality of power, decisiveness and rationality are in irreconcilable conflict, and compromises are unavoidable.

Since Arrow's work is not yet discussed in the educational literature, and since his arguments clearly apply to decision-making in education, the major part of this chapter describes the Impossibility Theorem and the various attempts at eliminating it, or at relaxing the constraints he suggested for the axiom. In the final part of the chapter I show how problematic the selection of a principal in fact is, when examined in the context of various possible, egalitarian decision procedures.

Arrow's Theorem

Taking his departure from what appeared to be 'just a mathematical curiosity' (Plott, 1976, p. 511) in majority rule, Arrow (1951, 1963) undertook what must surely count as one of the most significant investigations into the conditions of rational voting in a capitalist democracy. The question which guided what has come to be known as 'axiomatic social choice theory' seemed harmless enough. Arrow wanted to find out (1951, p. 2) 'if it is formally possible to construct a procedure for passing from a set of known individual tastes to a pattern of social decision-making, the procedure in question being required to satisfy certain natural conditions.' His quest was decidedly normative in that he wanted to find a set of ethical norms, or axioms, which could be imposed on the social choice process, and to find that process which would satisfy the axioms (Mueller, 1976, p. 185). Although Arrow posed the problem in terms of finding a suitable constitution by way of voting procedures, his study raises fundamental problems for egalitarian social choice processes in general which incorporate the preferences of individuals in order to reach the best choice.

The result of Arrow's enquiry was, in Plott's terms (1976, p. 512) 'broad sweeping, and negative', and gained him the Nobel Prize in economics in 1972. Simply stated, what does not exist in Arrow's view, and that of other political and social choice theorists, is a procedure for voting, or making formal choices, which is simultaneously rational, decisive and egalitarian. In fact, he proved that these criteria of an ideal system are incompatible, and that the only procedure which does satisfy all of them is that of a dictatorship. The general impact of Arrow's results was that, all of a sudden, he had opened 'a gigantic cavern into which fall almost all of our ideas about social actions. Almost anything we say and/or anyone has ever said about what society wants or should get is threatened with internal inconsistency. It is as though people have been talking for years about a thing that cannot, *in principle*, exist' (Plott, 1976, p. 512). To understand the impact of what Arrow has proved, let us begin by considering some anomalies of voting, and that of majority rule first.

Majority rule is a time-honoured, simple and egalitarian way of aggregating individual preferences by ranking them in pairs of candidates or alternatives. It runs into problems as soon as more than two alternatives are involved, giving rise to what, following Condorcet, is called the 'paradox of voting'. Imagine a three-member committee consisting of Tom, Dick and Jane who have to rank three candidates x, y and z. Using notational form, we have:

Tom $xPyPz$ (x is preferred to y, y is preferred to z)
Dick $yPzPx$
Jane $zPxPy$

Which candidate should be chosen by the committee? Of course, the candidate everyone wants, the one preferred by the majority. But the committee preference looks like this: $xPyPzPx$. In other words, we encounter a cycle. In this cycle x defeats y, y defeats z, and z defeats x, all by two votes to one (e.g. Blair and Pollak, 1983, p. 76). This outcome is called the 'majority rule cycle' or the 'majority preference cycle' (Plott, 1976, p. 514). Efforts which attempt to avoid it by adding more members to the number of candidates to be ranked have proven to be unsuccessful. Detailed discussions of this problem can be found in Sen (1970), Mueller (1979) and Plott (1976) in particular. The existence of a cycle means that majority rule, while being egalitarian, does not permit a best choice to be made; it is indecisive. Unfortunately, the problem does not disappear when turning to another, commonly used procedure, the Borda count, or point system. Since it is well known, it will suffice here to pinpoint the difficulty. Following Plott (1976), consider a four-option, seven-person group which, by allocating the relevant numbers to the candidates, gets a clear winner and a ranking. Now suppose the least preferred candidate is dropped off the list, necessitating an adjustment of scores from 1–3, rather than the previous 1–4. It now emerges that the group preference is exactly the *inverse* of that reached in the first counting. This is a very odd yet valid result according to the procedure. Which procedure and/or candidate is to be chosen? Again, a rational choice is not possible.

The problems inherent in majority rule and the Borda count led Arrow to ask whether such inconsistent social preferences arise in all voting systems or just in the ones described. Since it is practically impossible to list all possible ones, and the relevant configurations of individual preferences and their orderings, Arrow suggested instead some general principles, or axioms, which all procedures ought to meet and which would find general agreement. For ease of understanding, I follow a combination of Mueller's (1979) and Plott's (1976) reformulation of the axioms rather than Arrow's more technical account. The principles are those of:

1 *unanimity*, or the *Pareto principle*. If an individual preference is unopposed by any contrary preference of any other individual, this preference is preserved in the social ordering. Another way of putting it is to say that if everyone preferred option or candidate *x* over *y*, then society, or a committee, should neither be indifferent between them, nor perversely prefer *y* over *x*. This axiom has been misunderstood in the sense that it is seen to rule out conflict. This it does not do since, according to Plott (1976), 'if' has to be read as 'when'.

2 *non-dictatorship*. No individual should be in a position such that whenever s/he expresses a preference between any two alternatives and all others express the opposite preference, his or her preference is always preserved in the social ordering.

3 *preference transitivity*. If society prefers option *x* to option *y*, and it prefers option *y* to option *z*, then option *x* is preferred to option *z*. In notational form: $(xPyPz) (xPz)$.

4 *indifference transitivity*. Insert the term 'indifferent' in place of 'prefers' in principle 3. In notational form: $(xIyIz) (xIz)$.

5 *universal or unrestricted domain or scope*. This principle requires that a social choice be capable of aggregating every possible configuration of voters' preferences. It must be sufficiently general to be able to deal with all possible conflicts and controversies between opinions.

6 *independence of 'irrelevant' (Arrow) or 'infeasible' (Plott) alternatives*. The social choice between any two alternatives must depend on the ranking of individuals over only these two alternatives, and not on their rankings over other alternatives (Arrow's example, 1951, 1963, p. 26).

Now Arrow's theorem states that there is no constitution which satisfies all of these principles. He proved that the only ones which do are *dictatorial* (Arrow, 1951, 1963, p. 63). There is no doubt in the literature that the theorem is true (for simplified accounts see Sen, 1970, 1982; Mueller, 1979, p. 187; Plott, 1976, p. 524). The obvious question to be raised is, of course, what does all this mean, and how reasonable are the axioms anyway which apparently exert such enormous constraints?

To begin with, the intuition which underlies Arrow's proof is well captured by Mueller (1979, p. 188):

The unrestricted domain assumption allows any possible constellation of ordinal preferences. When a unanimously preferred alternative does not emerge, some method for choosing among the Pareto preferred alternatives must be found. The independence assumption restricts attention to the ordinal preferences of individuals for any two issues, when deciding those issues. But, as we have seen in ... majority rule, it is all too easy to construct rules which yield choices between two alternatives, but produce a cycle when three successive pairwise choices are made. The transitivity postulate forces a choice among the three, however. The social choice process is not to be left indecisive (Arrow, 1963, p. 120). But with the information at hand, individual ordinary rankings of issue pairs, there is no method for making such a choice that is not imposed or dictatorial.

The literature is replete with attempts to disprove this impossibility result and escape its 'unpalatable implications' (Blair and Pollak, 1983, p. 78), and 'Arrow-dodgers' (Sen, 1982, p. 165) have attempted, in particular, to relax Arrow's axioms in order to bypass, or eliminate, the result. The general agreement is, however, that while the discussion continues, the outlook is bleak. Just how significant and devastating Arrow's result is can be seen when one considers that his constraints are quite weak in that they constitute no more than plausible necessary conditions only. In fact, they appear to be weaker than appropriate for 'reasonable notions of distributional equity' (Mueller, 1979, p. 188). The first principle, *unanimity*, as well as (2) *non-dictatorship*, need not be discussed in the present context if we want to continue with such notions as individualism and democracy. The postulate of *transitivity*, axioms (4) and (5), demands that social choice produces a *consistent* social ordering. Arrow's reasons for this requirement are (1) 'that some social choice be made from any environment' (Arrow, 1951, 1963, p. 118), and (2) transitivity guarantees 'the independence of the final choice from the path to it' (Arrow, 1951, 1963, p. 120). As several writers have argued, however, these two requirements are really quite different ones, and are not necessary for transitivity. The first is reasonably easy to defend since deadlocks are undesirable in a democracy (see Mueller, 1979, p. 190). In order to make choices, however, Mueller, for example, argues that it is not necessary to assume a social preference ordering based on individual preference rankings. One only needs a social choice *function* in order to select the best alternative from a set (see also Sen, 1970, pp. 47–55). Full transitivity is not necessary. It is sufficient to rely on 'quasi-transitivity' or 'acyclicity'. 'Quasi-transitivity' requires transitivity of the preference relation, but not of indifference; acyclicity allows x_1 to be only 'at least as good as "x_n"' even though x_1px_2, x_2Px_3...., $x_{n-1}px_n$' (Mueller, 1979,

p. 190). The penalty for accepting quasi-transitivity, however, is that it produces an oligarchy which can force its preference on all other members. Adopting acyclicity, on the other hand, means that veto power is given to every member of a subset of a committee, a 'Collegium' in Brown's term. The result of relaxing the transitivity axiom is that dictatorial power is spread but does not disappear, and that arbitrariness is increased (Sen, 1970, pp. 47–55). In notational form, under quasi-transitivity *alb*, and *blc*. This can exist along with *aPc*. When two individuals disagree over *a* and *b*, however, the result is *alb*. When generalized, this result means that when conflicting interests are encountered in a society or a committee, the *rule of consensus* (Blair and Pollak, 1983, p. 79), which describes Sen's formulation of the relaxation of full transitivity, declares collective indifference. This is hardly a useful outcome. Sen himself questions whether the existence of a best alternative (in *a* and *b*) in each subset, while itself a sound basis for rational decision-making (Sen, 1970, p. 50), is satisfactory, particularly in view of the fact that as soon as a third option is added, *c* must be chosen (by the social preference transitivity).

Considering *path independence*, the assumption here is that the final choice is independent of how the initial decisions were made. This property implies what Sen calls 'property alpha'. It can best be shown by example. If Becker is the best tennis-player in the world, he is also the best tennis-player in Melbourne, Australia. Path independence here requires that his becoming the champion be independent of the ordering of prior matches. Sen complements the 'contraction-consistent' property alpha with an 'expansion-consistent' requirement, beta. It claims that if Becker and Cash tie for Wimbledon, then they must also tie for the world championships. While plausible as a constraint on a choice process where candidates are measured in one dimension only, very few social decision processes are this narrow. It is quite feasible that property beta might be violated without thus making the choice process either irrational or unfair. Property alpha is far more convincing. However, it is precisely path independence, together with alpha, which even in their weakest form lead to dictatorial or oligarchical social preference orderings (see Mueller, 1979, pp. 192–3). Finally, the notion of transitivity was inspired by the desire to avoid inconsistency and arbitrariness. But in doing that, Plott (1976) as well as Mueller (1979) argue that Arrow committed the fallacy of composition by illegitimately transferring the properties of an individual to that of a collection of individuals. Both writers draw the conclusion that the notion of a social preference must go. If the transitivity axiom is to stay, then, as Mueller argues, it must be shown that the arbitrary outcomes of cyclic preference rankings violate some basic ethical norm. But this is not necessarily the case. Procedures such as flips of a coin or the drawing of straws are often resorted to in small committees to resolve a conflict. The committee may be more interested in a 'fair' decision than a non-arbitrary one. The problem is, however, an obvious one. If the property of fairness were the overriding one, then, as Plott (1976, p. 544) points out, we can no longer speak of a social preference ranking. Since the selection process, as was shown above, merely throws up results which are as good as each other, social preference ranking is replaced by what Plott calls a 'social acceptability relation' (1979, p. 544), and Sen a 'Collective Choice Rule' (Sen, 1970). In this case it hardly makes sense to speak of an 'optimum' decision since the rationality criterion has been abandoned.

Consider next the principle of *universal domain*. This axiom captures in a general sense the liberal ideal of freedom of choice and expression. While appealing when considered on its own, conflicts arise quickly, however, since individuals have different, and often opposing, preference rankings. Cyclicity might occur, and if we also consider transitivity as necessary, an impossibility result is unavoidable. To attempt to avoid it, two options have been advanced in the literature. The first is to alter the principle so that the types of preference rankings be limited, which can be reflected in the social choice. The second is to restrict entry into a society or committee to those who possess the types of preference rankings which make collective choices possible.

It is possible to avoid Arrow's impossibility result on the assumption of a restricted domain if individual preferences satisfy a unimodal pattern called 'single-peakedness' (Black, 1971). For example, voters can only vote on the number of textbooks; they cannot consider their quality simultaneously. There are some situations which can be decided in this manner by majority rule, but it does not contribute to solving the problems of all those situations which are multi-dimensional and need to be decided in other ways which appear to be prone to Arrow's negative result. Another fundamental problem with single-peakedness is that it already assumes some consensus on the issue to be decided. If voter preferences become more homogeneous, the possibility of majority cycles decreases. How one gets such 'similar' preferences in the first place is described in theories of clubs and the voting-with-feet process, which still leaves many questions open. But even if decision-making can be carried out without violating Arrow's axioms which yield a 'best' decision, some decisions cannot be confined to clubs, etc., and the impossibility result looms again. Homogeneity of preferences can only be brought about if individuals adopt or already possess a common set of values. This solution raises more problems still, and since there are few if any issues which are of the requisite unidimensional quality, the option of single-peakedness does little to undermine Arrow's results.

Finally, the principle of *independence of irrelevant alternatives* has been the most controversial axiom, mainly because Arrow presented it in a confusing way (see Plott, 1976). Generally speaking, this principle states that the social choice ranking of any pair of alternatives depends only on individuals' rankings of those alternatives (Blair and Pollak, 1983, p. 78). It does not matter whether individuals change their preferences for *infeasible* options; the process outcome will remain invariant. According to Arrow's postulate, every process behaves in this way. It follows that if a process could be found which violates it, i.e., where, upon changes in some infeasible options the process outcome were also changed, the principle should be given up as invalid. While it appears that one process, the Borda count, indeed seems to violate the axiom, according to some, Plott (1976) advances an interesting argument that even the point system obeys the axiom. To see how this works, consider his example.

Suppose we are choosing from a list of candidates w, x, y, and z who is to receive an offer as full professor. We add four infeasible candidates to our list of four: James Maddison, Thomas Jefferson, J.S. Mill and Karl Marx. All candidates are ranked according to members' preferences with the lowest ranked receiving the number 1. The feasible candidate with the highest score will receive the offer. But this process can be said to violate the axiom because if you changed your mind about two infeasible candidates and ranked them below the feasible ones, then they would receive a higher score and hence the process outcome would be changed. Also, preferences for the feasible candidates remained the same since only the two infeasible ones were ranked lower. Hence, the argument goes, since this was not supposed to be happening according to the axiom, it must be false. Plott points out that this way of arguing rests on a questionable assumption, i.e., that the reporting of preference ranking was honest (Plott, 1976, p. 536). But according to game theoretic principles about how people behave in such circumstances, it is 'strategic' rather than 'honest' voting which must be assumed. Strategic voting means misrepresenting the actual ranking of the infeasible candidates to gain a more advantageous outcome. What are reported, according to Plott, are *strategic* advantages which have nothing to do with actual preferences for infeasible options. Since those do not change, and are not reported as changed, the process outcome remains invariant. Plott concludes 'that the proposed process could not behave as reported, and that the principle remains intact' (Plott, 1976, p. 536). Whether or not individuals always behave in a 'dishonest' manner is not at issue. Rather, the only way in which we could eliminate the principle is if we could be sure that people *never* behave strategically, clearly an impossibility. Does this axiom apply to all processes? The answer given through examination of non–cooperative and cooperative games is that it does. This concludes the overview of attempts of 'Arrow-dodgers' to evade the Impossibility Theorem. The result is, as Plott remarks in his very thorough and careful examination (1976, p. 553), that 'it is reasonable to suppose that the negative results should be taken at face value and that our philosophical positions must be altered accordingly.'

Do the logical inconsistencies Arrow exposed have anything to do with the 'real' world of educational decision-making, or are his considerations merely an exercise in logic?

Arrow's Theorem and Educational Decision-making

Insofar as school-based decision-making has to be concerned with 'social needs' and 'group wants', it has to be able to determine priorities and the ranking of options by some process. Ranking does not have to be expressed by preferences in the way Arrow does, but can be substituted for the concept 'better'. The technical properties apply equally to the latter concept. It is precisely these properties which pose the problem. To demonstrate the educational significance of Arrow's results, let us consider an example of educational decision-making, the selection of a principal. The relevant body for making this decision is the local school council. For the sake of the present argument, suppose that the council can potentially avail itself of a number of procedures of selection. In the following, let us consider what the selection process would look like by examining the properties of the most commonly used process, that of majority rule, as well as those of some alternatives. Suppose that our problem is to choose one candidate from a list of m candidates, where m is greater than three. Following Mueller's (1979, pp. 59ff) description, the procedures are as follows:

1 *majority rule:* choose that candidate who is ranked first by more than half the council members;
2 *plurality rule:* choose that candidate who is ranked first by the largest number of members;
3 *Condorcet criterion:* choose that candidate who defeats all others in pairwise elections using majority rule;
4 *Borda count:* give each of the m candidates a score of from 1 to m, based on its ranking in a member's preference ordering (as described above);

5 *exhaustive voting:* ask each member to indicate the candidate s/he ranks lowest from the list; remove that candidate who is ranked lowest by most members and repeat the process until a single candidate remains; he or she is the winner;

6 *approval voting:* each member casts a vote for all of the candidates on the list of whom s/he approves; the candidate with most votes wins.

The problems with majority rule have already been described. Since a voting cycle results when more than three options have to be considered, this method does not make selection of a winner possible. In practice, however, we do apply this procedure *and* select a candidate, thus doing what the process forbids. The question which needs to be asked is, what is that choice based on? I return to this problem later. While majority rule is the most egalitarian, it is also the most indecisive and the least rational.

Under plurality voting there is always a winner, but not a majority one. For example, in the following set of members' rankings over four candidates (adapted from Mueller, 1979, p. 60), x is the winner, but y recommends itself as the 'best' option because it is relatively high on all members' votes:

SCM$_1$	SCM$_2$	SCM$_3$	SCM$_4$	SCM$_5$	(SCM=school council member)
x	x	y	z	w	
y	y	z	y	y	
z	z	w	w	z	
w	w	x	x	x	

The problem with plurality voting is that it only takes into account information about the first preferences. The other four procedures do take into account more information about members' preference rankings. In this respect they have an advantage over the first two, but these are purchased at a price too.

According to the Condorcet rule, y in the above table is the winner since it defeats z and w in pairwise elections, 4 to 1. It also defeats x, the plurality winner, 3 to 2. Indeed, y is the winner by any of the other three voting procedures. The disadvantage of the Condorcet rule is that it, like majority rule, may not produce a winner. When a cycle over more than three candidates occurs, these may form a set of 'top' candidates who can beat all others but who do not allow the selection of a winner from among them. Even where there is a Condorcet winner, a candidate chosen by another procedure may be preferable. Consider the following:

SCM$_1$	SCM$_2$	SCM$_3$	SCM$_4$	SCM$_5$
x	x	x	y	y
y	y	y	z	z
z	z	z	x	x

According to this table, x is both a Condorcet and a majority rule winner. However, this situation looks like a 'tyranny of the majority' situation where the first three members can force their selection on the latter two who rank their candidate last; y emerges as a compromise candidate since it is ranked highly on all preference scales and may thus be the 'best' candidate. Using the Borda count for this example makes y the winner on average. This introduces a degree of stability or consistency which might be considered desirable on its own account. On the other hand, the Borda procedure, as discussed above, is open to strategic voting which is a potential threat.

Approval voting is an attractive idea when members agree to group candidates into two or three preference sets, as can happen when a large short-list needs to be reduced. Considering the last table, the first three members, although preferring x to y, would accept either x or y's victory over z. The gap between x and y is thus much narrower than that between y and z. These members might then vote for x and y, and y would be the winner. One might argue that the closeness of x to y in the first three members' ranking, plus y's top ranking for SCM_4 and SCM_5, lends intuitive legitimacy to being the winner.

The reason for there being agreement between the Borda count, the Condorcet criterion and other more complete information procedures regarding the winner is that these procedures pick out the candidate who ranks highest on average, and thus eliminate 'extremists'. Just how practically important this is can be seen in a study of the 1972 Democratic presidential primaries in the United States which are run under the plurality rule (Joslyn, 1976, as cited in Mueller, 1979). Under this rule the 'extremist' McGovern won overwhelmingly over the middle-of-the-road Muskie: 1307 to 271 delegates. Joslyn recalculated the final delegate counts under the rules we discussed above, and these show a dramatic increase in Muskie's delegate count in all but the plurality rule procedure. Mueller (1979, p. 65) comments that Muskie arguably should have been the Democratic Party's nominee, and that therefore, one of the other voting procedures is preferable to the plurality rule. But all this is a matter 'loaded with value judgements' (Mueller, 1979, p. 65).

What emerges quite clearly from the above examples is that the technical features of these egalitarian procedures are such that different procedures produce quite different results from the same list of four candidates. Although agreements have also been noted, these came about largely as a result of introducing extraneous considerations into the process such as judging candidates *on average*. On what grounds can these judgments be justified? This raises issues which can only be listed here. For example, the most urgent seems to be that, given the advantages and disadvantages of the procedures discussed, how do we select one to begin with? The question is important since results can diverge considerably. Also, what criteria come into play once we have adopted, say, majority rule, when we encounter a cycle? In fact, do we even follow the procedure at all, i.e., are we aware that cycles develop· when more than three candidates are on the list? The overriding worry is that since we obviously do make selections of principals in ordinary life, and since according to the technical features of egalitarian procedures we should not have been able to, we must have made these choices on criteria other than those specified by the rules. This is a question of considerable import which needs to be examined in the future.

References

ARROW, K.J. (1951, 1963) *Social Choice and Individual Values.* New York: John Wiley and Sons.

BLACK, D. (1971) *The Theory of Committees and Elections.* Cambridge: Cambridge University Press.

BLAIR, D.H. and POLLACK, R.A. (1983) 'Rational Collective Choice,' *Scientific American*, 249, 2, 76–83.

BURNHEIM, J. (1985) *Is Democracy Possible?* Cambridge: Polity Press.

MUELLER, D.C. (1979) *Public Choice.* Cambridge: Cambridge University Press.

PLOTT, CH.R. (1976) 'Axiomatic Social Choice Theory: An Overview and Interpretation,' *American Journal of Political Science*, 20, 3, 511–96.

SEN, A.K. (1970) *Collective Choice and Social Welfare.* San Francisco, Calif.: Holden-Day.

SEN, A.K. (1982) 'Social Choice Theory: A Re-examination,' in AMARTYA, A., *Choice, Welfare and Measurement*, pp. 158–200. Cambridge, Mass.: MIT Press.

Chapter 5

Functional Decentralization and Democratic Control

James C. Walker

The desirability of curriculum decision-making at the school level has been argued on grounds of both democracy and efficiency. These arguments have been part of wider debates on decentralization and accountability in educational policy and administration. In this chapter I shall argue that the discussion of school-based decision-making should not be separated from this wider context, nor should it be assumed that decentralized curriculum decision-making means decision-making at the level of the local school. I shall argue for the functional decentralization of schooling as a system of educational organizations.[1]

On the functional decentralization view schools can exist at any level of geographical generality: what is of primary importance is the functions they perform and the interests they serve rather than their physical location or the spread of their student populations. To determine which curriculum decisions should be made at a given level of generality, we identify the functions which are best served at that level of generality, and the legitimate social and individual interests affected. Schools performing these functions should be accountable to those legitimate interests.

Educational functions cannot be entirely separated from one another, of course. Nor can each legitimate interest be served in a way which takes no account of other interests. As a consequence, on the functional decentralization view, accountability should be a two-way process, running both up and down levels of generality in educational systems, for reasons of both efficiency and democracy.

Democracy and efficiency in education require more than accountability, however. In particular, they require appropriate forms of representation in decision-making. In considering representation, it is important to distinguish the democratic representation of students, parents and the general public in curriculum decision-making from the professional participation of educators. In this respect the position advocated here differs from theories of participatory and industrial democracy in curriculum decision-making at the school or any other level.

Functionally Decentralized Schools

Some goods and services are most efficiently produced in a centralized way, others in a decentralized way. Steel production, for instance, is not best conducted in backyards, as Mao's China discovered to its cost in the 'great leap forward'. Given moden technology, the same goes for many consumer goods, in addition to the extraction and refinement of primary products. The delivery of services, on the other hand, usually requires a degree of decentralization, with education being a case in point. Yet, as educators are well aware, decentralized production or delivery can occur within a framework of highly centralized decision-making; and issues of control and regulation can arise in a way which pits democracy against efficiency. Individual steel consumers may be content to go along with highly centralized decision-making in the steel industry, given broad agreement on how to produce sufficient quantities of good quality steel at an acceptable price; but in education what constitutes sufficiency and quality, let alone acceptable costs, is much more controversial, and clients have a greater diversity of educational needs and requirements than do steel consumers. Whereas the function of steel production can be relatively simply specified at a general, e.g. national, level, education is much more functionally complex and open-ended, and there is a greater variety of views and interests demanding political expression.

Prima facie, then, there would seem to be a case for decentralization of educational production and decision-making along functional lines.[2] Some educational functions may be of genuinely national interest, others of local interest, but there are parts of the curriculum which may be of special concern to particular groups and individuals who can be identified with neither a particular local level of interest nor with the national public interest as such: disadvantaged groups, individuals with particular interests or aspirations in music or mathematics, people with particular disabilities, people living in isolated communities in a variety of geographical regions and so on. Decentralization of decision-making for the education of these people is different from decentralization to local school decision-making. Functional decentralization takes account of more than geographical criteria.

The centralization/decentralization debate in education, however, has been conducted in almost exclusively geographical terms. 'Centralization' is usually taken to refer to authority wielded from a centre over a relatively large geographical area embracing many localities. In the school system 'decentralization' usually refers to a geographical breakdown through regions to localities, particular schools and classrooms. Considerations such as the interests of groups and individuals, the claims of various kinds of educational values and the requirements of administrative efficiency are appealed to usually in support of various views on the extent and composition of geographically centralized versus decentralized authority. These considerations become much more powerful when we think in terms of functional decentralization. Similarly, 'accountability' is most frequently used (especially by politicians) to refer to upward vertical relationships, rather than to downward vertical, or to horizontal, relationships, although there has been some interesting recent discussion of horizontal accountability (Rizvi, 1990).

A corollary of such thinking is the restriction of the idea of school to the local level. In challenging this, and arguing for a conception of schools, and therefore of school-based decision-making and management which is in principle applicable at any level of geographical generality, I shall use the word 'school' to refer to any organization involved in the direct production of educational outcomes among learners, and therefore in the distribution of knowledge and other resources. Thus the first dimension of functional decentralization is organizational. Schools are organizations operating at the end of the line in the performance of educational functions, working directly with students who are themselves the first objects of those functions.

Clearly, such organizations exist beyond the local level. Examples include organizations such as the New South Wales Conservatorium of Music and the School of the Air which serve a state or regional constituency, and organizations such as Britain's Open University or Australia's Deakin and New England Universities which conduct external studies or distance education serving geographically large, sometimes international, clienteles. The school level, then, is not to be identified with the local level; nor are problems of school-based decision-making and management to be identified with purely local problems. It seems possible that further development of the potential of modern communications technology will make purely local schooling of progressively less importance, and in time the functional decentralized school could become the norm. The question would then become whether there remains a case for local schools on the grounds of functional decentralization. As we shall see, there is no reason in principle why there should not be such a case.

For its productive and distributive functions to be planned and performed, the school needs to be organized in an appropriate way, having basic strategic (Etzioni, 1967) goals and problem-solving strategies informing its daily operations, and having the capacity to deal, through bit-by-bit incremental decisions (Braybrooke and Lindblom, 1963; Lindblom, 1959, 1979), with the responses of particular student individuals and groups, recognizing the practical limits of scope, the 'bounded rationality' of realistic decision-making (Simon, 1976). Moreover, in both strategic and incremental decision-making the school needs to be able to take account of alternative views of what the educational functions and methods of the school ought to be. Such a repertoire of strategic and incremental responses, or program for concrete performance of educational production and distribution, is the school's curriculum. A curriculum is a production/distribution program. A curriculum programs a school to perform its educational functions.

Yet, as discovery of the hidden curriculum has revealed, not all performance is carefully planned, or even planned at all. Learning outcomes are never always fully evident or fully under the control of educators. The curriculum actually programming a school need not be apparent in all respects to all teachers and students, nor need it (indeed nor can it) be entirely under the conscious control of any one individual or group in the school. A curriculum is inseparable from the whole culture of the school, and the distribution of resources and production of educational outcomes are not simply a matter of consciously deliberative strategic planning and daily decision-making. On the contrary, such deliberative behaviour is itself a form of cultural action. Intelligent curriculum decision-making requires continuous situational analysis of cultural patterns and processes in the school, to promote the achievement of desired objectives and enhance the performance of desirable functions (Walker, 1987a, 1987b).

I am suggesting, then, that although, broadly speaking, education can be distinguished as one public function distinct from others, such as the provision of health services, social security and defence, when examined internally, education has many subfunctions: it is itself multifunctional. One way of analyzing the curriculum is to identify the many functions it serves, the ends it is designed to achieve and the problems it is supposed to solve. These may relate either to specific fields, such as language, mathematics, science and the arts, or to broader, complex processes such as moral, social and political education and the provision of a productive workforce. Alternatively, they may relate to the education of particular groups, including local communities. If we conceive of the curriculum functionally, any one function can serve as the special basis for forming a particular kind of school. In this way we may distinguish functions prima facie suitable to local schools from functions better served at higher levels of generality.

Schools of music, for example, may be totally functionally specific (or instances of complete functional decentralization) and teach music alone. At the tertiary level functional decentralization of education in the arts is evident in functionally specialized institutions such as the New South Wales Conservatorium of Music. At the secondary and primary levels in the Australian states, on the other hand, this is rarely, if ever, the case. The New South Wales Conservatorium High School, for example, organizes a variety of the usual educational functions around a basic charter of producing competent musicians.

There are at least two ways of identifying functions. They may be depicted abstractly, relative to educational outcomes as such: the competent musician, the responsible citizen or the all-round educated person. They may also be identified concretely, relative to specific individuals and groups who instantiate the outcomes: defined by social class, age, gender, interest, aspiration, ability or disability, for instance. Thus a wide set of abstractly defined educational functions, generating a broad curricular program, may be performed in a school concretely functionally decentralized in the sense that it is serving the special needs of some particular group. The North Rocks School for the Blind and the Reiby Remand School for Girls are cases in point; so are single sex schools. Indeed, as I have suggested, we should conceive of the local school as functionally decentralized in this sense, as engaged in the production and distribution of educational outcomes among the members of a specifically identified group, the children of a particular locality.

From this point of view functional decentralization is the basic category, subsuming geographical decentralization, and justification of the latter hinges on the demonstration of concrete functions in reference to the problems, needs, aspirations and demands of the local group. Schools may, of course, be both abstractly and concretely functionally decentralized. The Conservatorium is like this: it performs the function of specialized musical education, and the function of meeting the needs of a special group, those who desire just such an education.

It follows that the geographical dimension, on its own, is an insufficient basis for sorting out which decisions ought to be made at which levels of generality. If we opt for functional decentralization, many functions, such as the education of the disabled, specialized musical education — indeed, perhaps many forms of specialized education — could be delivered and administered relatively independently of central authorities, in a manner which spreads across localities and regions, and, given modern communications technology, states and nations. Our notion of a school would then be construed in this functionally decentralized way, and the idea of the local school reconstrued as an appropriate functional unit.

There are at least two kinds of criteria for group identification by which we may identify concrete educational functions: need and demand. Short of thoroughgoing paternalism, we must take demand into account when determining which functions should be performed separately or decentrally, whether or not the functions are abstractly or concretely specified (i.e. whether or not we are deciding how education of particular kinds should be produced — together or separately — or how people with particular characteristics should be educated — again, together or separately). Supporters of privatization are simply the extreme limiting case, in effect advocating that we subsume need under demand: for privatizers, demand is the only appropriate index of need, if indeed need is thought relevant to educational policy-making.

The fact that demand can be used to identify functions, and market mechanisms used to indicate the appropriate level of geographical generality for functional delivery, is simply the most obvious illustration of the economic characteristics of functional decentralization. These may differ from the economic characteristics of other systems of educational organization, but on the present account all educational systems will have an economic dimension. For if we construe the curriculum as a program for production and distribution of scarce educational resources, and the school as the practical point of production and distribution, we are construing schooling as an educational economy, and curriculum decision-making as economic management.

Functional decentralization not only has organizational and economic dimensions, it also has a political dimension, explored further below. Fundamentally, what is proposed here is a political economy of education, where education is a process of cultural investment, production, distribution and consumption.[3] Functional decentralization will be a mixed economy in which public and private activity both have a part to play. Unless we agree to a completely free market in education, including curriculum development, the distribution of resources and the production of outcomes will need to be regulated in certain ways, at the levels of system development, general policy formulation and decision-making in the schools. Given our commitment to democratic accountability, this means that functional decentralization will have a coordinated rather than laissez-faire political economy. The question of what should be centrally and what decentrally decided and provided will depend on the identification, for each function, of a constituency with a legitimate interest in that function. For example, it could be argued that the nation as a whole retains an interest in certain forms of education, making comprehensive schooling at the local level desirable up to some point in secondary schooling. Although it is clear that this interest requires central decision-making and management in certain aspects of any school's curriculum, it is not clear that it requires them in all aspects. What is needed is an analysis of educational interests enabling us to see who has a legitimate interest in which educational functions, and at what levels and locations educational decision-making and delivery should occur.

Public and Private Interests

In Western liberal democratic societies people distinguish between matters of legitimate public interest, which are properly decided by public bodies and officials, and matters of private concern, which should be decided by individuals alone or in association with other individuals with whom they have voluntarily established relationships, such as families, clubs and firms. (This is not to say that once formed such associations cannot be subject to regulation in the general interest.) It is often controversial where the boundary between the public and private spheres should be drawn, but there is little or no disagreement that it should be drawn somewhere. Disputes over sex education, for example, are basically about where to draw the line. The commitment to a public/private distinction is therefore regarded as an element of the general interest, and as such the distinction is thought to be properly drawn by public procedures subject only to those procedures being compatible with the general interest as a whole.

Presumably it is part of the rationale for compulsory education that there are certain aspects of the curriculum which should be taught for reasons of general interest. It would seem that unless the state can show that some curricular elements should be required in the general interest, as determined by democratically legitimate procedures, enforced school attendance has no educational justification. Decisions concerning those aspects, then, should be made by publicly accountable bodies. Within a framework of state-imposed compulsory education, the complete privatization of education makes no philosophical sense — a point seemingly overlooked in much contemporary debate. Given a publicly determined curriculum, 'private' schools are by no means entirely independent institutions: they are simultaneously virtual subcontractors in the service of the state and private contractors supplying parents and students with particular variants of the state-ordained form of cultural production.

Once direct accountability to parents and students, in addition to accountability to governments, is admitted into 'public' schools, the qualitative difference between them and 'private' schools boils down to a variation in cultural product. This is not, in itself, an argument against 'private' schools; it is an argument against the speciousness of much privatization rhetoric. In the context of compulsory education, if there is an argument against private schools, it will be an argument against the political economy of their particular variants of cultural production and the compatibility of their products with the general interest.

Not all matters of public interest are of legitimate interest to all members of the public; not all are matters of general interest. The general public comprises more than one particular public, and the general interest consists only of those concerns of legitimate interest to all citizens, and therefore of all publics. It is a well understood principle of democratic theory that all those members of a public sharing that public interest should have a say in decisions affecting it. As Burnheim (1985, p. 5) has pointed out, however, there is much less appreciation of a correlative principle: that only those members of the public sharing that interest should have a say. As we shall see, this is an important part of the case for functional decentralization.

The question then arises: which matters of public interest are of general interest, and should therefore be the political responsibility of the most general level of government? This question cannot be answered in a purely abstract fashion. It requires an analysis of the actual interests served by the educational economy, a procedure for distinguishing legitimate from illegitimate interests, and a means of settling conflicts of interest.

Given that our educational interests lie in our satisfactory participation in the educational economy, I want to suggest that our approach to the question should be philosophically pragmatist — based on problem-solving — both in analyzing interests and in proposing decision-making procedures. Satisfactory participation means satisfactory problem-solving in a context of economic scarcity and therefore potential conflict of interests.

As a starting point, let us reduce our talk of interests to talk of problem-solving capacities, of forms of power over ourselves and our environment.[4] Let us assume that our interests lie in the solution and prevention of problems, in enhancing our chances of achieving our goals or ends. As private citizens and members of the public, therefore, we want some political power in the educational economy.

But which interests may we legitimately seek to satisfy, and where there is a plurality of sometimes conflicting interests, which should take precedence? To answer this, a distinction needs to be drawn between direct and indirect interests (Walker, 1987c). An individual or group has an indirect interest in a decision when the decision affects their problem-solving capacity only through its effect on the problem-solving capacities of others. A direct interest exists when the effect of a decision is not mediated through its effects on others. For example, an employer might have an interest in the production through education of a group of workers with certain narrowly specified skills and attitudes. This is an indirect interest in contrast to the direct interest of a student in gaining a broad general education which provides greater flexibility and statisfies other non-vocational needs. We need to distinguish between cases where a decision directly causally affects someone's problem-solving capacity, and cases where a decision affects someone's capacity only by changing the problem-solving capacity of another. In the first case, changes in the person are means to his or her own ends; in the second, changes in the person are means to another's ends.

If we accept something like Kant's practical imperative, 'So act as to treat humanity, whether in your own person or in that of any other, always at the same time as an end, and never merely as a means' (Kant, 1956), we have a reason for holding that indirect interests should not override direct interests. In our example the student's interest has prima facie moral priority over the employer's interest. The political consequence is that participation or representation in decision-making should be such that students' interests will have priority.

The moral priority of direct individual or sectional interest is only prima facie, however. Although it cannot be overridden by indirect private individual or sectional interests, it can be overridden by a general interest, which is equally shared and equally direct for all, and which is identified with the area of shared or overlapping private interests, and in particular with the infrastructural conditions for the pursuit of private interests. Such infrastructural conditions are commonly believed to include peace, personal security and, in liberal democratic thought, an educated population. Now the general interest is complex, and may conflict with private and other public interests; nevertheless, inasmuch as the general interest is the touchstone of all public and private interests, having no existence apart from their overlapping, when it conflicts with a given particular interest, this indicates not just a public/private conflict, but an internal conflict of interests of an individual or group. Since all individuals or groups have a direct interest in the general interest, it is in everyone's interest for that general interest to prevail.

Certain principles of educational planning and curriculum programming follow from this account. Most fundamentally, public decision-making procedures should be geared to the distinction between general and particular (whether public or private) interests, to ensure that the general interest is realized and that particular interests are left up to individuals and voluntarily formed associations to decide within a framework of justice and security. Educational functions should be decentralized accordingly. Given that there is compatibility with the general interest, functions relevant only to the problem-solving capacities of particular interest groups should be governed by members of those groups. The public/private mix in the educational economy in schools and school systems should be organized and regulated to enforce the conditions for realization of the general interest and to protect the freedom of private individuals and groups to pursue their legitimate interests. Each relevant interest group, from the general public to particular individuals and groups, should be represented, as a constituency, in making procedures affecting its interests, or have a say in any delegation of decision-making power.

A Democratic Political Economy of Schooling

From a pragmatist point of view the justification of democracy rests on the capacity of democratic procedures and institutions to solve the problems of constituents better than alternative methods, it being assumed that the basic political interests of people lie in the achievement of public solutions to their problems, and that the moral rights of people are to be understood as specifications of their legitimate interests. Democracy has no absolute political or moral value; its value is relative to its superiority as a practical decision-making procedure for solving publicly addressable problems of individuals and social groups. As a philosophical position, pragmatism is misrepresented if it is identified with opportunism or the pursuit of power for its own sake. Pragmatism is not unprincipled; its principles flow from a realistic analysis of practical problems and their material contexts. Pragmatism is taken to be the most acceptable theory of democracy.[5]

Within the above account of interests, accountability is a relation between representatives, and professionals, to legitimate constituencies, to those with a legitimate direct interest (granted the priority of the general interest) in the decisions made by representatives and professionals. Accountability needs to be understood in relation to the two basic principles of democratic theory outlined above: (1) that everyone with a legitimate interest in a decision has a right to representation in respect of that decision; and (2) that only those with a legitimate interest in a decision have a right to representation in respect of that decision. I now wish to add: (3) that those with legitimate direct interests in a decision should have majority representation with respect to that decision. An implication of the third principle is that since the general interest is a legitimate direct interest overriding all others, the general interest should have majority representation with respect to decisions affecting it.

It seems clear that students have legitimate direct interests (perhaps to be represented by their parents) in their own education. What, though, of those who perform educational functions? Teachers and other educational practitioners certainly have professional and industrial interests in educational decision-making. As professionals, they are concerned for the quality and efficiency of the educational process. As workers, they have industrial interests in their own working conditions and standard of living. The professional interest is an indirect interest in promoting the direct and indirect interests of others (students, employers, the general public); the industrial is a direct interest in not allowing the pursuit of the interests of others to be conducted in a way which treats educational practitioners merely as means to the ends of others, and not as people who have a right to be treated as ends in themselves.

Do educational professionals, then, have a right to participation or representation in curriculum decision-making? On the present account the possession of such a right hinges on the decisions affecting the welfare of professionals. The question here is not the democratic right of professionals to participate in decision-making; rather, the question is what decision-making procedure best serves the general interest and the interests of students compatibly with the welfare interests of professionals. From this point of view the legitimacy of professional decision-making depends on its delegated status, on the trust placed in professionals by those with legitimate direct interests, such as students and the general public through their representatives.

To deny that professionals such as teachers have a right to participate in educational decision-making flowing from their knowledge and experience as professionals will no doubt seem counter-intuitive to many professionals, and might appear to run counter to current practice of regarding teachers as 'stake-holders' or interested parties in educational decisions. I have already stated, however, the basis of professionals' legitimate stake — their own welfare interests. It could be argued that the well-being and professional development of the teaching service as a body is a material part of those welfare interests. It could also be argued that a healthy teaching profession is in the general interest and the interest of students. Nor need it be denied that many educational decisions are best made by professionals. The point is that the moral basis of whatever power and authority professionals might possess is the trust placed in them by the community as a whole and by individual students, the bearers of the general interest and legitimate direct private interests. Otherwise we run the risk of violating Kant's practical imperative, and of treating those whom the educational process affects educationally, the students, as means only to the ends of others. The extent to which professionals participate in educational decision-making, once procedures are instituted to safeguard their welfare interests, is not up to professionals to decide: their educational authority is delegated to them by others, those whom they serve, through their representatives.

How would these representatives be chosen in a system of functional decentralization? One of the shortcomings of modern electoral democracy is that representatives develop their own particular interests, as individuals and as a social (i.e. industrial) group in political activity. Electoral oligarchies or aristocracies develop, tied to unequal distributions of wealth and power. The resulting corruption and croneyism tend to thwart realization of the interests of constituents, to give undue political power to often self-appointed and questionably representative lobby groups and to discredit politics as an activity. Widespread cynicism about politicians and alienation from the representative system are now endemic in democratic societies, the system persisting largely for want of a better alternative. Moreover, the same geographically based thinking which distorts the debate over decentralization results in systematic violation of our second democratic principle, that only those with a legitimate interest should have a say in decisions affecting that interest. The worst extreme occurs when swinging voters in marginal seats both influence decisions on matters in which they have no interest at all and have a disproportionate influence on decisions which affect other voters equally. This, incidentally, is a further reason why geographical decentralization is unsatisfactory for decision-making on matters affecting the general interest and other interests beyond the locality.

Burnheim (1985, Ch. 3) has proposed a solution to these problems, which would ensure that decision-makers are a representative sample of those whose legitimate interests are affected by their decisions. Under a system of 'demarchy' (Hayek's term) or 'statistical democracy' (Burnheim's term) all individuals with legitimate interests would have an equal opportunity for nominating and being selected as a representative. Individuals selected at random from the nominees, and given strictly limited tenure of office, would have little incentive to do other than to promote the interests they represent. They would be more likely than career politicians to be in tune with the needs and views of those of whom they are statistically representative.

In a demarchic polity democratic representatives would form boards of trustees responsible for performance of particular functions affecting their constituencies, from transport and banking through to health and education. Such demarchy can commence at any site or level in existing systems where it is pragmatically possible; demarchic change is a strictly evolutionary proposal. If carried right through, it would eventually replace the state and electoral politics, coordination of functionally decentralized agencies being conducted by compulsory consultation and negotiation, and conflicts between agencies being settled by judicial arbitrating bodies representative of the general interest rather than by the market or state regulation. However far demarchic change can or would go, its success would be dependent on recognition of its merits as a practical decision-making structure by those whose interests were affected by demarchically governed, functionally decentralized agencies. That is, it would give the neatest and cleanest accountability routes to the general interest, to legitimate particular interests and to coordinating bodies, making functionally decentralized bodies accountable to one another as well as to their constituents.

Curriculum Decision-making at the School Level

Given that there is a general interest in education, expressed legally in the case of compulsory education, curriculum matters of general interest would be decided by a board of trustees representative of the general interest and legitimate particular direct interests. Whether indirect interests should be represented as such or by representatives of the general interest is a further question; I am inclined to support a minority representation, but this raises problems of proportion and balance among representatives of various indirect interests.

There are many practical questions to be addressed concerning procedures of statistical representation and the administrative arrangements for implementing it. Procedures would need to be devised for identifying interests and for carving the causal continuum of constantly changing, often attenuated influences on problem-solving capacities. Given our pragmatic orientation, we should be wary of generalizing abstractly about these issues. Being pragmatic, however, does require that we start with a recognition of where decision-making power presently resides, that we start with such institutions and organizations as we have. Steps need to be taken to identify the interests, legitimate or not, currently influential, and examine their relation to other interests lacking representation, or adequate representation. To change the balance and constitution of power means addressing the problems faced by the powerful, and making the case for statistically democratic functional decentralization as a set of solutions to them. It also means drawing the attention of the under- or unrepresented to the potential of such a system, and encouraging them to put pressure, through available means, on the decision-makers to move in a functional decentralization direction. In other words, discussion, debate and negotiation need to be instigated at all levels of educational systems, and between levels. Identification of latent unused power in the community and among students is another early step in ensuring adequate representation.

There are further familiar problems (to which I have alluded), characteristic of issues of educational policy and practice, related to the representation of the young and immature, which need to be addressed by proponents of demarchy. Who should represent the interests of those incapable of representing themselves? These issues, however, are faced by all theorists addressing problems of democracy and education. Space prevents me from tackling them her, but I would argue that a system of representation including parents and representatives of the general interest (which includes the education and upbringing of the young) is desirable. The role of professionals, as in educational decision-making generally, is to advise on and implement demarchically determined policy, where implementation will involve a greater or lesser degree of delegated decision-making.

There would be a strong and pressing obligation on a statistically representative board, at whatever level and in relation to whatever particular function, to show why its curricular policies were necessary for the general interest, since its justification depends in large part on this. As a first step, existing education ministers and their departments might attempt this exercise, though part of the present hypothesis is that demarchy would be a more reliable procedure for discovering what the general interest is. In this respect decision-making cannot be separated in practice from enquiry. Where it cannot be shown that control of curriculum areas at the most general level is in the general interest, control should be relinquished to further functionally decentralized boards at the school level, remembering that the school level is not equivalent to any particular geographical level.

At general and school levels the enquiry/decision-making procedure has one major objective, to identify problems of constituents to which educational solutions can be proposed, and to put into place curricular arrangements for testing those solutions. There is in principle no necessary limit on the sources from which proposals (or identification of problems) might come. One obvious source is professional educators, especially classroom teachers. Educators would potentially be in a much better position than they are in centralized bureaucratic systems to develop creative and innovative alternatives. There is no reason in principle why contracts could not be awarded to private individuals or firms for the performance of tasks required by trustees. Given overall democratic public control of educational distribution and the fixing of strategic directions for production, the nature of the public/private mix becomes a matter for further pragmatic enquiry. Trustee bodies would be free to encourage enterprising deployment of expertise in curriculum development, to choose between competing or alternative proposals, and to decide the degree of responsibility to be delegated to educational professionals. Arguably, the result would be much greater operational autonomy for teachers, successful solutions being rewarded and unsuccessful proposals being discarded. The cleaner accountability routes provided through a genuinely representative decision-making system would, according to our hypothesis, lead to greater efficiency and effectiveness, rather than less. Our hypothesis is that the present unfortunate clash often experienced between professional autonomy and public accountability could be short-circuited.

In this chapter I have concentrated on the political and economic conditions for implementation of functional decentralization. In practice the professional conditions are just as important and, if implemented, would likely raise the quality and status of the teaching profession. If professional rewards were dispensed for successful solutions to problems of school curriculum programming, with attention to both the distributive (input) and productive (output) aspects of the educational economy, there would be an incentive for professionals to give greater emphasis to research, development, experimentation and risk — to the development of an 'enterprise culture', and there would be an incentive for their employers, the trustee bodies, to allow time and other resources for research and professional education and training. Time, perhaps above all, will be needed for teachers at the school level to develop competitive curriculum materials and packages. The role of the teacher can become more that of an educator, as much concerned with curriculum development as with teaching per se.

Lines of communication with students and parents at the school level would be less ambiguous given the kind of accountability functional decentralization provides. For example, parental involvement at school level (or any level) would be a politically recognized and publicly supported activity. Trustees at general and school levels would be entitled to support such as compensation for income foregone in the conduct of their political duties, allowances, childcare and so on. In cases where trustee jobs were full-time, appropriate salaries would be paid, just as they are now paid to our political representatives. What would be missing, because of statistical selection and limited tenure, would be any career incentive. As well as avoiding the abuses of electoral politics, demarchy would include none of the inherent inequities of 'participatory' democracy such as the costs placed on the public spirited, or the unequal opportunities for participation imposed by unequal time and resources among participants.

Given our earlier claim that a curriculum is inseparable from the whole culture of the school, and the suggestion that the task of the local school is to address the problems of students in the local community, the major responsibility of each local school board is for curriculum policy, for strategic school-based decision-making concerning local educational distribution and production, in view of analysis of the cultural context of the school and the local community. This makes school-based curriculum a massive research and development task, a task which would require the assistance of well trained and resourced professional staff. If the idea that the school's function is to meet local needs is taken seriously, a coherent overall picture of those needs is necessary to produce an efficient program, and arguably the curriculum should be conceived holistically.[6]

This said, the interests of local communities have to be seen in relation to the general interest which is attended to by a board of trustees at the general level. I have suggested that the curricular elements identified by the general board should be present in the curricula of all schools. This does not, however, given functional decentralization, imply a hierarchical relationship between local and general levels; rather, it implies a coordinated relationship between different, more or less general, levels of functional decentralization, of which the general level is one. Relations between levels of functional decentralization are relations of mutual accountability, of negotiation rather than top-down authority. General boards may determine which aspects of the curriculum are necessary in the general interest, but the discovery of what that general interest is will require taking into account the problems of local communities, and there would seem a good case for representation of such particular interests on general boards as well as the mutual accountability requirement.

Moves towards a system of demarchic functional decentralization, as noted, can in practice occur at any level of decision-making generality. The functional decentralization proposal is a proposal for experiment, not a blueprint for rapid wholesale change. Many existing practices already have the potential for development in a demarchic direction, and functional decentralization schools already exist to some extent. The functional decentralization proposal is intended as a procedure of identification and extension of good current educational practice. There would seem to be little reason why those working at the school level could not commence experimenting in this direction.

Notes

1 The theory of functional decentralization has been expounded in the work of John Burnheim (see, especially, Burnheim, 1985). The theory has been applied to education within a pragmatist theory of democratic curriculum development in Walker (1987a).
2 Burnheim provides extensive general argument for functional decentralization on grounds of political democracy and administrative efficiency.
3 In my view the crucial theoretical problem to be addressed remains the question of the exchange value of the cultural product, or what is often (on the present account quite wrongly) described as 'the relation between education and the economy'. Bourdieu and Passeron's (1977) theory of cultural capital is suggestive in this regard, but does not in itself address the problem.
4 For expositions of the materialist pragmatist philosophy of education underpinning this approach see Walker and Evers (1984) and Evers (1987).
5 In the manner of Dewey (1916). This is not to deny that there are problems with Dewey's particular version of pragmatism (Walker, 1987a, pp. 5–6).
6 Some steps towards holistic cultural production of a coherent curriculum are suggested in Walker (1987d).

References

BOURDIEU, P. and PASSERON, J.C. (1977) *Reproduction: In Language, Society and Culture.* London: Sage.

BRAYBROOKE, D. and LINDBLOM, C.E. (1963) *A Strategy of Decision.* London: Collier-Macmillan.

BURNHEIM, J.B. (1985) *Is Democracy Possible? The Alternative to Electoral Politics.* Cambridge: Polity Press.

DEWEY, J. (1916) *Democracy and Education.* New York: Macmillan.

ETZIONI, A. (1967) 'Mixed-scanning: A "Third" Approach to Decision-Making,' *Public Administration Review,* 27, 5, 385–92.

EVERS, C.W. (1987) 'Naturalism in Philosophy of Education,' *Educational Philosophy and Theory,* 19, 2, 11–21.

EVERS, C.W. (1990) 'Schooling, Organizational Learning and Efficiency in the Growth of Knowledge,' in CHAPMAN, J.D. (Ed.), *School-based Decision-making and Management.* Lewes: Falmer Press.

HAYEK, F.A. (1960) *The Constitution of Liberty.* London: Routledge and Kegan Paul.

HAYEK, F.A. (1973, 1976, 1979) *Law, Legislation and Liberty.* 3 vols. London: Routledge and Kegan Paul.

KANT, I. (1956) *Groundwork of the Metaphysics of Morals.* Trans H.J. PATON. London: Hutchinson.

LINDBLOM, C.E. (1959) 'The Science of "Muddling Through",' *Public Administration Review*, 19, 2, 79–88.

LINDBLOM, C.E. (1979) 'Still Muddling, Not Yet Through,' *Public Administration Review*, 39, 517–26.

PEARCE, D.W. (Ed.) (1983) *The Dictionary of Modern Economics.* Rev. ed. London: Macmillan.

RIZVI, F. (1990) 'Horizontal Accountability,' in CHAPMAN, J.D. (Ed.), *School-based Decision-Making and Management.* Lewes: Falmer Press.

SIMON, H.A. (1976) *Administrative Behaviour.* 3rd rev. ed. London: Macmillan.

WALKER, J.C. (1987a) 'Democracy and Pragmatism in Curriculum Development,' *Educational Philosophy and Theory*, 19, 2, 1–10.

WALKER, J.C. (1987b) 'A Philosophy of Leadership for Curriculum Development,' in *Educative Leadership for Curriculum Development*, pp. 1–41. Canberra: ACT Schools Authority.

WALKER, J.C. (1987c) 'Interests, Rights and Educational Leadership,' Unpublished paper, University of Sydney, Department of Social and Policy Studies in Education.

WALKER, J.C. (1987d) *School, Work and the Problems of Young People: A Cultural Approach to Curriculum Development.* Canberra: Curriculum Development Centre.

WALKER, J.C. and EVERS, C.W. (1984) 'Towards a Materialist Pragmatist Philosophy of Education,' *Education Research and Perspectives*, 11, 1, 23–33.

Chapter 6

The Quality of Education and Accountability

John Hattie

Associated with trends to decentralize educational decision-making there is a concerted movement towards accountability via school-based management, standardized testing and performance indices. The prime movers behind these changes have been politicians rather than educators, and these politicians are particularly sensitive to financial expenditures and to the votes of their constituents. Politicians are keen to demonstrate that the 'education system' can deliver quality education at a cost that does not involve unreasonably increasing expenditures, while at the same time providing more opportunity, places, and sharing valuable resources. A constant theme accompanying these changes is the desire to hold those spending the money accountable.

When a central body devolves responsibilities typically it needs some system to ensure that its dollars are appropriately and well spent; it needs to ensure that quality education is provided, that the syllabus is followed and that schools are at least minimally efficient. How to do this, while saying that schools are primarily responsible, seems like a paradox. One way out of this paradox is to deny devolution actually occurs. The argument is that the central body has devolved only trivial power, as it determines the school grant, and this school grant is but a fraction of the total operating cost of the school. The salaries of staff, the indirect costs of infrastructure and buildings, the syllabus and the external examination procedures are not devolved. While these 'fixed' costs are large, there are many other aspects of schooling that have been devolved, such as the details and planning of the curriculum, who teaches what, under what physical arrangements and for how long. A lot of influence is being placed in the schools. Influence relates to power, and power relates to communication, persuasion and responsibility. It is possible to transfer much power when restructuring the administration of education, and discussion quickly turns to accountability of those 'in power'.

Under the centralized system, money was provided and usually tied to a particular project in a determined way. Accountability, therefore, appeared to take care of itself. As with many centralized schemes, special interest groups are powerful and provide an easier focus for accounting for the spending as well as determining specific educational outcomes. Parents are far removed from educational decisions, typically being the suppliers of toilet paper and light bulbs. Under a decentralized system, special interest groups have much less power and parents could become more involved in the checks and balances of educational accountability. Thus the forces and balances of powers can change. Although there is no inherent desirability in decentralization (or school-based decision-making, or giving power to school councils, etc.), there is a present perception (and rhetoric) that decentralized systems are more likely to improve education.

The accountability discussions initially focus on administrative and financial accountability, whereas educational accountability is left to later. Educational accountability relates to outcomes (cognitive, affective and love of learning) from schooling, teachers, etc., and thus also includes discussion about effects of the curriculum, processes and other inputs. Educational accountability, however, rarely is built into accountability models in a tight, logical and meaningful way.

What Is Accountability?

An accountability exercise involves a determination of goals and/or duties (see Scriven, in press, for a clear specification of such duties), a process to assess these goals, standards for the attainment of these goals, an attempt to measure the extent of achieving the goals or the duties, and an acceptability by various interest groups of this evaluation. There can be different sets of goals for different systems (or people), and different systems (or people) can tolerate different goals, different measuring in-struments and different outcomes. Administrators, for example, must be efficient, managerial and policy-oriented and their performance can be evaluated on appropriate performance-based indices. These goals are clearly different from those relevant for classroom teachers and students. Too many systems have confused the accountability issue by demanding the same performance indices of administrators, teachers and students.

A further confusion relates to whether the accountability is for improvement or effectiveness. It is possible to conceive of very effective schools that may need improvement, and very ineffective schools that cannot be easily improved (except, perhaps, with a dramatic change in the nature of the students enrolling, or the socio-economic background of the school district). Typically, accountability exercises from central authorities are more interested in effectiveness, whereas school personnel are more interested in improvement. The two outcomes do not have to be mutually exclusive; they only need to be recognized as different outcomes that may require different kinds of evaluation.

There are two major steps in an accountability exercise. In the first instance accountability involves answerability and responsibility. This presupposes that there are duties that the incumbents need to perform satisfactorily. Decisions need to be made about what evidence of quality is required, and the minimal and satisfactory standards for performing the duties. The participants have a key role in this stage. The outside authorities (e.g., parents, employers, politicians) may not like the performance/ quality indices or evidence and they may berate, criticize and/or praise the way in which the evaluation is done. They may argue against some of the indices and against the quality or extensiveness of the evaluation. This is very reasonable.

In the second instance there is an onus on the groups to which the participants are responsible (e.g., the employers and the parents) to evaluate the evaluation. These groups can aid in ascribing the duties, they can expect the participants to render an account of the performance of these duties, and they have the right of intervention if they do not accept the evaluation. This right could include non-acceptance of the evaluation (e.g., by denial of further funding by employers, or changing schools by parents), the public debating of the standards used in the evaluation and the quality of the evaluation, and the possibility of dismissal of the participants. It is possible to have evaluation without accountability, but it is not possible to have accountability without evaluation. It is not reasonable to have either accountability or evaluation without including a discourse about standards or quality.

Thus to be accountable involves the possibility of being called to account for what you do. There must be those accountable and those to whom these persons are accountable. The former can have a prime role in the evaluation phase, the latter in the acceptance of the evaluation. Both have a role in the ascription of the participants' duties and the standards of performance of these duties. This may involve teachers using the evaluation to improve, otherwise the evaluation may become mere window dressing. As the law stipulates that schooling is compulsory, then the legal authorities (the employers and maybe politicians) have the ultimate say in the ascription of duties and the standards of performance of these duties.

Given the above argument, an accountability exercise involves some generalizable statements about the value of schools, teachers and teaching as well as convincing others of the value of the schools, teachers and teaching. There is, however, often a trade-off between generalizability and the power to convince. If the exercise is aimed too narrowly at convincing one group (e.g., parents or professional educators), then it is less likely to generalize to other groups (e.g., employers or curriculum specialists). On the other hand, if the exercise is aimed to be too generalizable, it is less likely to convince any one group. My observation is that when criteria are set by 'outsiders' they tend to be too generalizable, and thus lack convincing power. The converse is often the case when criteria are set by teachers. Some balance is obviously necessary. My proposal is that the incumbents of the schools are initially responsible for the evaluation and the 'outsiders' are responsible for evaluating the evaluation. This check and balance is a reasonable and effective basis for accountability exercises.

An Example of Accountability in Action

In 1987 the Research Committee at the University of Western Australia decided that 15 per cent of the research budget over the next three years that would have normally gone to each of the sixty departments would be retained, pending an evaluation of the research productivity of the departments. As far as can be ascertained, this was the first effort by the central organizing committees on campus (and probably on any Australian campus) to tie funding with quality output. Of course, the sceptics said it could not be done.

Invitations were sent to department heads requesting submissions which outlined their productivity case. Examples of details included number of publications in refereed journals of repute, creative work which has a demonstrable research component, number of research theses successfully completed, outside grants, and evidence of the department's national ranking.

As this was the first time such an exercise had been undertaken, there was much discussion within the committee and university as to what should be included, and how quality should be evaluated. The committee was quite ruthless in its final determinations. Departments were classified into three categories: the eighteen A departments, which received 0 per cent of the 15 per cent retained; the twenty AA departments, which shared a small fraction of the 15 per cent retained; the ten AAA departments, which shared the bulk of the 15 per cent retained (quite a sizeable amount).

Department reaction was very mild indeed and there was hardly any criticism about the value of the exercise, the major sources of informations used or the relative performance of various departments. There was acceptance and even praise for the exercise both from the evaluated and from the senior administrators. The major effects of this accountability exercise were obvious. Although the committee was dealing with 15 per cent of the budget, the procedure has become the tail that wagged the dog. Departments are now geared primarily to enhancing the indices of quality performance.

In this example the appraisal was not completed by outside authorities looking in; it was not completed by dispassionate providers of the funds (they were one step removed) and it was not all-encompassing. Accountability does not have to be processed from outside, it does not necessarily involve the 'workers' meeting certain quotas, performance standards, etc. Accountability can mean that the 'workers' can be involved in agreeing on quality, they can apply these quality indices to themselves, and they can then be assessed on the quality of having completed this evaluation. The participants can be involved in the evaluation of their performance (this is not a call for action research with all its usual connotations, as the evaluation needs to be rigorous, does not need to be democratic and can be dispassionate; further, too often action research aims at convincing a small audience). They can be accountable for the standards they set, the nature of the standards and the meeting of the standards.

The point in relating this example is to demonstrate that such performance appraisals as outlined in the previous section can be done, and can be done with finesse and minimal criticism, provided that the evaluation involves the participants; the criteria become well known and generally accepted (they do not have to be well specified prior to the exercise); the evaluation is based primarily on quality and secondarily on quantity; the evaluation relates to a specific aspect of the total activities of the operation, although all aspects can be evaluated; the evaluators and those evaluated are involved in considering the merit of the procedure and the results; and those who requested the evaluation do not immediately involve themselves in the evaluation exercise. Rather, the administration sets expectations and evaluates the evaluation.

Outcomes vs Process

We know a lot about process in education, and good process obviously should be encouraged, particularly when it has effects on outcome —

such as increased retention, higher achievement levels and better work-force preparation. Process, however, is not the appropriate focus of accountability exercises. Two teachers may achieve the same outcome but by different processes. Process is but a correlate of outcome, and thus is no substitute for evaluating outcomes (see Scriven, in press). If the aim of the accountability exercise is improvement, then process may take a more dominant role; if the aim is to assess effectiveness, then process takes a secondary and very much subsidiary role.

There are many forms of educational accountability that relate to outcomes. In this chapter, the focus is on two major forms: the first relates to students and the second to schools. The latter is secondary to the former, but may be as important, depending on the purpose and audience of the accountability exercise.

Accountability of Student Performance

The quality of education for students should be primarily measured by its outcomes: cognitive gains, affective gains and love of learning gains. There remain, of course, contentious issues surrounding the content, or specific subject matter, which should make up these 'gains', and this is as it should be. An obvious corollary may be that the gains achieved by schools are indices of their effectiveness. The measurement implication leads to a totally different conclusion. Gain scores are notoriously problematic (for reliability, regression, factor structure and unit of measurement reasons) and should not be used (Cronbach and Furby, 1970; Rowley, 1977). Further, it would be easy to construct situations where a school could look effective or ineffective on the basis of gains, regardless of their performance. For example, to look good, a school would be encouraged to take many Asian overseas students who have steep learning curves. To look bad, a school could take many learning disabled children or children from impoverished backgrounds. Despite the desirable state of affairs regarding the value of measuring gains, it is not possible adequately to assess gain scores and thus they cannot and should not be used to evaluate effectiveness.

Further, elaborating on the point above, we should not confuse product gains with process gains. Recent trends towards process outcomes are seriously misguided in their attempt to specify educational outcomes, largely because they confuse process as outcome with process towards outcome. We may know a lot about 'how students learn' (to read, write, solve problems, etc.), but we know less about 'how students should be taught (to read, write, solve problems, etc.)'. The first concerns the theories as to how children learn, what goes on inside as they learn. The second concerns what teachers do to children to facilitate the learning process (see Hattie and Tunmer, in press). To ask for accountability in terms of the research on the first as if it applied directly to the second is incorrect.

Statements of standards are needed and these can only be judgment calls. Appeals to norms, means or percentiles are inappropriate as they cannot dictate or define a standard (see Glass, 1978). Standards, although difficult and controversial, need to be formulated. These standards could become the aim for schools, and form the basis for determining effectiveness. Such a procedure would highlight the desirability of the aims, the effectiveness of achieving the aims and the procedures for assessing the aims (both philosophically and psychometrically). Such aims could be written into school plans and thus become goals as well as benchmarks. The school plans can outline expectations, goals, etc. and these can be evaluated as can the success of school personnel to attain them.

In New York City schools were requested to set out clearly defined school improvement objectives. The accountability plan involved yearly evaluations of schools' progress towards meeting these improvement standards. Where objectives had been met, the school was required to set objectives for further improvement. Minimum and progress standards were set (by a lengthy consulting process) for all schools, and schools were required to reduce their deficits by 50 per cent within three years (see Spiro, 1988).

Accountability of School Performance

When assessing accountability of schools, researchers have found it difficult to measure the effects of schooling and those that try typically argue that schooling is not the major contributor to enhanced learning. Two major publications by Coleman et al. (1966) and Jencks et al. (1972) have dominated this research. They argued that there were no measurable school resources or policies that showed consistent relationships to a school's effectiveness in boosting achievement. Differences in schools had little to do with differences in students' performance. The major effects on achievement, they argued, were home-related variables. Since the publication of these studies, there has been a concerted effort to demonstrate the positive effects of schooling. These efforts have not been persuasive to the research community, and certainly the parents, community and politicians have not been easily convinced.

This dilemma can be resolved, however, by identifying the points of comparison used by each group. Those who claim that schools and teachers are in need of drastic improvement and who argue that the accountability needs standards, which are extremely high, are probably comparing schools and teachers to some ideal outcome of education. Those who claim that schools and teachers are effective (and maybe only fine tuning is necessary) may be comparing schools and teachers to more worldly expectations of the outcomes of education. The third group, typically researchers of education, compare schools and teachers to what would have happened if schools did not exist.

Despite its obvious importance, answering the question regarding the measurement of the effects of schooling is extremely difficult and rarely attempted. This is because schooling in most developed countries is compulsory, the drop-outs are self-selected, and thus there are no adequate comparison groups to contrast with those who are in school. Thus it is difficult to devise an experiment or directly test the effects of schooling.

The beginning of an answer is to ask: 'What are the "typical" effects of schooling?' and then to use this typical effect as a benchmark. The problem is how to ascertain 'typical effects' given the myriad of effects on schools, different teachers, subjects, school administration systems, ages of students, and other moderators like gender, prior ability, etc. The determination of the typical effect cannot be answered with any one study. Rather, the power of a simple statistical revolution will be harnessed to summarize over 22,000 previous studies (more details in Hattie, 1987).

Let me start by introducing a continuum on which the effects of schooling can be summarized. On this continuum the zero point means that there is no effect from introducing some teaching package, innovation or effect on schooling. A negative indicates that the innovation, etc. has a decreased effect on achievement, and a positive indicates that the innovation has an increased effect on achievement. For the present the line is constrained to achievement outcomes, but the line can be generalized to other outcomes of schooling (see Hattie, 1987, for such a generalization).

The aim is to place various innovations and effects of schooling along this line to identify the typical effects of schooling (and to identify the strengths, weaknesses and to allow for interactions). To do this, a scale is needed. The recommended scale is calibrated in effect-sizes. An effect-size provides a common expression of the magnitude of study outcomes for all types of outcome variables, such as school achievement. An effect-size of 1.0 indicates an increase of one standard deviation, typically associated with advancing children's achievement by one year, improving the rate of learning by 50 per cent, or a correlation between some variable (e.g., amount of homework) and achievement of approximately .50. When implementing a new program, an effect–size of one would mean that approximately 95 per cent of outcomes positively enhanced achievement, or average students receiving that treatment exceeded 84 per cent of students not receiving that treatment. Cohen (1977) argued that an effect–size of 1.0 would be regarded as large, blatantly obvious, grossly perceptible, and he provided examples such as the difference in IQ of PhD graduates and high school students. It is extremely unlikely that we could find an educational innovation that systematically leads to an effect–size of 1.0.

Let me give two examples to provide more meaning to the scale. The first relates to height. The difference between myself (at 5 feet 11 inches) and a person of 6 feet 2 inches would equal an effect–size of 1.0. This would be easily detectable. The difference between myself and a person of 6 feet 0 inches would be .34; difficult to detect, but leading to some important differences such as size of clothes and length of walking stick.

The second example relates to the introduction of computers in education and the consequent effects on achievement. It was possible to locate 557 studies that investigated the effects of introducing computers on students' achievement. Using a procedure called meta-analysis, it is possible to synthesize statistically these effects and also to assess the influence on differing groups of students (e.g., males versus females), different uses of computers, subject areas and so on. The average effect–size across these 557 studies was .31. Thus, compared to classes without computers, the use of computers was associated with advancing children's achievement by approximately three months, improving the rate of learning by 15 per cent, a correlation of .15; about 65 per cent of the effects were positive (that is, improved achievement), thus 35 per cent of the effects were zero or negative; and the average student achievement level after using computers exceeded 62 per cent of the achievement levels of the students not using computers. An effect–size of .31 would not, according to Cohen, be perceptible to the naked observational eye, and would be approximately equivalent to the difference between my height and a 6'0" person.

Of course, this is only an overall effect–size from introducing computers. There are many important moderators. For example, the effects decrease with age: primary students gain most (effect–size = .48), secondary students have medium gains (.32) and college and university students gain least (.25). There are no differences in effect–sizes on achievement between males and females in primary as opposed to secondary school.

We now have a unidimensional continuum that can serve to place the various effects of schooling. The scale is expressed in effect-size or standard deviation units such that 1.0 is unlikely although a very obvious change in achievement, and .31 is typical after introducing computers. This continuum provides the measurement basis to address the question of the effects of schooling. To answer this question, the results of a large number of studies were statistically synthesized, and thus it is possible to determine the typical effects of schooling, and to identify the innovations or changes that affect achievement in a systematic positive manner. Altogether 22,155 effect-sizes were calculated from 7827 studies, representing approximately 20–40 million students, and covering almost all methods of instruction, innovation, etc. The key question is: 'What is the typical effect of schooling?' The answer is .40.

Most innovations that we introduce in schools improve achievement by about .4 of a standard deviation. This is the benchmark figure. Most of what we do in classrooms should relate to improving education at least by .4 standard deviations, and preferably exceeding .4 standard deviations. This typical value is much more informative than the usual comparison figure of .0, and more meaningful than the ideals expected by some politicians, press writers and critics.

An example of the informative nature of this continuum relates to the effects of computers in schools. It can now be demonstrated that the effect of introducing computers in schools is close to the average effect after introducing most educational changes. Those who wish to argue that computers are effective would say 'yes' when compared to zero or classes without computers. When compared to typical effects, however, computers are not too different from the average. Thus it is perhaps not so surprising that teachers have found that the effect of introducing computers is not as dramatic as many advocates promised.

The continuum developed here provides a 'standard' from which to judge effects; a standard that is a real world comparison, based on typical, real world effects rather than on the strongest cause possible, or with the weakest cause imaginable. Comparisons with typical effects provide more meaningful estimates of the importance of effects of schooling. At least this continuum provides a method for measuring the effects of schooling.

The typical effect does not mean that merely placing a teacher in front of a class would lead to an improvement of .4 standard deviations. Some deliberate attempt to change, improve, plan, modify and innovate is involved. Similarly, this effect-size may not be uniform across all students. As already explained, while the typical effect relating to introducing computers is .31, the effect is greater for younger than older students. The major point of this continuum is that we now have a base to interpret the effects of change, both the overall effects and effects broken down by important moderators.

It is possible to use this continuum to answer one of the key questions: what are the schooling effects compared to the non-school effects. Recall the earlier statement by Coleman *et al.* (1966) that schools were not as influential in enhancing achievement as were home variables. The overall effect-size related to home and social influences is .38, whereas learning processes or presentation (usually controlled by the teacher) are .62; the background and style of teachers are .50, curricular differences .48, methods of instruction .36; and school environment (e.g., class size, environment) .36. (The student variables are .53.) Thus schooling does make a difference.

When we discuss accountability of teachers, there needs to be an expectation that teachers can enhance learning above and beyond the contributions from home, that there are measurable differences in the skill of teachers and that we can use the effect-size metric to guide some decisions. But this should be only a guide: the effects are not necessarily additive, they are typically but not always linear and there are individual variations. Further, it would be easier to obtain large effect-sizes from certain subgroups (e.g., senior students who have very steep learning curves compared to learning disabled students).

Teachers do make a difference and they do so in measurable ways. The procedure above can also lead to other corollaries which will merely be listed here.

1 While not advocating the use of process variables in accountability exercises, it is possible to ascertain which teaching attributes and learning processes tend to make a difference (e.g., the power of feedback and innovation) and which do not make a difference (e.g., individualization).

2 The effects are not necessarily cumulative. There are many examples where restructuring knowledge is more important or as important as learning gains.

3 The effects are also not necessarily additive. The effects probably follow a Cobb-Douglas function in that there are diminishing returns over time.

4 The findings have remarkable generality. The instances where the effect-sizes are subject or age dependent (etc.) are the exceptions.

5 The typical effects exceed what can be expected by maturation.

6 The scale can be used to compare the effects (e.g., costs in time, energy and money) of introducing various innovations relative to their benefits on achievement.

Further, there is compelling evidence that diversity, innovation and a constant attention to improvement are the foundations of successful outcomes of schooling. This is more likely to occur where diversity and innovation are encouraged, rather than where stability and consistency are favoured. The majority of political proposals for change concentrate on the peripherals of schooling: more funds, more time-on-task (without attention to quality of time), more time in pre- and post-service training, more evaluation, more accountability, more, more, more. The meta-analysis of research on the relationships between educational expenditures and student achievement indicates that educational expenditures have little effect on student achievement. 'There appears to be no strong or systematic relationship between school expenditure and student performance' (Hanushek, 1982, p. 1162).

The question may therefore be rephrased to ask *not*: 'Will changes to the schooling system lead to better (more effective) schools?' but: 'Will changes to the schooling system improve the overall gains by more than .4 standard deviations?' The odds must be stacked in favour of 'changes' with respect to encouragement of quality of feedback, although the lack of enthusiasm among teachers could be damaging.

A major implication for accountability is that it is critically important to assess competing claims: competing administrative systems, competing teaching styles, competing theories. It is critical to move away from the null hypothesis by which the accountability effects of innovation or intervention are assessed relative to no innovation or no intervention. The comparison must be between one 'supposedly' effective method and an alternative 'supposedly' effective method. The null hypothesis typically is not the question of interest, so it is no wonder that the answer is misleading; it typically subjects an innovation to a feeble danger of refutation and thus lacks vigour and convincing power, and the null hypothesis is virtually certain to be false before we start an analysis, and therefore lacks information. The above analysis stresses the need to structure accountability exercises to compare the effects of schooling with meaningful, real world effects.

Other School Measures: Performance Indicators

A recent trend in the evaluation of schools is to request performance indicators. These indicators can be requested for student outcomes, teacher satisfaction, parental involvement, etc. Performance indicators are defined in a multiplicity of ways, but usually in terms of the indicators themselves, rather than in terms of how they could be used, or how they are weighted to give an overall impression. Dunnell and O'Loughlin (1987) define them variously as 'statistically valid information related to significant aspects of the educational system', 'benchmarks for measuring progress or regression over time, or differences across geographical areas or institutions at one point in time such that substantive reference can be drawn from presentation of the data', and they require that performance indicators be representative of policy issues, easily interpreted, reliable and not subject to response errors. They then detail various indicators in terms of inputs, processes and output and cross these with student, teachers and system.

These performance appraisals often provide a broad brush to what is a delicate painting. In the quest for indices that apply to all schools they become generalizable but lose convincing power. They can miss the nuances of success and failure of the local school and become too related to gross overall indices. There is a place for such a global view, but it must be balanced with detail.

Other School Measures: Standardized Testing

In Britain the government's Task Group on Assessment and Testing has produced a report (Black, 1987) outlining procedures for measuring 'the delivery of the national curriculum'. It suggests an extensive system of assessment at 7, 11, 14 and 16 years via centralized tests and teacher judgments which are moderated to ensure comparability. This extends the present trend to develop league tables between various LEAs (and between states on the SAT in the USA). Goldstein and Cuttance (in press) argue that such comparisons using simple school averages or distributions would in part reflect differences between the social composition of schools and obscure any real 'effects' due to the schools themselves.

They contend that as more background factors are taken into account, the more unstable and unreliable become the resulting comparisons; such comparisons tell us nothing about the relative achievements of different types of pupils within the schools, and failure to take full account of the pupil intakes into schools is akin to assessing the performances of business without taking account of the cost of their raw materials. Goldstein and Cuttance propose that socio-economic background, prior achievement, mother's education, number of siblings in the family and gender should be partialled out of the final results. This, unfortunately, leads to another problem. If these factors are partialled out of a final achievement test, then there is probably only random error left; thus their tables reflect error and not reliable school differences.

There has been a move in the USA to compare the performance of schools on standardized tests on a state-by-state basis. Cannell (1988) has noted that the use of the tests has allowed all the states to claim to be above the national average! By this analysis, 90 per cent of the school districts would claim to be above the national average, and 70 per cent of the students are told they are performing above the national average. Such use of tests leads to much suspicion about the accountability methods primarily based on standardized testing, and the responses to Cannell have been most informative (e.g., Drahozal and Frisbie, 1988; Lenke and Keene, 1988; Phillips and Finn, 1988).

A further difficulty with using standardized tests relates to the dependability of measurement. Two critical aspects of dependability are that the measures are stable, and that the appropriate unit of analysis has been chosen. The research on stability of performance across years and across grades has not been encouraging (cf., Mandeville and Anderson, 1987; Matthews, Soder, Ramey and Sanders, 1981). The choice of unit of analysis (student, class or school) is critical when determining outcome effects, and the wrong design can lead to misleading inferences.

Other School Measures: Portfolios

Let us remember why we are discussing accountability. One reason is that government agencies need to be assured that political policies are in place, that taxpayers' dollars are well spent and that minimum standards (and better) are maintained. Consequently, parents (and students) need to be assured that quality education is provided, and that choice of schools is available. For devolution systems to be effective, parents (and students) must make *informed* choice. More information could be made available to parents (and students) about their relative choices. Parents already make a choice for their children to attend public and private systems and this choice needs to be extended such that parents are able to choose among government schools.

One method to ensure that schools are accountable directly to parents (and students) is to request that schools provide accurate information to parents about the school mission, success in achieving this mission, standards, teaching methods, etc. Some check on the accuracy of this information is necessary otherwise it may degenerate into a window dressing or sales pitch exercise. Similarly, the Ministry of Education could provide this information, but it tends to become based on more global assessments such as standardized tests and performance indices. An alternative could be to suggest that a private independent consulting business offers this information. This business would need to search the available evidence, seek cooperation with schools, demonstrate the value of its service to parents and insist on cooperation with schools to put their best face forward. This method would ensure that schools are accountable directly to parents (and students). It is noted, with support, that the British 1980 Education Act stipulated that schools publish information on curriculum, organization and examination results to facilitate informed parental choice. The 1986 Act further requested that school governors must convene annual meetings of parents to discuss the governors' written report.

The suggested form of accountability would be via school profiles. The school would be encouraged to provide a variety of evidence, such as attainment relative to similar school districts, and relative to previous years, course offerings, teaching style, etc. A further school measure that could be included in a portfolio is student evaluations. Many students, and certainly senior students, can make dependable evaluations about the teaching.

Conclusions

The emphasis on accountability has been regarded as an affront to the professionalism of teachers. There may appear to be a conflict between an emphasis on the accountability of performance in schooling on the one hand, and some critics' emphasis on the professional autonomy of teachers on the other. This does not need to be the case. In the model proposed in this chapter, teachers have a critical role in the accountability process. It is their task to be involved by using professional judgments to devise the goals, determine processes and be involved in conducting the evaluation. Evaluation is thus part of the teacher's duties. The emphasis here on learning gains highlights the pivotal part of teachers in the assessment and evaluation stage.

The move away from centralized control of schools in the name of greater autonomy contributes precisely to greater ignorance of what is going on in different schools. The second stage whereby the evaluations are evaluated is one means of breaking down this ignorance. A requirement to communicate results and/or at minimum to make the evaluation public would greatly offset this ignorance.

Accountability requires convincing others of the value of the enterprise. This convincing is relative. It is all too easy to be convinced of the value of schooling, if that comparison is to no schooling. That should not be the major question. Rather, the question relates to the effectiveness of schooling using this method, under these conditions, rather than the effectiveness of schooling using those methods and under those conditions. Parents and students need real options and much information about the relative effectiveness of different teachers and schools. It is incumbent on the administration (the agency that enforces the compulsory clause) to provide this relative information. Accountability is relative. Let us involve the participants — the students, teachers and administrators — to help formulate the evaluation plan to assess their methods, and let the meta-evaluators (e.g., the researchers, parents and politicians) assess the quality of the evaluations received from the many schools. A successful accountability program is an excellent method to enhance the quality of education both for the students and in the perceptions of teachers, parents, principals, administrators and politicians. If an accountability program does not enhance the quality of education and/or schooling, then the evaluators, teachers, parents, principals, administrators and politicians need to take action. Without accountability, all parties will continue in ignorance and this is a heinous crime in an activity aimed at increasing opportunities and enhancing learning.

References

BLACK, P. (1987) *National Curriculum: Task Group on Assessment and Testing.* London: Department of Education and Science and the Welsh Office.

CANNELL, J.J. (1988) 'Nationally Normed Elementary Achievement Testing in America's Public Schools: How All 50 States Are above the National Average,' *Educational Measurement: Issues and Practice*, 7, 5–9.

COHEN, J. (1977) *Statistical Power Analysis for the Social Sciences.* New York: Academic Press.

COLEMAN, J.S., CAMPBELL, E.Q., HOBSON, C.J., McPARTLAND, J., MOOD, A.M., WEINFIELD, F.D. and YORK, R.L. (1966) *Equality of Educational Opportunity.* Washington, D.C.: US Office of Education.

CRONBACH, L.J. and FURBY, L. (1970) 'How We Should Measure "Change" — or Should We?' *Psychological Bulletin*, 74, 68–80.

DAWKINS, J.S. (1988) *Higher Education: A Policy Discussion Paper.* Canberra: Australian Government Publishing Service.

DRAHOZAL, E.C. and FRISBIE, D.A. (1988) 'Riverside Comments on the Friends for Education Report,' *Educational Measurement: Issues and Practice*, 7, 12–16.

DUNNELL, P. and O'LOUGHLIN, M.J. (1987) 'A Framework for the Development of Performance Indicators in an Educational System,' Paper presented at the Joint Conference of the Australian College of Education and the Australian Council for Educational Administration, Perth, September.

GLASS, G.V. (1978) 'Standards and Criteria,' *Journal of Educational Measurement*, 15, 237–62.

GLASS, G.V., CAHEN, L.S., SMITH, M.L. and FILBY, N.N. (1982) *School Class Size: Research and Policy*. Beverly Hills, Calif.: Sage.

GOLDSTEIN, H. and CUTTANCE, P. (1988) 'National Assessment and School Comparisons,' *Journal of Educational Policy*, 3, 197–202.

HANUSHEK, E.A. (1982) 'The Economics of Schooling: Production and Efficiency in Public Schools,' *Journal of Economic Literature*, 24, 1141–77.

HATTIE, J.A. (1987) 'Identifying the Salient Facets of a Model of Student Learning: A Synthesis of Meta-analyses,' *International Journal of Educational Research*, 42, Ch. 4.

HATTIE, J.A. and TUNMER, W. (1988) Review of *The Process of Learning, Curriculum Perspectives*, 8, 1, 96–8.

INTERIM COMMITTEE FOR THE AUSTRALIAN SCHOOLS COMMISSION (1973) *Schools in Australia: Report of the Committee*. Chairman P. KARMEL. Canberra: Australian Government Publishing Service.

JENCKS, C., SMITH, M., ACKLAND, H., BANE, M.J., COHEN, D., GINTIS, H., HEYNES, B. and MICHELSON, S. (1972) *Inequality: A Reassessment of the Effect of Family and Schooling in America*. New York: Basic Books.

LENKE, J.M. and KEENE, J.M. (1988) 'A Response to JOHN J. CANNELL,' *Educational Measurement: Issues and Practice*, 7, 16–18.

MANDEVILLE, G.K. and ANDERSON, L.W. (1987) 'The Stability of School Effective Measures across Grade Levels and Subject Areas,' *Journal of Educational Measurement*, 24, 203–16.

MATTHEWS, T.A., SODER, J.B., RAMEY, M.C. and SANDERS, G.H. (1981) 'Use of District Test Scores to Compare the Academic Effectiveness of Schools,' Paper presented at the Annual Meeting of the American Educational Research Association, Los Angeles.

PHILLIPS, G.W. and FINN, C.E. (1988) 'The Lake Wobegon Effect: A Skeleton in the Testing Closet?' *Educational Measurement: Issues and Practice*, 7, 10–12.

ROWLEY, G. (1977). 'How Change Is Measured, and Why It Usually Isn't: Implications for Educational Research,' Paper presented at the Annual Meeting of the Australian Association for Research in Education, Canberra, November.

SCRIVEN, M. (1987) 'Duties-based Personal Evaluation,' *Journal of Personal Evaluation and Education*, 1, 9–23.

SPIRO, J. (1988) 'New York City's School Performance Indicators: A Collaborative Process,' Paper presented at the Annual Meeting of the American Educational Research Association.

WAINER, H. (1986) 'Five Pitfalls Encountered While Trying to Compare States on Their SAT Scores,' *Journal of Educational Measurement*, 23, 69–81.

WESTERN AUSTRALIAN GOVERNMENT (1986) *Managing Change in the Public Sector*. Perth: Government Printer.

WESTERN AUSTRALIAN GOVERNMENT (1986) *Financial Administration and Audit Act*. Perth: Government Printer.

Part 3
Perspectives on Practice

Chapter 7

Collaborative Decision-making at the School Level

Jim M. Spinks

In today's complex society many different values and expectations for education are being expressed. In this context governments and education authorities are determining key objectives and policies for education and empowering schools and communities to work within that framework in providing an education that is specifically suited to each community. This development is designed to enable schools and communities successfully to manage changes in education within the overall objectives, policies, strategic plans and curriculum initiatives of the government and education authorities.

Devolution places the emphasis for success on schools. In recognizes that a central authority can no longer quickly or appropriately respond to the changing needs of all communities. It acknowledges that only effective schools can lead to the development of an effective system. The situation requires that schools strive for excellence and this entails each school establishing a shared vision of a preferred and desired future for its students. The vision needs to include a pathway to that future. This pathway can be considered as the management of the school designed to ensure that students achieve the goals and outcomes encompassed by the vision of the future.

It follows from the continuing developments in devolution of responsibility for decision-making to schools and communities that schools now have three major tasks :

1 the development of a relevant curriculum to meet the needs of students;
2 the development of management skills to deliver the curriculum to students in the most effective and efficient ways possible through the resources available;

3   the development of approaches through which to manage change as a natural phenomenon in schools.

The development of collaborative decision-making at the school level is a response to these major tasks in the context of education today. It involves a systematic approach to decision-making and allows for appropriate participation by parents, students, teachers and other interested parties. Collaborative decision-making as an approach to school management is also often referred to as collaborative school management or policy-making and planning (key features of the approach). The term 'school self-management' is also used to describe the process.

Purposes and Guidelines

The specific purposes to be achieved in collaborative decision-making at the school level are detailed as follows:

1   to provide an approach to school management which clearly focuses on learning and teaching, the central issues of any school;
2   to facilitate sharing in the decision-making processes and the involvement of all possible participants in appropriate ways;
3   to identify clearly the management tasks and to provide direct and easily understood links between them and information about them;
4   to identify clearly responsibilities for decision-making and activities and to demonstrate lines of accountability;
5   to provide a means to relate resource allocations of all kinds to learning priorities for students;
6   to facilitate evaluation and review processes with the emphasis on further improving opportunities for students;
7   to limit documentation to simple, clear statements that can easily be prepared by those involved in their already busy schedules.

The achievement of these purposes is pursued through the following guidelines.

1   Goals for student learning are set on the basis of identified needs, the nature of the school community and the beliefs and values of the school.
2   Policies consisting of purposes to be achieved and broad guidelines are formulated on substantial issues related to goals. Priorities for student learning are established among policies.
3   Strategic and annual school plans are prepared as outcomes of policies and priorities.

4   Curriculum planning is undertaken for annual school programs involving both the design of courses and planning for delivery.

5   Program plans are used to identify and allocate all school resources. Proposed resource allocations are approved on the basis of learning priorities.

6   Learning programs are implemented on the basis of approved plans with guaranteed levels of resources.

7   Learning programs are evaluated with respect to both outcomes and methods of delivery to review goals, needs, policies, priorities and planning.

8   A policy group which always involves teachers and may involve parents and/or students identifies needs, sets goals, establishes policies and sets priorities.

9   Curriculum planning and implementation of learning programs are the responsibilities of teachers in their professional areas.

From this background it is now proposed to outline in some detail the features and processes of the collaborative school management model.

Collaborative School Management

The collaborative school management model identifies six key phases in the management of a school (or for that matter in any organization). These phases relate to *where* the school is going and *why*, *how* it is going to get there and then checking very carefully to see *if* and *when* it arrived. The six key phases are:

1   goal-setting,
2   policy-making,
3   curriculum planning,
4   resource provision,
5   implementation of learning program,
6   evaluation.

The relationships between these phases are illustrated diagramatically in Figure 7.1. With reference to Figure 7.1 the following details are provided in explanation (and in some cases illustration) of the various processes involved.

Need Identification and Goal-setting

A convenient starting point to explain the process is the top circle which represents need identification and goal-setting. Both of these aspects refer

Figure 7.1 A model for collaborative school management

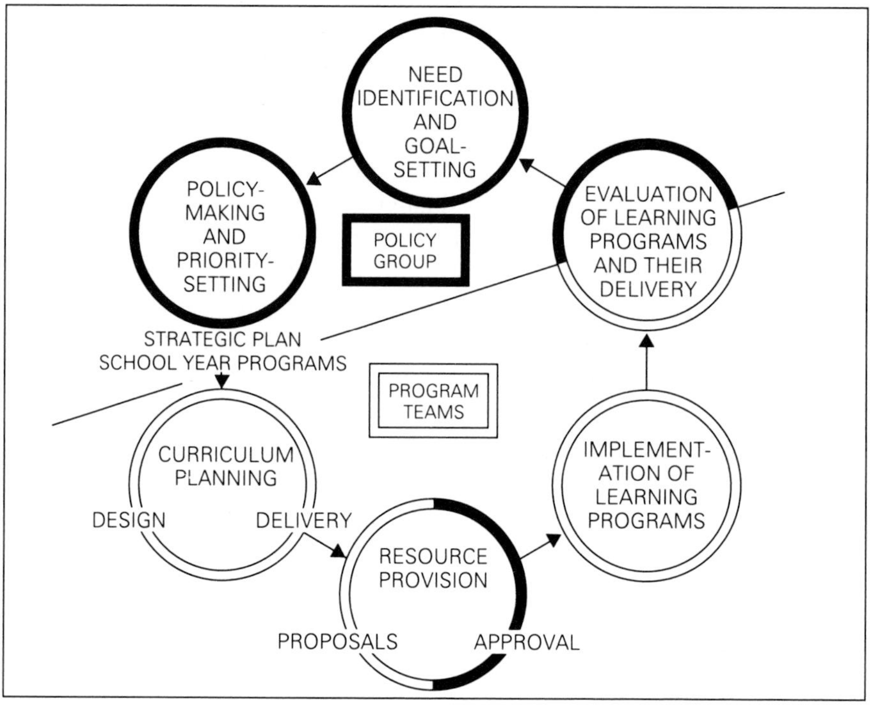

Source: Caldwell and Spinks (1988).

to the students and must always be the basis for all following actions. The completion of the management cycle through evaluation is beneficial in establishing whether goals have been achieved and needs met. It is also a key process in identifying further and emerging needs.

Policy-making

From the needs identified and the goals established, a set of key issues is identified that relate to student learning, resource provision and management of the curriculum. The determining of policy on each of these substantial issues is necessary to guide the overall development of the school curriculum. For each issue the purposes to be achieved are stated together with the broad guidelines for their achievement. Policies are written in clear, simple language and always limited to one typed page to facilitate their writing, preparation and eventual change.

Policies serve as the basis for programs within the school. Some policies specifically lead to programs, for example, mathematics and special education. Other policies do not lead to specific programs but are reflected across a range of programs. Policies on homework, discipline and reporting to parents fit into this category. Table 7.1 provides an example of a policy statement, in this case on drug education.

Priority-setting

With limitations on resources some policies become more important than others in meeting the key needs of students. This requirement is met through placing priorities on policies for appropriate periods of time. By relating priorities to policies the idea of placing priorities on areas of student learning is kept to the fore. Too often priorities become attached to the acquisition of equipment rather than to learning outcomes for students. Priorities are established for learning programs by transferring the priority of the key policy for each program. It is not practical to establish a large number of categories of priorities for policies. It suffices to indicate whether a priority is category 1, 2 or 3. In the resource allocation process every endeavour is made to satisfy priority 1 programs even at the expense of priority 3 programs, either in part or in whole if necessary. Further information is given on this process at a later time.

Strategic Plan

Not all policies and priorities can be achieved in any one school year. To facilitate planning and development it is desirable that key policies and priorities be identified and a long-term plan be produced outlining their proposed implementation over several years. Such long-term plans can be referred to as strategic plans, and planning of this nature serves two key purposes. First, it enables identification of planned major changes in the school over a period of years, and all programs can take these changes into account. Responsibility can be assigned on the strategic plan as to who is responsible for desired long-term action and the timescale for this action. Second, the existence and nature of the strategic plan assure teachers and others concerned that, although major changes are desired and planned, an appropriate period of years is being allowed for their occurrence and that a sequential and logical development within the constraints of the school environment is sought. Such an approach is reassuring to teachers who frequently feel pressure to ensure that changes are implemented immediately and in total. Naturally they reject the

Table 7.1   Policy statement: drug education

RATIONALE:

Drug education involves two key aspects. Firstly, it involves knowledge of drugs and an understanding of their effects on the body and mind. Secondly, it involves the social effects of drugs on the individual, the family, and society in general. It is considered appropriate that the school should deal with both aspects in drug education and in so doing encourage and invite the participation of parents and the community.

PURPOSES:

1.   To foster in students a feeling of self-worth and to develop their social and personal skills to better equip them to solve problems without the need to resort to cover-ups (drug misuse).
2.   To develop a drug education program in which students, teachers, parents and the community share in the learning and teaching.
3.   To provide an information base about commonly misused drugs and their effects on the human body and mind.
4.   To provide students with opportunities to explore and understand the social and human issues behind and associated with drug misuse.

GUIDELINES:

1.   The drug education program will commence from the first years of school. In the early years it will focus on the development of self-worth and personal and social skills.
2a. Learning programs relevant to Purposes 3 and 4 will commence in grade 5 and continue throughout the school life of the student along with a continued focus on the development of self-worth and personal and social skills.
2b. These learning programs will focus on identifying commonly misused drugs, their common names, effects on the body and mind and the effects of their misuse, both short term and long term.
2c. The learning programs will also address drugs in the sequence in which young people will most probably be exposed to them, e.g. medication, tobacco, alcohol, marijuana, narcotics.
3.   A parallel program for students (K-12) will promote the essentials of good health in body and mind.
4.   Our drug education program will be a part of our overall health education program. In K-6 this will be included within general studies. In 7–12 it will be offered as sequential half-year courses. It will be compulsory for 7–12 students to take a minimum of two half-year courses during their 7–12 years.
5.   Students, parents and community groups will be invited to be actively involved in preparing and participating in our school drug education program.
6.   Our drug education program will contain as essential elements: exploring and sharing ideas, role plays, time for reflection, understanding of issues and the development of values.

CONCLUSION:

This policy is to be viewed as an aspect of Health Education and should be considered in close association with all other policies related to the social, physical and emotional well being of students.

---

change not because of its real value but because of its supposed method of implementation.

An essential aspect of having a school strategic plan is that it be reviewed on an annual basis. Circumstances do change and it may be necessary to make adjustments to elements within the plan or the time-scale for achievement.

School Year Programs

For each school year it is possible to identify a set of programs to operate within the school through which policies and priorities are to be achieved. These programs need also to take into account the key elements of the strategic plan for that year and future years.

The set of school programs contains as elements all activities encompassed by the curriculum. The majority of programs will clearly be learning programs with a smaller number of support programs. It should be realized that the set of programs for any school will be unique, reflecting the differences among schools as they endeavour to meet their local community needs. Of course there will always be some programs basic to all schools.

Curriculum Planning

The third circle represents the curriculum planning that must take place for all programs identified earlier. This curriculum planning will be an outcome of the needs, goals, policies and priorities already established.

Curriculum planning involves two key aspects. First, it involves designing the curriculum or preparing the courses through which program purposes can be achieved. This course preparation must also take into account any relevant policy guidelines. Traditionally, schools have given considerable emphasis to this aspect of planning and have produced appropriate documentation. Further developments are to produce summaries to assist students and parents in course selection and in understanding the nature of courses. An example of such a curriculum summary is given as Table 7.2. It should be noted that the following aspects are highlighted.

> What will I learn?
> What must I have done to do the course?
> What is in the course?
> How will I know if I have successfully completed the course?

The summaries or guidelines are geared not only to help the teacher prepare courses and lessons but also importantly to assist students and parents in their understanding of courses.

The second key aspect to curriculum planning is planning how to deliver the learning programs to students, referred to as 'program planning'. Program plans are prepared as outcomes of relevant policies. To ensure that policies are the starting point, the first two sections of the

Table 7.2   Living skills curriculum guidelines

A. ADMINISTRATIVE INFORMATION				
Course Code I-174-5	Classification C	Cost to Student $3.00	What kind of Course?	
			Academic	
Additional Information (include program name) 9/10 LIVING SKILLS K-12 HEALTH EDUCATION			Non-academic	*
			Community-based	
			Practical	
Resources Required 'Approved' teacher as per policy. 'Flexible teaching environment' School Health Coordinator's Resource File and Directory			7/8 Course	
			9/10 Course	*

B.   LEARNING INFORMATION

1.   What will I learn?
a.   To appreciate the nature and importance of relationships with others.
b.   To develop an understanding of self and self-worth and how to cope with change.
c.   To further consider the implications of sexuality and reproduction, and how to care for the body.
d.   To learn about, recognize and practise safety at school, in a work environment and at home.
e.   To evaluate the relationship between good nutrition and good health.
f.   To understand the issues involved in decision-making about drug use.
g.   To understand how we relate to the environment.
h.   To identify community health services and their roles.

2.   What must I have done to do this course?
I-174-4 Grade 7/8 Living Skills

3.   What's in the course?
a.   Personal relationships, including sexuality and the importance of personal responsibility.
b.   Care of the body, including protection from and prevention of communicable diseases.
c.   The environment, and community health and social services.
d.   Constructive use of leisure time.
e.   Basic nutrition.
f.   Safety — at home, at school, at work and in the community.
g.   Use and abuse of drugs — legal and illegal.

4.   How will I know if I have successfully completed this course?
4.1 How Tested?
a.   Fact-based sections will be objectively tested, i.e. multiple choice or paragraph form tests.
b.   'Values' sections will be assessed through individual and group discussions and through written work.
c.   Self-evaluation.

4.2 How Told?
a.   Through individual and group discussions.
b.   In counselling sessions involving teacher, student and parent.
c.   Regular reports through the Student Performance Review Program.

program plans are summaries of the purposes and broad guidelines of the corresponding policies. A plan for implementation is then detailed as a series of elements, with each element being in keeping with the broad guidelines. The planning elements detail what activities are to take place, who will carry out those activities and what resources will be required. The elements are also placed in an order of descending priority with respect to their importance in achieving the program purposes. An example of a program plan is given in Table 7.3. It should be noted that program plans are always only two pages in length.

Resource Provision

The fourth circle refers to resource provision. In the program planning process a key aspect is to identify the resources, both human and material, required to carry out the program. The costing of these resources enables a budget to be prepared for each program, called a program budget. In the planning and related budgeting processes account needs to be taken of two key factors. These are the nature of the total resource package available and priorities for action. An overall increase in the total resource package can lead to an expansion of all or most programs. The converse is equally true and there are variations in between. However, changing program priorities from year to year are also relevant in anticipating planning and resource levels. An increased priority rating should be reflecting by an expanded or intensified plan with a subsequent increase in resources. A decreased program priority should result in the opposite. If the total resource package remains relatively stable and a program priority remains the same, then little change to program resources should be expected. The inclusion of additional programs or their omission can be another factor in these considerations. Indications in this respect would be identified in the strategic plan.

A summary of all program budgets allows a comparison with anticipated resources. This comparison leads to the balancing of the budget. Tables of expected resources and program budget summaries are shown in Tables 7.4 and 7.5 respectively. In these examples a balanced budget has been achieved. It is acknowledged that it is not possible to know the exact resources to be available when this program planning takes place. It is therefore necessary to work on predicted resources as a guide to including new programs and priority changes. Experience has shown that it is possible to predict the total resource package to be available with sufficient accuracy for planning purposes (usually in the order of 95–98 per cent). Fine tuning can then be carried out in the year of operation to

Table 7.3   Pastoral care program plan

PROGRAM: Pastoral Care	RESPONSIBILITY: J.M.S.	CODE: 105
KEY POLICY/S NO: 30, 07, 09, 33		PRIORITY: One

1. *PURPOSE:*
The first purpose stated below is the general or overall purpose of the program while those that follow are more specifically the purposes with respect to each individual child.
   1.1 To assist each child in reaching his potential in intellectual, physical, social and emotional development and to gain the maximum value possible from all school programs.
   1.2 To ensure that the child is familiar with the necessary school organization.
   1.3 To maintain communication with the parents on the child's development.
   1.4 To counsel the child on his school courses.
   1.5 To ensure that the child's social and emotional development is assisted and that any problems are resolved if at all possible.
   1.6 To give assistance and advice as may be required by the child.

2. *BROAD GUIDELINES:*
   2.1 It is considered that the above purposes are best achieved by each child being able to develop secure, warm and trusting relationships with the adults in the school and with other children.
   2.2 There are always two members of staff who specifically have responsibility for the overall well being and development of each child. A senior member of staff has the responsibility for all children in a grade area and works with the child's class teacher in caring for the child's best interests. Other staff share in this responsibility to some extent, especially in the more senior grades.
   2.3 It is recognized that time is a factor in the development of desirable relationships. For this reason, staff changes with respect to any child are kept to a minimum.
   2.4 Senior staff in charge of grade areas and class teaching staff are assisted by the Principal and Vice-Principals in their pastoral care roles; in particular with respect to children experiencing extreme difficulties in either the emotional or social sense. Support staff such as guidance and welfare officers are also able to assist in such circumstances.

3. *IMPLEMENTATION PLAN*
   3.1 Students are placed in grades K to 10 based on age according to Education Department regulations. Within each grade students are placed in class teaching groups with each group being no larger than 25. In some cases it is necessary to form composite groups across two adjacent age grades for reasons of economy. A class teacher is assigned to each class group. In K–6, the class teacher is also the 'usual' teacher for the class while in 7–10 every effort is made to ensure that the class teacher is also a subject teacher for the class.
   3.2 Senior members of staff are assigned overall responsibility for certain grades. These are detailed below:
   K–2: Infant Mistress   7,8,9,10: a SM* is assigned for each grade.   3–6: Senior Teacher (P)
   *It should be noted that where possible the SM and Class Teachers continue with the students as they progress from grade to grade.
   3.3 Additional senior staff support is provided to the program by the Vice-Principals (especially the VPO) and the Principal. The Principal also exercises overall program supervision.
   3.4 Class teachers report to parents on student development at regular intervals. This reporting is in the nature of both interviews and written reports. Grade area Senior Staff are responsible for this reporting as well as references for grade 10 students. Reports may also be initiated at any time by either staff, students or parents, should the circumstances deem it necessary.
   3.5 An excursion program is organized on the basis of individual grades and is the responsibility of the relevant senior staff. Costs associated are to be met by the students

participating but a contingency is made to assist individual students, should the circumstances require it.

3.6 Guidance and welfare support is provided through the Support Service Program (112).

3.7 Provision of an intense staff development program on the counselling of students and parents with respect to the student's overall development and course selections.

4. RESOURCES REQUIRED: Planning Elements	Teaching Staff	Materials	Travel
4.1 Class Groups K–6 9 7–10 13 22 22 × 3 × $652	43032		
4.2 Senior Staff Grade Area Responsibility K–2, 3–6, 7, 8, 9, 10 6 × 3 × $822	14796	600	
4.3 Senior Staff Support VPO 10× $891 VPC 5× $891 Principal 5× $1106	8910 4455 5530		
Program Supervision Principal 3 × $1106	3318		
4.4 Printing of student report forms		1500	
4.5 Excursion Contingency			500
4.7 Counselling Training (Costs to Dept. Support Services)			
TOTAL $82641	80041	2100	500

5. EVALUATION

The evaluation will focus on the effectiveness of the counselling training for staff and any resulting effectiveness of program delivery to students.

take account of minor discrepancies. Developments now taking place in many states with respect to resource provision and flexibility should reduce these problems.

The balancing of the program budgets is not a difficult task as relevant priorities related to student needs have already been established. There is a necessity, first, to consider all programs from the point of view of what is reasonable. Then every endeavour can be made to meet all resource requirements for priority 1 programs. The same can be applied to priority 2 programs, with priority 3 programs being cut in part or in whole to achieve the balance. Sometimes it is not acceptable to cut complete programs and even harsh reductions in resources do not always achieve the overall balance. In this case lesser reductions can be made to priority 2 programs. Where reductions are necessary, these can be made by eliminating the least important planning elements (always presented in

Table 7.4   Resources estimates

SUMMARY OF RESOURCES FOR 1988

Staff Resource

Teaching Staff	1014818
Clerical Staff	46069
Custodial Staff	83692
Department Teacher Aide Support	17941
Support Staff	10944
Relief Staff (PD)	1925
	1175389

Cash Grants and Subsidies

Annual Requisition Grant	12435
ARG — Cash Elective	9849
Australian Schools Commission	55130
Excursions	6000
Library Grant	3600
Resource Agreement Program	5000
Postage Subsidy	680
Telephone Subsidy	3200
Country Education	24068
Special Education	2200
Community Bus Grant	1000
Total	123162

Levies and Fees

K–6 General Levies	6598
7–11 Book Hire Fees	4484
9–11 Subject Levies	5555
7–8 Subject Levies	5900
	22537

School Initiated Activities

Booksales Profits	2500
Canteen Profits	3000
Investment Account Interest	1500
Gala Day*	1000
Fair*	1000
(*% to PP and B)	9000

Total Resources	$1330088

priority order) or making percentage reductions and each program in question accommodating the reduction within one or more planning elements.

Following achievement of a balanced budget the budget is presented for approval. Changes may be made in the approval process although the balance must be maintained. Additions to programs must equal deletions to other programs unless further resources can be found above those anticipated. However, the approval process should not concentrate solely on financial issues. The key purpose of the approval process is to ensure that programs are true reflections of policies and priorities and that

Table 7.5 Program budget summary

PROGRAM BUDGET SUMMARY SHEET FOR 1988

Program	Teaching Staff	Non-teaching Staff	Relief Days	Major Materials	Book Service and Hire	Minor Materials	Travel	Services	Reserve	Other	Program Total
102 Art Acquisition				2790							2790
103 Administration	105401	41023		4900		500		8600	169		160593
104 Community Bus											N.R.A.
105 Pastoral Care	80041			2100			500				82641
111 Curriculum Res.	15287	7110		4900				100	15		27412
121 Supp. Service	1644	17222						200			19066
113 Mus. S&D.	24042			3250	350	400	480	250	25		28797
124 Presentation Day				1000		220		260	15		1495
115 Year Eleven	54455		500	5000		480					60435
112 School Council	1782			175		130		750	50		2887
122 K–11 Phys. Ed.	32589		475	2500			1150	200	50		36964
123 7–11 Sport & Rec.	9475			750			700	120	50		11095
131 7–11 Soc. Sc.	60589			650	1700	700	700				64339
133 5–10 Trans. Ed.	8910					500		350			9760
134 7–10 Tr. Sup. Serv.		9634									9634
141 Lang. Studies	64285			886	1950			700		700	68521
144 Drama Festival	822										822
151 7–11 Maths	56689			3900	1050	200		560	40		62439
152 7–11 Science	59307		95	8500	1200	320	300	3600	40		73667
153 K–11 Comp. Educ.	24262		95	8234	300			320	140	5000	33617
161 7–11 Tech. Subjects	62299		95	3530	360	430	120	1600	100		73238
162 7–11 Visual Arts	19561		95		200	150		6784	50		30370
163 Home Skills	27287			2343	400	100		200	50		30475
164 7–11 Comm. Subj.	15353			1434	300	100	150	120			17457
172 K–2/3 Gen. Stud.	127746	13393	285	5200				150	125		146899
173 K–11 Spec. Ed.	48984	2511	95	1960				300	50	2200	56100
181 3–6 Gen. Stud.	108389	2512	190	3417		810		50	75		115443
191 Cleaning & Grounds		88107		4200		400			50		92757
193 Canteen		631									631
200 Student Council	822										822
195 C.C.A.R.S.	891			2050			1900	400	25	3650	8916
Rounding Error	6										6
	1014818	182143	1925	73669	7810	5440	6000	25614	1119	11550	1330088

program plans are in keeping with policy guidelines. Consideration of these issues may require planning changes before approval of the set of program plans and budgets is obtained.

The preceding information and the examples shown indicate that inclusion of the staff resource is a key feature of this approach to program planning and budgeting. The teacher is the most important resource in the delivery of the curriculum to students and omission would reduce program plans to plans to support delivery rather than plans to deliver the curriculum. It could be argued though that it is not necessary to cost the staff resource in dollar terms. Few would disagree as the staff resource could be expressed equally effectively as time. However, as devolution of responsibility for resources develops further, it is anticipated that the school will exercise even greater control over the nature of the staffing resource and will need to consider costs in exercising this responsibility. It should be noted that the staffing component of schools tends to increase with devolution, as savings achieved are translated into more teachers as a way of more effectively meeting the needs of students. The alarm that devolution will result in fewer teachers does not appear to be borne out in practice.

Implementation of Learning Programs

With completion of curriculum planning, including both design and delivery of the curriculum and approval of proposed resource use, implementation of learning programs can proceed. This is indicated by the fifth circle. Teachers and school staff can provide the planned learning activities for students with the sure knowledge that resources will be forthcoming as agreed to.

Day-to-day autonomy for the implementation can be assigned to those immediately concerned. This can include ordering and use of materials within the guidelines of the approved plan, allowing a quick response to learning needs as they emerge throughout the program period. There is no need for those implementing the programs to seek authority to acquire resources if the action is within the plan. The audit process is the later check as to whether this has proceeded as expected.

Evaluation

After implementation of the program plan for a suitable interval, it is appropriate to evaluate the program as indicated in the sixth circle. In the evaluation process it can be ascertained whether the program purposes have been achieved and to what degree. It is also appropriate to consider whether planning, budgeting and implementing can be improved. Overall the purpose of program evaluation is to investigate the effectiveness and efficiency of programs and their related policies.

Evaluation of programs can be a huge and time-consuming task for those involved and yet this undertaking is crucial to developing and improving policies and programs. The evaluations also serve a major role in the reconsideration of learning priorities. The time-consuming problem in program evaluation has been partially solved by adopting two approaches. For any one year most programs are only given a minor evaluation, while a smaller number are given a major evaluation. The differences between minor and major evaluations are shown in Table 7.6. A schedule of program evaluations is drawn up so that all programs receive a major evaluation in an agreed period.

Evaluations are not always useful in themselves. There is a need to use the information gained in later decision-making. This process is facilitated by evaluation reports being limited to one page for minor evaluations and two pages for major evaluations. In both cases the reports concentrate on reporting three aspects: the successes, the concerns, the recommendations relating to the concerns. Examples of program evaluations are given in Tables 7.7 and 7.8.

As indicated earlier, evaluations in themselves are not always useful. There is a need to use the information gained in later decision-making. This includes a consideration of recommendations at an appropriate time regarding whether they can be implemented, when and by whom. If a recommendation is to be implemented immediately, there is a need to decide who will do so and by when. Similarly, a recommendation can be put aside to be included in the next planning period. The above two cases relate to recommendations concerning implementation. If a recommendation concerns policy, it is necessary for this to be referred to those responsible for making policy for consideration and possible action.

Another way of using information gained in an evaluation relates to program priority. In the evaluation information is gained as to the effectiveness and efficiency of the program. However, the priority of the program is also important in deciding future action. For instance, an ineffective and inefficient program would not be deleted if it were also a high priority in relation to student needs. Instead, major changes to planning and implementation may be in order. On the other hand, an ineffective and inefficient program could well be deleted if it concerned a low priority in relation to student needs. Effectiveness and efficiency are also not necessarily simply linked. An effective program could be in-

Table 7.6   Major and minor program evaluation guidelines

Programs are subjected to either a MAJOR or a MINOR evaluation each year. Only one fifth of the programs receive a major evaluation in any one year but all programs receive a major evaluation in any given five year period. The nature of major and minor evaluations is detailed in the table below:

MAJOR EVALUATIONS	MINOR EVALUATION
1. All programs included in a cycle over a period of years.	1. Carried out on all non-major years for all programs.
2. In-depth considerations requiring an appropriate commitment of time.	2. Not time intensive.
3. Objective in nature if possible.	3. Subjective in nature.
4. A search for program outcomes and identification of inadequacies and areas of concern.	4. General identification of success indicators and areas of concern.
5. Focus on the purposes to be achieved by programs.	5. Related mainly to implementation of program.
6. Usually involve the employment of simple, information gathering techniques.	6. Rely on informed professional opinion.
7. Include coordination with similar programs in other grade areas (or schools).	7. Focus is within the program.
8. Carried out by a group including councillors, program team and possibly others as appropriate.	8. Carried out by the program team.
9. Two-page printed report.	9. One-page printed report.
10. Report presented to council or governors.	10. Report presented to council or governors.
11. Can lead to substantial policy and program changes.	11. Can lead to planning and implementation of changes or to bring forward scheduled major evaluations.

efficient in its requirement on scarce resources and deleted on the basis of a low priority in relation to student needs.

Documentation

A feature of collaborative school management is the simplicity and effectiveness of documentation. Policies are limited to one page and highlight purposes to be achieved and broad guidelines for achievement. Program plans and budgets are limited to two pages, with resources required for each planning element clearly identified. Evaluative reports are limited to one or two pages, with emphasis on reporting successes, concerns and recommendations to overcome concerns. In each case documents are printed and presented in booklet form as policy handbooks, program plans and budgets and program evaluations. These are distributed to all staff and to parents and student members of the policy group as working and reference documents. Easy access to information is in itself a benefit

Table 7.7 *Minor evaluation: computer education*

PROGRAM: K–10 Computer Education   RESPONSIBILITY: LM   CODE: 153

SUCCESS INDICATORS	AREAS OF CONCERN
1. All staff in the K–10 area have participated in school based professional development.	1. The availability of computers and printers within the school makes further development of the program difficult.
2. All students in K–10 have been involved in 'hands-on' activities with computers.	2. Staff involvement in professional development activities is limited because of time constraints.
3. The introduction of grade 7/8 computer awareness has been applauded by students and the community.	3. There are difficulties in transporting computers around the school.
4. Computer timetables in the K–6 area are working well.	4. The constant flow of new information and software makes it difficult for teachers to keep up with the latest brands.
5. Students are developing respect for and are comfortable using computers.	5. The collection of reference books for students in the library needs to be continually updated to keep up with innovations in this field.
6. Good maintenance services have been provided by the curriculum Services Branch.	
7. A wide variety of software is now available for use within the school.	
8. Students are regularly using computers outside lesson time.	
9. The central filing system in the computer room is working well.	
10. All computers in the school have Edword chips to enable wordprocessing.	

SUMMARY AND RECOMMENDATIONS
1. The replacement equipment policy is providing the necessary funding arrangements to overcome this problem.
2. Staff meeting time could be made available at the rate of approximately one per term to allow teachers to develop their expertise in this area.
3. Suitable trolleys should be purchased for the movement of computers around the school.
4. Staff members would like the opportunity to have 'experts' available from time to time to keep them informed of the trends in computing. Education Dept productions will also be made available to all staff in the same way as in 86 to help overcome this problem.
5. The staff will be asked to provide the librarian with a list of suitable references for future purchase.

to school effectiveness in reducing conflict which arises from perceived secrecy through lack of appropriate documentation.

Relation to the School Year

Collaborative school management requires that forward planning take place on a logical, sequential basis. It takes account of the busy schedules

Table 7.8   *Major evaluation: special education*

PROGRAM: Special Education   RESPONSIBILITY: M.S.   *CODE:* 173

INTRODUCTION:
The main emphasis in this evaluation was to identify the benefits and disadvantages of the Special Education program as perceived by parents, staff, and the student 'consumers' of the service. As the provision of the service necessitates an increased teaching commitment by all other staff, it was felt that the benefits must substantially outweigh the disadvantages in order for this step to be justified.
The following tasks were undertaken by the evaluating team:
— design of survey forms intended for use with parents, staff and students.
— administration of the survey across a randomly selected group of parents, staff and students.
— referral to assessments of students and records of student progress, within the constraints imposed by the need for confidentiality.
— analysis through lengthy discussion of the information provided by the surveys.
It was the feeling of the evaluation team, based on the information gained that the benefits of the program were perceived by all three groups surveyed as substantially outweighing the disadvantages.

INADEQUACIES AND PROBLEM AREAS:
1.   Teachers are not sufficiently aware of what children from their classes are doing during Special Ed. time.
2.   Some children's special needs are not being met to the fullest extent due to constraints on the amount of time available to them.
3.   The program has lapsed and or partially lapsed for a significant portion of this year due to lack of suitable Special Ed. staff.
4.   The program should make every endeavour to tailor its delivery more to the personality and teaching style of the individual classroom teacher and the learning style of the student, particularly with respect to choices between in class or extraction Special Education.
5.   Insufficient relief time available for the professional development needs of the Special Ed. program.
6.   The format of the policy statement on Special Education needs attention.
7.   New staff are not sufficiently aware of the services and procedures of the Special Education program.

SUCCESSFUL OUTCOME OF THE PROGRAM:
1.   The one to one or small group attention made available to children with special needs is highly valued by parents and teachers.
2.   Almost all children on the program who were surveyed reacted positively stating that they gained enjoyment and satisfaction from their Special Education time and saw value in it.
3.   The importance placed on the program by all three groups surveyed was highlighted by the fact that the temporary interruption to the program caused concern. It was noted that some children's progress has suffered, and many commented that the program should be resumed without delay, and maintained.
4.   Overall, children feel no stigma about being on the program. In fact the reverse often occurs, particularly with younger children. Occasional instances of 'testing' or 'embarrassment' occur to a mild extent in the Grade 8 age group.
5.   A general feeling was expressed that the performance of many of the children on the program has improved. In a small number at high school level this may have meant the difference between a failure, lower pass, or a pass. A related benefit for many children has been improved confidence, and ability to concentrate on a task.
6.   Effective liaison between Special Ed. staff and parents has been developed. Benefits for parents were expressed as
— 'more at ease and more aware of what was happening with my child'.
— 'more able to help my child at home'.

7. An encouraging start has been made on a provision for the very small minority of children who, because of severe behaviour problems or truancy, are resistant to remediation in the normally accepted ways. This provision will be further developed via the Country Education submission 'Educational Alternatives'.

SUMMARY AND RECOMMENDATIONS:
1. A systematic two-way communication process about the progress of children on the program needs to be set up between Special Education staff and classroom teacher. Techniques such as regular reports and discussions at Department staff meetings, or workshop sessions organized by Special Education staff, need to be utilized. Classroom teachers also need to be encouraged to make use of the consultation time available to them.
2. This will always be a problem, as the children with the most severe learning problems require almost constant one-to-one attention. There will be a continuing effort made to balance the needs of varying groups within the program e.g.
    — younger students vs older
    — those who will respond to short-term intervention vs those whose problems will always exist despite intervention.
3. Every endeavour has been, and will continue to be made, to employ highly suitable and satisfactory staff to fill Special Education positions. This is not always possible, due to state-wide lack of such personnel.
4. Improved liaison (see point 1 above) will ensure that the service more closely matches the learning styles of the students, and the teaching styles and requirements of classroom teachers.
5. Continued efforts should be made to budget for a reasonable relief time allocation for professional development in Special Education.
6. The policy statement on Special Education should be rewritten in the accepted format.
7. In the process of improving liaison between staff involved in the program, a special focus should be to ensure that all new staff are made aware, very early in the year, of the Special Education program services and the correct procedure for their use.

of schools in their day-to-day work and spaces out forward planning tasks over suitable intervals.

By the middle of the preceding year basically all policies to operate in the following year must have been adopted and priorities set. This is followed by the review and adjustment of the school strategic plan and the identification of the learning programs to operate. During the third quarter of the preceding year, program teams undertake curriculum planning in each program and prepare program plans and budgets. In some cases this involves new work, while in others it is a carrying forward of some previous work depending on the situation. In the last quarter of the year program plans and budgets are subject to the approval process and program evaluations undertaken. Evaluations belong in the latter part of the school year and are available in the early part of the year to modify the year's programs where possible and to serve as the basis for further policy development in the future. In this way the key tasks involved are spread over the school year to allow realistic undertaking by busy staff and policy group members.

Roles for Participants

It is not the intention of this chapter to detail role differentiations at length in relation to the collaborative management model. It is sufficient to say that a clearly identified group of parents, teachers and students (in secondary schools) shares responsibility for need identification, goal-setting, policy-making, priority-setting, budget approval and evaluation. This group is identified as the 'policy group' in the model diagram. Depending on the country or state, this group is referred to as the school council, board of governors, school board, etc., although some differences with respect to the role are evident.

The curriculum planning, budget preparation, implementation of learning program and evaluation are clearly roles for teachers in their areas of expertise. Teachers undertake these roles in teams centred on learning programs. Reference is made in the model diagram to these groups of teachers as program teams.

It should be noted that evaluation is listed as a role for both the policy group and the program teams. This is logical as the policy group is interested particularly in whether goals and needs are being met. Program teams are interested in this information but there would also be interest in evaluating the effectiveness and efficiency of delivery methods as well as reviewing the suitability of curriculum content and design.

Advantages and Concerns

Schools considering the introduction of collaborative school management will naturally want to weigh up the concerns and advantages. From the experiences of hundreds of schools which have adopted this approach the following key advantages have become apparent.

Information is readily available to all concerned. One-page policies, two-page plans and one- or two-page evaluation reports provide easily understood and quick reference information.

Policies and learning activities for students are clearly linked together. It is easy to see how resources are linked to policies and learning priorities through program plans.

It is easy for participants to see the relevance of their work to the overall process of providing an education to meet student needs.

Participants gain satisfaction and develop commitment as they are able to participate in a way that is relevant to them.

Most of the operations involved already exist in the school. There are policies, plans, budgets and sometimes evaluations. Collaborative school management logically links these operations together in a systematic and understandable manner.

It provides a clear method for accountability. Purposes or learning outcomes are known and clearly stated. The plans and resources by which the purposes are to be achieved are also known and clearly stated. There is an inbuilt path to evaluation with respect to whether purposes have been achieved or whether planning and resources are appropriate.

Openness of information is guaranteed. All concerned have copies of all policies, program plans and evaluations for reference. It is easy to know what others are doing and how one may assist or cooperate.

Program teams cooperate to benefit each other rather than compete for resources.

Priorities are known well in advance and are clearly linked to learning needs of students rather than items for expenditure.

The overall process is clear and easily understood. People know how change can be brought about.

There is inbuilt flexibility within programs to respond immediately to new or emerging student needs.

Naturally, there are also concerns as well as advantages. The key concern is always *time*. People fear that the processes commit them to a large number of tasks to fit into their already overcrowded schedules. They see that the process is another *add-on* to their lists of things to do. Experience shows that this does not occur. First, most of the tasks are already being carried out in schools, although usually in a manner where clear links are not established between the processes. All schools make policies, prepare program plans, allocate resources and evaluate. The approach helps schools to do these same tasks more effectively and with greater efficiency. There is a time input initially as tasks are clarified and skills developed. However, the eventual outcome is saved time through increased effectiveness and efficiency. There is also an increased satisfaction by participants as they make better progress in providing for the changing needs of students. Second, the approach needs to be implemented in a manner that does not produce work overload. It may take three to five years totally to implement the approach across the whole school. Its implementation can be gradual and voluntary and further implementation based on conviction from the advantages being experienced.

It is also appropriate to refer to the benefits and fears that are being expressed particularly in relation to the continuing devolution to the school level of responsibility for resources. This aspect of the collaborative school management model often receives particular attention from schools in the early stages of adoption of the model. Commonly expressed fears and benefits are listed below.

BENEFITS	FEARS
1 Able to manage money more effectively and create savings.	1 Principals would become more managers than educational leaders.
2 Better able to manage the educational business of the school.	2 Concern about principals having sufficient managerial experience and ability.
3 Better positioned to understand the financial position and an incentive to plan.	3 Suspicion that devolution is a device for making cuts and transferring the odium to schools.
4 Decisions best taken by those most affected by them.	4 Suspicion that the good managers in one year would be penalized in the next.
5 Opportunity for more upward flow of information.	
6 Opportunities for innovation.	
7 The good performers are rewarded.	

The benefits speak for themselves. The fears are real to those concerned and need to be addressed seriously if the benefits are to be realized in our schools. The issue of principals as educational leaders or resource managers is an interesting one. It arises from a misconception of the two roles. The role of the principal is to be an educational leader and part of that leadership involves effectively delivering learning programs to students through the best use of resources available. Too many existing problems in our systems and schools result from viewing educational leadership and managing resources as distinctly different roles. This leads to the second fear listed and perhaps this fear is an outcome of the focus of management in the past on separate compartments of management rather than management involving knowledge and expertise and delivery of that knowledge and expertise to the client in the best possible way. There is certainly an immediate need to provide management training for existing and potential senior personnel in schools as a very high priority.

The third listed fear is a political opinion being expressed. It needs to be dealt with through political assurances backed up with clear evidence that 'cuts' to schools are not the intention but rather to give schools the opportunities to use existing levels of resource in a more effective and efficient way with any savings made being available for redistribution within the school to the further benefit of students.

The fourth fear expressed is a sad indictment of some school systems of the immediate past. This has involved ensuring that all allocations are expended whether wisely or not so as not to lose the same level of funding for the next year. The approach of the end of the financial year should not be the sudden reason to spend surpluses. Good management should be rewarded with savings being used to pursue the goals in question in a planned manner.

Devolution of responsibility for decision-making to the school level does change the roles of the school and particularly leaders within the school. However, on the evidence these changes are not undesirable. They enable the educational leaders to exercise their leadership more effectively and to fulfil their responsibilities by giving them control over the means by which goals can be achieved. This involves changes in their roles but does not necessarily require additional time. Many frustrating practices are replaced through direct control of resources. The ultimate beneficiaries are the students through learning programs appropriately designed and delivered.

Development of the Model

The model for collaborative school management as described in this chapter was developed at Rosebery District High School in Tasmania, Australia. It was identified in relation to school effectiveness through the Effective Resource Allocation in Schools Project (ERASP), a Project of National Significance funded by the Australian Commonwealth Schools Commission and undertaken through the University of Tasmania and the Education Department of Tasmania. In this study Rosebery District High School received more nominations as highly effective in both a general educational sense and in the manner in which resources were allocated. Subsequent study of the school identified the relevance of the collaborative management model that had been developed over several years to the success of the school in catering for the needs of students.

Trial, Adoption and Appraisal of the Model

The model became the centrepiece of a professional development program which was trialled, refined and implemented in an extended consultancy in the state of Victoria, Australia, where the government was proceeding with plans for school self-management. Caldwell and Spinks conducted seminars for principals, parents, teachers and students from more than 1100 of 2200 schools, with senior officers in the regions of the state conducting others. A recent study (Victoria, Ministry of Education, 1987) found that 71 per cent of schools had made a decision to proceed, with the majority of schools making progress on one or more phases. While the government in Victoria did not proceed with plans for 'self-governing' schools, it is evident that the model will provide the framework for futher decentralization should that occur. An independent appraisal of its worth in this regard was offered in a recent report where it was identified as 'the preferred solution to the problem of allocation of block grants' because of the following characteristics:

* The ability [of the model] to link funding decisions with educational goals and policies;
* Developed management processes including mechanisms for establishing priorities, reconciling needs with scarce resources and resolving conflict;
* Careful design to control the level of complexity and work load involved in implementing the system. (Deloitte, Haskins and Sells, 1987, p. 49.)

The model was described in a more recent appraisal (Ashendon, 1988) as 'a major extension of possibilities in the use of information in Australian education' (p. 10) and as making 'a very exciting contribution' (p. 32) to the use of indicators in improving the quality of learning.

The model seems well suited to the requirements for school-site management in the United States, to the local management of schools in Britain, and to further developments in Australia. It offers a framework for resolving at the school level some of the critical issues involved.

> Successful adoption at the school level is a contribution to the relief of tensions currently encountered in shifting patterns of school governance. Schools can then work with a minimum of centrally determined rules and regulations and can develop the capacity to determine their own policies and curriculum to the extent desired.
>
> The focus of the model is learning and teaching and the support of learning and teaching. The basic unit of management in the school is a program unit of teachers with a common interest in an area of learning and teaching. The model addresses the contemporary view of equity in the manner in which it facilitates a matching of resources to the learning needs of each student.
>
> Guidelines for adopting the model (Caldwell and Spinks, 1988) call

for an evolutionary approach over three to five years, allowing adaptation to meet local needs, with schools encouraged to start at the phase in the management cycle which suits current approaches to management and the interests and capabilities of staff. In this fashion it is consistent with Miles' (1987) finding that an evolutionary approach, with empowerment of staff, is associated with success in school improvement.

The model is, of course, just a starting point. It is a framework for goal-setting, policy-making, planning, budgeting, implementing and evaluating. To make it work requires knowledge and skill related to learning and teaching, curriculum design and development, the gathering of information in program evaluation, and a capacity to exercise leadership in a fashion consistent with contemporary perspectives, namely, leadership which is widely dispersed, securing commitment to a shared vision for the school.

References

ASHENDON, D. (1988) *Indicators, Information and Education.* National Curriculum Issues Series No. 1. Canberra: Curriculum Development Centre.

CALDWELL, B.J. and SPINKS, J.M. (1988) *The Self-Managing School.* Lewes: Falmer Press.

DELOITTE, HASKINS and SELLS (1987) 'The Review and Development of Program Budgeting, Budgeting Processes and Financial Management and Accounting Systems,' Report to the Ministry of Education, Victoria.

MILES, M.B. (1987) 'Practical Guidelines for School Administrators: How to Get There,' Paper presented at a symposium on Effective Schools Programs and the Urban High School at the Annual Meeting of the American Educational Research Association, Washington, D.C., April.

NORTHERN TERRITORY. DEPARTMENT OF EDUCATION (1987) *Towards the 90s: Excellence, Accountability and Devolution in Education.* Darwin: Northern Territory Department of Education.

TASMANIA. EDUCATION DEPARTMENT (1987) *Secondary Education: The Future.* Hobart: Education Department of Tasmania.

VICTORIA. MINISTRY OF EDUCATION (1987) *Taking Schools into the 1990's.* Melbourne: Ministry of Education.

WESTERN AUSTRALIA. MINISTRY OF EDUCATION (1987) *Better Schools for Western Australia: A Program for Improvement.* Perth: Ministry of Education.

Chapter 8

Managing for Total School Improvement

Colin J. Marsh

Principals of schools have traditionally been seen as educational leaders with ultimate responsibility for the management of their respective schools (Hopes, 1986). But management is now perceived to be more creative and forward-looking than in previous decades when the emphasis was upon maintaining routines. Glatter *et al.* (1986, p. 128) highlight the intuitive, judgmental aspects of the management task in the 1980s compared with the more technical, scientific dimensions which were emphasized through much of the 1960s and 1970s. Other writers such as Schön (1983) emphasize the concept of reflective managers. Fullan (1985) identifies the need for school principals to have a 'leadership feel for the improvement process' (p. 401).

What Is School Improvement?

Miles and Ekholm (1985) define school improvement as a 'systematic, sustained effort aimed at change in learning conditions and other related internal conditions in one or more schools, with the ultimate aim of accomplishing educational goals more effectively' (p. 48). The statement begs many questions. What is considered to be a change for the better by some individuals might be deemed to be a worsening situation by others. The term 'school improvement' is an extremely value-laden, or normative term, and the literature is overflowing with divergent statements about what counts as school improvement.

It might be argued that knowing what is and what isn't school improvement is not as important as a commitment to want to change. Miles and Ekholm hint at this by their use of the phrase 'a systematic, sustained effort'. Greene (1986) reminds us that few of the participants involved in schooling reflect upon what they are doing: 'they proceed unthinkingly, caught up in dailyness, in the sequences of tasks and routines' (p. 13). What is needed is a commitment, especially by teachers and students, to examine their current practices and routines to see whether these are appropriate for their present situation. This takes a lot of time, perseverance and a considerable amount of collaboration.

'School improvement' can refer to relatively minor changes where there is some change to the program without any change in the basic goals and values; or it can refer to changes in the program and in the existing goals and values, which, in total, could amount to considerable change. An individual school community can become involved in minor or major changes, but the costs in time and resources usually limit their opportunities to minor changes. When major changes do occur in individual schools, such as those brought about by a charismatic energetic school principal, they are rarely publicized beyond the local community. By contrast, major changes are often initiated by state education systems and by federal government agencies.

Another way of considering the 'degree' of school improvement is to examine the type of decision-making that occurs between individuals and groups, especially within school communities. Involvement decision-making is where individuals or groups are present at meetings or informal conversations when policy matters are being discussed, but they do not have any direct influence on what policies are finally decided. There can be different degrees of 'involvement', as depicted in Figure 8.1, ranging from that of a passive member of an audience to that of an active member of a small advisory panel which does not have formal powers. Participatory decision-making is where individuals or groups share in the making of final decisions. It is typically referred to as a partnership arrangement, whereby various individuals openly discuss and collectively come to a consensus about the outcome and direction of a particular policy or action.

In terms of Figure 8.1, and using an example developed by Adams (1983), an 'involvement decision-making' mode might be where parents worked on a voluntary basis in the school canteen, under the supervision of a manager and directed by policy decisions made by the school principal. At the other end of the continuum a 'participatory decision-making' mode might consist of parents and teachers developing a nutritional policy for the school so that priorities about range of items sold and prices charged would be discussed and decided upon by this group.

It is evident that the 'participatory decision-making' mode involves far more negotiation, both informally and formally, among the main actors than tends to occur in the 'involvement decision-making' mode.

Figure 8.1 A continuum of decision-making

Involvement					Participation
			Examples:		
Member of an audience	Speaker at a meeting	Member of an advisory group	Member of a committee with formal powers	Chairperson of a committee with formal powers	One of a small group having executive powers

The sharing of ideas and the discussion of different stances rely upon some degree of consensus being finally achieved. The penalties are long periods of time needed to reveal and examine different points of view and the possibility that in some difficult situations no consensus can be negotiated.

Which Individuals/Groups Are the Targets for School Improvement?

Passow (1986) refers to students, staff and parents as the 'prime residents of schools', and so it might be assumed that these would be the major targets for school improvement. The traditional target for most school improvement endeavours is, of course, the student. The emphasis is upon ensuring that students — the clients of schooling — attain their highest possible levels of understanding, skills and values development. Unfortunately, the criteria used to measure these achievement levels are quite limited and tend to emphasize cognitive learning, as measured by various multiple-choice and essay tests.

Teachers are also a major client group in any school improvement activity. Teachers involved in implementing new curricula will need intensive, additional training. It cannot be assumed that a teacher will be able to adopt a new program and be proficient in its use without assistance and training. Even for minor changes it is crucial that teachers be given information about the new program and, where necessary, additional training for using it. For changes that involve teachers working together, either in their planning or in their instruction, there are additional interpersonal and small-group skills that need to be encouraged. Collaborative teamwork among teachers involves skills that may take long periods to develop.

Attention has been directed in recent years to another target, namely parents and community members. If the goal of school improvement includes having a higher level of parent involvement, then this must be an important focus. Unless parents have had other professional experiences which have equipped them with the skills needed for decision-making, special training sessions must be provided.

Who Initiates and Manages School Improvement?

There are sound reasons why school improvement actions should be initiated at the school level. For example, members of a school staff know their school situation best and can pinpoint areas of most need; they are the ones directly involved in implementing any changes. Yet in the literature on school improvement there are few examples where an individual school community has been responsible entirely for taking a particular initiative. There is usually an external source of funds which facilitates the initiative or other external personnel who contribute to the initiative in some way (see Table 8.1).

By contrast, there are examples in the literature of highly prescriptive, centrally initiated school improvement schemes that have been downright failures (Berman and McLaughlin, 1977; Corwin, 1981). Teachers' resistance to a centrally initiated program can be very strong indeed, to the extent that the program is either totally rejected or so drastically adapted that the original intentions are no longer possible.

A more typical situation is where state or regional education systems provide support for school improvement but do not prescribe how it is to be carried out. To this extent a state system can play an important role in maintaining a high profile for a school improvement program without being restrictive, such as by:

1 distributing clear statements on the goals of the program;
2 providing system level incentives that recognize and reward creditable school improvement efforts;
3 providing technical/advisory support for those schools needing assistance;
4 providing financial resources on a per capita basis.

This type of symbolic support by a state system for school improvement seems to be a pragmatic solution which allows individual school communities to work out their specific programs. By contrast, regulatory state approaches, although seemingly efficient in terms of rational-bureaucratic processes, are unlikely to gain the support of individual school communities.

Apart from questions of 'top-down' aspects of initiation there is also the matter of who initiates and manages within each school community. The school principal has a pivotal role to play as school improvement

Table 8.1   *Examples of groups involved in school decision-making*

School level	Regional/state level	Federal level
Principal	Regional directors/ superintendents	Department of Employment, Education and Training
Total school staff or departments	Advisory educaton officers	Curriculum Development Centre
Individual teachers	Directors-General and department heads	ACER
Parents	State Minister of Education and state government	Federal Minister of Education and federal government
School board/council	Professional association	Australian Education Council
Local community	Teachers' centres	Australian Teachers Federation
Students	Tertiary institutions	National pressure groups
	Media	
	Teachers' unions	
	Public examination boards	
	Church groups	
	Textbook writers and commerical suppliers	
	Employer groups	
	Law Courts	
	Citizen advocacy groups	

leader as attested by the voluminous literature over recent years on school principals (for example, Leithwood and Montgomery, 1982; Lieberman and Miller, 1981; Rutherford and Huling-Austin, 1985, in North America; Bolam, 1988; Glatter *et al.*, 1980, in the United Kingdom; Chapman, 1984; Angus, 1988; Caldwell and Spinks, 1988, in Australia; and the International School Improvement Project publication by Van Velzen *et al.*, 1985, Stego *et al.*, 1987; Hopes, 1986).

The principal as the major school improvement figure is examined in detail in subsequent sections of the paper. Notwithstanding, it is worth noting that there can be other key leaders on a school staff (Vandenberghe and Hall, 1987; Stego *et al.*, 1987; Hord *et al.*, 1984). Corbett and Rossman (1988) suggest that empowering teachers is a necessary aspect of sound school improvement practices. Angus (1988, p. 37) suggests that other staff members can exercise their own creative initiatives and that each school site is a complex web of ideological, economic and social relationships.

How Do We Know When School Improvement Has Occurred?

School improvement programs can vary enormously in terms of being locally or centrally initiated, and in terms of contexts and level of schooling. As a result it is extremely difficult to use any standard evaluative approach to ascertain whether a program has been successful or not.

Commonly used methods in the United States include the use of standardized tests to measure student achievement gains in basic subjects such as reading and mathematics. These methods enable school districts and states to make comparisons about the relative success of their school improvement endeavours; the results are widely published and are readily understand by the general public. Yet these measures are extremely narrow, they can lead to teachers teaching to the test, and they tend to ignore important affective states of students.

If standardized tests are not an adequate measure of school improvement, are there any alternatives? A more preferable method seems to be a qualitative approach which attempts to document the feelings, aspirations, successes and failures of the chief participants in any school improvement program. This is especially important because such programs take a considerable time to develop and to be fully implemented. A longitudinal approach to evaluation which attempts to pinpoint the various stages of success, as they occur, seems to be infinitely better than a snapshot view which may be taken before any satisfactory level of implementation has been achieved.

But qualitative methods of evaluation also have their problems. Unless care is taken to verify comments and conversations made between the evaluator and the participants and to seek out major issues for in-depth analysis, it is likely that qualitative evaluations will be little better than a collection of superficial descriptions provided by those who are ego-involved and prone to give positive, glowing accounts (Tangerud and Wallin, 1986).

A major reason for concentrating upon qualitative methods — such as observing participants, individual and group interviews and the use of checklists — is to provide ongoing feedback to allow for fine tuning of the school improvement program in operation. Implementation of a program will rarely occur in accordance with the original plan, and various adjustments have to be made. Evaluation data can be extremely valuable in providing a justification for changes in direction and emphasis.

There is a place for more measurement of student outcomes in a total package of evaluation measures, but such student tests should be far wider in scope than the traditional standardized tests and should only be undertaken toward the end of the school improvement program when teachers and students have become very familiar and practised in their new activities.

Management Patterns

Lloyd (1985) considers that school management should be considered in terms of planning, organizing for implementation and exercising control. The planning phase involves identifying school-wide problems, and searching for and choosing solutions. Establishing effective processes for communicating, delegating, consulting and coordinating is the major task for managers involved in the second phase. The third phase of exercising control includes using various ongoing assessments and evaluations. It seems more appropriate to consider management in terms of these processes than in traditional terms of management responsibilities for expenditure, personnel and curriculum. After all, the last three terms are inextricably included in any processes of planning, implementation and control.

Caldwell and Spinks (1988) emphasize the planning and implementation aspects, although implicit within their approach is a strong control element. They emphasize the need for a management or policy group in each school. Teams are appointed to deal with specific school improvement tasks. Paperwork is kept to a minimum. Strict time schedules and achievable goals are stressed. Glatthorn (1987) prefers school managers to consider the 'taught curriculum' and the 'supported curriculum'. Manager leaders need to devise ways to supervise the taught curriculum. Where deficiencies are noted, this provides the incentive for mounting specific school improvement efforts. The school leader supervises the 'supported curriculum' by marshalling appropriate resources, appointing and training committees. Glatthorn (1987, p. 255) also emphasizes the implementation phase as crucial in any school improvement endeavours, but it is interesting to note the high priority he accords to curriculum alignment — the process of ensuring that there is a high degree of congruence between the district guides, teachers' instructional plans and the assessment measures.

For teachers and principals to operate effectively in school improvement endeavours can often require the attaining of new skills and understandings. Various authors stress teachers' professional development needs (Lieberman, 1986; Harisun, 1987). School principals need special assistance in such areas as interpersonal relationships (Chapman, 1985; Duignan, 1984) and problem-solving skills (Leithwood and Montgomery, 1986).

Many writers report the non-rational element of school management. Patterson *et al.* (1986) remind us that schools do not have a single set of stable goals and power is not a fixed entity. The school environment is far from stable and predictable. Lieberman (1986) also refers to the non-linear aspects of much of school management.

Approaches to School Improvement

Many writers remind us that there is no single optimal way to embark upon school improvement. Each school will have its own unique agenda, participants, resources and priorities. The literature abounds with various recommendations and caveats, and somehow each school has to take these on board in determining what is best for it. Notwithstanding, it is possible to coalesce these ideas into 'general approaches' or 'models' which provide conceptual maps for participants, which they can and must vary to suit their own particular schools.

Situational Analysis Model

Reynolds and Skilbeck (1976) popularized the situational analysis approach to school level planning in the 1970s, although it depends heavily on models developed previously by Tyler (1949) and Taba (1962). Users of the situational analysis model appear to be particularly attracted by its management aspects, but it also allows for a consideration of the culture of the school and the needs of the various subgroups that comprise the school community.

A major focus of the model is upon the needs of the participants, as reflected in the term 'situational analysis'. Persons involved in school improvement activities need to determine the gap between the current situation and what is desired. This involves collecting a considerable array of data about the activities of persons internal to the school (for example, teachers and students) and those external but influencing the school (for example, education system officials). Some of the data will be collected informally via conversations and discussions, and some will be collected by more formal methods such as surveys and questionnaires.

The other phases of the model are closely aligned to other linear models and include:

goal formulation,
program building (especially scope and sequence),
interpretation and implementation,
monitoring, assessment, feedback reconstruction.

The situational analysis model provides practical procedures for undertaking school improvement projects. An overriding emphasis is management and ways in which staff activities and energy at the school level can be channelled effectively.

Collaborative School Management Model

The collaborative school management model, advocated by Caldwell and Spinks (1986), provides individual schools with a thorough, integrated set of practices to achieve policy-making, planning, resource allocation and evaluation. It is a resource-focused approach to planning and enables various groups operating within a school community to work out manageable priorities to ensure that planned tasks are achieveable.

Concerns-based Adoption Model

The concerns-based adoption model (CBAM) was developed by researchers at the University of Texas Research and Development Center for Teacher Education in the 1970s. It has been used by school districts and individual schools as part of school improvement programs in many areas of the USA and Canada, and also in Western Europe and in Australia.

The overriding emphasis in upon the individual teacher and how he or she can accommodate various concerns in adjusting to innovatory practices and curriculum products. Various diagnostic instruments have been identified such as 'Stages of Concern', 'Levels of Use' and 'Innovation Configuration' to assist schools develop effective in-service programs for their staff. Of interest here is not the diagnostic instruments and how they have been used successfully in various settings, but an appreciation of the values embedded in this approach. Various authors such as House (1979), Olson (1982) and Popkewitz (1982) maintain that the CBAM approach is technological in intent. The CBAM instruments measure the degree to which curriculum innovations are being used or not. There does seem to be a heavy emphasis upon ensuring that high fidelity of use levels is attained by teachers.

People-centred Action Model

A school improvement approach that has been advocated by Loucks-Horsley and Hergert (1985) could perhaps be most appropriately labelled a 'people-centred action model'. The authors provide practical no-nonsense suggestions about how school improvement activities can be initiated and completed successfully. Their emphasis is more on actions and interactions between participants than on involvement in protracted periods of planning.

This approach has some of the data-collecting techniques advocated in the concerns-based adoption model, and the series of steps appears to have the trappings of other rational, means-end models. Nevertheless, the emphasis is predominantly on political matters, on gaining support from other participants, understanding their concerns and preferences, and trying to find mutually acceptable solutions.

Organization Development Model

This model has been widely used in the USA and Europe (Schmuck and Miles, 1971; Fullan, Miles and Taylor, 1980) and more recently in Australia (Mulford, 1979; Henderson, 1985; Johnston, 1985). The model uses behavioural science techniques to solve problems for groups working in organizations. The emphasis is on the organization or system and the role of groups within the system. This is in marked contrast to other models, such as CBAM, which emphasize the role of individual teachers.

Unlike other models, organization development (OD) is more concerned with process than any specific outcomes of school improvement. In fact, the major purpose of OD might be stated as the improvement of the functioning of groups (communication skills, organization skills). Often external consultants are used to assist with the OD process, as the initial activities of reflection and analysis are difficult to achieve without outside help. However, once the group processes are in train, it is possible and most desirable for groups to take over their own actions and to renew themselves in subsequent problem-solving activities.

There is considerable emphasis on reflecting upon current activities in this model. To jolt participants into action, data on present actions of teachers and students are usually needed, and as a result of this feedback, particular plans and strategies are put forward by the group. These actions are evaluated in turn, and new cycles of OD are initiated.

Case study examples of school improvement at the primary school level (Johnston, 1985) and at the level of technical and further education (TAFE) (Henderson, 1985) indicate that OD can be a powerful tool for energizing a staff to become involved in school improvement practices. The various group meetings required are very time-consuming, and prolonged arguments can occur between participants, but they do enable staff to develop as a cohesive group and gain confidence in planning and executing their school improvement endeavours. The OD model emphasizes political and cultural perspectives, and very minimal attention is given to the technological perspective.

Action Research Model

Stenhouse (1975) was one of the first educators to promote the idea of the 'teacher as researcher'. Subsequently, educators in the United Kingdom such as Elliott and Adelman (1973) and May (1981), and in Australia Kemmis (1982), Kemmis and McTaggart (1981), Grundy and Kemmis (1981) and Tripp (1985) have been strong advocates of this approach to school improvement.

'Action research' involves groups of teachers systematically analyzing an issue or problem of concern to them and then planning action programs, executing them, evaluating their efforts and repeating the cycle if necessary. A key element of the approach is the participation by teachers in the self-reflection, discussion and argumentation.

Trends and Developments in School Improvement

As a result of major projects on school improvement occurring in a number of countries and cross-national projects such as the International School Improvement Project, there is considerable material available on trends and developments. The six aspects described below are those which have been frequently cited.

1 Researchers are now beginning to study school improvement settings in terms of a conflict paradigm rather than a rationalist paradigm. For example, Huberman and Miles (1986) argue that there is far more explanatory power in examining such aspects as careerism, interpersonal conflict, politics, power plays and opportunistic coalitions.

2 Collaboration and voluntarism among participants are perceived to be critical elements in school improvement, even though various conflicting situations may occur en route! Lieberman and Miller (1986) refer to the need for teachers to have early participation in the thinking and planning of school improvement efforts. High participating levels cannot be mandated by superordinates. Fullan *et al.* (1986) refer to the need for an open climate where participants can discuss, raise issues and be willing to look at things.

3   Time is being recognized as a crucial element in school improvement endeavours. It may take a considerable period of time for some persons to be willing to commit themselves to a project. Building collegiality among staff is something which has to be nurtured patiently. In primary schools in particular, teacher isolation is a major problem to overcome.

4   Administrative firmness and follow-through are most important aspects of school improvement endeavours. Although the literature has been largely sceptical of 'top-down' and authoritative edicts (for example, House, 1979; Berman and McLaughlin, 1977), more recent studies support the need for 'administrative decisiveness, bordering on coercion, but intelligently and supportively exercised' (Huberman and Miles, 1984, p. 66). They suggest that powerful managers can exert directional control and reduce uncertainties for participants, so long as they provide sufficient resources and assistance and maintain this for extensive periods.

5   School improvement endeavours when successful can destabilize rather than stabilize school communities. A number of studies refer to school settings which become hotbeds of change once the initial inertia is overcome. Participants may develop very different career aspirations. Complacency among staff is no longer tolerated when they have visions of better alternatives and structures. This educational turbulence may need to be kept within bounds, but it is evident that succesful school improvement ventures can develop a new momentum of its own.

6   Effective school leadership is dependent upon appropriate system level support. Principals need assistance and support in experimenting with new projects. They need access to resources and informaton to implement their projects. It is not realistic to allocate entire responsibility for school improvement on the building principal (Patterson *et al.*, 1986).

Concluding Comment

Improvement at the school level has its own special priorities and rhythms. The actions of various participants at the school level are important: teachers, administrators, students, parents. The managers of school improvement, whether they are school principals or school management teams, have a crucial role to play in providing the opportunities for collegial planning and the organizational structures, resources and time for intentions to be realized.

References

ADAMS, D. (1983) *Community Participation in Schooling*. Perth: Education Department, Western Australia.

ANGUS, L.B. (1988) 'School Leadership and Educational Reform,' Paper presented at the Annual Conference of the American Educational Research Association, New Orleans.

BERMAN, P. and MCLAUGHLIN, M.W. (1977) *Federal Programmes, Supporting Educational Change*. Santa Monica, Calif: Rand Corporation.

BOLAM, R. (1988) 'Role of the National Agency and the United Kingdom Context,' Paper presented at the Annual Conference of the American Educational Research Association, New Orleans.

CALDWELL, B.J. and SPINKS, J. (1986) *Policy-Making and Planning for School Effectiveness*. Hobart: Education Department, Tasmania.

CALDWELL, B.J. and SPINKS, J. (1988) *The Self-Managing School*. Lewes: Falmer Press.

CHAPMAN, J.D. (1984) *A Descriptive Profile of Australian School Principals*. Canberra: Commonwealth Schools Commission.

CHAPMAN, J.D. (1985) 'Professional Development: The Role and Needs of the School Principal,' in HUGHES, P., *Better Teachers for Better Schools*. Melbourne: Australian College of Education.

CORBETT, H.D. and ROSSMAN, G.B. (1988) 'How Teachers Empower Super Ordinance: Running Good Schools,' Paper presented at the Annual Conference of the American Educational Research Association, New Orleans.

CORWIN, R. (1981) 'Patterns of Organisational Control and Teaching Militancy: Theoretical Continuity in the Ideas of "Loose Coupling",' in KERCKHOFF, A. and CORWIN, R. (Eds), *Research in Sociology of Education and Socialisation*. Greenwich, Conn.: JAI Press.

DUIGNAN, P. (1984) *The Australian School Principal: A National Study of the Role and Professional Development Needs of Government and Non-Government School Principals*. Canberra: Commonwealth Schools Commission.

ELLIOTT, J. and ADELMAN, C. (1973) 'Reflecting Where the Action Is: The Design of the Ford Teaching Project,' *Education for Teaching*, 92.

FULLAN, M. (1985) 'Change Processes and Strategies at the Local Level,' *Elementary School Journal*, 85, 3.

FULLAN, M., MILES, M. and TAYLOR, G. (1980) 'Organisation Development in Schools: The State of the Art,' *Review of Educational Research*, 50, 1.

FULLAN, M., ANDERSON, S. and NEWTON, E. (1986) *Support Systems for Implementing Curriculum in School Boards*. Ontario: Ministry of Education.

GLATTER, R. et al. (1986) *Understanding School Management*. Milton Keynes: Open University Press.

GLATTHORN, A.A. (1987) *Curriculum Leadership*. Glenview, Ill.: Scott, Foresman and Company.

GREENE, M. (1986) 'How Do We Think about Our Craft?' in LIEBERMAN, A. (Ed.), *Re-thinking School Improvement*. New York: Teachers College Press.

GRUNDY, S. and KEMMIS, S. (1981) 'Educational Action Research in Australia: The State of the Art,' Paper presented at the Annual Conference of the Australian Association for Research in Education, Adelaide.

HARISUN, M. (1987) 'Professional Development through Participation in School-Focused Curriculum Development and Implementation,' in HUGHES, P., *Better Teachers for Better Schools*. Melbourne: Australian College of Education.

HENDERSON, J.C. (1985) Organisation Development and the Implementation of Planned Change, Unpublished PhD thesis, Murdoch University, Perth.

HOPES, C. (Ed.) (1986) *The School Leader and School Improvement: Case Studies from Ten OECD Countries*. Leuven: ACCO.

HORD, S.M. *et al.* (1984) 'How Principals Work with Other Change Facilitators,' *Education and Urban Society*, 17, 1.

HOUSE, E.R. (1979) 'Technology versus Craft: A Ten-year Perspective on Innovation,' *Journal of Curriculum Studies*, 11, 1.

HUBERMAN, A.M. and MILES, M. (1984) *Innovation Up Close: How School Improvement Works*. New York: Plenum Press.

HUBERMAN, A.M. and MILES, M. (1986) 'Re-thinking the Quest for School Improvement: Some Findings from the DESSI Study,' in LIEBERMAN, A. (Ed.), *Re-thinking School Improvement*. New York: Teachers College Press.

JOHNSTON, S.E. (1985) A School Consultant in Action, Unpublished Master of Educational Studies thesis, University of Queensland, Brisbane.

KEMMIS, S. (1982) 'Research Approaches and Methods: Action Research', in ANDERSON, D. and BLAKERS, C. (Eds), *Transition from School, an Exploration: Research and Policy*. Canberra: ANU Press.

KEMMIS, S. and McTAGGART, R. (1981) *The Action Research Planner*. Geelong: Deakin University.

LEITHWOOD, K.A. and MONTGOMERY, D.J. (1982) 'The Role of the Elementary School Principal in Programme Improvement,' *Review of Educational Research*, 52, 3.

LEITHWOOD, K.A. and MONTGOMERY, D.J. (1986) *Improving Principal Effectiveness: The Principal Profile*. Toronto: OISE Press.

LIEBERMAN, A. (1986) (Ed.) *Re-thinking School Improvement*. New York: Teachers College Press.

LIEBERMAN, A. and MILLER, L. (1981) 'Synthesis of Research on Improving Schools,' *Educational Leadership*, 38, 7.

LIEBERMAN, A. and MILLER, L. (1986) 'School Improvement: Themes and Variations,' in LIEBERMAN, A. (Ed.) *Re-thinking School Improvement*. New York: Teachers College Press.

LLOYD, K. (1985) 'Management and Leadership in the Primary School', in HUGHES, M. *et al.* (Eds), *Managing Education: The System and the Institution*. London: Holt Rinehart and Winston.

LOUCKS-HORSLEY, S. and HERGERT, L.F. (1985) *An Action Guide to School Improvement*. Alexandria, Va.: ASCD.

MARSH, C.J. (1988) *Spotlight on School Improvement*. Sydney: Allen and Unwin.

MAY, N. (1981) 'The Teacher-as-Researcher Movement in Britain,' Paper presented at the Annual Conference of the American Educational Research Association, Los Angeles.

MILES, M. and EKHOLM, M. (1985) 'What Is Good Improvement?' in VAN VELZEN, W.G. *et al.*, *Making School Improvement Work: A Conceptual Guide to Practice*. Leuven: ACCO.

MULFORD, W. (1979) *The Role and Training of INSET Trainers: Synthesis Report*. Paris: OECD.

OLSON, J.K. (1982) 'Three Approaches to Curriculum Change: Balancing the Accounts,' *Journal of Curriculum Theorizing*, 4, 2.

PASSOW, A.H. (1986) 'Beyond the Commissioned Reports: Toward Meaningful School Improvement,' in LIEBERMAN, A. (Ed.), *Re-thinking School Improvement*. New York: Teachers College Press.

PATTERSON, J.L. *et. al.* (1986) *Productive School Systems for a Non-rational World.* Alexandria, Va.: ASCD.

POPKEVITZ, T.S. (1982) 'Motion as Education Change: The Misuse and Irrelevancy of Two Research Paradigms,' Unpublished paper, University of Wisconsin.

REYNOLDS, J. and SKILBECK, M. (1976) *Culture in the Classroom*. London: Open Books.

RUTHERFORD, W.L. and HULING-AUSTIN, L. (1985) 'Changing the American High School: Descriptions and Prescriptions,' Paper presented at the Annual Conference of the American Educational Research Association, Chicago.

SCHMUCK, R.A. and MILES, M. (Eds) (1971) *Organisation Development in Schools,* La Jolla, Calif.: University Associates.

SCHÖN, D.A. (1983) *The Reflective Practitioner*. New York: Basic Books.

STEGO, N.E. *et al.* (Eds) (1987) *The Role of School Leaders in School Improvement.* Leuven: ACCO.

STENHOUSE, L. (1975) *An Introduction to Curriculum Research and Development.* London: Heinemann.

TABA, H. (1962) *Curriculum Development: Theory and Practice.* New York: Harcourt, Brace and World.

TANGERUD, H. and WALLIN, E. (1986) 'Values and Contextual Factors in School Improvement,' *Journal of Curriculum Studies*, 18, 1.

TRIPP, D.H. (1981) 'Action Research on the Child's Televisual Experience in School,' Working Paper No. 9 of the Active Eye Project. Perth: Murdoch University.

TYLER, R.W. (1949) *Basic Principles of Curriculum and Instruction.* Chicago, Ill.: University of Chicago Press.

VANDENBERGHE, R. and HALL, G.E. (Eds) (1987) *Research on Internal Change Facilitation in Schools.* Leuven: ACCO.

VAN VELZEN, W.G. *et al.* (1985) *Making School Improvement Work: A Conceptual Guide to Practice,* Leuven: ACCO.

Chapter 9

Schools: Places Where Teachers Learn

Lawrence Ingvarson

Places Where Teachers Learn

School A

A couple of years ago a teacher in an independent private secondary school happened to say to me over morning tea, 'I get a tremendous sense of professional development working here compared with the last school I was in.' When asked why that was, she said, 'I think it's mostly because of our head of department and the way we talk about our work here in our regular departmental meetings, as well as over lunch or during morning tea. She is always finding interesting articles which she asks us to look at to see if there is something worthwhile to pass on to the rest of the staff. We often go into each other's classes when we are trying out something new or when there's some problem with a particular student, and talk about that. We talk about where we are going, we plan things together, and we're on the look-out for courses that might be useful for what we are trying to do. Judy (the Head of Department) is always encouraging us to go to courses that look as if they tie in with what we are trying to do and we talk about those when we get back to see what might be worth trying out. It's challenging really. We learn a lot from each other and I don't feel like I'm in a rut any more. I feel supported and that I'm treated like a professional.'

This school has developed a five-page professional development policy which includes a rationale for professional development; principles which link professional development to the school's capacity to adapt to changing circumstances; mutual responsibilities of staff and the school; strategies for implementing the policy; and priorities established by the Professional Development Committee for the allocation of its budget of approximately $20,000 to courses, conferences, school-based activities and professsional reading.

School B

During the year a group of ten teachers at this outer suburban high school arranged their timetables so that they had a common free period for weekly meetings. They shared a concern that their students had a passive attitude to learning, that they were not teaching their students *how* to learn, nor how to take more responsibility for their own learning. At the weekly meetings they talked about their teaching, what they had tried and what effects it had had. They learned to be open about what did not work and how to turn this knowledge to their advantage. They came to call their joint exploration and evaluation of teaching strategies to solve this problem the Project for Enhancing Effective Learning.

Initially the teachers worked with ideas on 'meta-cognition' from outside consultants, but after the first term they assumed control over the direction of the research. By the end of the first term the usual experiences of uncertainty and 'deskilling', which accompany any serious attempts to bring about change, were in evidence, and the students were less than impressed with what some of them thought to be clumsy and unwelcome attempts to make them think. 'But when are we going to do some work?' said one. However, the regular interaction and emotional support of the group overcame any long-term threat to their commitment to the project. And their collaborative research produced a wealth of insights and shared understandings about how to promote greater critical engagement by students in what they were learning. It also turned out to be an enterprise of peer evaluation and accountability which led to profound changes in teaching behaviour and professional self-esteem.

By the end of the first year these teachers produced a book documenting their research findings and what they had learned about how to support their own professional development (Baird and Mitchell, 1986). Throughout this year the group experienced difficulty in gaining any funding support from system school improvement programs and professional development committess. One refused because parents were not involved; another because university researchers were involved and, 'therefore, they did not need further support.' The group continued for a second year, and another book. There is considerable interest in the project among teachers from other schools, and the original teachers are in constant demand to share their expertise.

These examples serve the purpose of indicating a direction for professional development policy-making in the future; conditions are needed which stimulate such policy-making at system, regional *and*, most importantly, school levels. Staff development in these cases is more than a matter of attending outside courses or occasional school-based in-service days, valuable as these can be. It has become an ordinary and ongoing condition in the workplace itself. It is an outcome of the kinds of staff talk, observation, mutual assistance and peer evaluation of teaching made possible when staff share expectations of collegiality and experimentation (Little, 1982). The staff in these schools have assumed a collective responsibility for the nature and direction of their professional development. It is rooted in their practice and the natural desire to enhance their competence. Most importantly, the nature and direction of this group enterprise are in their control and integrated with the needs of the school to implement its curriculum effectively. In turn, this change in staff relationships has expanded the way these teachers conceive of the job of teaching and has enhanced their professionalism. The turbulence and buffeting of schools by categorical 'programs' has been replaced by the 'steady work' of educational reform (Elmore and McLaughlin, 1988), based on a better understanding of how the overall conditions of work and school organization affect teachers' motivation and opportunities for professional development (Little, 1989).

The workplace conditions and attitudes in these schools represent a 'professional culture' (Lieberman, 1988) that is paradoxically a precondition for, and an outcome of, effective staff development policies; an environment different from the customs and habits into which teachers are usually socialized, which reinforce isolation and make conversation about teaching a staffroom social indiscretion. But establishing such a work culture represents a major innovation in itself for many schools.

Is it realistic for a school system to plan to support the building of such culture? Or are examples such as those above mainly fortuitous? Can such changes be achieved through gradual means, or are they dependent on prior radical shifts in social and economic contextual demands and constraints that shape the role of schooling? The purpose of this chapter is to argue that it is realistic, and that it can only be gradual. We have grossly underestimated the scale of the task, particularly, for example, in terms of identifying the necessary enabling balance between school level autonomy and system control (Stevenson, 1987), the required shift in the agendas of employer-union agreements (Kerchner and Mitchell, 1988), the specialist training required, especially for principals and teachers in leadership roles (Astuto and Clark, 1986), and the stable system of external support (Louis *et al.*, 1985) which must be in place before it can happen in the majority of schools and involve a majority of teachers.

We have some idea of what this innovation, if we can call it that, looks like in practice from examples such as those above, and research on educational change is starting to provide some useful guidelines about how such a change could be managed with good chances of success (e.g. Fullan, 1985; Miles, 1987). But before exploring the kind of planning that would be needed to support the implementation and institutionalization of practices such as those in the examples above, it is necessary to take a brief look at some recent history of school-focused in-service education.

A Brief History of School-focused In-service Education

The schools above are manifestations of an idea that has been around for many years: the idea that the most effective forms of in-service education occur as an integral and routine part of the work of the school, not just isolated courses. It has also long been common knowledge that working relationships between staff that encourage the sharing of experience and experimentation with teaching ideas are rated by teachers much more highly than official in-service activities as an avenue for their professional development (Ingvarson, 1982). The James Report (DES, 1972) captured the spirit of the idea well:

> In-service training should begin in the schools. It is here that learning and teaching take place, curricula and techniques are developed and needs and deficiencies revealed. Every school should regard the continued training of its teachers as an essential part of its task, for which all members of staff share responsibility. An active school is constantly reviewing and reassessing its effectiveness, and is ready to consider new methods, new forms of organisation and new ways of dealing with the problems that arise. It will set aside time to explore these questions, as far as it can within its own resources, by arranging for discussion, study, seminars with visting tutors and visits to other institutions. It will also give time and attention to the introduction of new members of staff, not only those in their first year of teaching but all those who are new to the school. Heads of schools, heads of departments and other senior teachers should be especially concerned to assess the needs both of their schools and of teachers on their staff and to encourage teachers to take the opportunities offered outside the school for in-service education and training.... (p. 12)

The James Report was an inspiration in the world of in-service education during the 1970s. Like the curriculum reform movement in the UK during this period, it reflected a high point in a 'professional' view of teaching and in the level of influence of teachers' organizations over the nature and direction of educational change. The image which the James Report sought to convey, in these pre-oil crisis, pre-Thatcher days, was one of a relatively autonomous community of responsible professionals, naturally oriented toward personal development, open to innovation and evaluation, capable of identifying needs, and able to plan wisely a program for staff development focused on school-wide needs as well as the needs of individual teachers. Teachers' centres were another manifestation of this professional self-confidence, as was the idea of school-based curriculum development (Skilbeck, 1974). It became part of the conventional wisdom in this post-1968 period that anything 'top-down' was autocratic and ineffective, and that the research, development and dissemination model, when applied to education, was fundamentally flawed.

The concept of school-focused in-service education emerged from the James Report, and became something of a movement across several countries (Bolam, 1980). It was paralleled by a number of seductive images of the school as a development-oriented, intelligent organism, such as the 'creative school' (Nisbet, 1973), the 'problem-solving school' (Bolam, 1982) and the 'autonomous school' (Van Velzen, 1979). School-focused in-service education became a major component in a collaborative project involving nine countries and sponsored by the Organization for Economic Cooperation and Development (OECD) during the late 1970s. The OECD project defined school-focused in-service education as follows: 'school-focused training is all the strategies employed by trainers and teachers in partnership to direct training programs in such a way as to meet the identified needs of the school and to raise the standard of teaching and learning in the classroom.' Howey (1980) prepared a synthesis of four national case studies of school-focused education (Australia, Canada, New Zealand, UK) for this OECD project. Toward the end of this project it became clear that the idea of school-focused in-service education was in need of a major overhaul. The case studies read more like gallant, but amateurish and isolated, attempts to tackle a task that required much more system level planning and coordination of resources than had been anticipated. Relying on local development and the idea of the autonomous school, so far as professional development was concerned, was beginning to look more like neglect than planning, especially in the face of increasing pressures on schools for curriculum reform and adaptation to economic circumstances. There were major policy and resource questions that had to be, and could only be, addressed at the system level before schools could be expected to implement change and incorporate additional roles and expectations for staff.

A Shift in Strategy: The School Improvement Perspective

In 1982 the OECD initiated another collaborative project called the International School Improvement Project (ISIP). The main areas of study within this project such as school-based review, principals and internal change agents, external support systems, and the development and implementation of school improvement policies by employing authorities indicated that a significant shift from a relatively laissez-faire local development to a system level management of change perspective had taken place. In-service education was now seen as one component, albeit a crucial component, within a broader set of conditions and arrangements which needed to be in place if teachers were to have a realistic chance of improving schools. For each of the areas of study, case studies and syntheses of research have been published by the OECD. They are a valuable resource for anyone with responsibilities for planning for school improvement at the system or the school level.

This shift to a managed change perspective has been influenced in part by US research on change, particularly that concerned with factors influencing the implementation of specific educational innovations. Three influential examples of this research are:

1   the concerns-based adoption model (Hall and Hord, 1987);
2   the Rand study of federal programs supporting educational change (Berman and McLaughlin, 1978);
3   the study of dissemination efforts supporting school improvement (Crandall *et al.*, 1982).

The need for such a shift has also been reinforced by recent research on in-service education (e.g. Joyce and Showers, 1980, 1988; Little, 1986; Guskey, 1986), which shows that new teaching strategies may take as long as two or three years to be assimilated into routine practice, and that effective in-service training needs to be a careful blending of theory, demonstration and practice with long-term follow-up 'coaching' and feedback in the regular classroom.

Fullan (1985) analyzes the implications of this research for the planning of change at the local level. One finding is that for certain kinds of teaching innovations, commitment to the change emerges after changes in behaviour are attempted; that is, after new ideas and skills are tried and evaluated in terms of their effects on students. It may be wiser, therefore, for staff developers to invest heavily in classroom experimentation with the few, rather than protracted mass conversion exercises on whole-school in-service days. We have learned that significant change in teaching is a long-term and difficult process of personal learning which requires peer support and technical assistance in the classroom if new ideas are to have a chance of being implemented. This calls for a strong capacity for long-term staff development planning within the school which matches the difficulty of the task.

Another key finding in this area of research indicates that external support personnel have a significant impact on the receptivity to new ideas and the use of information (Louis, 1981; Emrick and Peterson, 1978). Huberman and Miles (1984) go so far as to claim that: 'Large-scale, change-bearing innovations lived or died by the amount and quality of assistance that their users received once the change process was under-way' (p. 273). This research has led several countries to give priority to the development of an external support system. Louis *et al.* (1985) provide a detailed review of the forms of external support systems which OECD countries are developing and a framework for making decisions about their design and management.

The Provision of Support for Schools

External support refers to the process of aiding school improvement through means such as consultation, training, provision of information or materials and resources such as funding and replacement staff. 'System' implies that there are mechanisms for coordinating the efforts of the various agencies which might provide these forms of support, both with each other and with the needs of schools. The major elements of external support include policy units, curriculum and research branches, consultants or advisers, school support centres, colleges and universities, and special purpose programs. The purposes of external support systems vary from country to country in the degree to which they are instruments primarily for the implementation of government policy, or for generating improved operation based on locally identified needs.

In essence, an external support system is the means used by a school authority for generating educational ideas, for keeping them circulating and available to teachers, and for providing teachers with adequate opportunities to learn how to use them. Underpinning any support system will be assumptions about where new knowledge about teaching practices, programs and models comes from and how teachers are expected to make sense of and learn how to use these new skills. There is a range of strongly held views about the appropriate answers to these questions which are discussed, for example, in Ingvarson (1987) and Day (1985). Models of in-service education fall into two major categories: action research models (Elliott, 1985); and training (Joyce and Showers,

1980) or 'innovation-focused' models (Fullan, 1985). These represent very different answers to questions about where pedagogical knowledge comes from and how teachers learn how to use it. But there is agreement that there are no short cuts to professional development.

The Dutch School Support System

The Dutch school support system for schools was formalized in 1986 by an act of parliament. It is largely independent from the system for administering schools, a feature which arises from the fact that the majority of its schools (70 per cent) are privately run, although all schools are 100 per cent government funded. Schools are largely 'self-governing' and receive recurrent grants which include a specific element for school improvement and in-service education. The main components of the school support system are national institutes for curriculum development, educational research and educational measurement, the universities, and sixty-five local education centres each with a staff of about fifty consultants. The local centres are partly instruments for supporting, through training and consultation, the implementation of national policy. But they are also agencies for bringing together local needs and ideas for the development of curricula and national policy.

After eight years of negotiation and preparation, legislation for the 'Support Structure' was passed in 1986. It is

an acknowledgement of the fact that Dutch schools require external support which is not of a merely occasional or temporary nature. Consequently the government states in the Bill that educational support, like education itself, is so essential that it has to be considered as a basic provision, and as such available to everyone, regulated and financed on a central level in order to ensure its quality. (Köllen, 1988)

The educational support system is an attempt to coordinate the external resources which schools can call upon; both to maintain and improve the quality of education, and to assist with the implementation of national policies and innovations. A fixed proportion (about 2 per cent) of the annual education budget is allocated to the Dutch support system. While much in-service education for teachers is still provided through part-time, external courses in teacher training colleges, an increasing proportion is in the form of long-term staff development programs tied, through the local centres, to school-identified needs and 'national innovation projects'.

The local centres must establish long-term 'contracts' with schools concerning the focus for the improvement effort and the plan for within-school support during the implementation phase. They are dependent for about half their funding on establishing these contracts or 'agreements' with schools (which must be at the request of schools). Three things are impressive about these arrangements: the quality of planning for implementation; the degree of control which the schools exercise over this planning; and the long-term nature of the work which centre consultants do with schools, which is consistent with research on effective forms of in-service education.

The Dutch have returned, in part, to using a 'dissemination of innovation' approach after some disillusionment with other change strategies such as 'local development' and the 'problem-solving school'. In a sense they are looking for a more effective marriage between the two. They believe that good ideas do not make their own way into routine use in classrooms without 'job embedded' training and support.

The Netherlands case indicates that it is no longer appropriate to examine the in-service education area in isolation from system level planning for managing change and the coordination of the resources necessary if governments are serious about the implementation of new educational policies. This integration of in-service education with system level planning may mean some reduction in the control that teachers have over their own professional development, but there is the trade-off, or security, that when the Dutch government introduces new policies and programs, it has guaranteed that the resources will be around for long enough for teachers to have a chance to learn how to put them into practice.

The Australian Experience

There are signs that Australia is starting to move in a similar direction to that outlined in the Dutch case. The recent report of the policy development project on Teacher In-service Education of the Commonwealth Schools Commission, called *Teachers Learning* (Department of Employment, Education and Training, 1988), recommends that state systems work toward the development of a coordinated external support system for schools, which includes:

> establishing a school support infrastructure of consultants and resource centres;
>
> greater coordination with higher education institutions;

requirements for schools to develop school improvement plans as a basis for the schools' allocation for training and development activities;

allocating 60 per cent of training and development funds to support school-focused programs linked with school development plans;

union-employer agreements to enhance career paths for teachers and establish a training and development culture by various promotion and incentive schemes in which prominence is given to evidence of recent and sustained professional development; and

following more carefully principles of good practice concerning in-service education activities and systematically evaluating them.

The report also recommends a national target for expenditure on in-service training and development of 1 per cent of the total expenditure on schools. These recommendations represent a recognition of the kinds of structural and budget conditions which need to be in place if schools are to have the discretionary resources, the external support and the incentives required to plan and carry out effective staff development programs. They cannot, of course, guarantee that the kind of staff development illustrated in the two vignettes will happen. But it is unrealistic to expect a permanent shift in working conditions, one which affects the professional development of most teachers, not just volunteers, to take place without them.

What matters is system policies which stimulate, rather than replace, the need for teachers and parents to discuss, set priorities and plan their own long-term policies as a routine part of the school's responsibility for curriculum evaluation and improvement (Coulter and Ingvarson, 1985). This position is supported by a recent synthesis of research on the contribution of staff development to the creation of characteristics associated with secondary school effectiveness, where Stevenson (1987b) reports that

the most important impact of collaboratively planned staff development is enhancing collegial relations among teachers, and administrators, in their daily work: a key characteristic of effective schools. The strongest enhancement, irrespective of the specific purpose of staff development, occurs when the governance of staff development involves a participative structure which provides teachers and administrators at the school building level with a sense of ownership of the program. (p. 246)

The same study confirmed the effective role which external technical support plays in staff development, particularly in a context where 'the locus of control of problem-solving and decision-making resides within the school staff' (p. 246).

Teachers Learning also recognizes that the agenda for teacher union-employer agreements must broaden considerably into more general areas of educational policy and resource allocation if a serious effort is made to improve working conditions for professional development. A similar recognition has led some US educationalists to advocate a shift from an industrial to a professional model of unionism, and the development of education policy trust agreements negotiated between unions and managers which move well beyond the usual agenda of work rules and terms of employment (Kerchner and Mitchell, 1988). The shift in the locus of control and the responsibility for staff development toward the school community, for example, implies that teachers themselves take greater responsibility for the evaluation of teaching, developing more professional models of peer appraisal and accountability (Darling-Hammond, 1986; Ingvarson, 1989). It will no longer suffice to regard teacher evaluation as management's problem. As the work of some researchers on planned change indicates (e.g. Huberman and Miles, 1984), support needs to be combined with pressure.

Recent Developments in the USA

A conception similar to school-focused in-service education has been given impetus recently in the USA by a coalition of researchers, unionists and others (e.g. Lieberman, 1988; Goodlad, 1987). They want to provide an alternative image for the direction school reform should take to the knee-jerk, 'first wave' policy reactions which ensued in the wake of the doom-oriented report, *A Nation at Risk* (1983). This image is well captured in the title of Lieberman's recent book, *Building a Professional Culture in Schools*.

The first wave reformers commonly pressed for 'standardization' (Darling-Hammond and Wise, 1985), 'aimed at stemming the "crisis" of American education by setting uniform minimum standards for school practices' (McNeil, 1987, p. 93). Teachers were seen to be part of the problem, not the solution; objects of reform rather than the active shapers (Bascia and Sisken, 1988). A whole raft of regulations and policies for reform focused directly on teachers and their recruitment, training and evaluation, whereas in the 1970s they would have focused on new curriculum materials or innovatory programs (Darling-Hammond and Berry, 1988). The reforms were predicated on the pessimistic assumption that the 'problems' of American education were 'problem' teachers. But, as McNeil (1987) points out,

> the irony of the reforms built upon these negative assumptions, is, however, that *they help to bring about* mechanistic, disengaged, depressed teaching, or at best boring teaching. They are also helping bring about the exit of some of our best teachers, who see their professional, creative teaching threatened, even negatively rewarded, by standardised reforms which disregard teacher initiative. (p. 93)

The alternative 'second wave' reformers put their faith in a cluster of policy initiatives which aimed to 'professionalize' teaching, as they perceived that the sorry state of public education was a legacy of years of undervaluing, underrewarding and underestimating teachers. Foci of their research and discussions include the way in which different workplace conditions facilitate or inhibit learning *for teachers* and opportunities for teachers to exercise professional leadership through the development of what Little (1982) calls 'norms of collegiality and experimentation'.

In summarizing her research on the relationship between workplace conditions and school improvement, Little notes,

> School improvement is most surely and thoroughly achieved when:
>
> Teachers engage in frequent, continuous and increasingly concrete and precise *talk* about teaching practice (as distinct from teacher characteristics and failings, the social lives of teachers, the foibles and failures of students and their families, and the unfortunate demands of society on the school). By such talk, teachers build up a shared language adequate to the complexity of teaching, capable of distinguishing one practice and its virtue from another....
>
> Teachers and administrators frequently *observe* each other teaching, and provide each other with useful (if potentially frightening) evaluations of their teaching. Only such observation and feedback can provide shared *referents* for the shared language of teaching, and both demand and provide the precision and concreteness which makes the talk about teaching useful.
>
> Teachers and administrators *plan, design, research, evaluate and prepare teaching materials together.* The most prescient observations remain academic without the machinery to act upon them. By joint work on materials, teachers and administrators share the

considerable burden of development required by long-term improvement, confirm their emerging understanding of their approach, and make rising standards for their work attainable by them and their students.

Teachers and administrators *teach each other* the practice of teaching. (pp. 12-13, her emphases)

Lieberman's (1988) book is an examination of the conditions which need to be present to enable the school culture to move in this direction. The contributors share the view that 'professionalizing teaching and building a more collaborative culture in schools can profoundly change the way both staff and students in the school grow and learn' (p. vii).

But the establishment of values and norms which make professional development opportunities a routine part of the job will be a major innovation in itself in many schools. As Beverley Showers (1985) points out, with reference to teachers 'coaching' other teachers, an important component of effective in-service training: 'the social changes required by coaching in the workplace represent a major departure from the traditional school organization. The building of collegial teams that study teaching on a continuous basis forces the restructuring of administrators and supervisory staff' (p. 48).

How realistic or feasible is this conception of workplace conditions and staff relationships as a goal to work towards? Anyone familiar with the experience of attempting to bring about change, or the research on the fate of educational innovations, would have to be pessimistic. House talks of schools as 'frozen institutions' (1974). Simons' (1987) research work on self-evaluation in English schools, using principles of 'democratic evaluation', has led her to use the analogy of a club with tacit rules such as 'mind your own business', 'stick to your own patch' and 'don't get ideas above your own station'.

These values of *privacy, territory and hierarchy* underpin the organizational structure of schools and act as constraints upon the apparently informal nature of most staff relationships. An evaluation exercise threatens to break such rules and one that is initiated by members themselves may be seen as a serious breach of long-established and widely accepted conventions.

She argues that collaborative self-evaluation practice, linked into the organization of the school, is dependent on 'the possibility of dismantling the value structure of privacy, territory, and hierarchy, and substituting the values of openness, shared critical responsibility, and rational autonomy.' This will require, she thinks, an extended period in which schools are surrounded, so to speak, by high walls which protect staff members who are taking risks in learning how to carry out collective self-evaluations from the additional risk of observation by outsiders.

In an extensive review of research literature on the possibilities and limits of collegiality among teachers, Little (1987) identifies forms of support which are necessary for collegial relations to be enhanced in schools.

> For teachers to work often and fruitfully as colleagues requires action on all fronts. The *value* that is placed on shared work must be both said and shown. The *opportunity* for shared work and shared study must be prominent in the schedule for the day, the week, and the year. The *purpose* for work together must be compelling and the task sufficiently challenging. The *material resources and human assistance* must be adequate. And the *accomplishments* of individuals and groups recognised and celebrated. (p. 513)

This represents a formidable agenda for those with responsibilities for the preparation of school administrators who are key figures in providing such recognition and support. It implies a need for decision-making structures which embody the principle that staff development policy and practice is a shared responsibility. It also implies a need for positions of responsibility within schools for suitably trained teachers, with time release, to orchestrate staff development planning and activity. Whether this is best done within existing structures, by expanding the role definition of subject department heads or chairpersons, for example, or by the creation of new roles such as 'staff development officers' is not clear. But there is now much useful material for people who may have responsibilities for establishing a professional development program in their schools, and the emphasis is decidedly on thinking *programmatically*; that is, developing a formal structure within the school dedicated to long-term planning and ongoing professional development to complement system-provided external support structures (for example, Loucks-Horsley and Hergert, 1985; Loucks-Horsley *et al.*, 1987; Miles, 1987; Joyce and Showers, 1988).

Planning for Staff Development

Staff development planning at the school level will make it more, rather than less, likely that schools will make demands upon a system of external support and policy guidelines. The research and experience outlined above makes it clear that schools should not be left to their own devices in this difficult enterprise. A concerted effort is needed at all levels of educational policy-making.

One approach to the problem of supporting the kind of occupational culture for staff development described above is to treat it as if it were an innovation, and to apply what is known about effective planning for its implementation. A range of strategies, such as the following from Fullan, Miles and Anderson (1987), would be required.

1. *competence development* (enlarging and developing skills of teachers and administrators in managing staff development through training);
2. *consultant development* (identifying teachers who can act as regional or district facilitators, enhancing their skills and building a support structure for them in their work with schools);
3. *stimulation/facilitation of naturalistic efforts* (supporting grass roots staff development initiatives at the school level, including experiments, pilots, demonstrations);
4. *diffusing and supporting effective practice* (disseminating well developed staff development practices and supporting users in implementation of them);
5. *networking* (linking staff developers within and across schools and regions for mutual enhancement);
6. *organizational capacity building* (strengthening the ability of regions and schools to manage the multiple innovations involved in the change process; developing a good infrastructure of supporting agencies).

In addition, a form of reasoning called 'backward mapping' might be useful (Elmore, 1979); working backwards from descriptions of the desired practice, such as those provided at the beginning of the chapter, to the policies and planning which would be required at school, regional, union and system levels, if the practice were to have a chance of being implemented. Backward mapping is a fancy name for the common-sense (but not common) practice of clarifying what a change or innovation is supposed to look like in practice, before rushing into policy edicts: a matter of ensuring that there are answers to questions such as: 'What would it look like in practice?'; 'What would be going on?', 'Who would be doing what?'; 'What kind of training would they need?'; 'What resources would be required?'; 'How will their provision be coordinated?'; 'Who is going to orchestrate the change process?'; and 'How is the change going to be embedded into the hard part of system and school level budgets?'

Backward mapping, in other words, is an approach to implementation planning. It involves reasoning through implementation problems *before* policy decisions are firmly made. It implies that 'we do not clearly understand what a policy should be until we have thought about how it will be implemented' (Elmore, 1983). It rests on the assumption that implementation occurs at the bottom, not at the top; that in education the kind of control which policy-makers are wise to promote is delegated control rather than hierarchical control because implementation is fundamentally dependent on individuals exercising responsibility, initiative and control over their own actions.

Elmore provides a set of steps in backward mapping that can be translated and applied to the case of staff development. Each step can only be treated here in an illustrative rather than an exhaustive manner.

1 *Define and clarify the nature of the problem:* for example, inadequate motivation and opportunities for professional development in many schools in relation to the kinds of changes teachers are expected to bring about.

2 *Where do we attack the problem?* In the school.

3 *What has to happen in the school and the classroom to bring about an effective staff development program?* There has to be time, leadership, expertise, discretionary resources and incentives. For example, many principals would need skills in the management of change. Teachers would need training for leadership roles such as professional development or curriculum coordination; skill in orchestrating change efforts; specific training for change facilitator role and how to ensure in-service education is effective; and how to organize contracts for effective use of external support systems.

4 *What needs to happen at the regional level to increase the likelihood that these things will happen in the school?* Learning to play a responsive and facilitating role, developing clear guidelines for 'school development agreements', enhancing the skills of consultants, networking.

5 *What can employing authorities do to increase the likelihood that these things will happen in the regional offices?* Better integration of in-service education with system policy-making and planning for the implementation of change; strengthening of links between professional development and the evaluation of teaching; act on the assumption that teachers are the most important educational resource they possess, and that there is a need for greater teacher participation at all levels in policy-making and decisions about their own professional development; negotiate clear expectations

about mutual responsibilities and conditions for professional development in employer-union agreements.

6 *What can the government do to increase the likelihood that the state education department and regional offices will successfully address the staff development problem?* Recognize that there is a clear link between the quality of education and the quality of opportunities for professional development for teachers by setting aside a stable proportion of recurrent funding (2–3 per cent?) for this purpose.

Conclusion

If professional development is to be adequate to meet the demands placed on schools for change, system level policies and planning for change must pay equal attention to strategies which stimulate and support the development of an environment of collegiality and a formal program for professional development within schools (the internal system), and to the planning of a well-designed 'external support system' to support the dissemination and implementation of government policy. Without a strong internal support structure in schools for professional development, external efforts to bring about change will largely fail. This is a pressing need in school systems where responsibility for educational policy-making has been devolved in large part to schools. To be effective, the purposes of staff development policies must be conceived as much in terms of influencing relationships between staff (such as the level of collegiality) and mutual professional responsibilities (such as the evaluation of teaching) as in terms of individual teacher development.

References

ASTUTO, T.A. and CLARK, D.L. (1986) 'Achieving Effective Schools,' in HOYLE, E. and McMAHON, A. (Eds), *World Yearbook of Education 1986: The Management of Schools.* London: Kogan Page.

AUCHMUTY, J.J. (Chairman) (1980) *Report of the National Inquiry into Teacher Education.* Canberra: Australian Government Publishing Service.

BASCIA, N. and SISKEN, L.S. (1988) 'A Teacher's Eye View of Educational Reform,' Prepared for Teacher Context Center, Stanford University, Palo Alto, California.

BERMAN, P. and McLAUGHLIN, M. (1978) *Federal Programs Supporting Educational Change*, 1–8. Santa Monica, Calif.: Rand Corporation.

BOLAM, R. (1980) *Innovations in the In-service Education and Training of Teachers: Final Synthesis Report on an OECD/CERI Project.* Paris: Centre for Educational Research and Innovation/Organization for Economic Cooperation and Development.

BOLAM, R. (1982) *Strategies for School Improvement*. Paris: OECD.

BAIRD, J.R. and MITCHELL, I.J. (Eds) (1986) *Improving the Quality of Teaching and Learning: An Australian Case Study — the PEEL Project*. Melbourne: Monash University Printery.

COULTER, F. and INGVARSON, L.C. (1985) *Professional Development and the Improvement of Schooling*. Canberra: Commonwealth Schools Commission.

CRANDALL, D.P., *et al*. (1982) *People, Policies and Practices: Examining the Chain of School Improvement*. 10 Vols. Andover, Mass.: The Network.

DARLING-HAMMOND, L. (1986) 'A Proposal for Evaluation in the Teaching Profession,' *The Elementary School Journal*, 86, 4, 531–51.

DARLING-HAMMOND, L. and BERRY, B. (1988) *The Evolution of Teacher Policy*. Santa Monica, Calif.: Rand Corporation.

DARLING-HAMMOND, L. and WISE, A. (1985) 'Beyond Standardization: State Standards and School Improvement,' *Elementary School Journal*, 85, 315–35.

DAY, C. (1985) 'Professional Learning and Researcher Intervention: An Action Research Perspective,' *British Educational Research Journal*, 11, 133–52.

DEPARTMENT OF EDUCATION AND SCIENCE (1972) *Teacher Education and Training*. London: Her Majesty's Stationery Office.

DEPARTMENT OF EMPLOYMENT, EDUCATION AND TRAINING (1988) *Teachers Learning: Improving Australian Schools through In-service Teacher Training and Development*. Canberra: Australian Government Publishing Service.

ELLIOTT, J. (1985) 'Educational Action-Research,' in NISBETT, J., MEGARRY, J. and NISBETT, S. (Eds), *World Yearbook of Education 1985: Research, Policy and Practice*. London: Kogan Page.

ELMORE, R.F. (1979) 'Backward Mapping: Implementation Research and Policy Designs,' *Political Science Quarterly*, 94, 4, 601–61.

ELMORE, R.F. (1983) 'Complexity and Control: What Legislators and Administrators Can Do about Implementing Public Policy,' SHULMAN, L.S. and SYKES, G. (Eds), *Handbook of Teaching and Policy*. New York: Longman.

ELMORE, R.F. and McLAUGHLIN, M.W. (1988) *Steady Work: Policy, Practice and the Reform of American Education*. Santa Monica, Calif.: Rand Corporation.

EMRICK, J. and PETERSON, S. (1978) *A Synthesis of Findings across Five Recent Studies in Educational Dissemination and Change*. San Francisco, Calif.: Far West Laboratory.

FULLAN, M. (1982) *The Meaning of Educational Change*. New York: Teachers College Press.

FULLAN, M. (1985) 'Change Processes and Strategies at the Local Level,' *The Elementary School Journal*, 85, 391–421.

FULLAN, M. (1986) 'The Management of Change,' in HOYLE, E. and McMAHON, A. (Eds), *World Yearbook of Education 1986: The Management of Schools*. London: Kogan Page.

FULLAN, M. (1988) 'Change Processes in Secondary Schools: Toward a More Fundamental Agenda,' Prepared for the Teacher Context Centre, Stanford University, Palo Alto, California.

FULLAN, M., MILES, M. and ANDERSON, S. (1987) *A Conceptual Plan for Implementing the New Information Technologies in Ontario Schools*. Report to the Assistant Deputy Minister for Educational Technology, Ontario.

Goodlad, J. (Ed.) (1987) *The Ecology of School Renewal: NSSE Yearbook.* Chicago, Ill.: University of Chicago Press.

GUSKEY, T.R. (1986) 'Staff Development and the Process of Teacher Change,' *Educational Researcher*, 15, 5, 5–12.

HALL, G.E. and HORD, S.M. (1987) *Change in Schools: Facilitating the Process.* New York: State University of New York.

HENRY, N.B. (Ed.) (1957) *In-service Education.* Fifty-sixth Yearbook of the National Society for the Study of Education. Chicago, Ill.: University of Chicago Press.

HOUSE, E. (1974) *The Politics of Educational Innovation.* Berkeley, Calif.: McCutchan.

HOWEY, K.H. (1980) *School-focussed In-service Education. Clarification of a New Concept and Strategy. Synthesis Report.* Paris: Centre for Educational Research and Innovation/Organization for Economic Cooperation and Development.

HUBERMAN, A.M, and MILES, M.B. (1984) *Innovation Up Close: How School Improvement Works.* New York: Plenum Books.

INGVARSON, L.C. (1982) *School-focused In-service Education for Teachers: Some Australian Experiences.* Paris: Centre for Educational Research and Innovation/Organization for Economic Cooperation and Development; Canberra: Curriculum Development Centre.

INGVARSON, L.C. (1987) 'Models of In-service Education and Their Implications for Professional Development Policy,' *Independent Education*, 17, 2, 23–32.

INGVARSON, L.C. (1989) 'Linking Teacher Appraisal with Professional Development: A Challenge for the Profession,' in MCKENZIE, P. and LOKAN, J. (Eds), *Teacher Appraisal.* Melbourne: Australian Council for Educational Research.

JOYCE, B. and SHOWERS, B. (1980) 'Improving In-Service Training: The Messages of Research,' *Educational Leadership*, 37, 379–85.

JOYCE, B. and SHOWERS, B. (1988) *Student Achievement through Staff Development.* New York: Longman.

KERCHNER, C.T. and MITCHELL, D.E. (1988) *The Changing Idea of a Teachers' Union.* Lewes: Falmer Press.

KÖLLEN, E. (1988) 'The Dutch Eductional Support Policy,' in VAN DEN BERG, R., HAMEYER, U. and STOKKING. K., *Dissemination Re-considered: The Demands of Implementation.* Leuven: ACCO.

LIEBERMAN, A. (Ed.) (1988) *Building a Professional Culture in Schools.* New York: Teachers College Press.

LITTLE, J.W. (1982) 'School Success and Staff Development,' *American Educational Research Journal*, 19, 3, 325–40.

LITTLE, J.W. (1986) 'Seductive Images and Organizational Realities in Professional Development,' in LIEBERMAN, ANN (Ed.), *Rethinking School Improvement: Research, Craft and Concept.* New York: Teachers College Press.

LITTLE, J.W. (1987) 'Teachers as Colleagues,' in KOEHLER, V. (Ed.), *The Educator's Handbook*, pp. 491–518. New York: Longman.

LITTLE, J.W. (1989) 'Conditions of Professional Development in Secondary Schools,' Prepared for the Teacher Context Center, Stanford University, Palo Alto, California.

LOUCKS-HORSELY, S. and HERGERT, L.F. (1985) *An Action Guide to School Improve-*

ment. Andover, Mass.: Association for Supervision and Curriculum Development, The Network.

LOUCKS-HORSLEY, S., HARDING, C., ARBUCKLE, M., MURRAY, L., DUBEA, C. and WILLIAMS, M. (1987) *Continuing to Learn: A Guidebook for Teacher Development*. Andover, Mass.: Regional Laboratory for Educational Improvement of the Northeast and Islands.

LOUIS, K.S. (1981) 'External Agents and Knowledge Utilisation: Dimensions for Analysis and Action,' in LEHMING, R. and KANE, M. *Improving Schools: Using What We Know*. Beverley Hills, Calif.: Sage.

LOUIS, K.S., VAN VELZEN, W., LOUCKS-HORSLEY, S. and CRANDALL, D. (1985), 'External Support Systems for School Improvement,' in VAN VELZEN, W. *et al. Making School Improvement Work: A Conceptual Guidebook*. Leuven: ACCO.

MCNEIL, L. (1987) 'Exit, Voice and Community: Magnet Teachers' Response to Standardization,' *Educational Policy*, 1, 93–113.

MILES, M. (1987) 'Practical Guidelines for School Administrators: How to Get There,' Paper presented at the annual meeting of the American Educational Research Association.

NISBET, J. (Ed.) (1973) *Creativity of the School*. Paris: OECD.

SHOWERS, B. (1985) 'Teachers Coaching Teachers,' *Educational Leadership*, 42, 7, 43–9.

SIMONS, H. (1987) *Getting to Know Schools in a Democracy: The Politics and Process of Evaluation*. Lewes: Falmer Press.

SKILBECK, M. (1974) *School Based Curriculum Development and Teacher Education Policy*. Paris: OECD.

STEVENSON, R.B. (1987a). 'Autonomy and Support: The Dual Needs of Urban High Schools,' *Urban Education*, 22, 2, 366–86.

STEVENSON, R.B. (1987b) 'Staff Development for Effective Secondary Schools: A Synthesis of Research,' *Teaching and Teacher Education*, 3, 3, 233–48.

VAN VELZEN, W.G. (1979) *Autonomy of the School*. S'Hertogenbosch: KPC (Catholic Pedagogic Centre).

VAN VELZEN, W.G., MILES, M., EKHOLM, M., HAMEYER, U. and ROBIN, D. (1985) *Making School Improvement Work: A Conceptual Guide to Practice*. Leuven: ACCO.

Chapter 10

Information Needs for Decision-making at the School Level

Phillip N. McKenzie

The prospect of a broader range of decision-making responsibilities being exercised at local school level raises questions of the ways in which schools go about the decision-making task and the information base that they draw upon. The nature of that information base is the focus of the present chapter. Its premise is that if schools are to be allocated expanded responsibilities, it is critical that they have access to the information necessary to carry out those tasks in an effective manner. The discussion attempts to identify the likely dimensions of those needs and the ways in which the existing information sources available to schools may have to be extended. In so doing, criteria to guide the development of school level information systems are suggested.

A potential increase in school autonomy also raises questions of the consequent information needs of school system administrators and parents. At the very minimum central administrations will require information that allows the impact of the decentralization policies themselves to be monitored and evaluated. Further, since there is unlikely to be any fundamental shift away from government financial responsibility for public schools, it is inevitable that system administrations will need information that assists state-wide goals and broad accountability requirements to be met. The work on education indicators that is currently underway in many school systems reflects these concerns. Consideration of education indicators is also relevant to the information needs (and rights) of parents faced with a more decentralized school system. Any genuine increase in school autonomy will increase school diversity and, if the current controversy in England is any guide (see Fairhill, 1988), the debate on the sorts of information that parents need to choose among government schools has the potential to be extremely divisive.

A detailed discussion of the information needs of system administrators and parents and the extent to which they overlap with those of schools is beyond the scope of this chapter. However, two general points can be made. First, it may be difficult for any one information system simultaneously to meet the needs both of schools and of central administrators. For example, it may be counter-productive for school systems to use for purposes such as teacher assessment the sorts of information generated by schools to assist local efforts in program evaluation and improvement (Sawin, 1986). As noted by Simkins (1983, p. 57), 'when information systems are seen to be politically threatening, few [providers of information] find it difficult to devise means of resistance.' Second, as is argued below, local decision-making is likely to be assisted when schools are able to view their own operations from the broader perspective offered by comparable data from other schools. This suggests that the school system has an important role to play as a provider of contextual information to assist with school-based decision-making.

A first step in discussion of the prospective information needs of schools is to identify those areas in which greater school decision-making responsibilities are likely. Illustrative material for this discussion is drawn from the administrative reforms either being implemented or under consideration in several Australian government school systems at present.

The Dimensions of School-based Decision-making

Broadly speaking, there are two major dimensions along which government schools may be allocated decision-making responsibilities: curriculum determination and resource management. Figure 10.1 shows these dimensions in simplified form. The rows express an increasing degree of school autonomy in determining the aims of school programs and in developing curricula to achieve those aims; the categories concerned are taken from Deschamp and McGaw (1979). The columns attempt to identify the major stages as schools are allocated greater responsibility for the specification and management of educational resources. (The term 'block grant' refers to the allocation from the centre of a sum of money or other form of resource entitlement that the school is basically able to use as it sees fit.) Note that the figure refers only to government schools; to express the resource autonomy of private schools it would be necessary to add a fourth column concerned with school responsibility for revenue generation.

Australian government school systems exhibit considerable differences in the extent and detail of school decision-making responsibilities (McKenzie and Keeves, 1982). However, at the risk of oversimplifying a

Figure 10.1   Dimensions of school-based decision-making in government school systems

	Central specification and supply of all resources	Central appointment of teachers; block grant for other resources	Block grant for school determination of all resources
Central aims with curriculum guides	1	2	3
Central aims with school-based curriculum development	4	5	6
School aims and curriculum development	7	8	9

complex picture, it is possible to discern some general patterns. The common practice over the past twenty years has been to devolve greater curriculum responsibilities to schools and for those moves to be followed, at a lag of some years, by policies that provide schools with increased power to determine the mix and nature of the resources that they use. In terms of Figure 10.1 the general shift in the pattern of governance of Australian school systems has been from Cell 1 to Cell 4 and thence to Cell 5.

Government schools now have more freedom to develop curricula appropriate to local circumstances but, despite some earlier indications to the contrary, that freedom has generally not extended to the determination of broad curriculum aims. Thus, for example, the curriculum role of the centre is made quite explicit in the state of Victoria: 'To enhance the capacity of schools to determine their own educational programs within the framework provided by central policies and guidelines ...' (Ministry of Education, Victoria, 1987, p. 3). A similar policy emphasis applies in most of the other Australian government school systems.

In a comparable manner Australian government schools over the past twenty years have gained greater freedom to determine the resources that they use, but it is a freedom largely confined to non–teacher resources. It is now common for schools to be allocated a block grant to cover items such as equipment, supplies, public utilities, and even some non-teaching staff, and to have the freedom to apportion funds across and within categories. However, in regard to the most important resource — teachers and their time — schools are still largely dependent upon staffing schedules, appointments and working conditions determined by central authorities. There have been recent signs, though, of prospective changes in this regard. Under proposals advanced by the Education Department of Western Australia (1987) each government school would have the right to receive a block grant for the purchase of goods and services, be able to determine the mix of teaching and other staff and, within central guidelines, have the authority to deploy resources according to local judgment. In terms of Figure 10.1 these proposals would have the effect of moving Western Australian government schools towards Cell 6. The proposals, which are comparable with some aspects of the 1987 British Education Reform Bill, have generated substantial opposition, particularly from teacher unions, and are unlikely to be implemented in full. Nevertheless, they point the way to the prospect of the curriculum responsibilities of government schools being supplemented by significant new tasks in determining the level, nature and mix of the resources that they use.

The Western Australian proposals, and those of the Northern Territory Department of Education (1987), are similar in flavour to those advanced in Victoria a little earlier (Ministry of Education, Victoria, 1986) for the creation of 'self-governing' schools. The Victorian proposals also attracted substantial opposition, particularly in regard to the notions that government schools should be able to determine the mix of teaching and other resources and employ the teachers of their choice. In the event those elements of the proposed reforms have not been adopted. However, as Table 10.1 shows, the package of administrative changes being implemented in Victoria still entails a substantial degree of school level responsibility. In terms of other Australian government school systems it is probably only matched in the Australian Capital Territory.

For the next few years at least the types of school-based decision-making inherent in Table 10.1 will probably form the boundaries of government school autonomy in Australia; it is on the types of information necessary to support that level of decision-making that the rest of the chapter concentrates. Over the longer run it is likely that the pressures to provide government schools with greater freedom to determine the resources that they use will re-emerge. This is especially likely in regard to the number and composition of the teaching staff. In those circumstances the sorts of information discussed below could be considered as a necessary but far from sufficient aid to effective school decision-making.

Table 10.1   Roles and responsibilities of the school council and the principal

School council	Principal
1 Deciding the education policy of the school within Ministry guidelines and requirements.	1 Providing educational leadership and support for the operations of the council.
2 Deciding the major directions of the school program by determining curriculum objectives.	2 Supporting, promoting and implementing the policies of the Ministry, and the policies and decisions of the school council.
3 Ensuring that school policies are relevant to local needs.	3 Ensuring the effective and efficient management of the school.
4 Strengthening the relationship between the school and the community.	4 Determining (with the staff) the most appropriate educational means of realizing council policy and decisions.
5 Being responsible for defined areas of school operations such as: — budget approval; — monitoring of financial management; — selection of ancillary staff; — approval of camps and excursions.	5 Helping council members to become involved in policy formation in all the major areas of school policy.
6 Determining how much of the defined council responsibilities is to be delegated to the principal.	
7 Planning on a long-term basis.	

Source: Ministry of Education, Victoria (1987), p. 15.

Identifying School Information Needs

A useful schema for considering the information needs of school-based decision-making is provided by Simkins (1983) in a discussion of the implications of the increasing use of curriculum analysis models in British school administration. He identifies two broad purposes for any management information system, namely to supply: 'information required for planning and decision making — to enable the manager to assess the organization's future needs and problems and to develop appropriate strategies to meet them — and that required for evaluation and control — to permit the organization's past and present activities to be assessed in the light of some appropriate criteria of performance' (p. 49).

The two broad aspects of school management outlined above enable the identification of four major points at which information is required to assist with school-based decision-making. Three of these are suggested by Simkins (1983) in his discussion of the major stages in the general decision-making process:

1   intelligence: searching the environment for conditions calling for a decision;

  2 design: inventing, developing and analyzing possible courses of
     action;
  3 choice: selecting a particular course of action from those avail-
     able.

To these may be added:

  4 evaluation: making judgments on the effectiveness of the strategy
     adopted.

In practice these four categories of information are likely to be inter-
twined. However, their separate treatment provides a useful means of
identifying gaps in the existing information base available to schools and
the ways in which that base may need to be extended.

Intelligence: Searching the Environment

In principle, the identification of the conditions calling for a decision is
the simplest function that an information system needs to perform. It is
one that poses particular difficulties for schools because it brings into
focus those perennial problems of determining just what it is that school
programs are trying to achieve and the standards by which those achievements should be judged.

The complexity of the issue is implicit in the call by Sirotnik (1987,
p. 78) for a 'multicontent, multisource, and multimethod' approach to
understanding the 'circumstances, activities and meanings' of schooling.
Although couched in terms of the changing nature of educational evaluation, his argument is relevant here. He contends that:

> the 'program' for evaluative focus is now the ongoing constella-
> tion of daily activities and programs constituting the program of
> the local school. This suggests the need for information — actual-
> ly a considerable variety of information — designed to facilitate
> any number of evaluative purposes from appraising the impact of
> specific programmatic interventions, to informing organizational
> and instructional planning and development activities, to, perhaps
> most importantly, monitoring the periodic health of the school
> work and learning environment. (p. 77)

The last of these — the health of the school environment — is of
particular concern in this context for it provides (or at least should
provide) a major influence on when and how school-level decision-

makers should act. What sorts of information are needed for a school to monitor its institutional health? There are at least four major types:

1   educationally relevant information on the nature of the student population and community that the school serves;
2   a description of the nature of the school program and its objectives;
3   information on school outcomes such as students' cognitive and affective growth, teachers' attitudes and behaviour, and community support for the school; and
4   comparable material from other schools that enables individual school information to be placed in a broader perspective and evaluative judgments made.

The collection, processing and analysis of the volume of information outlined above might appear daunting. However, in a number of respects the required information is already available in one form or other. All government schools complete administrative returns that contain detailed material on their programs and patterns of resource deployment. Almost all schools collect extensive background information on incoming students and maintain detailed records of students' performance and behaviour over the course of their school life and, in some instances, their post-school lives as well. Further, most Australian government school systems now require schools to engage in a process of formal self-evaluation on a periodic basis, commonly every three to five years (McKenzie and Harrold, in press). Those evaluations typically include the collection and collation of a substantial body of qualitative and quantitative information relevant to at least the first three of the categories listed above. Technically at least, it would not be difficult to construct an information base that integrates the variety of forms of information that schools currently generate.

The problem is not so much the lack of information that schools can use in 'searching the environment'. If anything, most school administrators probably already have so much information about their schools that it is difficult for them to identify the major problem areas that should engage their attention. As the American economist Kenneth Boulding once said, knowledge comes from the orderly loss of information. The challenge is to provide schools with the incentive and the analytical means to use readily available information in a more systematic and focused manner. Fundamental to this is the identification of what it is that school decision-makers need to know and how it may be best presented to engage their attention (Simkins, 1983).

What it is that school administrators need to know is difficult to specify in advance and without detailed knowledge of individual school circumstances and priorities. Their needs are also likely to change over time. This suggests that any school-based information system should have sufficient flexibility to provide data on a wide repertoire of measures from which schools could select those best suited to their current needs. Important evidence on the potential and feasibility of this approach is provided by recent projects in several government systems to develop packages that enable schools to draw comparisons between their own programs and performance and state-wide norms. For example, under Project Baseline the Research Branch of the Western Australian Education Department worked closely with schools over several years to identify their information needs for self-evaluation purposes and to produce materials that enable those needs to be met. Measures and supporting software have been developed in areas such as student attitudes and achievement; teachers' perceptions of organizational climate; and parents' views of school-community relationships. The Baseline materials illustrate what Cumming (1987) has termed a trend towards the use of 'quality information' in school self-evaluations and help to dilute the criticism of Foon (1986, p. 3) that 'the lack of a comparative data base does not allow judgements of schools or processes to be made against any criteria except themselves.'

The advantages for schools of packages like Project Baseline are four-fold. First, the school is spared the cost of developing valid and reliable outcome instruments. Second, choice can be made from a wide variety of measures. Third, the technology allows the speedy turn-around of information, the display of results in easy-to-use form, and for the data to remain confidential to the school concerned. Fourth, schools are provided with norms against which their own programs and performance can be judged. It is suggested here that such comparisons are an important means of attracting school administrators' attention.

Similar processes can also be applied to much of the information that schools generate in the process of routine administration. In Victoria, for example, secondary schools complete an annual Staff Duties Analysis which contains a wealth of information on the allocation of teacher time between teaching and other duties, curriculum provision across the year levels, and class sizes. Comparable returns are completed by schools in the other government systems. If it were possible for central administrations to process such returns quickly, abstract from them key curriculum and resource usage indicators, either for the population of schools or for relevant subgroups (based on enrolment size, the nature of the catchment area and so on) and feed them back to schools, the capacity of schools to judge the adequacy of their programs would be considerably enhanced.

Design: Analyzing Possible Courses of Action

It is one thing to identify the need for change in a school program; it is another to develop possible approaches to achieve that change. This suggests the need for an information system that can assist school decision-makers to explore 'what if' questions by examining the implications of alternative strategies.

The work of Davies (1969) is an important illustration of the sort of approach that is required. He sought to provide school administrators with an analytical framework that would enable them to look afresh at the possibilities of school organization by freeing them of the mass of detail that is normally needed to describe school operations. His approach has two major elements: a notation that enabled the complexity of curriculum provision and resource use to be expressed in simple terms; and a set of relationships between key elements of the curriculum — the number of students, the number of classes that each student takes, and the number of classes provided by the school — that allowed alternative patterns of school organization to be explored: 'instead of taking a week, or weeks, or even months, to produce just one promising alternative to the school's existing curriculum, it should be possible by the use of this ... technique to compose, say in the course of the morning, two or three feasible patterns of a kind representing, perhaps, a revolutionary departure from the arrangements at present in force' (Davies, 1969, p. 65).

Davies' approach to unravelling the complexities of school organization has been influential in the United Kingdom since the early 1970s and has inspired attempts to refine and extend his model, most notably by Wilcox and Eustace (1980). The latter is an important contribution because it allows for a more fine-grained analysis of curriculum provision and the ways in which class groups are formed than was possible under Davies' earlier formulation. As with Davies' model, its basis is the use of a system of notation to extract from documents such as school timetables or curriculum statements essential aspects of school operations and the links between them. Without such abstracting and summarizing tools the valuable information that most schools already hold about themselves is difficult to unlock and use.

Approaches such as these have received only limited use in Australian schools (see Loader, 1978; Ellem, 1986), in part due to the lack of incentive to invest in their development and implementation. The moves towards greater school autonomy, however, change the structure of incentives faced by schools. School-based decision-making puts a premium on the capacity to view the school as a whole and to discern the linkages between its major elements. The interrelationships of curriculum, teachers, students, facilities and finance are of such importance that a focus on any one of these in isolation from the others can lead to unanticipated, if not undesirable, consequences. This is particularly the case in the present climate where the resources for government schools are severely constrained and likely to remain so.

In times of growth and (relatively) abundant resources incremental decision-making — responding to individual problems or opportunities without a systematic regard for how the decision may affect other parts of the organization — may suffice because the costs of mistakes can be easily absorbed (Levine, 1978). More austere times do not provide this cushion. Unfortunately, they also make it more difficult to find the resources to develop and implement the necessary early warning and decision support systems.

Choice: Selecting a Course of Action

Simkins (1983) suggested that as British schools gain experience with local decision-making and that as the issues that confront schools become clearer, efforts will be made to design information systems that not only provide alternative approaches but which also, on the basis of stated values and objectives, are able to recommend which approach should be adopted. An example of this type of development is provided by Levin (1986) who has outlined the features of an interactive computer-based approach to assisting those undertaking cost-effectiveness analyses in school settings.

The obstacles in the path of this feature of school information systems are, however, formidable. Apart from the ever-present problems of establishing the links between particular school strategies and educational outcomes, the diversity of value positions that is present in any school community underlines the risk of having any one set of values in-built into some form of automatic decision-making process. More positively, the mere possibility of such a development could stimulate interest in exploring ways of encouraging school decision-makers to make their own value positions more explicit and open to scrutiny.

An interesting illustration of this type of approach is provided by Harrold and Hough (1987). Their emphasis is on assisting schools to evaluate the ways in which resources are deployed and they attempt this through a grid — with subject departments and year levels forming the axes — that enables comparisons to be made between where pupil learning activities are concentrated and teacher time is deployed. Initially, the analysis assumes that the teaching time of all teachers is equally effective and that all pupil learning opportunities are of equal worth. Subsequent comparisons are then made under different assumptions, thereby focusing decision-makers' attention on important issues underlying the differential treatment of various groups of pupils in the school. The analysis builds on the workbook developed by Harrold (1988) to assist Australian non-government schools better to understand the ways in which their patterns of fee structure, curriculum provision and teacher time usage shape the flow of resources to different groups of students within the school. Without the documentation of resource use that a tool such as the work-book provides, it is difficult for schools to engage in any systematic examination of the value positions that underpin their operations.

Evaluation: Making Judgments

Almost by definition school-based decision-making compels local admin-istrators to be involved in the evaluation of school policies and practices. Of the four major elements of decision-making identified in this chapter, it is probably in this regard that Australian government schools have gained most experience over the past decade. As noted earlier, most government schools are now required to engage in some form of periodic, institutional self-evaluation. The lessons gained by teachers from their participation in school self-evaluation — in areas such as gaining the cooperation of major interest groups and the processes of information collection, analysis and report writing — and the supporting materials developed by school systems and others provide important resources for the new decision-making responsibilities that many schools now face.

Institutional self-evaluations of the large-scale and periodic type will almost certainly continue to be undertaken in Australian schools, if only for accountability reasons. The pressures of school-based decision-making are likely to mean, however, that such evaluations will need to be supplemented. For one thing, most school self-evaluations have been of the formative type (McKenzie and Harrold, in press). The prospect of increased decision-making responsibilities, particularly in the area of re-source management, will mean that schools will also require evaluations that are summative in focus. For another, it is unlikely that the needs of school decision-makers will be satisfied by evaluations that occur only every few years; schools may require evaluation approaches that are more readily integrated with the ongoing management of the school.

A promising development in the latter regard is the 'Collaborative School Management Cycle' elaborated by Caldwell and Spinks (1986) and described by Spinks elsewhere in this volume (see Chapter 7). This approach to school-based decision-making employs a participative model to identify school objectives, plan and cost appropriate programs, and evaluate the results. The model does not differ markedly from other Australian approaches to school evaluation in the evaluative techniques that are used. Its promise, however, lies in the way in which evaluation is conceptualized as an integral part of school management:

> Policy making, program planning and budgeting thus facilitate evaluation because the base-line information is readily available. Time can therefore be devoted to measuring the outcomes of programs. The evaluative task becomes realistic rather than a task in which large amounts of time are spent casting around, wondering what one is really trying to measure. (Caldwell and Spinks, 1986, p. 111)

Approaches such as these, by making school-based evaluation more focused and feasible, may help to overcome the concerns noted by Cumming (1987) and others that many teachers express about evaluation in Australian schools, namely, that it is ritualistic, time-consuming and of little apparent relevance to subsequent decision-making.

Developing School-based Information Systems

This discussion has outlined a number of forms of information that are needed by schools to assist with local decision-making responsibilities. It has also suggested that in most instances the necessary raw data already exist in some form or other. Moves towards school-based decision-making need not unleash a massive new round of information collection, collation and analysis. Rather, the emphasis should be on assisting schools to use more effectively the existing information that surrounds (and possibly overwhelms) them.

A possible exception to this lies in the field of financial management. Government schools have traditionally had little financial autonomy and have tended to need budgetary information of only a rudimentary kind. Recent moves to devolve some financial responsibilities have led several school systems to develop accounting information packages to support school-level program budgeting. In the main this sort of information is new to school administrators and its collection and analysis are undoubtedly causing anguish, even in those schools that are now supplied with specialist financial personnel such as bursars. However, until government schools are allocated direct financial responsibility for the major resource that they use, namely teachers, information of a non-financial kind — relating to the nature of the school program and its impact on students — should form the focus of efforts to aid school decision-making.

To assist schools to use more effectively the information that is already available requires effort on four major fronts.

1 Schools have to become convinced that an investment of time and resources in local school decision-making is worthwhile. Incentives for effective school-based decision-making need to be provided or, less constructively, penalties for poor decision-making imposed.

2 Existing forms of information held within schools and central administrations need to be catalogued, integrated and key indicators of school operations extracted. In this regard the new generation of inexpensive and powerful computing equipment has much to offer (Sawin, 1986).

3 Summary information on other schools and their programs needs to be provided by central administrations so that individual schools have a broader context for understanding their own operations.

4 Analytical frameworks need to be developed which enable schools to assess the implications of the information available to them and to explore alternative ways of using school resources.

This chapter has outlined approaches adopted in various school systems to the provision of better information to aid school decision-making. It is unlikely that any one model could be successfully transplanted without substantial modification for local circumstances. Therefore, it will be necessary, as several school systems have already recognized, to invest resources in developing support systems for their own schools. In this, care will need to be taken that attempts to improve the information base available to schools are in themselves cost-effective. That is, the improvement in practice made possible by a more informed approach to school decision-making should outweigh the costs involved. Since those costs and benefits are difficult to specify in advance, a prudent initial step would be to work closely with a small group of schools to identify their information needs, examine the existing information sources that they could tap and, where these prove inadequate, experiment with the development of purpose-built information systems.

The value of moves to encourage school-based decision-making will ultimately depend upon the fostering of a climate that enables 'critical discourse [to become] a way of organizational life in schools' (Sirotnik,

1987, p. 88). In this process school-based information systems, if they permit schools to have access to information that is timely, relevant to their needs and expressed in meaningful form, can play a major part.

References

CALDWELL, B.J. and SPINKS, J.M. (1986) *Policy-making and Planning for School Effectiveness*. Hobart: Education Department of Tasmania.

CUMMING, J. (1987) 'What's Happening in School Self-evaluation in Australia?' *Curriculum Development in Australian Schools*, 3, January, 42–4.

DAVIES, T.I. (1969) *School Organisation*. Oxford: Pergamon.

DESCHAMP, P. and McGAW, B. (1979) 'Responsibility for Curriculum Evaluation in Centralized Systems,' *Australian Journal of Education*, 23, 209–26.

EDUCATION DEPARTMENT OF WESTERN AUSTRALIA (1987) *A Program for Improvement: Better Schools in Western Australia*. Perth: Education Department of Western Australia.

ELLEM, G. (1986) 'Timetable Analysis: A Tool for School Administrators,' *Journal of Educational Administration*, 24, 18–37.

FAIRHILL, J. (1988) 'Curse of the Black Spot,' *Education Guardian*, 1, March, 25.

FOON, A. (1986) 'Evaluative Procedures and Accountability in Australian Schools: A Review of Practice 1980–85 and a Prelude to the Future,' *National Council of Independent Schools Newsletter*, 4, 3, Supplement, 1–4.

HARROLD, R.I. (1988) *Curriculum and Financial Performance: A Workbook for Non-government Schools*. Hawthorn, Vic.: Australian Council for Educational Research.

HARROLD, R.I. and HOUGH, J. (1987) *Curriculum, Finance and Resource Deployment: Toward School Self-Evaluation*. Loughborough: Loughborough University of Technology, Department of Education.

LEVIN, H.M. (1986) *What Have We Learned about Cost-Benefit and Cost-Effectiveness Analysis?* Palo Alto, Calif.: Center for Educational Research at Stanford, Stanford University.

LEVINE, C.H. (1978) 'Organisational Decline and Cutback Management,' *Public Administration Review*, 38, 4, 316–25.

LOADER, D. (1978) 'The Allocation of Teachers in Schools: An Alternative to the Class Size Dialogue,' *Unicorn*, 4, 253–64.

McKENZIE, P.A. and HARROLD, R.I. (in press) 'Tools for School Self-evaluation: Developments in Australia,' *Studies in Educational Evaluation*.

McKENZIE, P.A. and KEEVES, J.P. (1982) *Eight Education Systems: Resource Allocation Policies in the Government School Systems of Australia and New Zealand*. Hawthorn, Vic.: Australian Council for Educational Research.

MINISTRY OF EDUCATION, VICTORIA (1986) *Taking Schools into the 1990s*. Melbourne: Ministry of Education.

MINISTRY OF EDUCATION, VICTORIA (1987) *The Structure and Organisation of the Schools Division*. Melbourne: Ministry of Education.

NORTHERN TERRITORY. DEPARTMENT OF EDUCATION (1987) *Towards the 90s*. Darwin: Department of Education.

SAWIN, E.I. (1986) 'Microcomputers and Local Curriculum Assessment: Potentials and Problems,' *Studies in Educational Evaluation*, 12, 109–17.

SIMKINS, T. (1983) 'Some Management Implications of the Development of Curriculum Information Systems,' *Journal of Curriculum Studies*, 15, 47–59.

SIROTNIK, K.A. (1987) 'The Information Side of Evaluation for School Improvement,' *International Journal of Educational Research*, 11, 77–90.

WILCOX, B. and EUSTACE, P.J. (1980) *Tooling up for Curriculum Review*. Windsor: National Foundation for Educational Research.

Chapter 11

Program Budgeting: A Way Forward in School Management

Brian J. Spicer

Since the early 1980s many Western governments have progressively pursued policies directed at providing a stronger economic base for future development and at ensuring a fundamental restructuring of the economy. In full recognition of the need for international economic competitiveness both public and private enterprise and the workforce as a whole have been encouraged to pursue goals of greater efficiency and productivity. These goals have also been carried over into the educational sector with the emphasis increasingly on greater effectiveness and efficiency in resource management.

In such an economic and political climate effective resource management is essential and it is no less essential in the case of the individual school than it is for the large university or for the education system as a whole. In the foreseeable future, with limited budgets, educational change to meet current goals and to attain emerging goals more effectively must depend on improved resource management — whether those resources be raw dollars, the existing educational stock of land, buildings and other physical resources, the human resources of teachers, administrators and other personnel, or those other community resources which can be accessed by educational institutions. Quality education will increasingly demand quality resource management. Our decision-making about how resources are to be used must be less haphazard and more carefully attuned to real priorities than may hitherto have been the case. Moreover, our management and monitoring of the use of these resources must be elevated to the standards accepted as the norm for the corporate world.

This is not to argue that a country's economic ills will be cured simply by applying tighter rules for resource management. It is a reasonable proposition that whilst such an approach will reduce resource wastage and will assist in the achievement of priorities, it may well be impossible to raise educational standards to the level demanded by the post-industrial society unless an even higher proportion of GNP is provided for educational purposes. However, until our political masters determine that such increases are both economically and politically desirable and feasible the emphasis for our educational leaders must be on more effective management. In the long term as, hopefully, more resources do become available we will find that our educational institutions, and the educational systems of which they are part, will have in place resource management strategies which will ensure the application of those resources in the most efficient and effective way possible.

This chapter examines an approach to more efficient resource management which has been developed in this specific context of tighter budgetary control but also in the more general context of global change. Some of the key trends which can be identified will add further strength to the calls for better resource usage and for greater resource accountability.

Key Trends

Two of the major pressures impacting on our society and hence on our education system are the growth of high technology and the emergence of the 'information society' in which the newly valued resource is knowledge. Both have tremendous significance for education and for resource demand and usage in education. A major goal for education must be to ensure that people can live and work in a high technology age. The computer is changing our lives and is likely to effect changes at an even faster pace in the future. Such changes will be inescapable. But, whilst we must ensure that our new generations of adults can work effectively with this high technology, so we must also recognize that they must have the ability to translate the new knowledge of the world into appropriate ideas, theories and practices. Failure to meet the demands of these emergent pressures will almost certainly mean a languishing at the lower end of the development table. On the other hand, to meet these demands will require different resources and hence either more money or a change in our educational priorities. Given the lack of budgetary support, there will need to be a shift in priorities but, in addition, we shall probably see a further escalation of the trend towards institutional 'self-reliance'.

Increasingly, we will find schools and colleges and universities going out into the wider community to seek alternative resource sources. There will be a move towards more entrepreneurship in education, at every level and no matter what size the institution. Whether they like it or not, educators, and educational administrators above all, will become much more responsible for both resource acquisition and resource maintenance. This move towards self-help and self-reliance, as distinct from the government being seen as responsible for everything, will be paralleled by another related trend which is for an increasing involvement by external stakeholders in school management and decision-making. The move towards the wider community as a major source of resources will inevitably mean that the community will want a 'voice' in planning and management. Of course, specific stakeholders such as parents and students can be expected to demand more of a role in curriculum and resource management, because they are the ones most directly affected by school decisions. They will want a say and a genuine role in policy-making.

Significantly, this trend for an increased stakeholder and participant role in school-based decision-making should be the catalyst for the further growth in education of a trend which is increasingly impacting on the corporate world, namely, the shift from 'top-down' hierarchical management structures such as are typical of governments, the military and the church towards a marked 'team' orientation in which we are all 'as one'. This is a most exciting prospect because the team is more likely than the hierarchy to bond effectively and, through 'networking', generate new understandings and innovative solutions to problems. It does, however, require that we manage our most important resource — the 'human' resource — in a way different from that which has been typical of the past. Creating and managing a 'team' are very different from being a 'top-down' autocrat. The development of team skills is essential if the generative process outlined above is to emerge.

If these trends grow in importance, it is likely that they will also engender the desire to develop long-term goals rather than merely to consider short-term goals. Within our various educational institutions we shall be asking: 'What are we on about?'; 'What sort of business are we really engaged in?' Our answers will reflect not only the reality of the context of our own country but the twin reality that the world is changing and changing rapidly, and that no single part of the globe is further away than the touch of a button. The tyranny of distance which so frustrated mankind for generations is virtually non-existent. We must educate our children to meet the demands of tomorrow but we must also work to ensure that they can meet the demands of the decades from now. Certainly, and it follows from all that has been argued thus far, the era upon us will often many options. The world is changing so quickly, knowledge is expanding at such a rate, technology is wreaking havoc with our imaginations to such an extent that to believe we can be educated in a few brief years at school for a lifetime of productive involvement in the real world is no longer either tenable or realistic. These elements must surely have important consequences for the decisions we make about resource priorities and resource management.

There are two other important trends which will have a major impact on our schools. Although they seem to derive logically from the spirit of this era, they represent the possibility for tension and pressure within our institutions. The first is the move towards greater decentralization and devolution in education. The trend is to give greater control to the local communities and the local stakeholders for the decision-making in their schools rather than simply decreeing that all power and authority should radiate from the centre. This trend sits very comfortably alongside trends for more networking and teamwork, for greater mobilization of community resources, etc. mentioned earlier. It is at the very core of the move towards devolution and reinforces the establishment of a situation in which educators and administrators will be increasingly responsible for the management of the total school — finance, personnel, buildings, etc. — as well as curriculum. Our school leaders will, of necessity, become de facto entrepreneurs.

Yet there is an enormous possibility of conflict arising from the coexistence of this move towards devolution and the second major trend which is increasingly obvious in much of the world today, namely, the shift in attitude by governments towards demanding greater accountability for the effective and efficient use of resources from all of its agencies and enterprises, including educational institutions. Governments, like communities, are seeking to ensure that educational priorities are achieved through the appropriate application and management of the resources available to our schools. The problem of tension arises partly because the government's educational goals are not always long-term and more often than not they tend to be limited in scope and are not necessarily fully shared by the community at large and by the community of professional educators and teachers in particular. However, potentially more explosive tension is likely to occur because educational issues do not always translate readily into money equations.

Overall, these trends and pressures have a direct impact on us as educational leaders and as educational managers; they mean change at a pace which we have probably never before witnessed. In turn this means that, as educational managers, we shall be responsible for ensuring that the quality of the resource management system in our schools and colleges is upgraded and developed to meet the challenges of this rate of change. This will mean much greater stress and responsibility on our educational managers to put in place appropriate management systems. We shall be forced to adopt 'strategic management' as our key approach.

Figure 11.1   Strategic management in educational institutions

Strategic management is a *total process*

from

— initial appraisal of present position or state of school or college

to

Strategic planning　　　— formulation and publication of mission statement

to

— finalization of a set of goals and objectives

to

— development of plan of action (including general and specific curriculum decisions, program budgets, staffing decisions, etc.)

to

Operational planning　　— implementation of plan (activation of school program)

to

— evaluation and review

Strategic Management

Strategic management is a concept derived from the corporate sector which should now be applied to individual educational institutions in much the same way as it is being increasingly applied to government authorities and instrumentalities. Whilst many education idealists might express concern about the notion of applying a major corporate concept to an institution such as a school, close analysis should reveal that the underpinning logic is not very different from that which underpins much of traditional curriculum theory; and we should be more concerned with the strength of that logic than with fear of adopting a concept with such clear business overtones.

In brief, strategic management (see Figure 11.1) involves two vital stages of planning and action: the 'strategic' and the 'operational'. In the first stage of strategic planning the educational institution must undertake a thorough appraisal of its current position which will, in turn, provide the raw material, the basic knowledge, leading to the formulation and publication of a mission statement and subsequently to the finalization and adoption of a set of appropriate and relevant goals and objectives. These elements are the backdrop for all subsequent resource management as well as curriculum management decisions. Perhaps the only aspect which needs further elaboration, and then only because of its relatively recent application to education, is the development of the mission statement (see Figure 11.2).

This is a most significant achievement, certainly the first major task,

Figure 11.2 Key elements of mission statements

1 Why do we exist?
2 What dimensions of education will we concentrate on?
3 What distinctive role will we aim for?
4 How shall we conduct our educational enterprise? (management values and style)

of the stage of strategic planning because of its emphasis on clarifying the distinctive purposes and roles for the institution and specifying the styles and values to be adopted in conducting the business of the institution. It is also a major statement of strategy: a statement of the way the institution defines its relationship with both the micro and macro environment. Many school 'policy' statements do embrace elements of good mission statements but the process must be developed and formalized.

During the second phase of operational planning the focus is on action. Initially there is the development of a plan which reflects general strengths and weaknesses, richness and poverty in various resource areas, determines priorities, prepares program budgets and sets the parameters for staffing and other resource decisions. This plan will be implemented and then, both as part of the action process and as part of a summative approach, the effectiveness of the plan in theory and practice will be the subject of close and rigorous monitoring, evaluation and review. Whereas during the planning phase the leading question should be: 'Are we doing the right thing?', during the operational phase the 'team' must continually ask itself: 'Are we doing things right?'

Strategic Management in Education:
A Case Study — Victoria (Australia)

In the USA and Canada, as well as in Australia, the move towards strategic management at the school level has been facilitated, indeed positively encouraged, by adopting an approach linking available resources directly to school policy and priority decisions via program budgeting and strongly reflective of the collaborative management cycle (Caldwell and Spinks, 1985) with its emphasis on devolved and 'team' decision-making.

Initially, the policy was communicated to schools through official memoranda then via demonstration using a pilot school program and ultimately through professional development programs for ministry support staff and school principals. Principals then became the diffusers of the idea in schools through the active introduction of program budgeting. Indeed, the real strength of the change process adopted in Victoria has been the role of the school principal as 'entrepreneur' within his/her own school. In accord with House's theory of personal contact in the spread of innovation (House, 1974), principals have adopted the entrepreneurial role as change agents and, through personal contact with their school communities, executed the introduction and adoption of program budgeting in their schools (Kayak, 1988).

The consequences of this change have been far-reaching, shaping not only current and new programs and the associated allocation of resources but generally having an impact upon the social fabric of the school system itself. One case study (Kayak, 1988) reported that the introduction of program budgeting and its associated management changes fundamentally altered relationships between staff members in that the majority of staff became involved in active decision-making relating to the curriculum and to the process of resource allocation, and hence the hierarchical power of the senior staff was diminished. Whilst the spread of program budgeting throughout Victorian schools is incomplete, the program budget innovation has represented, both directly and indirectly, a substantial response to many of the key trends apparent in the wider community and described earlier. Specifically, program budgeting has provided a foundation for school level entrepreneurship, for increased stakeholder participation and the development of a team ethos, placed a new emphasis on 'goals' in educational planning, and represented a significant step towards decentralization and devolution of power and authority. In so many ways the school of today is beginning to take on the characteristics of the corporate world with smaller and accountable units of work with a higher level of collegiality and co-ownership. Staff are stakeholders and not merely employees. Schools are encouraged to be more adaptable and responsive to the needs of the community and to recognize their responsibility for greater efficiency and productivity.

Program Budgeting

In Victoria the concept and practice of program budgeting was introduced to government departments in December 1983 with the intention of effectively eliminating traditional line item budgets by the end of the 1985 financial year.

As can be seen from Figure 11.3, the line item budget is essentially a financial accounting base specifying the amounts to be spent on particular objects of expenditure: staff salaries, travel costs, materials, etc. These

Figure 11.3   Sample line item budget (system level)

		1982–83 Payments	1983–84 Estimate
		$	$
DIVISION No. 308 — REGIONAL SUPPORT SERVICES			
1 Salaries and Payments in the nature of Salary —			
2 Salaries and allowance		37 070 135	37 882 000
4 Payments in lieu of long service leave, retiring gratuities ..		151 354	300 000
		37 221 489	38 182 000
2 General Expenses —			
1 Administrative expenses		2 002 848	2 243 000

	Payments 1982–83	Estimate 1983–84
	$	$
1 Travelling and subsistence	1 149 018	1 182 000
2 Office requisites and equipment, printing and stationery	114 100	127 000
3 Books and publications	24 051	31 000
4 Postal and telephone expenses ..	270 570	307 000
5 Motor vehicles — Purchase and running expenses	167 087	287 000
6 Fuel, light, power and water	185 971	212 000
7 Incidental expenses	92 051	97 000
	2 002 848	2 243 000

		1982–83	1983–84
23 Curriculum materials		138 743	154 000
26 Cleaning — Wages, contracts, etc.		195 534	207 700
27 Grants to schools		109 000	160 300
		2 446 125	2 765 000
3 Other Services —			
1 School camps — Somers, Rubicon and Bogong		447 587	505 000
Total Division No. 308		40 115 201	41 452 000

Source: State Board of Education, Victoria (1984), p. 10.

objects of expenditure are resource 'inputs' to the particular service activity involved. However, the line item budget tells virtually nothing about the particular services to be provided or about the policies currently being pursued by the government or service authority, nor does it provide any notion of the performance expectations for the year.

Program budgeting, on the other hand, is a much more embracing planning tool. It is far more than a mere accounting process. It is a means of facilitating the management of programs and providing the means by which programs can be monitored, performance assessed and future plans and action amended. It is very much a complete planning cycle, operating within the larger cycle of strategic management, the key elements of which are the establishment of priorities against an assessment of needs and the evaluation of the program against established objectives (Policy and Planning Unit, Victorian Ministry of Education, 1984a, 1984b).

As an accounting mechanism, and it must be stressed that this is not program budgeting's main feature, it is a system for classifying expenditures by purpose rather than by resources and, therefore, for 'facilitating the understanding and therefore the involvement of lay persons in planning budgets, choosing priorities among options available and evaluating effectiveness. Program managers are given greater flexibility in resources management in return for closer control over policy' (State Board of Education, Victoria, 1984, p. 1). The State Board in Victoria, whilst noting that program budgeting is 'essentially a device to improve policy control by linking financial inputs to performance outputs' (State Board of Education, Victoria, 1984, p. 4), was very keen to ensure that a mechanism to deliver better programs would not have the effect of recentralizing an education system which was becoming increasingly devolved in its control and management. As a result of its concern, the State Board reiterated its belief that

> the situation of schools themselves, complex and diverse as they are, imposes requirements for unique local solutions which, articulated through councils, parents and teachers' organisations, make it politically sensible to separate program budgeting in education into two levels of programs — those of the State, concerned with resourcing and supporting schools, and those at the school level, concerned with planning and managing each school's own policies and programs. (State Board of Education, Victoria, 1984, p. 5)

By the beginning of 1987 between 40 and 45 per cent of all Victorian schools had prepared program budget documents in at least some areas of school operation, and nearly 60 per cent of schools had taken the initial steps to become informed about program budgeting and its implementation (Policy and Planning Unit, 1987)

The planning model which was provided to Victorian schools drew heavily on the pioneering work of Caldwell *et al.* in Tasmania. For example, the Policy and Planning Unit in its *Resource Booklet* published in January 1984 provided a list of budgetary tasks adapted from Caldwell (1983a).

1 Development of an Educational Plan
    — establishing priorities; needs assessment; budget calendar

   2   Collection and Appraisal of Data
        — enrolment projections; personnel requirements; salaries; re-
        source inventories; etc.
   3   Preliminary Expenditure Plan
        — allocation of resoures to priorities; initial program identifica-
        tion
   4   Preliminary Revenue Plan
        — estimated revenue from central and local sources
   5   Formal Budget Document
        — Final program identification; program descriptions, commen-
        tary and budget summary
   6   Adoption of Budget
   7   Administration of Budget
   8   Review and Audit (Policy and Planning Unit, Ministry of Educa-
        tion January, 1984a)

This list of tasks reflects the fact that program budgeting is very much a
'... financial translation of an education plan ... with a systematic
matching of resources to priorities within and among programs for
meeting the learning needs of pupils' (Caldwell, 1983b).

However, as the State Board pointed out, 'efficient corporate planning requires adequate advance timing for the effective participation of all
concerned in the development of a plan that is likely to work ... [and
outlined] three stages, progressively more specific in budget terms, but in
each of which there is a role for council, principal and staff to interact on
the specifics of proposed action' (State Board of Education, Victoria,
1984, p. 30). These three stages are illustrated in Figure 11.4.

It would be apparent, even from this brief review, that program
budgeting has the potential to facilitate long-term ongoing planning
which is systematic, relevant and capable of integrating other key management functions at the school level, including collaborative planning
and decision-making, communication, conflict resolution and evaluation.
It will also assist schools to clarify their objectives, determine priorities
which reflect local needs and preferences, facilitate the evaluation of
educational programs and enable the assessment of resource allocations
(Policy and Planning Unit, 1984a, 1984b). It can, and should, be a
valuable mechanism for the school.

Increasingly, one of the major problems confronted by schools involved in implementing a policy of program budgeting has been to find
an appropriate conceptualization for the various subprograms within the
school. Traditionally, in the curriculum area the practice has been to tie
the new program budget structure to conventional subject areas rather than

Figure 11.4   Cycles in a one-year period of corporate planning at the school level

STAGES LEVELS 1	CYCLE 1 STRATEGIC PLANNING	CYCLE 2 PROGRAM PLANNING	CYCLE 3 PROGRAM BUDGETING
COUNCIL	1 3	5	7
SENIOR STAFF	2		
STAFF		4	6

1. Levels of *responsibility* for plans: *communication* flows up, down and across lines of authority and responsibility.

Steps

1. School Council establishes goals, strategies, policies and objectives for school as a whole with *input from principal, staff and community as appropriate.*

2. Principal and other senior staff, *in consultation with teachers and support staff where appropriate,* prepare goals, strategies, policies and objectives for each program in a manner consistent with those for the school as a whole.

3. Consolidation of goals, strategies, policies and objectives for the school as a whole.

4. Development of detailed plans with priorities among programs and program objectives, *with further input from staff, students and the community as appropriate.*

5. Consolidation of program plans for school.

6. Preparation of program budgets in the light of available revenue.

7. Consolidation of program budgets for the school.

Source: State Board of Education, Victoria (1984), p. 31.

to identify a smaller number of key areas whilst still preserving the identity and integrity of component subprograms. For example, there is no particular reason why all performing and creative arts should not be grouped together — visual and plastic arts, music, physical education, drama — in a way which maintains the individual integrity of the component subprograms but also provides for their relatedness to be considered in planning and in decision-making as to funding priority. Such an approach also encourages groups of 'related' staff to examine critically the relative priorities they accord to the individual elements prior to the consideration of the overall school budget by the relevant school committee. If a school program structure could present thirty to forty subprograms grouped in seven or eight major areas, this would be a significant step towards more effective policy-related and flexible management.

Indeed, to maintain the conventional subject areas as the organizing framework may be a severe constraint on our ability to adapt the curriculum to the changing needs of tomorrow's society. Brown (1983) offers alternative structural possibilities including programs by year level or class groupings, by subschools or by skill development (e.g. literacy, numeracy, communication, problem–solving, social development). Other possibilities could well include programs to cover specific areas of need: e.g. multicultural learning, and computer and technology education.

Program budgeting must necessarily recognize that apart from the traditional curriculum areas (compulsory and elective) there are many other activities which require planning and budgeting action. These activities, covering areas such as buildings, grounds, equipment, including operations and maintenance, administration and general services, pupil welfare, educational resource centres, professional development, community education, parent/community activities, etc., represent other significant and potentially significant areas for which the school must have goals, program descriptions, objectives and evaluation strategies and for which the school must determine priorities in resource allocation.

Once the program structure for the school has been determined, there are alternative frameworks which may be adopted for developing program descriptions.

Framework A

1   Program goals — where a goal is a statement of broad direction, general purpose or intent.
2   Program description — setting out what is currently offered in the program and including a description of resources and services provided.
3   Program objectives — a list of desired outcomes toward which program activities are directed within a given timeframe (usually the school year).
4   Program evaluation — how effectiveness is to be determined.

Framework B

1   Purpose of program
2   Nature of program
3   Planning for implementation
4   Resources required
5   Proposed evaluation

Framework C

1   Condition statement — describing those 'external' circumstances which result in a need for the program. For example, changing demographic characteristics in local area; changing community expectations in some subject areas, such as computer studies; etc.
2   Description statement — outlining the tasks or activities associated with the carrying out of the program; the units responsible for the program; the organizational arrangements made and the identified beneficiaries of the program.
3   Objectives — what the program is expected to accomplish. These objectives should be directional and measurable.
4   Indicators — the basis for evaluation. These data must be logically related to the program objectives and be usefully applied in the decision-making process.
5   Policy initiatives — indicating how the program is responding to specific policy directions.
6   Resource allocation — a financial statement providing information on the estimated cost of maintaining the existing program and of implementing the proposed program. (Policy and Planning Unit, 1984a, 1984b)

There are many examples of program budgets in the literature (Caldwell, 1983a; State Board of Education, 1984; Policy and Planning Unit, 1984a, 1984b) which reflect the use of this kind of framework. Figures 11.5 and 11.6 provide examples of primary school program budgets for Language/General Studies, P-2 (Creed, 1988) and Physical Education (Kayak, 1988).

Conclusion

Government desire to improve the efficiency and effectiveness of resource usage in all areas of public expenditure has led to the growth of program budgeting as a major strategy in all educational institutions. It brings together the essential and significant characteristics of modern corporate and strategic management within the context of a collaborative style of school management. Figure 11.7 illustrates this interrelationship.

The school policy group headed by the principal and the leaders of the school community (council, staff associations, etc.) is responsible for assessing the internal and external factors which are of major importance in the school environment and for providing the leadership in strategic

Figure 11.5 Exemplary primary school budget

PROGRAM: LANGUAGE/GENERAL STUDIES, P.2 RESPONSIBILITY: CODE 5.1

1. PURPOSE
— To develop the literacy skills of all children.
— To foster a love of literature and encourage a desire to read.
— To ensure that language is seen as an integral part of the health, social studies and science components of this program.
— To be responsive to the physical, intellectual, social and emotional needs of all children.
— To develop desirable attitudes — perseverance, independence, cooperation and responsibility.

2. BROAD GUIDELINES
— The program should accommodate and build on the learning that has already taken place prior to the child entering school.
— The program should ensure that learning proceeds at the rate best suited to the individual child.
— The teaching program should be activity-centred, enabling children to learn through direct experience in a secure and stimulating environment, taking into account children's interests and capabilities.
— The program should maintain a balance of components of each curriculum area.
— The program should involve parents wherever possible.

3. IMPLEMENTATION
The six grades involved in the above program are divided into two areas of coordination responsibility (Pre/1, and 2).

Each program member, although considered to be a contributing member towards all aspects of the program, will become independently 'identified' with a particular curriculum area and will be responsible, in conjunction with the team leader and the Curriculum Resource program leader, for the following duties.

* disseminating information
* attendance at meetings arranged outside the school
* attendance at in-services
* purchasing or processing aids and equipment
* maintaining inventories of aids and equipment

Each grade teacher will include all curriculum areas in the total program. The library item of the reading component will mainly be the teaching and program responsibilities of the Curriculum Resources Program team leader. The curriculum areas of Art, Music, Phys. Ed. will also be implemented, for the most part by support staff. The library program forms an integral part of the total program, and other support staff areas will be suitably integrated with the class teachers' programs. It is necessary that class teachers liaise with the support staff to ensure optimum program integration to the children's benefit. It is also recognised that each curriculum area requires its own development for each component. Thus a 'unit' approach will be incorporated.

The established school language courses will continue to provide a reference point for the specific language skills aspect of the program. The Social Studies course (Chelsea Inspectorate 1981) will remain the reference point for the thematic/concept and content-cluster approach which is continuing to provide the basis for the integration of the curriculum areas. Science and Health programs utilised in 1984 will be reviewed on planning day, term 1 1985. Science, in particular, is suited to 'unit' program development.

Excursions will be planned to enhance, (by introducing, consolidating or concluding), those themes which most directly exemplify the Aims and Assumptions of the General Policy. Camping program activities are to be reviewed.

1984 Objectives and evaluations will be reviewed for their application to 1985 programs and revised where necessary on the planning days.

4. RESOURCES
Staffing:
Class teachers × 6 × 15.4 units = 92.4 units
B.3 × 9 units   =   9   units
                                    101.4 units   . . .   89232

Curriculum Needs:
   Language, general   420   . . .
   Reading   370
   Word Study   69
   Social Studies   125
   Science   88
   Health   23
   Storage   100   1195
Children's Requisites:
   Education Department Allowance 2000
   Area Allowance   750
   Religious Instruction   213   3163
Reserve: 200   4558
                                                           93790

5. EVALUATION (MAJOR)
An on-going subjective and objective evaluation program will occur. The main criteria for evaluation will be the noted improvement in achievement and attitude of the children. Methods for evaluating this will include:

* Achievement tests where appropriate
* The keeping of anecdotal and cumulative records of children's work including subjective teacher observation/assessment of the quality of children's participation in all curriculum areas.
* The continuation of the established verbal and written parent/teacher contacts to provide information and ascertain parental opinion of children's progress.
* Teacher comment on the appropriateness of teaching materials and methods being employed.
* The involvement of School Council, and of external agencies (CGCS, SEU, etc.) as required in the assessment of the program

Source: Creed (1988).

and operational planning. It is that group which is responsible for the initial appraisal, for the statements, and for the determination of goals, objectives and priorities and general plans for action. Whilst their decisions feed in to the deliberations of the 'predominantly' staff teams working on specific program developments, in the final analysis the policy group also has the task of assessing and approving both the programs and the budgets. It is a corporate management structure because all parts of the system of a particular school have a part to play in the governance of that system.

Whilst more time must elapse before a summative judgment can be reached as to the quality of the import of program budgeting on Victorian schools, it appears that in those schools where its role has been clearly established the benefits may be very substantial indeed. The man-

Figure 11.6 Physical education program budget

CODE:	PROGRAM: Physical Education	RESPONSIBILITY: P.E. SPECIALIST/ CO-ORDINATOR	CHAIRMAN/PRINCIPAL

1.0 *PURPOSE:*
1.1 To develop in children an enthusiasm for physical activity and to maintain and encourage that enthusiasm so that they become committed to pursuing an active lifestyle.
1.2 To develop and maintain self-esteem, self-confidence, team-spirit and physical fitness.
1.3 Sportsmanship, self-improvement and attitudes to be emphasized.

2.0 *BROAD GUIDELINES:*
2.1 To achieve our principle aim we shall endeavour to develop our specific aims by involvement in:–
fitness and skill components in Dance, Gymnastics, Games, Water Safety, Swimming and survival skills.
2.2 Students will develop and maintain physical fitness (Huff 'n Puff Program).
2.3 Develop the skills needed to control and manage the body and to be able to move to a variety of rhythms.
2.4 Develop pupils' bodies, with particular emphasis on improving strength, joint mobility, balance, co-ordination and posture.
2.5 Develop good judgement and co-ordination in the basic physical skills associated with the use of small equipment.
2.6 Develop confidence in ball control skills in a wide range of games situations.
2.7 Develop an awareness and understanding of the elements of team play and good sportmanship.
2.8 Develop knowledge of rules and strategies appropriate for a variety of games.
2.9 Develop confidence in, on, under and around water.

3.0 *PLANS FOR IMPLEMENTATION:*
3.1 A P.E. specialist (.5) will provide each class with one (1) 30 min. physical education session per week.
3.2 Each class teacher will be responsible for the continuation of P.E. on a regular basis with own class.
3.3 All teachers will follow the South Australian Daily Physical Education Lesson Plans in accordance with their own and their children's needs. This program to be stored in Teachers' Reference section of library.
3.4 Fitness activities of fifteen mins. duration will be conducted on a daily basis by P.E. specialist and/or class teacher.
3.5 Swimming lessons of 10 sessions a year, will be conducted throughout the school by qualified 'private' instructors for all children.
3.6 A perceptual motor program will be conducted at Prep level for 1½ hours per week by class teacher in first and second terms.
3.7 The P.E. specialist will be responsible for the purchase, maintenance, storage and distribution of materials, equipment and resources.
3.8 Children will have approximately 2–3 hours of P.E. per week.
3.9 Sport will be conducted in the 5–6 area at a district level. Sports practice of 1 hr. per week additional to P.E. lessons and fitness activities. Teams should be selected on the basis of encouraging participation rather than only the most capable being chosen.

4.0 *RESOURCES REQUIRED:*
4.1	Physical Education materials and equipment (Replacement and new additional)	400.00
4.2	Purchase of resource materials (e.g. Sth Aust. Lesson Plans/Games Books/ Kanga Cricket etc.)	400.00
4.3	Swimming (refer S.G.P.)	3200.00
		$4000.00

5.0 *EVALUATION:*
5.1 Careful and continual observation of children's progress.
5.2 Note improvements in children's fitness, skills and attitude.
5.3 Each child should have an individual record card for recording progress and which can be used as the basis of a report to parents.

PROGRAM TEAM: D.A.; P.G.

Source: Kayak (1988).

Figure 11.7 *Program budgeting within a collaborative yet corporate and strategic management structure*

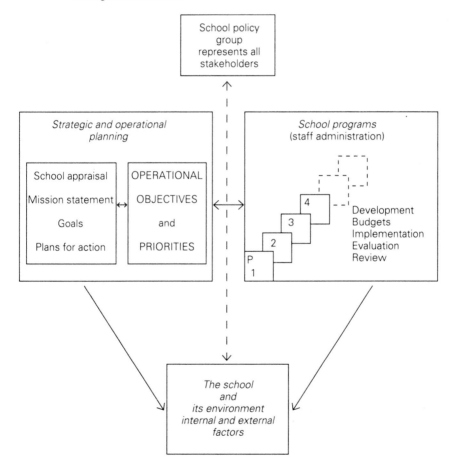

agement process implicit in program budgeting does provide a significant stimulus for schools to be self-directed, to be responsible to the stakeholders, to be accountable and yet to be so within a collaborative setting. It provides an appropriate strategy for educational improvement by enabling all stakeholders to have a role in decision-making and by ensuring that the decisions are 'owned' by all the stakeholders rather than being imposed from the top. The commitment to collaboration, for sharing and for interaction in all places of management process is much more likely to create a more demonstrable relevant education and one far more likely to influence in a positive fashion the life of the community it serves.

The approach also encourages and provides for the growing professional development of teachers. It asks for them to exercise their professional expertise and judgment. Yet it does so in a context which stresses the equality of colleagues and the importance of teamwork in the determination of final goals and plans.

In terms of responsiveness to change, program budgeting, once established, allows via its annual cycle of decision-making for schools to adapt more quickly and to respond to altered circumstances and changes in values (Kayak, 1988). Yet it encourages and allows for forward planning of curricula, it demands that schools recognize priority areas for development and, by placing high value on evaluation and linking that evaluation to the program objectives, ensures a professional rather than statutory concern for accountability. Of course, whether all of these potential benefits are realized will only become apparent some years from now. However, the introduction of program budgeting represents a major management change strongly underpinning the general move towards decentralization and devolution within the government school sector in Victoria towards the 1990s. That there are potential dangers is also true. It may well be that a school with the level of self-governance encouraged by, and implicit in, a program budgeting structure may become more restricted in its perspectives and outlook. However, provided that the curriculum support centres are maintained to provide some new input of ideas and stimulus, then such dangers are probably relatively small when weighed against the potential benefits.

Whilst the stress in this chapter has been on program budgeting strategies, it should also be clear that it argues most strongly for the integration of decision-making. Ultimately, resource management decisions are integral to, not separate from, decisions about educational goals, curriculum, student evaluation, etc. If we recognize the significance of this integration, we shall avoid the danger that the movement towards the 'business model' in educational management will place more stress on money than on people and learning. We must not allow the criticisms to develop of the type reported in 1986 in relation to school-based budgeting systems introduced in parts of British Columbia, Alberta and Ontario:

> Although School-Based Budgeting has been promoted as an answer to many of the problems faced by our school boards, the evidence suggests that it clearly is not.
>
> Our schools *do* have serious problems however. The answers to these problems, however, lie not in management systems designed to facilitate the imposition of fiscal restraint, but rather in the restoration of adequate funding levels and the development of new community-based structures to give parents more input into their schools.
>
> The introduction of business management techniques such as School-Based Budgeting only serves to worsen the problems facing our schools. (Calvert, 1986)

References

ADMINISTRATIVE STAFF COLLEGE (1988) *Observer Checklist-team Effectiveness Factors*, Working Papers. Mt Eliza, Vic.: Administrative Staff College.

BROWN, IONE (1983) 'Programming a School Budget: Principles and Techniques,' in FITZGERALD, R.T. (Ed.), *Budget Design and Education Policy*. Burwood: Victoria College.

CALDWELL, BRIAN, J. (1983a) *Program Budgeting at the School Level*. A workshop package. Hobart, Tas.: Centre for Education.

CALDWELL, BRIAN, J. (1983b) 'Resource Allocation at the School Level,' in FITZGERALD, R.T. (Ed.), *Budget Design and Education Policy*. Burwood: Victoria College.

CALDWELL, BRIAN, J. (1983c) *Corporate Planning Processes in Education*. Hobart: University of Tasmania, Centre for Education.

CALDWELL, BRIAN, J. and MISKO, J. (1984) 'School-based Budgeting: A Financial Strategy for Meeting the Needs of Student,' *Educational Administration Review*, 2, 1, pp. 29–59.

CALDWELL, BRIAN, J. and SPINKS, JIM, M. (1985) *Policy Making and Planning for School Effectiveness: A Guide to Collaborative School Management*. Hobart: Education Department of Tasmania.

CALDWELL, BRIAN, J. and SPINKS, JIM, M. (1988) *The Self-managing School*. Lewes: Falmer Press.

CALVERT, JOHN (1986) 'School-based Budgeting: "The Facts",' *Journal of Canadian Union of Public Employees*, 8, 5.

CHAPMAN, J. (1988) 'Decentralisation, Devolution and the Teacher,' *Journal of Educational Administration*.

CREED, PHILIP (1988) *Progress and Prospects in School-level Program Budgeting in Victoria*, State Board of Education Working Paper. Melbourne: State Board of Education.

FITZGERALD, R.T. (Ed.) (1983) *Budget Design and Education Policy*. Burwood: Victoria College.

HOUSE, ERNEST R. (1974) *The Politics of Educational Innovation*. Berkeley, Calif.: Mu-Cutchan.

HUFF, A.S. and RANNEY, J.M. (1981) 'Assessing the Environment for an Educational Institution,' *Long Range Planning*, 14, 3, 107–15.

HULLS, C.A. (1983) Risk and Receptivity Relating to Space Management Innovations in Tertiary Institutions. Unpublished PhD thesis, Monash, University, Melbourne.

HYMES, D.L. (1982) *School Budgeting: Problems and Solutions*, Sacramento, Calif.: Education News Services.

KAYAK, M. (1988) Introduction of Program Budgeting at Hawksburn Primary School, Unpublished Masters Paper, Monash University, Melbourne.

POLICY AND PLANNING UNIT (1984a) *Program Budgeting at School Level: A Resource Booklet*. Melbourne: Victorian Department of Education.

POLICY AND PLANNING UNIT (1984b) *Program Budgeting at School Level: A Supplementary Paper*. Melbourne: Victorian Department of Education.

POLICY AND PLANNING UNIT (1987) *Implementation of School-level Program Budgeting: Progress Report*. Melbourne: Ministry of Education, Victoria.

STATE BOARD OF EDUCATION, VICTORIA (1984) *Program Budgeting in Victorian Education*. Melbourne: Government Printer.

VICTORIA. TREASURER (1983) *Program Budget 1983–84*. 4 Vols. Melbourne: Government Printing Office.

Part 4

Research Findings

Part 4
Research Findings

Chapter 12

School-based Decision-making and Management: Implications for School Personnel

Judith D. Chapman

School-based Decision-making and Management in Australia

The Tradition of Centralism

In the state systems of education established in Australia in the late nineteenth century administation came to be characterized by a high degree of centralized control, a clearly defined hierarchy of authority and an extensive set of regulations designed to ensure uniformity and fairness in the provision of resources and services, together with efficiency and accountability in the management of schools.

Under these arrangements all major decisions, both professional and managerial, were made by senior officers of the education departments of each state. The state education department prescribed curriculum, enrolment procedures and school organization. Schools were evaluated annually by inspectors. The principal acted as an agent of the department, implementing policies and decisions made by officials in central office. Staff and parent involvement at the school level was limited. Pressure from interest groups was channelled through formal bodies of unions and parents who negotiated or consulted directly with the respective state minister or director general.

The Changing Context: The Commonwealth Role in Education

Since 1972 educational reform in Australia has been accompanied by a distinctive rhetoric centred on democratization and devolution (Blackmore, 1986). The Karmel Report (1973), considered among the most influential documents in the history of post-war education in Australia (Ashenden and Gallagher, 1980), established one of its principal values as the 'devolution of responsibility to schools'.

> The Committee favours less rather than more centralized control over the operation of schools. Responsibility should be devolved as far as possible upon the people involved in the actual task of schooling, in consultation with the parents of the pupils whom they teach and at the senior levels with the students themselves. Its belief in this grass roots approach to the control of schools reflects a conviction that responsibility will be most effectively discharged where the people entrusted with making decisions are also the people responsible for carrying them out, with an obligation to justify them and in a position to profit from their experiences. (Karmel, 1973, p. 10)

The Karmel Report proposed a multi-faceted response to the difficulties perceived to exist in the Australian schooling system. Among its recommendations were:

> an erosion of the monopoly of the state bureaucracies (largely through the establishment of the Commonwealth Schools Commission);
>
> a move towards decentralized and more personal styles of educational management; and
>
> a refurbishment of school syllabi and teaching styles, stressing relevance, child-centredness, personal development and more humane relationships between staff and students.

An era of reform and renewal of Australian schools emerged with the establishment of the Commonwealth Schools Commission in December 1973. Concerned to provide for the needs of the disadvantaged, to encourage diversity and innovation in schools, curricula and teaching methods, to promote public support for school improvement, and to promote economic use of resources (The Schools Commission Act, 1973), the Schools Commission supported a series of programs — such as the Priority Schools Program and the Innovations Program — which provided seed money to enable school staff, often with the assistance of community representatives, to identify school level priorities and to devise programs which more adequately met school-based needs.

Collaborative school level decision-making and the transformation of the quality of the educational experience through the improvement and development of school-based personnel were highlighted in a series of reports from the Schools Commission including *Educational Leadership for*

Responsive Schools (1985). These reports emphasized the images of 'adaptive', 'innovative' and 'responsive' schools characterized by leadership teams, collaborative school-based decision-making and local community involvement.

Although not a specific program for implementation, the Schools Commission also brought into national focus international developments in the field of school improvement which emphasized the school unit as the focus for change, and the empowerment of school-based personnel and the involvement in the decision-making process of all partners in the school community.

State Developments

In 1973, coinciding with the release of the Karmel Report and the creation of the Schools Commission, the establishment of the ACT Schools Authority provided for the first time in the Australian context a school system founded on respect for the principles of devolution and the involvement of members of the community in the decision-making of schools.

Contemporaneously, in some of the more established, traditional systems, policy-makers and administrators, recognizing that they were no longer providing effective administration for rapidly expanding and increasingly complex school systems, began to consider alternative forms of system organization and school administration. The most far-reaching changes in this regard were to be found in the state of Victoria.

In 1972 it became the Victorian Liberal Government's policy to decentralize administrative arrangements pertaining to education. This decentralization process had two dimensions. One was associated with the creation of regional directorates and the other with the granting of increased authority to the principals of schools. 'The central authority, the regional directors and school principals now share the total decision making arena which hitherto was the sole preserve of the central authority' (Mr T.J. Moore, Assistant Director of General Education, in Moore, 1975, p. 26).

Principals became responsible for the budgeting and accounting for equipment, furniture and fuel. In addition, they became responsible for determining staffing needs for instruction, support services and administration. The withdrawal of the Board of Inspectors in the secondary division also resulted in principals becoming responsible for the maintenance of staff discipline, reporting on unsatisfactory teachers and the maintenance of school standards.

In 1976 the enactment of the Education (School Councils) Act added another dimension to the administration of schools. The Act, which reformed the composition and function of school councils, reflected a new direction in government policy: the devolution of authority from the bureaucracy of the education department to the *community* of the school. Whilst the principal remained ultimately responsible for the determination of the school's educational policy, members of the school community as represented on council were, for the first time, given statutory authority to advise the principal on the development of that policy. Whereas prior to 1975 there was only limited interaction between the school and its community, after the passing of the Act it became councils' responsibility to ensure effective interaction, initially through the wider use of school facilities in the community's recreational, cultural and continuing education activities.

The passing of the Act, however, found many principals opposed to the reforms. The threat of more open structures and increased accountability, the suspicion that council members might use control over finance to become involved in the day-to-day running of the school, the fear of ideological influences and the loss of their recently gained but not inconsiderable autonomy caused disquiet to many (Fitzgerald and Pettit, 1978). Initially, despite the changes in structure and function introduced by the 1976 Act, some principals at least, through their control of the council agenda, their linguistic skills in persuading and influencing councillors, and their monopoly of information about the day-to-day operation and internal administration of the school, were able to ensure their dominance in relationships with council members (Gronn, 1979).

In 1981 a White Paper on restructuring the Victorian Education Department recognized some of the problems that had been encountered in the implementation of the original school councils legislation.

In 1981 and early 1982 there were massive structural changes consistent with the recommendations of the White Paper at the central and regional levels of the Victorian Education Department. But in the midst of these changes came a further dramatic upheaval. In the election of 1982 the Liberal Government was toppled from power after ruling Victoria for twenty-seven years. The new Labor Government halted further implementation of the recommendations of the White Paper and undertook a ministerial review of education. The results of that review were published in a series of ministerial papers in which the new government announced its intention to go well beyond the plan of the Liberal Government in terms of devolution of authority. It established as a major objective a shift in the focus of education to the school level. Embodied in the ministerial papers was the principle that all sections of the school community should work as partners in the interests of school and students. Particular emphasis was placed upon:

general devolution of authority and responsibility to the school community;

collaborative decision-making processes;

a responsive bureaucracy, with the main function of serving and assisting schools;

effectiveness of educational outcomes; and the active redress of disadvantage and discrimination.

In December 1983 the State Minister of Education released a statement on the *Role of Principals*. While reiterating the central role played by principals in the life and work of the school, the statement emphasized that 'this important leadership function is to be exercised in cooperation with the School Council and the staff of the school.' In the same year the Education Act was amended to provide that 'the School Council shall determine the general education policy of the school within guidelines issued by the Minister.' Contemporaneously, changes were made to the composition of school councils to provide for a higher proportion of teacher representation. These amendments placed a new emphasis on local responsibility and shared decision-making on educational policy matters.

In 1984 the role of the school council was extended further with the introduction of school council involvement in the selection of principals and deputy principals. In the same year, and as a result of negotiations between the unions and the department, it was announced that within each school administrative committees were to be established to offer advice to the principal on the implementation of the industrial agreement and on general school operations. Whilst principals retained the right of veto on the administrative committees, reasons were to be given for any advice that was disregarded.

On 11 November 1985 the Minister announced another major restructure of education with focus on coordination and devolution. The position and role of director general was abolished and replaced by the position of chief executive, responsible for coordinating the total educational portfolio. Simultaneously, five major investigations of various aspects of education were set in process. These culminated in mid-1986 with the publication of a series of reports: The Corporate Structures Report; The Structures Working Party Report; The Ministerial Statement on Post-Compulsory Education; The Re-organization of Schools Taskforce Report; and Taking Schools into the 1990s.

The '1990s Report' recommended the most complete school-based decision-making and management approach yet to be proposed for introduction into any Australian government system. When it was released in June 1986, however, the Report provoked an outcry from wide sections of the educational community.

The 'self-governing schools' recommended in the Report were to be funded on the basis of a single grant, which would cover all aspects of school operations excluding only major works and services. Functions to be performed by the self-governing school were to include:

determination of the school's educational policy and approach to curriculum development;

selection and promotion of teaching staff and approval of staff leave;

employment of consultants;

payment of salaries;

allocation of resources to best serve the need for curriculum development and review; and

management of the budget based on the school's assessment of its priorities.

Alarm at the radical nature of the proposals, resentment over the manner in which the Report was prepared, with little or no consultation with interest groups, and realization that self-governing schools would undermine the central bargaining powers of established interest groups were, however, to make inevitable the Report's rejection by an educational community totally unprepared for the reforms it proposed.

Nevertheless, by 1986, the Victorian education system had moved to more school-based decision-making and management than had hitherto been known in any school system in Australia. The implications of these changes, derived from research conducted in the Victorian setting, are the subject of the remaining sections of this chapter.

The Implications for School Leadership

A New Conception of the Principalship

As Kaufman (1977) has noted, one of the main effects of reorganization is to redistribute influence. In school systems which move to devolve more responsibility for decision-making and management to the school level substantial change is inevitable in this regard. Many relationships will be altered and many people will be forced to play new roles. This is clearly seen in the new conception of the principalship which has emerged in the school system of Victoria, Australia (Chapman and Boyd, 1986). Here, within a context of economic restraint and fewer resources for education, the principal has found him/herself working with new values, new decision-makers and a new set of management decisions and responsibilities. In this context the principal is no longer able to see him/herself as the authority figure, supported and at times protected by system-wide and centrally determined rules and regulations. Instead the principal must become a coordinator of a number of people representing different interest groups among the school community, who together will determine the direction the school is to follow. In the words of the past president of the Victorian Primary Principals Association, 'The Principal now becomes relocated from the apex of the pyramid to the centre of the network of human relationships and functions as a change agent and resource' (Wilkinson, 1983). The transition to this new conception of the principal's role, however, is not without difficulty.

Power and Authority

In the traditional, highly centralized systems of public education, evident in many countries, considerable power and authority have resided in the bureaucratic position of school principal. In the process of devolving more decision-making to the school level this bureaucratic authority may be severely eroded.

Initially, in Victoria, the most extreme response to the changed bases of the principal's power and authority was to interpret the decreasing importance attached to bureaucratic position as a complete diminution of the principal's power (Chapman and Boyd, 1986). Although this was not the case, the situation for principals functioning in a more school-based system can be paradoxical. Whilst principals become more visible and accountable to their local community, they remain the system's most senior officer in the school. This dual responsibility carries with it considerable role ambiguity. On the issue of accountability, for instance, many more traditional principals are likely to continue to defer to the central legal authority, steadfastly guarding their claim to 'ultimate' responsibility in the school; others may query, 'Who is the master to be?'

Not surprisingly, the confusion of principals confronting this issue will be exacerbated during the early stages of school-based management when they perceive their newly created councils or school-based committees as inexperienced and uninformed and when they find the central office transformed by new administrative arrangements and changed personnel who are possibly unknown and perhaps unable and/or unprepared to offer the support provided in the past by the 'centre'. The sense of isolation engendered by this situation is likely to become particularly acute on legally contentious issues or on problems that could involve industrial action.

Decision-making

In a school-based system the expanded role of 'councils' and other school-based decision-making committees, and the general expectation that, having been created, they will be consulted on a wide range of issues, operates to limit significantly the principal's decision-making discretion. At the same time, however, the principal's decision-making arena will be expanded as he/she is asked to make decisions in response to new questions. In answering these questions, however, principals will be working with new groups of people, new participants in the decision-making process. Often these new decision-makers will have different values from those possessed by principals and from those possessed by people with whom principals interacted in the past. Frustration at being forced to consult with younger, inexperienced teachers and resentment at being expected to assume responsibility for implementing decisions, determined by groups, which would not have been made by themselves, are the potential negative results.

Having been schooled in traditions where principals were expected to be prime sources of authority and decision-making at the school level, it is not surprising that many principals responsible for implementing school-based policies will not possess the skills to adapt to the new decision-making and management style. Unless adequate provision for professional development is provided by the system, the danger is that 'crisis management' will be the basis for professional development. Whilst on-site learning in response to immediate events is appropriate for some skill development, it is not sufficient for the thorough development of an overall philosophy or approach.

Of course, unless principals are properly prepared to facilitate participative decision-making, it is inevitable that they will encounter problems in managing the conflict which will arise when attempts at collaboration fail. Diminished bureaucratic authority and external support make it harder for principals to deal with such situations.

There are also problems for many principals of balancing collaboration with supervisory duties. It is often difficult for a principal to discipline a teacher in one context, with regard to student supervision for example, and then work again with that teacher on another matter in a collaborative setting. Wounds are frequently hard to heal!

Administrative Complexity

A multi-faceted system of education, in which resources and services are allocated from either centre or region and in which authority resides with both the official offices of 'the centre' and with the community of the school, offers considerable complexity for the principal. In Victoria, Australia, rather than facilitating the provision of services to schools, regional offices have frequently been considered by principals to be impediments to effective school management, placing another bureaucratic step in the process between the school and the central office.

In the initial stages of decentralization in Victoria this problem was compounded by a lack of clarity in respective roles and responsibilities. This frustration was exacerbated when principals were requested to duplicate effort in response to similar requests from both centre and region. This, in addition to the demands of the community, has meant that principals spend much of their time running to the behest of an assortment of agencies external to the school.

Internally, the plethora of committees will also contribute to organizational complexity. Principals must form, liaise and interact with consultative groups, attending not only to the interpersonal dynamics that such intensive interaction produces but also ensuring that, in the overall organizational design, overlapping functions are avoided and lines of communication are clear.

The Different Nature of Professional Life

Increased school management, as a result, dramatically alters the nature of the principal's professional life. Principals are forced to assume a more public role, interacting with people in the wider community, forging links with the school and its environment. In schools located in areas where parents are not accustomed to participating in school decision-making, principals must also assume an 'educative' role in respect to the public, increasing their awareness and facilitating their involvement in the processes of school decision-making and management. While such activities contribute to a more varied and fragmented professional life than experienced by principals in the past, they may also contribute to a greater incidence of stress. The high proportion of principals in Victoria taking sick leave and early retirement during the implementation of the devolution process is evidence in this regard.

School-based Principal Selection

In many countries throughout the past decade the selection of principals or school leaders has been the focus of considerable attention. The POST project (Morgan, Hall and McKay, 1983), funded by the Department of Science in the UK, the Baltzell and Dentler study (1983), funded by the National Institute of Education in the US, the Musella study in Canada (1983), the Hopes study (1985) in the Federal Republic of Germany and the Commonwealth Schools Commission study in Australia (Chapman, 1984a) have all highlighted the need for improvement in the practices employed in the selection of school principals. Of central concern in more decentralized systems has been the need to achieve some 'match' between the needs of the particular school and the skills, knowledge and attitudes of individual applicants.

In Victoria, Australia the provision for local school-based committees to select their principals and deputy principals has represented at a most practical and vitally significant level the effective devolution of decision-making from the central offices of the Education Department to the school. Overall this policy has received considerable support from the school community, with many school communities indicating that they have felt a greater commitment to their incoming 'leaders' as a result of participating in their selection. Notwithstanding this overall support, a review of the implementation of the policy does highlight some major concerns associated with devolving responsibility for the selection of school leadership to the level of the school (Chapman, 1986). Process issues, including lack of clarity and specificity in criteria, insufficient evidence, excessive emphasis on 'intuitive judgment' together with issues of principle, e.g. regarding confidentiality and equity, are among the major concerns.

The Implications for the Teaching Profession

The Individual's Sense of Efficacy

The theory of participatory democracy asserts that the major function of participation is an educative one, including the psychological aspect and the gaining of practice in democratic skills and procedures. As Pateman

(1970) points out, one of the most important correlations that has emerged from studies of political behaviours and attitudes is that between participation and the individual's sense of political efficacy/competence. People who have a sense of political efficacy are more likely to become involved in decision-making in the first instance and are more likely to gain from involvement in the longer term. Underlying this sense of political efficacy is a sense of general personal effectiveness which involves self-confidence in one's dealing with the world. Notwithstanding the importance of childhood experience and socialization in the family and at school, Almond and Verba (1968) suggest that crucial to the development of a sense of political efficacy are adult experiences, in particular the provision in the workplace of a structure of management which provides the opportunity to participate in the making of significant decisions.

Research (Chapman, 1988) clearly reveals the extent to which the experience of participation in school management can contribute to an increased sense of personal and political efficacy among a considerable number of teachers. Through participation teachers claim to have gained an increasing sense of mastery over the destiny of the school and of themselves in that school. Associated with the sense of mastery and control is the increasing sense of 'one's place' — one's identification and affinity with the school and with fellow teachers and parents. The sense of powerlessness and isolation which so many teachers, regardless of status, have traditionally experienced as a result of being an employee of a massive government bureaucracy would thus appear to have the potential of being considerably reduced.

Increased Trust in the Administration of the School

Together with an increasing sense of personal and political efficacy and a broadening of professional understanding, involvement in school decision-making and management has been found to have the potential to develop, among participants, an increased trust in the organization of the school. Associated with the increased trust is the knowledge that structures and mechanisms now exist to reduce excessive influence being exercised by the few. Staff now feel they have someone apart from the principal from whom they can acquire information. As information is now readily known and available through staff representatives, the matters which 'niggled and irritated', such as suspicions about inequitable allotments, are now less likely to 'explode'.

The development of trust in the organization and a belief in the individual's ability to influence that organization provides the basis for an improved relationship between principal and staff. In part this is the result of the improved dialogue, both formal and informal, between principal and staff, made necessary by the participatory decision-making process. Reduction in the 'them vs us' mentality is also the result of a wider range of staff becoming aware of the complexity of problems which have always challenged the administration of the school.

It is interesting to note Driscoll's findings (1978) that a more significant indicator of satisfaction in an organization is trust rather than level of participation. Paradoxically, one may well speculate that as a direct result of this increased trust derived from increased participation, individuals may feel less strongly about the need to participate in the decision-making process.

The Involvement-Influence Distinction

It should be emphasized, however, that the factors which have been found to enhance an individual's sense of efficacy, produce satisfaction and contribute to ongoing teacher involvement in school decision-making and management have been found to be significant only when teachers are confident that they do have influence over the important decisions that are made and implemented (Chapman, 1988). When teachers feel that their time is spent on decisions that are not important or decisions which will not be implemented due to constraints either internal or external to the school, frustration, disillusionment and at times cynicism result. The most immediate impact is experienced when constraints are imposed by principals at the school level. More significant in the longer term may be the constraints which are imposed by forces external to the school, especially those associated with the demands of a centralized system in a time of economic constraint.

The Costs of Involvement

Not all teachers will choose to become involved in decision-making and management at the school level. Chapman (1988) found that there are many teachers who, although they are not satisfied with the decisions made in their school, choose not to become involved in decision-making and management on the basis that the perceived costs of involvement exceed the benefits.

As Duke, Showers and Imber (1980) found, for teachers to choose to devote some of their professional time to participate in school decision-making, they have to view such participation as more rewarding than their teaching activity. For participation to be attractive for such a group, organizational arrangements must ensure that participation in decision-making does not detract from teaching.

The evidence is conclusive, however, that one of the most immediate costs of increased teacher involvement in school management is 'time'. For many teachers the additional time associated with committee work, and the need to balance priorities among administration, teaching and personal life contributes to increased tiredness and stress which in turn affect classroom practice and attendance. For some teachers, the response is to alter priorities, opting for the investment of time and energy in administration/decision-making at the expense of teaching. For others, the response is to opt out of decision-making, sometimes with the result that those 'less able' obtain committee membership by default. In this context the need for administrators to understand the 'zones of tolerance' of organizational members is clear.

One other disturbing effect of limited time is its impact on the decision-making process itself and the quality of the decisions made. When there are time constraints and difficulties associated with coordinating a wide range of people and organizing them to meet and achieve some agreement, it is often difficult to evaluate issues critically and to develop considered responses. Too often committees go for quick solutions, adapting and modifying but never really innovating (Chapman, 1988).

The Influence of the School Leader on Teacher Participation

Despite the provision of structures to enhance teacher involvement in decision-making and management, the evidence reveals that the influence of the principal remains fundamentally important in determining the extent, nature and pattern of teacher participation in the decision-making of schools. In the Australian context it has been found that the most widely representative committees evolve in schools where principals actively encourage participation, acknowledge individual contributions and ensure effective implementation of committee decisions. In direct contrast, in schools where principals are viewed as authoritarian in approach, despite democratic procedures and the electoral system, power tends to remain concentrated in the hands of a select few. Anger, cynicism, apathy and withdrawal characterize the responses of staff in such settings. This is consistent with the findings in California (Duke, Showers and Imber, 1980), where the establishment of formal groups and representative school governance bodies was found to promote teacher participation most successfully in those schools where principals supported the notion of shared decision-making. It also offers support for the Imber and Duke (1984) hypothesis that formal governance and decision-making committees tend not to be satisfying modes of participation in themselves unless there is an actual de jure transfer of power. Whilst principals have a right of veto, and readily exercise that veto, the potential for disillusionment and frustration with the participative process will always exist. This element can be addressed by school systems; more disturbing, however, is that Chapman's research also reveals the extent to which the principal determines participation through his/her interpersonal relationships with staff (Chapman, 1988). Those who relate best to the principal are most likely to become involved in school decision-making in the first instance and they are most likely to gain satisfaction from their participation in the longer term.

Whilst such positive feelings may be applauded, they may also contain within them a new 'circle of exclusion'. Among those who perceive themselves among the less powerful in the school, the existence of a principal operating in a selectively collaborative way and allied with a group of influential staff can in itself present a formidable threat. To ensure the widest possible level of representation and involvement, it would seem desirable, perhaps essential, that principals adopt an approach which avoids the perception of selective support and/or the existence of principal cliques.

Who among Teachers Participate and Why?

Gender.   Pateman in her introduction to Mason's book, *Participation and Workplace Democracy* (Mason, 1982), highlights the contrast between formal political equality and the substantive inequalities that structure social institutions. As Blackmore (1986) argues, patterns of participation are thus explained, not simply by formal access or the psychological attributes that motivate individuals to participate, but by social structures and institutional configurations which exclude those who are already powerless. In systems which have promoted increased teacher participation in decision-making this has worked to exclude women from a significant decision-making role. In the participatory decision-making structures introduced into the schools of Victoria, Australia, men not only hold the overwhelming majority of principal, deputy principal and senior teacher positions, but now also hold two-thirds of the positions in the decision-making committees of schools (Chapman, 1988). This existence of a gender imbalance in participation rates confirms trends from elsewhere. In the USA, for example, Alutto and Belasco (1972) found that women participate in decision-making less than men and desire lower levels of participation. Similarly, Riley (1984) found that men are more militant than women and are therefore more inclined to use the available avenues for participation at the school and district/regional level than are females. This has serious implications for system-wide educational policy, particularly at a time when concurrent with the implementation of increased school-based management some systems have been promoting policies of equal opportunity for female personnel.

Seniority and Organizational Responsibility. In an Irish study Conway (1976) found that the relationship between formal status and participation in school decision-making bodies, while positive and direct, was only a weak association. He suggested that position in the school hierarchy in Ireland, where length of service has been traditionally employed as the most important criterion for promotion, may best be viewed as an indicator of ascribed status which may not be congruent with social power or achieved status. A similar study conducted by Conway (1978) in England, where promotions are determined at the school level, found a stronger positive relationship between formal status and teacher participation in decision-making. In Australia somewhat more equivocal findings have emerged in respect to the relationship between seniority and administrative responsibility and patterns of participation in schools. No doubt, this is related to the existence of a two-tiered system for obtaining promotion and assuming responsibility. Traditionally, teachers received promotion in the government school system, largely on the basis of seniority. Alternatively, teachers can be allocated special duties or responsibilities in a particular school on the basis of assessments conducted by a panel, composed of the principal, the deputy principal and two peers.

The existence of this two-tiered system, which has emerged as a result of the attempts to integrate democratic school-based decision-making within a traditional bureaucratic system, has led to many serious tensions. Disrespect for senior personnel, whose power resides in formal status and 'seniority' rather than in commitment and expertise, has created the condition in some schools, where staff are using the democratic process deliberately to block the access of senior personnel to decision-making committees. This produces a 'rump' of senior, highly paid staff, frequently bitter and disgruntled and without a great deal of actual influence in the decision-making and management of the school.

Age and Teaching Experience. In Australia it has been found that the majority of teachers on decision-making committees are in the 30–40 age group. Similarly, in the US Alutto and Belasco (1972) found that teachers with between five and twelve years' experience are those desiring the highest levels of participation. Sergiovanni (1969) suggests that this constitutes the groups of teachers with the highest need deficiencies.

It should be noted, however, that in the Australian context the high proportion of teachers in this age group on school committees also reflects the high proportion of men and women in this age group in the teaching service. It is yet to be seen whether teachers, as they grow older in the teaching service, will relinquish their committee positions or hold on to them in quest of promotion, promotion which due to declining enrolments will come later in their careers but which due to changed criteria and selection procedures will place considerable value on participation in the decision-making committees of schools.

The Implications for the Teaching of the Educational Program

Although the direct impact on curriculum development is only beginning to emerge, increased school-based decision-making and management does appear to have some positive impact as more teachers are being forced to address issues, to consider alternatives and to establish and defend their positions (Chapman, 1988). The cross-faculty interaction arising from committee work focused on the school as a whole rather than subject or departmental concerns is reported to be of particular value in enabling people to gain a wider perspective on educational issues. Teacher involvement is also seen as enhancing curriculum development insofar as teachers are more committed to the curriculum decisions that are made.

These perceptions support the belief that there may be a direct positive relationship between increased school-based decision-making and improvements in educational outcomes. The argument is further strengthened if one considers the cognitive and motivational mechanisms by which participation has been conceived as affecting output in the business field (Locke and Scheiger, 1979). Predominant among the cognitive mechanisms are the increased information, knowledge and creativity brought to bear on decision-making, the greater understanding of decisions derived from enhanced goal clarity and the improved understanding of the reasons and methods for change. Among motivational mechanisms are increased feelings of trust, an increased sense of control and greater commitment.

There appears to be no direct and positive relationship, however, between teacher involvement in decision-making and management and improved teacher practice. In fact it has been suggested that the short-term impact of increased teacher participation in decision-making on face-to-face teaching may be more negative than positive as teachers report that involvement in committee work distracts teachers' energy away from teaching, correction and classroom practice (Chapman, 1988). Conway (1984), having reviewed the literature on this topic, concluded that some consultation is critical for quality teaching so that teachers are informed, but that participation should not create a situation in which the teacher is distracted from the teaching function. Similarly, from a student perspective, Greenblatt, Cooper and Meeth (1983) in a study of the relationship between participation and quality teaching found that students identified as effective those teachers who were freed to teach rather than expected to perform administrative tasks.

The Implications for Relationships between the School and the Community

The Distribution of Power

In North America, where members of the community have traditionally participated in district level decision-making, the relationship between the professional educators and members of school boards has been the subject of considerable investigation. The difficulties in reconciling the seemingly inherent tension between representation and administration, democracy and efficiency has been acknowledged as a major factor contributing to the relationship's problematic nature. Despite a long tradition of community participation in North America, considerable research suggests that a hierarchical model of decision-making based on professional values and technical authority prevails (Zeigler and Jennings, 1974).

Initially, with the creation of school councils in Australia, the threat of more open structures and increased accountability, the suspicion that council members may use control over finance to become involved in the day-to-day running of the school, the fear of ideological influences and the loss of their not inconsiderable autonomy caused disquiet to many school principals (Fitzgerald and Pettit, 1978). Despite legislation, some principals at least, through their control of the council agenda, their linguistic skill in persuading and influencing councillors and their monopoly of information about the day-to-day operation and internal administration of the school, were able to ensure their dominance in relations with council members (Gronn, 1979).

More recent research (Chapman, 1984b), however, informed by the more complex model of relationships between professional educators and members of the community, developed by Boyd (1975) and stressing the importance of both 'community derived' and school-system professional forces when analyzing the social control of public education, suggests that in council operation the desire to exercise control shifts with the nature of the issue under consideration. Thus for principals, a perceived challenge to their authority is likely to bring forward a mobilization of their power resources. Similarly, in matters of finance and information transmission community members are likely to exercise more power than they may otherwise do during the course of council operations. Furthermore, personal factors (sex, age, educational level, occupational status) will affect the degree of control which community members exhibit. In addition, conditions associated with the school itself (the extent to which it is considered successful in the achievement of its educational goals and the extent to which it is seen as maintaining effective interaction with its community) together with conditions internal to the operation of council (people's satisfaction with council operation and their satisfaction with the relationship between the principal and council members) will affect attitudes to participation and control.

Who among the Community Participate in School Management and Whom Do They Represent?

School councils or boards throughout the world have been found to be composed of occupational elites. Individuals, involved in the education profession but serving on boards/councils in their capacity as community representatives, also tend to be overrepresented in proportion to their numbers in the community (Charters, 1953; Ornstein, 1981; Chapman, 1984b).

As Stroud (1986) points out, one of the consequences of this elite occupational composition is the increased availability of leadership and management skills. This may make the work of the school administration more effective, but it also ensures that the actions of the professional educators are more open to scrutiny.

In association with the high representation of people from professional and managerial occupations, research has revealed that council/

board members tend to have a level of education which is higher than the average for the community served (Zeigler and Jennings, 1974; Chapman, 1984b). Research is somewhat contradictory in its finding as to the impact this has on council board operation. In the US setting Gross (1958) found a positive relationship between the educational level of board members and their adherence to 'professional standards' and a professional orientation suggesting that such members tend to take on the public relations function of promoting the school in the community rather than representing community views to the professional educators. In contrast, in Australia this group was found to be least susceptible to professional control. It is interesting to note that Kerr (1964) found that dependence on professional educators had the effect of reducing pressure for meaningful educational change.

Discussion: Learning from the Australian Experience

The problems encountered in the introduction of increased school-based decision-making and management in Victoria, Australia have in large measure an historical basis. From 1872 to 1968 the education system had operated on the principles of centralized bureaucracy. School personnel had been schooled in this tradition, they had undertaken their initial teacher training and received their early professional experience within this context.

The year 1979 heralded the first major shift to a more decentralized system. With virtually no additional preparation or training, principals were told to 'run their own schools'. Heavily reliant upon departmental support, principals came to expect to be the prime decision-makers and ultimate source of authority within schools. They adjusted to the new role with varying degrees of success.

The years 1981 through 1984 saw two successive governments conduct major reassessments of the education system. Poised to implement its policy of decentralization and devolution at the school level and having already effected changes at the centre and region, the Liberal Party was ousted after twenty-seven years of state government. On coming to power, the Labor Government faced the problem that there was no strongly articulated majority sentiment for devolution and school-based management. At the grass roots teachers and parents seemed to be either ambivalent or only mildly supportive, whilst many principals were openly opposed. Moreover, when the time came to devolve further powers to schools, even the union and parent leaders became less enthusiastic when they recognized that school-based management ran counter to the interests they had developed in centralized bargaining power.

An enormous amount of momentum is needed to change a large education system. Changed administrative arrangements require that an entirely new communication network be established. The new 'appropriate' people must be identified, working relationships must be built up. New values require that the heritage, the folklore, the understandings of people must be reassessed; this within a context where many people are experiencing some personal and professional threat and insecurity.

Notwithstanding the problems associated with the implementation of any system-wide change, much of the confusion and anxiety associated with the Victorian experience of increased school-based management must be directly attributed to the nature of the implementation process. Although the devolution effort accomplished part of its objective to share decision-making more broadly, it is clear that the implementation of the plan suffered from a gross neglect of the need for retraining and in-service activities designed to foster the learning of the new attitudes and roles that were fundamental to the new style of decision-making and management that was mandated.

Further, the entire process took place with considerable haste, placing enormous pressures on people's energy level and time. Sources of power and authority that were evident under the traditional bureaucratic arrangements were not precisely transformed or delegated, and new sources of authority and power were unclear. School personnel could no longer act with the certainty of the past. In addition, the advantages of a school-based approach were at no time adequately communicated in sufficient detail to enable school-based personnel fully to understand and accept the policy. People's fears of the new and unexplored were never significantly allayed.

Finally, whilst in the North American experience of school-based management the principal was acknowledged as pivotal to success, in Victoria the government's perceived disrespect for principals severely limited the degree to which the policy was implemented at the school level. Whilst in the tradition of the Education Department, many assumed 'their duty' to implement the plan, the trust, commitment and ownership, so lauded as outcomes of teacher and parent participation at the school level, were never developed among principals by their own participation in the development of the devolution plan. With their sense of loyalty and identity with 'the system' undermined, the successful implementation of school-based decision-making and management could never be assured.

Future Trends

Throughout this decade educational theorists and researchers have promoted the notion that a school that was relatively autonomous, self-appraising and aware of its own strengths and weakness was most able to address problems of quality (OECD, 1987, p. 3). In many countries the effective implementation of increased school-based decision-making and management would have required a radical reshaping of the relations between the centre and the periphery of the education system and consequently a revision of the principles governing the organization and operation of schools. In this chapter the implications of this reshaping, based on research conducted in school systems where reorganization has taken place, have been explored.

In more recent times, however, some nations have switched to a more specific, direct and short-term approach to 'quality' issues. In many countries the most recent educational debate has been conducted in a context of alarm regarding the state of the economy and national competitiveness. Whilst there has been no proven relationship between educational achievement measured by specific tests and international productivity comparisons, in some countries education has received much of the blame for the nation's relatively poor economic performance in respect to productivity, product quality and technical development (Clayton Felt, 1985). The 'language of crisis and mobilization in the face of threats to national survival' (Seddon *et al.*, 1990), as highlighted in reports such as *The Nation at Risk* in the US (1983) and the *QERC Report* in Australia (Quality of Education Review Committee, 1985), reflects the concerns of politicians and policy-makers operating in an economic context which forces governments to question the nature and cost of existing educational services. Associated with these demands has been an increased demand for public accountability, and the emergence of a new group of interests and agencies, who with their own assessments of education and training needs arising from structural changes in the economy, industry and the international economic environment, have driven the educational debate towards a redefinition of the main objectives and outcomes of education from a fundamentally utilitarian and instrumental philosophy.

In response, central administrations in some countries have moved towards placing a greater emphasis on:

setting quality targets and providing the means to attaining them;
monitoring the implementation of the appropriate strategies;
conducting appraisals of performance.

In the immediate future the challenge facing many countries is to resolve the dilemmas and the unquestionable tensions which exist between an emphasis on improvement through increased school-based decision-making and management and the emerging political concern for centrally determined quality control.

References

ALMOND, G., and VERBA, S. (1968) *The Avec Culture.* Boston, Mass.: Little-Brown.

ALUTTO, J. and BELASCO, J. (1972) 'A Typology for Participation in Organizational Decision Making,' *Administrative Science Quarterly,* 17, 1, 117–25.

ASHENDEN, D. and GALLAGHER, M. (1980) 'The Political Context in Australian Schooling,' Discussion Paper. Canberra: ACT Schools Authority.

BALTZELL, C. and DENTLER, R. (1983) *Selecting American School Principals: Research Report.* Washington, D.C.: National Institute of Education.

BLACKMORE, J. (1986) 'Tensions in Participation and School Based Decision Making,' *Educational Administration Review,* 4, 1, 29–48.

BOYD, W. (1975) 'School Board-Administrative Staff Relationships,' in CISTONE, PETER, J. (Ed.), *Understanding School Boards,* Lexington, Mass.: Heath.

CHAPMAN, J. (1984a) *The Selection of Australian School Principals.* Canberra: Commonwealth Schools Commission.

CHAPMAN, J. (1984b) 'Towards an Understanding of Administrator Dominance,' *Educational Management and Administration,* 12, 167–80.

CHAPMAN, J. (Ed.) (1986) *School Council Involvement in the Selection of Administrators.* Geelong: Institute of Educational Administration.

CHAPMAN, J. (1987) *The Victorian Primary School Principal: The Way Forward.* Report to the Victorian Primary Principals Association.

CHAPMAN, J. (1988) 'Teacher Participation in the Decision Making of Schools,' *Journal of Educational Administration,* 26, 1, 39–72.

CHAPMAN, J. and BOYD, W. (1986) 'Decentralization, Devolution and the School Principal: Australian Lessons on Statewide Educational Reform,' *Educational Administration Quarterly,* 22, 28–58.

CHARTERS, W. (1953) 'Social Class Analysis and the Control of Public Education,' *Harvard Education Review,* 24, 268.

CLAYTON FELT, M. (1985) *Improving Our Schools.* Mass.: Education Development Centre Inc.

CONWAY, J. (1976) *Organizational Structures and Teacher Participation in Decision Making in Selected Schools in Ireland.* Social Sciences Research Centre, Monograph 8. Galway, Ireland: Social Sciences Research Centre.

CONWAY, J. (1978) 'Power and Participatory Decision Making in Selected English Schools,' *Journal of Educational Administration,* 16, 1.

CONWAY, J. (1984) 'The Myth, Mystery and Mastery of Participative Decision-making in Education,' *Educational Administration Quarterly,* 20, 3, 11–40.

DRISCOLL, J. (1978) 'Trust and Participation in Organizational Decision Making as Predictors of Satisfaction,' *Academy of Management Journal,* 21, 1, 44–56.

DUKE, D., SHOWERS, B. and IMBER, M. (1980) 'Teachers and Shared Decision

Making: The Costs and Benefits of Involvement,' *Educational Administration Quarterly*, 16, Winter, 93–106.

FITZGERALD, R. and PETTIT, D. (1978) *The New Schools Councils*. Burwood Monograph Series No. 3. Burwood State College.

GREENBLATT, H.R., COOPER, B. and MEETH, R. (1983) 'School Management and Teacher Effectiveness: Finding the Best Style,' Paper presented at Annual Conference of the American Educational Research Association, Montreal.

GRONN, P. (1979) The Politics of School Management. Unpublished doctoral thesis, Monash University, Melbourne.

GROSS, N. (1958) *Who Runs Our Schools?* New York: Wiley and Sons.

HOPES, C. (1985) *Auswahl und Ausbildung von Schullectern in Hessen*. Frankfurt am Main: Deutsches Institut für Internationale Pädagogische Forschung.

IMBER, M. and DUKE, D. (1984) 'Teacher Participation in School Decision Making: A Framework for Research,' *Journal of Educational Administration*, 22, 1.

KARMEL, P. (1973) *Schools in Australia*. Canberra.

KAUFMAN (1977) 'Reflections on Administrative Re-organization,' in PEAKMAN, JOSEPH, E. (Ed.), *Setting National Priorities: The 1978 Budget*. Washington, D.C.: The Brookings Institute.

KERR, W. (1964) 'The School Board as an Agency of Legitimation,' *Sociology of Education*, 38, 34–59.

LOCKE, E. and SCHWEIGER, O. (1979) 'Participation in Decision Making: One More Look,' *Research in Organizational Behaviour*, 1, 265–339.

MASON, R. (1982) *Participation and Workplace Democracy. A Theoretical Development in the Critique of Liberalism*. Carbondale, Ill.: Southern Illinois University Press.

MOORE, T. (1975) 'Administration in the Late 1970's. Proceedings of a Seminar for Principals and Senior Teachers.' *Continuing Education Centre, Wangaratta, Victoria*, Series 3, No. 1, 1975, p. 26.

MORGAN, C., HALL, V. and McKAY, H. (1983) *The Selection of Secondary School Headteachers*. Milton Keynes: Open University Press.

MUSELLA, D. (1983) *Selecting School Heads*. Toronto: Ontario Institute for Studies in Education.

NATIONAL COMMISSION ON EXCELLENCE IN EDUCATION (1983) *A Nation at Risk*. Washington, D.C.: Government Printing Office.

OECD. EDUCATIONAL COMMITTEE. (1987) *Quality of Schooling: A Clarifying Report*. Paris: OECD.

ORNSTEIN, A. (1981) 'Composition of Boards of Education in Public School Systems,' *Urban Education*, 16, 232–4.

PATEMAN, C. (1970) *Participation and Democratic Theory*. London: Routledge and Kegan Paul.

QUALITY OF EDUCATION REVIEW COMMITTEE (1985) *Quality of Education in Australia (QERC Report)*. Canberra: Australian Government Publishing Service.

RILEY, D. (1984) 'Teacher Utilization of Avenues for Participatory Decision Making,' *Journal of Educational Administration*, 22, 1.

SCHOOLS COMMISSION (1985) *Educational Leadership for Responsive Schools*. Canberra: Commonwealth Schools Commission.

SEDDON, T., ANGUS, L. and POOLE, M. (1990) 'Pressures on the Move to School-based Decision-making and Management,' in CHAPMAN, J.D. (Ed.), *School-based Decision-making and Management*. Lewes: Falmer Press.

SERGIOVANNI, T. (1969) 'Factors Which Affect Satisfaction and Dissatisfaction of Teachers,' in CARVER, F. and SERGIOVANNI, T. (Eds), *Organizations and Human Behaviour: Focus on Schools.* New York: McGraw-Hill.

STROUD, T. (1986) 'School Councils: The Professional Educator and the Community Members in the Governance of Schools,' PhD Colloquium Paper, Monash University, Melbourne.

WILKINSON, V. (1983) *President's Report.* Primary Principals, VPPA, 1, 19.

ZEIGLER, L.H. and JENNINGS, M.K. (1974) *Governing American Schools.* North Scituate, Mass.: Duxbury Press.

ZEIGLER, H., TUCKER, H.J. and WILSON, L.A. (1977) 'Communication and Decision Making in American Public Education: A Longitudinal and Comparative Study,' in SCRIBNER, J.D. (Ed.), *The Politics of Education.* Chicago, Ill.: University of Chicago Press.

Chapter 13

School-based Decision-making and Teacher Unions: The Appropriation of a Discourse

Jill Blackmore

This chapter analyzes the activity of teachers and more specifically teacher unions in policy-making in education in the state of Victoria, Australia, since the 1970s. It argues that the increase in teacher union participation in policy and decision-making, the consequence of numerous administrative restructurings and teacher activism since the 1970s, indicates an ongoing process of democratization in educational decision-making. This reorganization has focused on schools as the unit of decision-making, and encouraged the representation of various interests (students, parents, teachers, business, community) on school-based administrative and curriculum committees, local school councils, regional boards and state level policy-making bodies. The chapter looks to contextualize the emergence of school-based decision-making and management as a form of democratic educational governance in Victoria during the 1970s and to consider how the school-based decision-making and management discourse has been co-opted by corporate managerialism since the mid-1980s.

Three ideological positions constituted a discourse of 'participatory' school-based decision-making which emerged during the 1970s. These positions were not necessarily mutually exclusive nor only associated with particular social groups. One perspective, perhaps best represented by the Victorian state Labor Party educational policy committee, the now defunct independent advisory Australian Commonwealth Schools Commission and parent organizations, suggests that the educational bureaucracy would be more egalitarian and responsive to the community through the active participation of parents, teachers and students (Johnston, 1983; Tanner, 1983). A second ideological strand focused on the notion of the ability of teachers to make decisions about their work on the grounds of professional expertise, a position strongly held by teacher unions (Hannan, 1985). The third strand drew from orthodox organizational theory regarding the value of participative decision-making as a strategy of control favourable to middle and central management (Blackmore, 1986). Each ideology displayed different views on the relationship between capital and labour, democratic theory and anticipated educational outcomes. Each position had political, professional and strategic implications for teachers. At the same time there was a common thread emphasizing the value of participatory democratic processes throughout this earlier discourse surrounding school-based decision-making (Blackmore, 1986).

In the 1980s government reports throughout Australia have also focused upon the school as the unit of decision-making, but within a framework of corporate management. Policy statements such as *Better Schools for WA* (Western Australia, Ministry of Education, 1987), *Towards the 1990's* (Northern Territory, 1987) and *Into the 1990's* (Victoria, Ministry of Education, 1985) utilize the language of collaborative decision-making whilst effectively rendering school-based decision-making outside the control of teacher unions, local bodies and the majority of parents by other centralizing tendencies (national curriculum, assessment procedures, funding). School-based decision-making in this form ultimately serves particular managerial and class interests. Although the language of parental choice and community is evident in the plethora of government reports, they are within a broader frame of entrepreneurial local schools, incentives and markets. The most extreme example of this more conservative interpretation of school-based decision-making is the Baker Bill introduced by the Thatcher Government in 1987 in Great Britain. This Bill allows state funded schools to opt out of the local education system and 'go it alone' whilst retaining per capita funding from the national government. Such a policy effectively disenfranchizes a wider representation of parents, teachers and students in determining resource allocation and educational values but embodies popular notions of choice and community (see Sallis, 1988; Western Australia, Ministry of Education, 1987). This signifies a shift in the discourse surrounding school decision-making away from an earlier focus around the key concepts of collaboration and participation.

In a period of expansion in educational provision this earlier view of school-based decision-making and management was adhered to by an uneasy alliance between advocates of industrial democracy, professional autonomy and more humanistic administration. In a period of a crisis of contraction in the 1980s the tension between the underlying democratic and political motivations has brought about new discursive formations. The earlier conception of participation has been 'captured' since the mid-1980s by corporate managerialists who redefine the concepts of participation and collaboration at school level in economic rationalist terms by shifting the focus of the discourse onto new concepts of account-ability, parental choice, efficiency and effectiveness.

Theoretical Comments

Any analysis of the effect of structural change on social and political relations must involve consideraton of the socio-political and economic arrangements in a wider historical context. Habermas argues that there are 'crisis tendencies' in advanced capitalism rooted in the economy and the administration, as well as crisis tendencies in legitimation and motiva-tion. That is, these 'tendencies' are no longer located immediately in the economic sphere but also in the socio-cultural sphere because 'the prob-lem, in short, is to distribute socially produced wealth inequitably and yet legitimately' (McCarthy, 1984, p. 358). Gramsci also emphasizes socio-cultural relations. He argues that dislocations in economic and cultural experiences brought about by structural change since the 1960s have resulted in a crisis in the 'ideological hegemony' of ruling interests (Gramsci, 1971). Johnston expands on Gramsci's argument:

> Over long periods, the dominant groups in the social formation, through their control of economic and cultural production, lay down hegemonic beliefs and practices that become sedimented into commonsense knowledge. At any one time, particular indi-viduals or groups draw upon this armory of words and social images to develop particular forms of public representations. These articulated discourses are mediated through institutions such as the media, church and university into the public arena. At times of social and economic dislocation, they hook into hegemo-nic meanings at the level of popular belief and experience and gain the consent of subordinate groups in society. (Johnston, 1987, p. 3)

As the notion of a national economic crisis comes to be assumed in popular common sense, it provides a rationale for the need to renegotiate political and social arrangements, whilst redefining the boundaries, key concepts and issues of that debate.

In Australia the economic crisis of the 1980s has been manifested in the articulation of a perceived crisis in education which has been created and defined by the New Right, but which has gained wider credibility within both political parties, the Labor Party and the Liberal (conserva-tive) Party. In turn, this 'crisis' has provided a justification for the reorganization of schooling to make it more efficient and effective (Johnston, 1987). Central themes in the discourse of educational reform are the 'market' and 'user pays' which focus on concepts of choice, individualism and excellence. Such concepts are well embedded in liberal democratic theory, and fit with a particular view of democratic process. The difference lies in the way in which participation is conceptualized. The emergent discourse of educational reform of the 1980s, which focuses upon school-based decision-making, is based upon what Pateman calls elitist notions of democracy rather than participatory notions (Pateman, 1970). Whilst Victoria could be seen to be unique in terms of the extent to which participation and collaboration between teachers, parents and government in policy-making at the school level has developed in practice, it is worthwhile to consider some commonalities, in particular the 'crisis in state education' (see Sallis, 1988; Wexler and Grabiner, 1986).

Wexler and Grabiner depict a primary contradiction in the 'rightist social movement' in the USA which is reflected in a similar educational discourse around the need for the reorganization of public education. On one side is the language of the *market* which stresses laissez-faire arrangements, gives pre-eminence to individual freedom and encourages the commodification of social relations. On the other side is a language of *morality* which appeals to social integration, minimizes diversity and wishes to restore the patriarchal family. Both can be attributed to different class factions and social groups. Whilst the language of morality is less obvious in the Australian reform rhetoric, perhaps with the exception of Queensland, the dominance of economistic views of education using the language of the market has strong parallels (Scott, 1980). Furthermore, Wexler and Grabiner's view that a particular political formation, that of corporatism, is evident in the sectoral reorganization of education in America has application in Australia. The importance of corporatism as a social form in this context, according to Wexler and Grabiner, is that it resolves this contradiction in the short term 'in that it surpasses or supersedes the contradiction with a higher and less democratic form of capitalism' — a view of representative rather than participatory democracy (Wexler and Grabiner, 1986, pp. 14–16). The marketization of education is further legitimated by the reassertion of the need for standards and accountability in education.

Political formations which have become evident in the state of Victoria since the 1970s can also fit the 'corporatist model'. There has been an ongoing process of 'incorporation' of teacher unions, union representatives as well as individual teacher unionists into governmental and policy-making processes. According to Panitch, the 'corporatist' model is 'a political structure in advanced capitalism which integrates organised socio-economic producer groups through a system of representation and co-operative mutual interaction at the leadership level and mobilisation and social control at the mass level' (Bowen cited by Panitch, 1977). The corporatist model is characterized by collective agreements concluded among organized and voluntaristic 'communities of interest' centred on the interaction of central trade unions and business organizations in national planning and incomes policy. Thus it appears not to be state imposed, but merely state coordinated. The collaboration between corporate capitalists and corporate labour representatives appears to be among equals (Wexler and Grabiner, 1986, p. 15). Triado argues that corporatism is a response to the problems of governability created by increasingly complex situations and administrative overload (Triado, 1984, p. 37). In the Victorian instance the administrative resolution which meets such contradictions is that of structural decentralization which focuses upon the school as the unit of decision-making. This effectively incorporates local and central interest groups into the decision-making process whilst maintaining control by the state through other centralizing mechanisms, such as program budgeting and perfomance indicators (Pusey, 1981; Johnston, 1987).

This incorporation has produced dilemmas for teacher union leaders at both the centre and in schools. First, it has widespread political consequences for teacher unionism in general in terms of their relationship with the state, union organization and rank and file support (Goldman and van Houten, 1977). Ironically, whilst teacher control of their workplace has been facilitated by the move towards school decision-making and management, this process of incorporation has effectively quieted their opposition. The extent to which the institutionalization of democratic decision-making procedures at school level has produced a more equitable distribution of power in schools, given the external, system level constraints, is questionable (Watkins, 1988). Instead, there exists a feeling of malaise and professional powerlessness amongst government school teachers at the school level despite the moves towards greater administrative decentralization.

Second, the rhetorical links between school-based decision-making and management, professionalism and teacher unionism are highly problematic. School-based decision-making and management based on market rather than participatory principles has unfortunate implications for teacher professionality and autonomy. One explanation may lie in determining how the ideology of professionalism has the potential either to emancipate or to disempower teachers in particular historical contexts (Lawn, 1985; Grace, 1985). As yet the notions of school-based decision-making and participation have become, in the context of the late 1980s, a controlling rather than liberating force over teachers and state education, even to constitute a threat to the very existence of a state system. This is not irreversible. Teachers and their unions can, within their own particular school sites, maintain and/or regain the more democratic and participative connotations of school-based decision-making and management which have been practised, albeit with some difficulty and with differing degrees of success, since the mid-1970s.

Given this theoretical starting point, this chapter goes on to discuss, first, how the justification for restructuring of education in Victoria since the early 1970s has taken up this particular strategy of voluntaristic 'representation' (whether of parent, teacher, or business interest groups) through emerging 'corporatist' structures. Second, it considers why this reorganization has taken on a particular administrative form of school-based decision-making and management. Despite the specificity of the Victorian situation in terms of its industrial relations and school governance, this analysis is readily linked to trends in other Australian states, the USA and the UK in response to perceived crises in public education. First, there is a tendency towards corporatist strategies in the USA and a 'disintegration' of corporatist structures in the UK (Wexler and Grabiner, 1986; Sharp, 1986). Second, there is the move in the UK to a philosophy of educational marketing as embodied in self-governing institutions whilst facilitating unprecedented state intervention in education in the form of a national curriculum and the funding of self-governing schools (Sharp, 1986).

School-based Decision-making and Participation: Three Interwoven Strands

Participation in decision-making has a long history in organizational and political theory (Pateman, 1970). In Victorian state education it is a more recent phenomenon. Historically, the state system has excluded the community from involvement in schools by a highly centralized bureaucratic structure. There has been a redistribution of power over policy among professional interests (teachers, union officials and bureaucrats) since the Second World War. In part this is due to the 'professionalization' of teaching (in the conventional sense of upgrading qualifications, extending training and gaining control of the professional knowledge base), the increasing complexity of administration and the growing disillusionment within the community over the ability of experts, either educational or administrative, to solve social problems (Bessant and Spaull, 1976, pp. 191–3; Larson, 1977).

Since the 1960s teachers have gained greater autonomy in classrooms with the demise of direct supervision by inspectors (Connell, 1985; Lortie, 1975). Whilst teacher unions were able to negotiate with the director general and minister on salaries and conditions through formal and quasi-legal channels until 1982, political pressure by community (largely represented by white and some blue collar wage-earners) was limited to delegation by representatives of voluntarist associations such as the Victorian Council of State School Organizations, the Parents' Federation of Victoria and employer interest groups such as the Chamber of Commerce and the Employers' Federation. Prior to the 1970s locally elected school councils and parent associations served primarily in a fund-raising capacity at school level, and were merely one of the various bodies which could petition the Minister. Policy was largely in the hands of the central educational administrators (the director general and the inspectors).

The rapid expansion of secondary education in the 1960s brought a crisis in the provision of secondary education by the mid-1960s. This led to increased teacher union activity, particularly by the more militant post-primary teacher unions, the Victorian Secondary Teachers Association (VSTA) and Technical Teachers Union of Victoria (TTUV). Union activity encouraged the upgrading of teacher qualifications (both pre- and post-entry), opposed inspection for teacher assessment and demanded improved working conditions with the view to improving 'professional status' through control of the workplace. The success of VSTA branch activity in individual schools over campaigns for control of entry and against inspection (1968–74) meant that what began as an industrial strategy became a principle of union organizational development. Thus the school developed as the unit of professional and autonomous decision-making. The strength of the union/school branch was maintained by the ability of representatives to act often more swiftly than principals or head office on matters of teacher welfare or to call disruptive stop-works.

During the 1970s it was the unions which took the policy initiative. Unions, often at branch level, were actively involved in policy formation and implementation on diverse issues ranging from sex and health education through to curriculum and assessment reform. The post-primary unions were particularly active in developing alternative modes of school organization, assessment and curriculum. For example, several Melbourne working-class schools established the STC (Schools Tertiary Entrance Certificate) as an alternative to the Higher School Certificate which was the selector used for tertiary entrance (Suggett, 1986; Fitzgerald *et al.*, 1977). The union essentially became the vehicle for the intellectual and professional energies of teachers, and influenced school policy through the dissemination of well-known publications such as *The Secondary Teacher* (later *The Victorian Teacher*) (Blackmore and Spaull, 1987, p. 211).

The evolution of policy at branch level and branch decision-making procedures had an impact upon the organizational and curriculum structures in schools during the early 1970s. In particular, the relationship between teaching staff and the school principals was openly questioned by such notions as that of replacing principals with a staff executive. Such proposals contested the paternalistic and authoritarian control of principals who were perceived to be the representatives of an inefficient, intransigent and insensitive educational bureaucracy. In principle, it claimed the right of staff members as professionals to determine the distribution and use of resources and personnel in schools. The principal was to 'fit' the school and not vice versa. The traditional hierarchical principal/staff relationship in schools was further challenged by the activity of staff associations which, with the influx of more highly qualified, specialist trained young staff into schools during the 1970s, became a powerful professional force for administrative and curriculum change in schools (Hannan, 1985). A third factor reducing principal control was the development of elected school committees during the 1980s which determined the allocation of school resources and staff and undertook peer evaluation. Finally, since 1983 principals have been selected by local selection committees appointed by school councils (Chapman, 1986). Whilst the increased push for greater professional control over the administration of schools confronted the very nature of traditional educational leadership in schools, it also opened up further questions regarding community involvement in school decision-making (Meier and Welsh, 1981, p. 187). The union view, although ready to consult with parents and community, tended to cast teachers as the 'experts' in the client-teacher relationship. As such, teachers were seen to be sufficiently capable of 'representing' the interests of students and parents in matters central to education: curriculum, school organization and resource allocation.

At the same time the socio-economic dislocation of the 1960s highlighted the contradictions between the rhetoric of equality and the existence of inequality and poverty in an apparently wealthy society. Whilst the 1960s saw the reappearance of child-centred, progressivist ideologies supported by a new class of educated professionals, it was also a period of intense activity of institutional pressure groups over the funding of education. As Johnston describes the period: 'Around the issues of funding, equality, and rich and poor schools, the parent and teacher groups took active positions in making education a key political issue' (Johnston,

1983, p. 21). The focus of this activity was the Australian Labor Party (ALP), which was, as an opposition party, susceptible in the late 1960s to the active alliance of parents, teachers, tertiary students and academics. In Victoria there was a networking of individuals between the Victorian ALP Policy Committee, Parent Federation and teacher unions (Tanner, 1983). By 1972, when Whitlam won government as leader of the Federal Labor Party, a policy focusing upon devolution and democratization had been adopted, a policy which was to be put into practice through the Commonwealth Schools Commission after 1974. Central to the social democratic discourse of the Schools Commission, which comprised representatives from peak teacher unions, parent organizations, employers and the Commonwealth government, was the notion of administrative devolution of power to the schools and their community. In 1973 Karmel wrote: 'The grass roots approach to the control of schools reflects the conviction that responsibility will be most effectively discharged when the people entrusted with making decisions are also the people responsible for carrying them out, with an obligation to justify them, and in a position to profit from their experience' (quoted in Johnston 1983, p. 26). Schools which were more accountable to their community were also seen to be less alienating of particular social groups and able to recognize and address more adequately the issues of access and equality. Participation and school-based decision-making were key themes of the discourse of the Schools Commission and parent organizations by the mid-1970s. In Victoria parent organizations were a powerful lobby for increased parental say in school policy through school councils.

During the same period (1968–79) the state educational bureaucracy faced increasing criticism as to its lack of responsiveness, its alienation from the community and its ponderous bureaucratic decision-making processes. In 1974 the Director General, Laurie Shears, backed by a Liberal Minister of Education, implemented the first attempt at administrative decentralization in Victoria in the form of regionalization. By 1976 parents, teachers and students were representatives on school councils, although these councils had little control over school curriculum or policy at this stage. This was an administrative solution to the problem of an unresponsive bureaucracy, premised upon the belief that decisions should be made more by those who were directly affected. At the same time it was intended to reduce the 'span of control' between the centre and the schools. It did little to alter the bureaucratic control from the centre, which was retained in practice. A new phase of administrative restructuring was initiated by the Victorian Liberal Government from 1979 to 1982 as part of a direct attack on teacher union initiatives. This more radical restructuring was based, after private management consultancy advice, upon an 'undisguised industrial model based upon line-management principles and the division of labour between an hierarchy of individual specialists in a "top-down model"' (Deakin Institute of Education, 1986, pp. 9–13). Policy was at the centre, administration was to be by the regions, and operations carried out by the schools (Macpherson, 1983, p. 7).

These earlier phases of restructuring, although generally couched in a rhetoric of community participation and devolution of responsibility to the schools, depicted a particular view of school administration which was derived from the organizational theory and literature of the time (Blackmore, 1986, pp. 30–4). Decision-making in conventional administrative literature was seen to be the 'central administrative act'. The structural reform in Victoria under the Liberals reflected a move in organizational theory towards participative decision-making since the Second World War. This human relations movement emphasized the need to develop worker morale and satisfaction because it was seen to increase organizational effectiveness. A number of 'myths' had developed in organizational theory to surround participative decision-making which have little empirical evidence to support them. For example, the belief that worker involvement in decision-making demanded greater commitment by the individual to the decision and therefore productivity (Alutto and Belasco, 1972; Lock and Schweiger, 1979; Imber, 1983; Conway, 1984). Despite the empirical failure to justify such claims of causality between participation, satisfaction and productivity, the 'bottom line' of the assumption of participative decision-making by business and administrators was that it was seen to be a managerial *strategy* to increase control, not reduce it.

At another level, the motivation for the implementation of participative decision-making processes in schools or industry from above is suspect in that it implies a particular view of democratic process. As Foster suggests, participative decision-making was a way of assisting administrators to 'ensure the successful psychological fit' of the individual to institutional goals (Foster, 1986, p. 20). Ramsay argues that employers were willing to introduce participatory measures as they 'seek to gain control by sharing it'. The paradox of workplace democracy as perceived in organizational and management terms is that it can just as readily be used as a means of 'sustaining the status quo by being conciliatory and containing disruptive measures' (Ramsay, 1983, p. 206).

Historical circumstance is therefore significant. In a time of economic constraint ideology disguised as a scientifically neutral managerial strategy has effectively controlled teachers by relocating the arena of contestation over limited resources away from the centre and to the school level. First, participative and school-based decision-making in this context can be seen merely as another step in the move from job redesign of the 1920s and the human relations movement of the 1930s and 1940s, which were themselves a gloss over the early scientific management of Taylorism. Certainly the Liberal phase of restructuring was intended to maintain and not disperse central control over decision-making in schools. Macpherson suggests that 'the metaphors of control and economy were widely evident in the rhetoric of decentralisation, which in turn masked a low commitment to devolution' (Macpherson, 1983, p. 7). Second, governments and bureaucracies, confronted with a 'legitimation crisis' in the sense of their professional and technical capacity to produce socially equitable outcomes, met with an increased demand for accountability (McCarthy, 1984). Education systems in the USA, the UK and Australia have stressed increased community and parental participation through school-based decision-making as a means to resolve the credibility gap between client and institution (Dawson, 1982). With the defeat of the Victorian Liberal Government in 1982 by the Labor Party the rhetoric of decentralization and devolution was taken to its logical conclusion (Blackmore and Spaull, 1987). It was a rhetoric which owed much to the interorganizational networking between Labor Party state Education Committees, teacher unions, the Federal Schools Commission (established by Labor in 1972) and parent organizations (Tanner, 1983; Johnston, 1983).

The school was to become the unit of decision-making. The social democratic principles under which this was to occur were outlined in the Victorian ministerial papers on decision-making, schools councils, school improvement, curriculum, program budgeting and regional boards (Minister of Education, Victoria, 1983–85). The papers reflected much of the conceptual confusion over the notion of democratic participation present in the three perspectives already described. At a fundamental level, the ministerial papers displayed a confusion between notions of participatory and elitist views of democracy; between direct and representative notions of participatory democracy (Pateman, 1970). On the one hand, school-based decision-making and management was linked to school improvement in the sense of community and school self-evaluation, thus presenting a view of professional accountability as a sharing of information. Workplace democracy was a right and simultaneously humanized the bureaucracy. On the other hand, the papers established structures which relied upon representative notions of democracy with the proliferation of representatives of the various voluntary organizations on policy-making bodies. The tension between 'participation' and 'representation' as an elite democratic form became a central problem on committees at school, regional and central levels (Watkins,

1988; Blackmore and Spaull, 1987). As Watkins points out, the confusion between notions of representative and participatory democracy implicit in the ministerial papers did not countenance the differing power relations within, for example, the regional boards, between teacher and parent representatives with fixed organizational constituencies and agendas, and locally elected parents without clear constituencies or platforms. Nor did the papers imagine the complexity of representative practice which is 'primarily a public, institutionalised arrangement involving many people and groups, and operating in complex ways of large-scale social arrangements. What makes it representative is not any single action by one participant, but the overall structure and functioning of the system, the patterns emerging from the multiple activities of many people' (Pitkin quoted in Watkins, 1988, p. 25).

Critical to any such arrangement are the legal/managerial and economic parameters which legitimize the form and extent of participation. Thus 'moves towards increased devolution are likely to lead to an inherent antagonism between greater community participation at the local level and the overall economic and managerial imperatives of the state' (Watkins, 1988, p. 25).

For the initial years of the Labor Government (1983–86) there appeared to be some temporary and partial convergence between the ideological justifications for school-based decision-making and management as the most appropriate administrative form of governance (Boyd and Chapman, 1987). The devolution of responsibility to schools through the school councils and regional boards by the Labor Government also affected union structures and decision-making processes in schools. The first response was the need for branch revitalization and membership education. Furthermore, the ideological commitment of the Labor Party towards industrial democracy was now supported by the belief that administrative moves towards decentralization and devolution were politically essential. The evolution of more democratic committee systems in most schools during the 1970s both facilitated and encouraged, together with the ministerial papers, the greater expectation of teachers and parents to be involved in decision-making.

Thus the stage was set for a unique set of direct negotiations on school management between the Minister of Education and the teachers' unions between 1983 and 1985 in the form of three separate, and later joint, industrial agreements. These industrial agreements determined in detail the nature of staffing, conditions *and* school organization (Agreement Implementation, *VSTA News*, 1985). The agreements were welcomed by teacher unionists as the single annual log of claims minimized the need for action on one-off issues and created a comprehensive industrial approach. It was argued that the democratic process underlying the formation of policy was maintained through branch representation and the ballot at the annual general meeting (*Victorian Teacher*, 2, April 1983, p. 16). The agreement was significant in that it institutionalized the committee structures which had partially evolved during the 1970s; it consolidated the union branch as the negotiating body for teachers in schools; and it established and legitimized the principle of union representation on major committees.

Furthermore, the reduced need for branch action meant less conflict between branch and school administration. These improved relations allowed teachers to direct their attention to educational issues of curriculum, transition education and retention. Numerous schools reported increased branch membership participation due to the industrial peace, with over 80 per cent of all teachers belonging to a union. But teacher response to the annually renegotiated agreement has become progressively more pessimistic with the worsening economic climate. Many foresaw a new apathy among teachers, a willingness to give over trust to a new Labor Government, whilst the cynics perceived the unions as being 'hamstrung and degutted by the agreements', as 'the cream of our industrial leaders have been enticed into Ministerial appointments' (*Victorian Teacher*, 1983, pp. 6–10). The central union executive was also seen to be increasingly compromised in its close relationship with the Labor Government. One teacher was critical of the mythology and reification of an agreement that meant disadvantaged schools and committed teachers were forced to accept a lowest common denominator of conditions. Whilst the agreements standardized conditions across the state, they also reduced hard won individual school flexibility in staffing to meet special needs (disabled, non-English-speaking, economically disadvantaged). The reluctance with which the 1987 agreement was ratified by the membership in the face of no viable alternative was evident at the meeting of branch representatives (*VSTA News*, 1987). Teachers were now soured by the rapid, often coercive closures and amalgamations of schools by centrally appointed delegations upon which their own union representatives were seen to be active members.

The industrial agreement in this instance has tended to minimize rather than extend the ability of branches to carry out their previously independent action to meet the specific needs of schools. At the same time the incorporation of teachers as representatives demands a commitment to the decisions made by the administrative committees and central union executive. The coincidence of the new form of school governance brought about by the agreement and a period of economic contraction, declining enrolments and reduced expenditure has thus committed union members to decisions which have often been detrimental to individual unionists and the branch itself, and to students and the school community. The centralistic tendencies, characteristic of industrial negotiations intent on establishing uniform sets of conditions, have worked against the essential democractic principles upon which they were founded. School-based decision-making, initially seen to be 'an integral plank of the Government Ministerial Papers and the Industrial Agreements', has produced unexpected results. A VTU survey reported in 1984:

> The process of change to decentralised decision making according to some teachers had outstripped the teachers' abilities to participate in the process. On the other hand, many teachers have eagerly adopted the philosophy of school based decision making. They are keenly aware of the importance of involving the whole community. Teachers report improved staff morale and job satisfaction. Others say they value working closely with their colleagues on local innovations. (*Victorian Teacher*, 10 July 1984, p. 13)

But lack of support facilities and resources, as well as reduced time allowances for staff involved in such time-consuming processes, endanger the success of such devolution (*Victorian Teacher*, 5, 1985, p. 5). Participation has come to be seen by many teachers to lead to 'busy work' without the real capacity to influence change, since the power lies at the centre. Watkins appropriately reflects that:

> School democracy might also be looked at in a sceptical fashion, as a covert method of controlling formerly militant unions. From this viewpoint it could be argued that increased participation may be a means to reduce any union discontent and to minimize its effectiveness. By being actively integrated in to the decision making process, teachers are less likely to act against any decision for which they are partially responsible. This ensures a high degree of stability in what has been a highly volatile industrial arena. The resultant stable and predictable educational situation becomes a major achievement for politicians extolling a mandate for good industrial relations. (Watkins, forthcoming)

School-based decision-making and management therefore gained impetus from three ideological strands during the 1970s: industrial democracy, professionalism and organizational theory. It is the very 'rhetorical mix' of these strands which has allowed the rhetoric of school-based decision-making to be readily immersed within the emergent 'corporate management' logic, therefore giving rise to differing, often contradictory, expectations of how such 'democratic processes' are to work and with what consequences. The apparent inroads of teachers as active decision-makers into the traditional hierarchical administration of schools and educational bureaucracy have been undermined by worsening economic conditions. Since 1979 the formerly proactive role of the teacher union in determining the agenda of reform has been subsumed under a more conservative governmental reform agenda of corporate management common to all political parties by the mid-1980s. The dominant managerialist perspective of state and federal Labor governments derives from their concern that Labor governments be seen both at home and overseas as good financial managers. Consequently, the three major teacher unions have assumed a more reactive position than in the previous decade, despite their alliance with, and electoral support of, the Victorian Labor Government in 1982.

At the same time there has been a politicization of the management of education. The locus of power in education has moved from the administrative head to the political head under the guise of administrative efficiency. Under both Liberal and Labor governments the role of the director general was increasingly circumvented by ministerial control. Furthermore, the three administrative divisions of technical, high and primary were combined into a single schools division under a chief general manager, thus undermining historically entrenched power relations within the educational bureaucracy. Administration in the 'corporate management logic' is seen to be a neutral and efficient form of decision-making over scarce resources. Regardless of the nature of the field of government or specific needs of a sector or of particular policy domains, e.g. welfare, health, education, administration is now carried out by 'administrators', not social workers, teachers or nurses.

Restructuring based upon corporate management principles has also affected the nature of the previous decade's 'incorporation' of individuals and interest group representatives. Restructuring for corporate management has meant many of those individuals recruited from key union positions into the central policy and planning during the early stages of radical administrative restructuring and curriculum reform have now been 'relocated' back to the newly amalgamated regions and schools. Thus key personnel, particularly women, have either been alienated from their support networks or removed from central policy-making arenas. Finally, those individuals remaining in central positions are constrained by the need to be seen to be loyal to the corporate management ethos of efficiency and effectiveness. Efficiency, effectiveness and increased 'productivity' are seen to be causally linked to line-management structures, clear organizational objectives, instrumental relationships between education and industry, and, more significantly, self-governing institutions, whether schools or universities. This is not seen to be in direct antithesis to the state intervening to pursue policies directed towards the 'national interest' (Blackmore and Kenway, 1988). How then are these inconsistencies and contradictions between the centralism of corporate management and the decentralization of school-based decision-making and management reconciled?

Corporatism and Democracy

The political formation of educational decision and policy-making particularly evident in Victoria can be depicted as fitting a 'corporatist' model. As Hyslop (1988) argues, the position of the state and in particular the political and ideological aspects of the state have been ignored by theorists in industrial relations and only more recently seen to be a site for investigation by educational theorists. This is a consequence of the dominance of viewing industrial relations in education as an administrative 'problem' and the emphasis upon the voluntaristic nature of industrial relations (Hyslop, 1988, p. 53).

Orthodox adherents to corporatist theory argue that corporatism is a strategy, a method of interest representation (Cawson, 1983), or a preferable mode of policy-making (Schmitter, 1983). Such theories of corporatism adhere to the liberal theory of political pluralism. Democratic process is seen to be brought about by the voluntary involvement of union, business and other interest group representatives who actively lobby the state on an equal footing. In this manner the neutral state effectively mediates between legitimate and competing social and political interests in order to produce a harmonious accord about the distribution of limited resources in the public interest. The intervention of the state is legitimized by an appeal to national unity and socio-economic consensus, and is seen to be a necessary strategy to meet the demands of industrial concentration, technological development, increased international competition and declining profits (Hyslop, 1988, p. 58). It has also been argued that such intervention is based on the principle of equity of representation of interests. It is exemplified in the incomes policy in Great Britain and Australia, in particular the economic accord of 1983 and the apparent arrangement on wage justice. Hence in Australia of the 1980s the public interest (civil) is equated to a favourable balance of payments (economic).

This author adopts the radical perspective of Panitch (1981) who links the growth of the corporatist state since the 1970s as a by-product, and essential element, of a crisis in capital accumulation. Panitch's interpretation is radical in that he depicts corporatism as a form of capitalist social-political organization, a specific conjuncture of class relations and only one facet of a social formation whereby capital displays power over labor (Hyslop, 1988, p. 62). Corporatism (based upon consent) is, therefore, in the Gramscian sense an alternative to coercion in responding to the crisis of legitimation and accumulation in capitalism. The 'pluralist' interpretation of the 'incorporation' of interest groups is inadequate because of its assumption of the neutrality of the state and the acceptance of elite democratic theory implicit in it. Pluralism emphasizes the 'fallacious pretence of egalitarianism in the corporate organisation of society'. The lack of neutrality of the state is most evident in the link between 'corporatism' (the representation of elite interests in the governmental process) and the emergence of a less democratic civil and economic administration in the form of corporate management. In the latter the spirit of corporatism is evident since the 'authority remains with the employer, it is he [sic] who still controls. But those who are controlled are taken into his [sic] confidence, their views are solicited and so the control, by becoming less of an imposition, is made to operate more effectively (and legitimately)' (Wexler and Grabiner, 1986, p. 16). Any discussion of corporatism requires a theory of the state which accounts for its relationship to voluntarist or 'private' organizations such as trade unions. In this sense Gramsci's emphasis on how the organic relations between the governmental apparatus and civil society are critical to the unification of ruling classes is valuable. Specific institutions (trade unions, education) are treated not merely as the technical apparatus of government. Rather, Gramsci 'relates them to their social bases and stresses the ways in which their functions and effects are influenced by their links to the economic system and civil society' (Jessop, 1982, p. 146). In so doing he gives precedence to class relations over the specificity of institutional structures of the state, and stresses the modalities of state power in particular periods. Thus school-based decision-making and management and corporate management are both administrative reforms or modes which must be seen as institutional instances maintaining particular social formations in specific historical contexts.

Furthermore, it is the hegemony of consent implicit in corporatism which makes Gramsci's conceptualization of the state most appropriate in this analysis. In Jessop's words:

> ... hegemony involves the successful mobilisation and reproduction of the 'active consent' of dominated groups by the ruling class through their exercise of intellectual, moral and political leadership.... For the maintenance of hegemony involves taking systematic account of popular interests and demands, shifting

position and making compromises on secondary issues (without however, sacrificing essential interests) and organising this support for the attainment of national goals which serve the fundamental long-run interests of the dominant group ... hegemony is crystalised and mediated through a complex system of ideological (or hegemonic) apparatuses located throughout the social formation. But the practice of hegemony is nonetheless concentrated in the sphere of the civil society or so called 'private' organisations, such as the Church, trade unions, schools, the mass media or political parties. (Jessop, 1982, pp. 148–9)

Corporatist theorists argue that there are implications for political practice and equity. Triado discusses the inherent tensions between the functional characteristics of corporatism and the normative dimensions of democracy. He argues that 'corporate' representation is denied to certain groups and classes without corporate status, and narrows the scope of political activity in conformity with the given social order. Those individuals outside the voluntarist organizations go unrepresented. Corporatism is an instrumental means of going about public policy formation within a liberal democracy. It is a form of political rationality premised upon consensus which is increasingly distanced from more participatory democratic expectations:

Corporatism furnishes the institutional means to mediate the demands of *functional* interest groups ... with the aim of developing an administrative *consensus* over resource allocation, investment planning, industry restructuring, the introduction of high technology, economic performance, full employment, wage levels, price controls, and various policies to augment the 'social wage', all pursued with the aid of certain ideological and cultural accoutrements stressing the overriding 'national interest'. (Triado, 1984, p. 40)

Ultimately, corporatism reduces to conventional pluralist notions of elite democracy, the political orthodoxy of the post-war period which denies the importance of class conflict and the manipulative and coercive role of the state. It takes on a view of democracy that is non-participatory and links it with a view that the 'national interest' can be represented by elites within interest groups. Democracy is not pursued in the normative sense of 'classical democracy' or, as Pateman calls it, participatory forms of democracy, but rather the elite notions of representative democracy (Pateman, 1970). Thus national interests can be linked more effectively with specific elite interests, and capital accumulation and concentration become a means to achieve the common good.

The inclusion of unions or unionists in decision-making diverts attention away from more significant trends in the economy relating to the rapid accumulation of capital by a few 'entrepreneurial individuals' and creates tensions within the union organization on ideological grounds. Furthermore, tension develops organizationally as increasing bureaucratization and top-down policy decisions by union leaders enforced through this new corporatism conflict with the union rhetoric of democratization of decision-making (Ozga and Lawn, 1981, p. 23). Corporatism raises issues of representativeness and the nature of *participatory* democracy both at the macro-political level (economic summit) and the organizational level (educational and union bureaucracies) (Blackmore and Spaull, 1987; Watkins, 1988).

Thus decentralization and devolution to schools as the units of decision-making have not been unproblematic for the unions both organizationally and politically. The earlier decentralization into regions in 1974 had forced the unions to reorganize on similar bureaucratic lines, to provide union representation on all committees and centralize policy initiative and action away from the branches. Participatory decision-making has made increased demands on all unionists and on teachers' time and, one could argue, increased accountability of teachers to both their clients and the bureaucracy.

In the union bureaucracies themselves the incorporation of individual unionists and union representatives into the decision-making process has highlighted the tension described by Triado (1984). It has altered the relationship between the union leadership and bureaucracy (union officials) and the 'rank and file'. 'Trade union bureaucrat' has become a term of deprecation, representing union officials as scapegoats for the contradictions which are inherent in the nature of trade unionism within a capitalist system (Hyman, 1979, pp. 54–5). Hyman, in attempting to understand the vilification of union leaders, argues that union officials, although initially more progressive than their constituents, frequently appear to perform a conservative role in periods of membership struggle and activism. This is because of the contradictions inherent in their ongoing mediating role between employers and unions which favours sustaining an accommodative rather than a confrontationist relationship with employers and the state, given the current non-revolutionary stance of unionism. Together with the union officials' self-interest to maintain an image of professional competence in collective bargaining, public opposition is effectively 'quieted'. Thus trade union consciousness interrelates intimately with material and ideological influences which mean that the politics of trade unionism constitutes a totality often 'resistant to major strategies of radicalisation and democratisation' (Hyman, 1979, p.

63). This is most evident in the masculinist resistance, for example, within the union movement (and administration in general) to greater participation at leadership level by women (Blackmore, 1989).

Furthermore, the consensus mode of conflict resolution which accompanies incorporation in a period of crisis and conflict in fundamental values leads rank and file members to perceive their leaders as forgetting their democractic constituencies whilst individual unionists are trapped within their own decision-making processes at school level (Hyman, 1979). In the past appeals to the ideology of professionalism as opposed to unionism have been used to constrain teacher opposition. Now appeals to union loyalty within the framework of 'corporatist structures' both legitimate union organization while simultaneously controlling the rank and file through an ideology of representation and consensus. The ideological hegemony of a corporate managerialist logic, which demands individual employee loyalty to efficiency and effectiveness as organizational (and national) imperatives, works against participatory democracy because the corporate logic gives pre-eminence to product rather than process and to elite forms of representation which remove all power from the very participants such representation is meant to empower (Pateman, 1970; Mason, 1982; Watkins, 1988). The power of ideology as a means to maintain an hegemony of consent is critical here. The next section will illustrate how ideological persuasion is perpetrated through the production and reconstitution of particular discourses central to the educational debate around state educational reorganization, focusing upon school-based decision-making and management.

Marketing Education: 'Choice, Fairness, Standards'

Kenway (1987, p. 191) elaborates upon how the political right in Australia has 'sought to achieve a hegemonic discourse, to establish closure around certain key concepts, to have its definitions accepted as universally valid and its sectional interests defined as general interest.' Such concepts would include notions of fairness, choice, standards, accountability, efficiency and effectiveness. The power of ideology in this particular instance lies in its potential for hegemony, its absorption into the common sense. It is a discourse not exclusive to a particular class, but constitutes elements of an ideological field which can be picked or adopted by governments, parties or social groups, forming temporary alliances to maintain their own interests (Kenway, 1987). In this sense school-based decision-making and management (which involves the effective incorporation of community and professional interests), which in the past was seen to promise democratization of schooling, is now seen to be an administrative solution for contradictory elements in the demands for reform from the right. On the one hand, it meets the demand for individual parental choice critical to the marketing of education, whilst on the other it allows for increased central control and social integration through establishing processes of accountability within standardized and mechanistic corporatist structures.

Driven by the belief that Australia is increasingly subject to the perversity of international money markets sensitive to 'impressions of sound economic management', all major party policy-makers in education have taken on corporate managerialism as their creed. The argument is as follows. Education, so critical to national survival, has to be further deregulated on the grounds that schools and tertiary institutions are more efficient and productive if they meet local community and/or national needs (Blackmore and Kenway, 1988). Previous deregulation of local education with the demise of zoning in many states has meant government schools already compete with each other and with non-government schools for a declining pool of clients. It is assumed that market forces, in this context, determine what is a 'good' school, on the presumption that parents (not students, teachers or the state) make informed choices. The emphasis by the right on parental 'choice' has been seen to complement and stimulate corporate managerial moves towards deregulation, particularly as expressed in the extreme version of school-based decision-making and management, the self-governing school (for example, Victoria, Ministry of Education, *Into the 1990's*, 1985). At one level the educational market rests upon the principle of individual choice. At the macro level the aggregate of individual choices presents a model of consensus and social integration to the benefit of the 'national interest'. That is, there is a shift in the rhetoric from the individual to the government. Education thus becomes an instrument of national policy and not merely of individual social mobility.

Another key concept connected to national efficiency is that of educational standards. The 1970s trend towards administrative decentralization and teacher autonomy in assessment and curriculum, part of a strong tradition in English education through the local education authorities, and more recent tradition in Australia, has been reversed in the 1980s as conservative interests redefine the central issues in the assessment/ curriculum debate as being efficiency and choice, not diversity and equity (Sharp, 1986). The tension between the notion of participative decision-making at the school level (dominant early in the Victorian Labor Government's administration) and the centralizing tendencies of stringent financial policies by the politicians has also been reconciled through collaborative school-based decision-making in the form of program budgeting (Blackmore, 1986). Economic crisis has created pressures for greater 'educational efficiency' in terms of instrumentally meeting industrial needs (preparing youth for work and training) and economic accountability (in terms of expenditure and standards). In this debate teachers have become the scapegoats.

Thus schools are said to have more autonomy and control over resources. But whilst the controlling influence of the conservative discourse focuses upon particularly narrow conceptualizations of educational choice, standards and accountability, central authorities are encouraged to adopt less educative responses. Individual schools (and thus teachers and students), in competing for clients, are prepared or expected to submit to monitoring in order to be seen to maintain mythical standards of the past (State Board of Education, Victoria, 1987). Standardized testing is valued because it promises comparability among individual schools and systems (government and non-government), because of its perceived objectivity and fairness (in minimizing teacher subjectivity) and 'quality' control in maintaining basic standards. The necessity of schools in a contracting system to conform superficially to such imposed external criteria of 'worthwhile' practice devalues the more educative aspects of school-based decision-making and school-based curriculum development which were products of the 1970s. It also devalues the ability of teachers and students to inform the nature of their interaction in the learning situation. Thus standardized testing (as have examinations in the past) features in plans for administrative devolution towards schools recommended by the Quality of Education Committee (1985), the Keeves Report in South Australia (*Final Report*, 1982), *Better Schools in WA* (Western Australia, Ministry of Education, 1986) and *Towards the 1990's* in the Northern Territory (1987).

McNeil (1987) expresses little surprise that, given such a context, schooling presents an 'incongruous clash of individual performance and evaluation models and a setting that often subordinates individuality to aggregate "processing" as in standardised tests.' She argues that teachers are subjected to two subtle sets of pressures:

> One of these I term 'participatory de-skilling' of teachers — abrogating their own role, and in doing so, assigning students a passive role in an aggregate instructional situation. The other pressure is the imposition of standardized measures which also militate against teachers' attention to student differences. The standards lead to an 'imposed de-skilling'; by preventing teachers from exercising instructional choices that reflect the differences they see among their students. (McNeil, 1987, p. 106)

System level standardized testing has an implicit view about teaching and learning and indicates, according to Ryan: 'the narrowly technical view of teaching as "competent delivery of prescribed educational services"; an abstract assessment of learning in terms of discrete measurable performances; and increased "steering capacity" for increasingly conservative and powerful educational elites' (Ryan, 1982, p. 36). School-based decision-making and management as conceptualized within the corporate managerial logic thus effectively reduces teacher professionality and autonomy and makes teachers increasingly powerless both in their classrooms and in their staffrooms.

Control of curriculum has also become an industrial issue during the 1980s because it cannot be separated from volatile questions regarding the relationship between credentialling, assessment, school organization and structure, and how particular arrangements continue to benefit particular social groups. It is the focal point of the VSTA's long-term opposition to university influence over what is the 'worthwhile' knowledge to be taught and how it is to be assessed in secondary schools (Blackmore and Kenway, 1988). The focus is on the role and composition of the new Victorian Curriculum and Assessment Board (VCAB) and its first task of creating a single Victorian Certificate of Education (VCE) to carry out the dual (and contradictory) functions of certifying the successful completion of twelve years of secondary education whilst acting as a selection mechanism for higher education and training (Blackmore, 1988). The VSTA has been singularly active in promoting public debate intended to highlight the oppositional role of the more conservative universities to reform, and their refusal to review their own curriculum, assessment and teaching practice. Yet the unions have been relatively quiet in the public debate over the VCE, given the high level of union representation together with other 'interests' on all curriculum committees. Radical rank and file unionists see past progressive educational achievements such as the School Tertiary Entrance Certificate (STC) alternative to traditional curriculum under threat with the dilution of its essential principles within the VCE (Hannan, 1985). It is more likely that the new educational settlement currently under negotiation will diminish the influence of the union and its members on school-based curriculum and assessment development (*The Age*, 11 March 1988). Curriculum frameworks, new fields of study and assessment procedures are being introduced at a time when structural reorganization and drastic financial cuts in teacher development and support services by federal and state governments will further undermine teacher autonomy and ability to influence the direction of educational change. The state is thus regaining control of school decision-making, and, in so doing, mediates the New Right's influence through the state's capacity to steer debate within specific boundaries and around particular concepts which constitute an economic and instrumental ideology of schooling.

Similarly, conservative forces have also indicated a capacity to steer the educational discourse by facilitating a shift towards an economic rather than an educative notion of accountability since the 1970s. This shift is premised upon apparent evidence of falling standards, a perceived economic crisis and the need for increased educational productivity. Educational accountability became an issue in the 1970s when it was argued that the massive expenditure of funds of the reform era of the 1960s failed to reduce social inequalities. Public confidence in the expertise of the professionals who had supervised such 'reforms' has been challenged in the context of 'the legitimation crisis of late capitalism' (McCarthy, 1984). This lack of public faith in scientific rationality as mediated by the state through professional experts and bureaucrats was, and is, apparent in the increased demands for community and citizen participation and initiatives in educational planning, health, welfare and the legal system. It is fundamentally an appeal for greater accountability which involved equalizing power relations between teachers as experts, students and parents. In that sense it favoured communitarian forms of decision-making.

Again conservative interests have been able to redefine the meaning of accountability towards an economic view premised upon market demand. Earlier demands for greater accountability took the form of *professional* accountability which led to the development of professional and institutional self-evaluation in the local education authorities in Britain (Simons, 1987), action research (Carr and Kemmis, 1986) and the School Improvement Plan (SIP) in Australia. Integral to the rhetoric initially associated with such programs was an educative notion of accountability which suggests a mutual sharing of information for the purpose of improved communication, interpersonal relations and learning between teachers, students and parents. It exploited the educative potential of school-based decision-making and management.

With the redirection towards efficiency and effectiveness, accountability has taken on economic and bureaucratic meaning. At system level this can be seen in the market philosophy pushing for self-governing schools; at school level with the increased competition between individual schools; and at classroom level with teacher competency being judged by student testing (Blackmore, 1988). This form of accountability assumes the view of being accountable *to* an audience (both client and bureaucracy) in a hierarchical, coercive sense. It targets perceived administrative inefficiencies and teacher incompetencies as in the New South Wales

Swan Report on *The Quality of Teachers* (New South Wales, Department of Education, 1985). In the USA, for example, the recent Holmes Report on teacher education equates improvement of teacher 'quality' with up-grading certification. Furthermore, it seeks to ensure pupil achievement by increasing the differentiation of titles and roles among teachers, thus reinstating professional hierarchies premised upon academic qualifications and formal patriarchal authority, while simultaneously reasserting the dominant market orientation of schooling (Darling-Hammond, 1987; Blackmore, 1987). Teachers are expected to solve society's economic and social problems with the 'production' of excellence and socially critical students, whilst simultaneously undergoing an erosion of their conditions of work and suffering denigration of their intelligence, judgment and experience through increased technicist/managerialist control of curriculum (Pusey, 1981). Learning becomes a management problem; that is, how to allocate resources to produce the maximum number of certified students within a designated time at minimal cost. If offers a pay-off for the school system as good public relations are made possible as school administrators can be seen to 'provide technical solutions to the complex economic, social and political problems that plague their schools. Simultaneously, they invoke the tenets of accountability as indicators of success', rather than emphasis on the individual and successful learning experience (Aronowitz and Giroux, 1985, p. 29). As Grace points out:

> Politically it is clear that the growing emphasis in ministerial and official statements upon the existence of 'incompetent teachers in our schools' has not emerged in this particular historical juncture merely by chance. Such an emphasis serves a number of useful ideological functions. In the first place, it diverts attention away from the effects which educational expenditure cuts per se are having upon educational standards and achievements by concentrating upon purported teacher deficiencies. In the second place, it legitimates policies for closer control and monitoring by implying that excessive teacher autonomy exists, and in the third place it provides a useful 'quality control' argument to be used in strategies involving the reduction of teacher numbers and their training institutions and in decisions involving teacher redeployment and redundancy. (Grace, 1985, p. 4)

The irony is that via the combination of corporate management techniques and collaborative rhetoric, school-based programs in Victoria, such as the Participation and Equity Program (PEP) and School Improvement Program, both of which advocated and practised participative and collaborative processes to bring about school improvement and greater educational equity in the early 1980s, have now been 'incorporated' and transformed within the conservative framework. Program budgeting at school level effectively facilitates centralized system accountability by linking local participative processes and shared accountability through school-based decision-making and management with central economic control and accountability. As Ryan points out, 'the collapse of any practical distinction between "community" and "state" achieves educational expression in the centralisation of control over curriculum and pedagogy' (Ryan, 1982, p. 32). Similarly, performance indicators, as a means of judging teacher, school or student quality, return to notions of teaching and learning as linear, means-end processes which can be categorized and quantified. In so doing, performance indicators de-skill teachers, reducing their possibilities for professional development in the educative sense. Ryan again argues that the technocratic imperative and commitment of corporate managerialism to planning erode teachers' craft responsibilities:

> The perverse consequence for the teacher is that she is held more 'accountable' for the execution of the teaching task, that is represented as simplified by the 'expert' management of planning and difficulties. Increasingly then, the tendency will be to internalise failure and to seek narrow technical redress (a new motivational trick, perhaps a little more muscle). As a consequence, teachers will be even more disinclined to discuss their origins in the wider school and social context will be less and less recognised: any holistic and experiential view of teaching and learning difficulties has no part to play in a developing managerialist ideology legitimated by the dominant social sciences (including accountabilitist pedagogical theories). Thus are collective and necessary strategies pre-empted. (Ryan, 1982, p. 32)

Past successes of teachers, parents and local school communities in achieving some level of shared or professional accountability through such programs as PEP have not defused what Habermas calls the 'steering capacity' of the government to determine the direction and character of the discourse away from those notions of accountability which emphasize educative processes towards managerial objectives of efficiency and effectiveness (Ryan, 1982, p. 198). In this way the language of participative and democratic school governance has been co-opted for managerialistic purposes.

Conclusion: The Ideology of Professionalism and Teacher Strategies

Two aspects need mentioning here regarding fundamental differences in participatory and corporate management approaches to school-based decision-making and management with respect to teachers. First, there is the dichotomizing of teaching from administration which is implicit in the corporate management model of school-based decision-making and management which assumes the conventional conceptualization of 'administration'. Such a dichotomy dominates administrative theory and perceives of administration as a technical problem intent on seeking and achieving consensus over objectives. This view needs to be critically appraised because it ignores the role of teachers as policy-makers (Blackmore, 1986). It also portrays all conflict to be destructive, and considers teacher opposition, whether individual or collective, as being a consequence of 'maladministration' rather than acceptable conflict over values, interests and resources, conflict which occurs in all organizations and social situations (Blackmore, 1987). Administration is non-political, a technical strategy. Implicit in the participatory notions of school-based decision-making was that educational administration cannot be separated from what is taught and learnt in schools, that administration cannot be separated from what is taught and learnt in schools, that administration is value ridden and that schools are the sites of cultural conflict. The administration of schools perceived from a cultural perspective involves the social distribution of power and knowledge — what is taught, how it is taught, by whom and whom.

Second, implicit in the ideology of professionalism which underlies the corporate approach is a presumption that teacher professionality, as an individualized technical activity, can be separated from teacher collective and political action as unionists. Coporate managerialism elicits notions of administrative hierarchy with the emphasis on formal role. In the practice of school-based decision-making which evolved in Victoria, unionism and professionalism were inseparable (Ozga and Lawn, 1981; Ginsburg *et al.*, 1980). Teachers have developed expectations through professional and union action to have a say at all stages of the policy process: problem definition, policy formulation, implementation, evaluation and even the demise of programs. Maintenance of a particular notion of professionalism as being mutually exclusive of unionism is critical from the corporatist view in that:

> ... teachers have been unproblematically defined as divided from other workers. Definitions which drew on the ideas of non-

productive labour, middle class status seeking professionalism or collaboration with the state have all been used, sometimes in combination, to differentiate teachers; that is to isolate them, by means of their assumed ideology, or economic or social location from other workers. Yet all workers ... have similar difficulties depending on their level of political development, their class consciousness, the nature of their work under monopoly capital or the complexities or contradiction of their class position. The determination to classify teachers in ways which do not correspond at least to some of their actions suggests an unwillingness to recognise the ways in which teachers and other workers share the same problems. (Ozga and Lawn, 1981, pp. 67–8)

As Lawn points out, the ideology of professionalism has empowered teachers on the one hand in particular historical contexts. For example, in the late 1960s and 1970s teachers gained increased autonomy by making claim to their increased right to develop curriculum and gain control of the workplace as professionals. Professionalism here offered teachers possibilities of empowerment. At the same time it was this increased teacher autonomy promised by school-based decision-making which was interpreted by teachers as evidence 'that they were regarded as professionals of expertise and integrity' (Grace, 1985, p. 212). School-based decision-making meant that they were entrusted to carry out this professional task. On the other hand, not only does the invoking of professionalism separate teachers from other workers, but it is a political strategy which makes teachers loyal to the existing order in the sense that they wish to attain the status accompanying the professionality of an occupation (Lawn, 1978, p. 15). It is how this ethic of legitimated teacher professionalism is perceived which has been, according to Grace, a controlling influence through a 'partnership' between teacher unions, local authorities and the school in the 1950s and the 1960s in Great Britain:

> For teachers, the ethic of legitimated professionalism provides, at a structural and economic level, only a partial realisation of their occupational aspirations but at a cultural level it provides a strong sense of professionalism through the experience of workplace autonomy. For the state, the ethic of legitimated teacher professionalism provides some sort of ideological guarantee that 'the teachers of the people' can be relied upon to be loyal professionals within the existing social order. (Grace, 1987, p. 222)

Professionalism is a problematic concept. The evoking of the ideology of professionalism by particular interests can work against the professionality of the teachers they claim to protect.

How can the participatory notion of school-based decision-making and management be regained? It can be restored through teacher unions and unionists, both individually and collectively, at central, regional and local levels reclaiming control of the discourse. The inherent contradictions outlined indicate that current proposals for school-based decision-making and management cannot be justified under persistent discursive scrutiny. Second, teachers must reappropriate control of their practical craft knowledge. Elliott argues that progressive teachers have complied with the official rhetoric while resisting its distorting influence on their practice by recognizing the significance of control of practical knowledge. Elliott argues that teachers' 'practice based on craft knowledge is highly resistant to the bureaucratic tendency towards standardisation of performance because such knowledge is not only largely tacit, but also bound to particular contexts of experience.' This resistance can only be overcome by 'eliminating the conditions under which this knowledge is constructed and transmitted ie. professional privacy and freedom from external regulation' (Elliott, 1987, p. 8).

The strategies he suggests for opposing the gaining of control over teachers' practical knowledge by transferring the responsibility for the generation of teacher knowledge to outsiders differ from more recent union practices. Instead, teachers must state that they *are* already accountable in that they can make informed judgments in concrete situations about how to teach particular individuals and groups, and these judgments can be transmitted to those with educational interests (Ryan, 1982, p. 33). Teachers must re-establish their power base in their practice in the classroom and in school administration, and privilege the valuing of educational processes over other end-products of efficiency and effectiveness. In so doing, teachers must recognize the nature of power.

Already teachers and parents had forged new alliances to defend the state system in terms of public statements of support and joint policy. Similar alliances need to be reconstructed at the school level. In the political context of the 1980s different demands have arisen and the focal point of the local organization, the union branch, will again need to adapt and, in so doing, to make demands upon its central representatives. Ironically, Bill Hannan, former editor of the *Secondary Teacher*, ministerial adviser and now Chairman of the State Board (a body which is perhaps the best example of 'corporatism'), foresaw the need to reconceptualize the role of the union branch in 1983: 'Up until 1982–3 the branch's strength was largely measured by their capacity to impose union conditions and respond to provocation.... In the future a strong branch will be the one which pervades the school structures and which brings the kind of educational democracy expressed in teacher union policy to bear on the administration and the curriculum of the school' (Hannan, 1982, quoted in *Victorian Teacher*, p. 3).

References

ALUTTO, J.A. and BELASCO, J.A. (1972) 'A Typology for Participation in Organisational Decision Making,' *Administrative Science Quarterly*, 17, 117–25.

APPLE, M. (1984) 'Conditions of Labour, Conditions of Teaching', *The Review of Education*, Summer, 259–65.

ARONOWITZ, S. and GIROUX, H. (1985) *Education under Siege*. Hadley, Mass.: Bergin and Garvey.

BEARE, H. (1983) 'The Structural Reform Movement in Australian Education during the 1980's and Its Effect on Schools,' *Journal of Educational Administration*, 21, 2, 149–68.

BESSANT, B. and SPAULL, A. (1976) *Politics of Schooling*. South Melbourne: Pitman Pacific.

BLACKMORE, J. (1986) 'Tensions to Be Resolved in Participation and School Based Decision Making,' *Educational Administration Review*, 14, 1, 29–47.

BLACKMORE, J. (1987) 'Contradiction and Contestation: Theory and Ideology in Teachers' Work in Victoria, Australia,' Paper presented to British Educational Research Association, Manchester, September.

BLACKMORE, J. (1988) *Assessment and Accountability*. Geelong: Deakin University Press.

BLACKMORE, J. (1989) 'Educational Leadership: A Feminist Critique and Reconstruction,' in SMYTH, J. (Ed.), *Critical Perspectives on Educational Leadership*. Lewes: Falmer Press.

BLACKMORE, J. and KENWAY, J. (1988) 'Rationalism, Instrumentalism and Corporate Managerialism: The Implications for Women of the Green Paper in Higher Education,' *Australian Universities Review*, 42–8.

BLACKMORE, J. and SPAULL, A. (1987) 'Australian Teacher Unionism: New Directions,' in BOYD, W.L. and SMART, D. (Eds), *Education Policy in Australia and America: Comparative Perspectives*. Lewes: Falmer Press.

BOYD, W. and CHAPMAN, J. (1987) 'State Wide Educational Reform and Administrative Reorganisation,' in BOYD, W.L. and SMART, D. (Eds), *Educational Policy in Australia and America*. Lewes: Falmer Press.

CARR, W. and KEMMIS, S. (1986) *Becoming Critical: Knowing through Action Research*. Geelong: Deakin University Press.

CAWSON, A. (1983) 'Functional Representation and Democratic Politics: Towards a Corporatist Democracy?' in DUNCAN, C. (Ed.), *Democratic Theory and Practice*. Cambridge: Cambridge University Press.

CHAPMAN, J. (1986) 'The Changing Nature of the Principalship in a Decentralised and Devolved System,' *Educational Administration Review*, 4, 1, 48–68.

CONNELL, R.W. (1985) *Teachers' Work*. Sydney: George Allen and Unwin.

CONWAY, J.A. (1984) 'The Myth, Mystery and Mastery of Participative Decision Making in Education,' *Educational Administration Quarterly*, 20, 3, 11–40.

DARLING-HAMMOND, L. (1987) 'Schools for Tomorrow's Teachers,' *Teachers College Record*, 88, 3, 354–8.

DAVIS, E. (1981) *Teachers as Curriculum Evaluators*. Sydney: George Allen and Unwin.

DAWSON, D. (1982), 'Educational Hegemony and the Phenomenology of Community Participation,' *Journal of Educational Thought*, 16, 3, 150–60.

DEAKIN INSTITUTE OF EDUCATION (1986) *Restructuring of Victorian Education*. Geelong: Deakin University Press.

ELLIOTT, J. (1987) 'Knowledge, Power and Teacher Appraisal,' Paper presented to the British Educational Research Association Conference, September, Manchester.

Final Report of the Committee of Enquiry into Education in South Australia: Education and Change in South Australia (1982) Chairman: Dr J. KEEVES. Adelaide: Government Printer

FITZGERALD, R., MUSGRAVE, P. and PETTIT, D. (1977) *Participation in Schools?* Hawthorn, Vic.: ACER.

FOSTER, W. (1986) *Reconstructing Educational Leadership*. Geelong: Deakin University Press.

FREEDMAN, S., JACKSON, J. and BOLES, K. (1983) 'Teaching an "Imperilled Profession",' in SHULMAN, L. and SYKES, G. (Eds), *Handbook of Teaching and Policy*. New York: Longman.

GINSBURG, M., MEYENN, R.J. and MILLER, H.D.R. (1980) 'Teachers' Conception of Professionalism and Trade Unionism: An Ideological Analysis,' in WOODS, P. (Ed.), *Teacher Strategies*. London: Croom Helm.

GOLDMAN, P. and VAN HOUTEN, D. (1977) 'Managerial Strategies and the Worker: A Marxist Analysis of Bureaucracy,' *Sociological Quarterly*, 18, Winter, 108–25.

GRACE, G. (1985) 'Judging Teachers: The Social and Political Contexts of Teacher Evaluation,' *British Journal of Sociology of Education*, 6, 1, 3–16.

GRAMSCI, A. (1971) *Prison Notebooks*, Trans Q. Hoare and G. Nowell-Smith. New York: International Publishers.

HANNAN, W. (1985) *Democratic Curriculum*. Sydney: George Allen and Unwin.

HOLMES GROUP (1987) 'Tomorrow's Teachers,' *Teachers College Record*, 88, 3, 2–85.

HYMAN, R. (1979) 'The Politics of Workplace Trade Unionism: Recent Tendencies and Some Problems for Theory,' *Capital and Class*, 8, 54–67.

HYSLOP A.G. (1988) 'Trade Unions and the State since 1945: Corporatism and Hegemony,' *International Journal of Sociology and Social Policy*, 53–90.

IMBER, M. (1983) 'Increased Decisionmaking Involvement for Teachers: Ethical and Practical Considerations', *Journal of Educational Thought*, 17, 1, 36–42.

JESSOP, B. (1982) *The Capitalist State: Marxist Theories and Methods*. Oxford: Martin Robertson.

JOHNSTON, K.M. (1983) 'A Discourse for All Seasons? An Ideological Analysis of the Schools Commission Reports, 1973–81,' *Australian Journal of Education*, 27, 1, 17–32.

JOHNSTON, K.M. (1987) 'Popular Discourse about Schooling: A Cultural and Ideological Analysis,' Paper presented to the AARE/NZARE Conference, University of Canterbury, Christchurch, New Zealand.

KENWAY, J. (1987) 'Left Right Out: Australian Education and the Politics of Signification,' *Journal of Educational Policy*, 2, 3, 189–203.

LARSON, M.S. (1977) *The Rise of Professionalism: A Sociological Analysis.* Stanford, Calif.: University of California Press.

LAWN, M. (Ed.) (1985) The Politics of Teacher Unionism', *International Perspectives.* London: Croom Helm.

LOCKE, E. and SCHWEIGER, D. (1979) 'Participation in Decision Making: One More Look,' in STRAW, B.M. (Ed.), *Research in Organisational Behaviour.* London: Heinemann Education.

LORTIE, D. (1975) *School Teacher: A Sociological Study.* Chicago, Ill.: University of Chicago Press.

McCARTHY, T. (1984) *The Critical Theory of Jürgen Habermas.* Oxford: Polity Press.

McNEIL, L. (1987) Talking about Difference: Teaching to Sameness,' *Journal of Curriculum Studies,* 19, 2, 105–22.

MACPHERSON, M. (1983) 'An Analysis of Some Current Events in Educational Administration in Victoria,' Unpublished paper, Monash University, Melbourne.

MASON, R.M. (1982) *Participatory and Workplace Democracy: A Theoretrical Development in the Critique of Liberalism.* Carbondale, Ill.: Southern Illinois University Press.

MEIER, A.J. and WELSH, D.H. (1981) Conflict in Victorian High Schools, 1965–75, MEd thesis, Monash University, Melbourne.

MINISTER OF EDUCATION, VICTORIA (1983–85) *Ministerial Papers 1–6.* Melbourne: Victorian Government Printer.

NEW SOUTH WALES. DEPARTMENT OF EDUCATION (1985) *Quality of Teacher Review* (Swan Report). Sydney: NSW Government Printer.

NORTHERN TERRITORY. DEPARTMENT OF EDUCATION (1987) *Towards the 90s: Excellence, Accountability and Devolution in Education.* Darwin: Department of Education.

OZGA, J. and LAWN, M. (1981) *Teachers, Professionalism and Class.* Lewes: Falmer Press.

PANITCH, L. (1977) 'The Development of Corporatism in Liberal Democracies,' *Comparative Political Studies,* 10, 1, 61–91.

PANITCH, L. (1981) 'Trade Unions and the Capitalist State,' *New Left Review,* 125, 21–43.

PATEMAN, C. (1970) *Participation and Democratic Theory,* Cambridge: Cambridge University Press.

PUSEY, M. (1981) 'How Will Governments Strive to Control Education in the 1980's?' *Discourse,* 1, 2, 9–17.

QUALITY OF EDUCATION REVIEW COMMITTEE (1985) *Quality of Education in Australia (QERC Report).* Canberra: Australian Government Publishing Service.

RAMSAY, H. (1983) 'Evolution or Cycle? Worker Participation in the 1970's and 1980's,' in CROUCH, C. and HELLER, F. (Eds), *Organisational Democracy and Political Processes.* London: John Wiley and Sons.

RYAN, B. (1982) 'Accountability in Australian education,' *Discourse,* 2, 2, 21–39.

SALLIS, J. (1988) *Schools, Parents and Governors: A New Approach to Accountability.* London: Routledge and Kegan Paul.

SCHMITTER, P.C. (1983) 'Democratic Theory and Neo-corporatist Practice,' *Social Research,* 50, 4, 885–95.

SCOTT, R. (Ed.) (1980) *Interest Groups and Public Policy*. South Melbourne: Macmillan.

Secondary Teacher [various issues].

SHARP, R. (1986) 'Thatcherite Schooling: Break or Continuity?' in SHARP, R. (Ed.), *Capitalist Crisis and Schooling: Comparative Studies in the Politics of Education*. Melbourne: Macmillan.

SIMONS, H. (1987) *Getting to Know Schools in a Democracy: The Politics and Process of Evaluation*. Lewes: Falmer Press.

STATE BOARD OF EDUCATION (1987) *Monitoring of Achievement in Schools*, Working Paper, December.

SUGGETT, D. (1986) The STC Course: Towards a Radical Practice, MEd thesis, Latrobe University, Melbourne.

TANNER, L. (1983) 'The Policy Formulation Process of an Australian Political Party in Opposition: A Case Study of the Australian Labor Party's School Commission Proposal,' in PALMER, I. (Ed.), *Melbourne Studies in Education*, Melbourne: Melbourne University Press.

TRIADO, J. (1984) 'Corporatism, Democracy and Modernity,' *Thesis Eleven*, 33–51.

VICTORIA. MINISTRY OF EDUCATION (1985) *Taking Schools into the 1990's*. Melbourne: Ministry of Education.

Victorian Teacher [various issues].

VSTA News [various issues].

WATKINS, P. (forthcoming), 'Devolving Educational Administration in Victoria: Tensions in the Role and Selection of Principals,' *Journal of Educational Administration*.

WATKINS, P. (1988) 'Representative Democracy in a Regional Board of Education,' *International Journal of Educational Management*, 2, 1, 18–25.

WESTERN AUSTRALIA, MINISTRY OF EDUCATION (1987) *Better Schools for Western Australia: A Programe for Improvement*. Perth: Ministry of Education.

WEXLER, P. and GRABINER, G. (1986) 'The Education Question: America during the Crisis,' in SHARP, R. (Ed.), *Capitalist Crisis and Schooling: Comparative Studies in the Politics of Education*. Melbourne: Macmillan.

Chapter 14

Curriculum Decision-making at the School Level

Andrew Sturman

Smith (1983) commented that although one finds within the research literature numerous references to 'factors affecting' or 'constraints' on curriculum decision-making, these are usually presented as a list of items rather than as elements of some coherent framework describing the teacher's operational space. Smith argued that one potential basis for the development of a framework was the concept of 'frame' which was originally introduced by Bernstein (1971) to describe the degree of control that teachers and students possessed over selection, organization, pacing and timing of knowledge. As Smith described, this concept has been extended by Dahlöff (1969) who categorized two types of frame factors, physical and administrative, and elaborated by Kallos and Lundgren (1976) who referred to 'higher order' frame factors far removed from the teacher and 'proximal' frame factors in which the teacher was directly involved.

Smith's (1983) concept of perceived curriculum decision-making space was an attempt to provide a conceptual framework for the description and analysis of individual teachers' curriculum decision-making. Its strength rests in the acknowledgment that curriculum decision-making takes place within an operational space defined by each teacher. The ultimate space within which teachers operated was, according to Smith, the result of the interaction of a number of frame spaces which represented the degree of restriction of freedom that individual teachers perceived. Various frame spaces — the central administration, assessment authorities, individual schools, faculties or classrooms — would affect individual teachers, although not all would necessarily affect all curriculum decisions. Smith acknowledged that frame spaces were dynamic across time and context, although he argued that some, more likely the higher order frames, would remain stable over a long time.

Smith's research revealed the importance to secondary school teachers of two administrative frames: the system and school. Of these, the system frame was reported to be the most important. Teachers felt constrained by the system authorities and by certification authorities in four curriculum areas: the selection of knowledge, its sequencing, methods and approaches to teaching, and time spent on units of knowledge. The school frame was also important, particularly in knowledge selection, its organization and pacing, and assessment and evaluation of student learning. In addition to these frames, two others — the community and the individual — have been highlighted in research into curriculum decision-making.

This chapter reports findings from a study that examined the effects upon the curriculum of moves to decentralize educational decision-making in Australia. The study sought to investigate the effects on the curriculum of the four frames of influence that emerged from the research. The system frame was conceptualized to refer to the state educational system in which teachers work. Of particular importance within this frame are the central and regional offices of education and the assessment authorities. The school frame was conceptualized to refer to the extent to which individual teachers within schools were granted freedom to influence the curriculum or, put another way, the extent of 'loose' or 'tight coupling' within schools (see Weick, 1976). The community frame was conceptualized to refer to the influence on the curriculum of parents and other community members within the catchment areas of the schools. Finally, the individual frame was conceptualized to refer to the effect upon a school's curriculum of the epistemological preferences of teachers (see Young, 1979, 1981).

These frames relate to different types of decentralization that have emerged or been advocated in Australia: regionalization, school-based decision-making, teacher-based decision-making and community participation in curriculum decision-making. For example, the effects on the curriculum of regionalization and of changes to the role of assessment authorities, which marked early decentralization initiatives in Australia, can be examined through reference to the system frame. The effects upon the curriculum of school-based curriculum decision-making, which marked later policies related to decentralization (see Interim Committee of the Australian Schools Commission, 1973; Rawlinson and Spring, 1981), can be examined through reference to the school frame. The effects upon the curriculum of policies and practices designed to enable greater teacher participation in decision-making can be assessed through reference to the individual frame. Similarly, the effects of policies and practices designed to grant greater curriculum decision-making authority to the community, a type of decentralization that is particularly relevant to certain Australian states, can be studied through reference to the community frame.

Methods and Measures

The research reported in this chapter was based on a number of case study visits to schools in three states of Australia. One region within each state was selected and within these regions three schools were selected for case study. Each of the schools was visited for one week and in that time interviews were conducted with the administrative staff, other staff with special responsibilities in the curriculum area and teachers in two faculty areas — science and social science. In addition to the interviews, the teachers completed a questionnaire which sought information on the organization of the curriculum, the teaching practices employed in the school, teachers' views of knowledge and teachers' views of the work environment. Similarly, the administrators completed a questionnaire that was concerned with school level organization and decision-making.

The term 'curriculum' was conceptualized to distinguish 'curriculum' from 'instruction' and the ideal program from the program in practice. In addition, two year levels were included in the study: Year 9 as an example of the compulsory years and Year 11 as an example of the post-compulsory years.

The System Frame

To analyze the effect of this frame, states were selected which were positioned at different stages along a continuum which could be visualized as having centralization at one extreme and decentralization at the other. In this way it was hoped, in line with some of the strategies employed in comparative methodology (cf. Lijphart, 1975), that differences in some of the key concerns of the study would be maximized, thereby enabling an examination of how such differences emerged and what effects they have.

Models of Educational Governance

It is possible to depict three hypothetical models of educational governance which can be applied to educational systems in Australia: administrative, professional and participatory. Although it is not argued that the system of education in any one Australian state or territory exactly fits any one model, systems will resemble one model more than another.

The administrative model postulates that educational governance should be primarily the responsibility of the central office which, although accountable to the parliamentary system through the Minister, would receive little interference from that system unless controversy evolved. Schools would have little autonomy, with the major decisions being made at the centre to be implemented by the school. The central office would evaluate schools, assess students and teachers, and monitor programs. School councils would, if they existed, be advisory only, and regional offices, if they existed, would be designed only to lighten the administrative workload of the central office and would not develop any real identity or autonomy.

The professional model postulates that the educational system should be primarily left to the school professionals (principals and teachers) on the grounds that they are best able to determine the needs of students and best capable of developing structures to satisfy such needs. Regions and central offices would be facilitators, that is, they would provide the services needed by the schools. School councils, where they existed, would be advisory, uninvolved in any 'professional' issues, and would be expected to act as a service to the school, supporting that school in its local community. Schools would be responsible to the community and the parliamentary system at large, but no formal methods of evaluation would be used.

The participatory model postulates that representative democracy, as exemplified in the Westminster system, should be supplemented with a type of participatory democracy aimed at involving 'lay' people, communities and parents. Although the parliamentary system would hold the ultimate authority, that authority would be devolved to various other bodies set up to allow participation at regional and school levels. The central and regional offices would be facilitators, facilitating at the regional level the regional councils and at the school level the school councils. These councils would be representative of the 'communities' they serve, accountable to them and responsible for educational provision within those communities. At the central level the opportunity for community participation in statutory bodies would also be available.

Public education in Australia, from its inception in the nineteenth century until the 1960s, could in many ways be characterized by the 'administrative' model. Although some devolution of authority to schools or regions had occurred, the traditions guiding education encouraged centralization. Kandel (1938) wrote of Australian education as education for 'efficiency'. Connell, as late as 1970, still referred to the 'prudential' and 'administering' traditions of Australian education.

Commentators on Australian education writing at the time of the establishment of the Australian Schools Commission and shortly afterwards might possibly have visualized that governance of education was moving, to a lesser or greater degree depending on which state was discussed, from the administrative model to the professional model with the participatory model as the ultimate end. The move towards the professional model was characterized by the relaxation of controls upon teachers. More and more examinations were abolished; the inspectorate became more advisory; evaluations of schools were encouraged to be school-based; and central office involvement in the curriculum became less prescriptive, leaving more and more scope for school-based decision-making.

The move towards a 'participatory' model was characterized by increasing powers being granted to school councils such that, in theory at least, they extended their influence from administrative to educational issues, and support services were developed for schools and their councils in the educational regions. The extent to which different states have adopted the participatory model has varied. Most systems have provided opportunities for broad representation of parents, professionals, administrators and the community on state advisory bodies, but the extent of representation on school level bodies, and their respective powers, has varied greatly.

The categorization of states within these broad models is likely to be controversial and only partially accurate. As a result of the review of research and an historical analysis of issues related to decentralization, Victoria was selected as an example of a state operating within the participatory model (the Australian Capital Territory was similarly categorized), Queensland as a state where the administrative model was more appropriate (New South Wales or Western Australia could also have been selected) and South Australia as an example of the professional model (Tasmania and the Northern Territory were also considered to fall within this classification).

The System Frame and the Curriculum

Perhaps one of the most notable facets of the results which compared the curriculum patterns in the three states was the similarity in responses of teachers. Although this was most apparent in the ideal program, it was also a feature of the program in practice. The greatest degree of congruence existed in relation to various broad emphases in the program, teachers' freedom over instructional practices and the use of different instructional practices. The greatest dissimilarity occurred with regard to specific emphases in the program, the use of materials and, to a lesser extent, sources of authority for the curriculum.

Although, compared with the other states, Queensland teachers attached somewhat greater importance to source of authority outside the school, in all states sources within the school were accorded the most importance. In Queensland within the school greater authority was attributed to those in positions of authority, which suggested that external structures of control were to some extent mirrored by intraschool structures. Administrators' responses to questions pertaining to sources of authority for the curriculum provided a somewhat different perspective from those of teachers. In those states where school councils existed, parents and the community were seen by administrators to have as much influence on the curriculum as central or regional offices.

The analyses suggested that, with respect to curriculum organization and structure, the South Australian schools were the least traditionally organized. In that state there was greater use of a semester system, there was a more flexible approach to student groupings, greater time devoted to elective offerings, more elective subjects offered in total and more school-developed courses. Victoria displayed many characteristics of a more traditional pattern. In all states content was rated as the most important curriculum emphasis and context the least important. With regard to more specific emphases it was the South Australian teachers who placed the greatest emphasis on values, personal and social skills and skills of originality, decision-making and enquiry. Conversely, they placed least emphasis on factual knowledge related to the disciplines. The Victorian teachers were similar to their South Australian counterparts with regard to cognitive skills, but more similar to Queensland teachers with regard to social and personal skills, values and subject content.

When the ideal program was examined, a more integrated program was considered desirable in each state and greater stress was also placed on both process and context. Process was the most important emphasis at each year level in the ideal program. With the exception of subject content all specific emphases were rated as more important in the ideal program, but on the whole the relative differences in emphases remained. However, the Victorian teachers' responses were closer to those of the South Australian teachers than Queensland teachers.

Although there was considerable similarity in the responses of teachers in the three states to the use of various teaching practices, there was a tendency for the South Australian teachers to favour what might be called an 'open' teaching style. Teachers in that state placed relatively greater emphasis on curriculum negotiation, an enquiry approach to learning, the use of a wide range of materials and groupwork. Conversely, they made less use of more traditional practices such as whole-class instruction, testing and grading, exercises to practise work, textbooks and giving students advanced knowledge of the curriculum to be covered. There were somewhat greater differences between states with respect to the use of different materials, and there was a tendency for Queensland teachers to make more use of traditional materials such as textbooks and the chalkboard. In the ideal program there was surprisingly less congruence in the responses of teachers than there had been in the program in practice. Victorian and South Australian teachers, compared with their Queensland counterparts, placed greater emphasis on a more 'open' style of teaching and less on a traditional style.

The School Frame

Corwin (1974) has described how researchers cope with organizational diversity by constructing models that seek to describe complex patterns of relationship among a large number of key variables. These models, he argued, are able to serve as preliminary guides to research by providing a basis for both anticipating and interpreting empirical relationships and for comparing (and classifying) organizations in terms of how well they conform to different models.

Corwin described several primary models, as well as additional derivative models, which had been applied to educational organizations. He viewed the primary models as two sets of polar types: the closed and open model and the rational and natural-systems model. The open and closed models are based upon different assumptions about the extent to which organizations are autonomous from the environmental and how important the environment is for understanding processes internal to the organization. The closed model assumes that internal organizational characteristics function independently from external influences, while open models emphasize environmental influences upon organizations.

The rational model assumes that organizations have clear-cut goals, planned and closely coordinated activities and tight control by officials. Perhaps the best example of this model is bureaucracy as an ideal type (Hall, 1963; Weber, 1952). The natural-systems model emerged as a result of accumulating evidence that organizations frequently do not conform to the rational model. Although Corwin was writing before the notion of 'loose coupling' emerged in the literature, it is clear that he saw this concept as one derivative of the natural-systems model. He referred to research into patterns of autonomy in schools (Katz, 1964), 'structural looseness' (Bidwell, 1965) and zones of autonomy (Lortie, 1969). More recent work has extended these arguments. The notion of schools as loose coupled systems has been described by Weick (1976, 1980), March and Olsen (1976) and in other theoretical writings (Firestone, 1985; Herriott and Firestone, 1984; Miskel, McDonald and Bloom, 1983), and Davis and Stackhouse (1983) have described two theoretical approaches that seek to explain these observations: the 'schools as institutions' model (Meyer and Rowan, 1977) and the 'organized anarchies' model (Cohen and March, 1974).

There is a tendency in much of the research and theorizing into schools as organizations to search for one model which can describe all schools. For example, Stackhouse (1978, p. 39) argued: 'We have seen that a conventionally bureaucratic diagram does not accurately fit the patterns of structure and co-ordination mechanisms found in contemporary high schools. More recent sociological literature presents another view of school organization which seems to fit the evidence somewhat more closely.' This more recent literature related, in fact, to the concept of loose coupling. Although the concept of loose coupling can be usefully applied to organizations (see Ainley, 1984; Sturman, 1986), it is not argued that all schools should be viewed as loose coupled. Rather, the concept is better viewed as a continuum along which schools can vary. Variations may even exist within schools. For example, relationships between teachers and administrators may be loose coupled, while those between students and teachers are tight coupled.

While it is argued here that organizational modelling is a useful device for understanding the operation of schools, it must be acknowledged that running contrary to this is another view (Greenfield, 1980) which would seem to reject the attempt to apply a body of theory and principle to organizations. This view criticizes attempts to separate people and organizations, and sees the latter not as structures subject to universal laws but as cultural artefacts dependent upon the scientific meaning and intention of people within them: 'Theory thus becomes the sets of meaning which yield insight and understanding of people's behaviour. These theories are likely to be as diverse as the sets of human meanings and understandings which they are to explain' (Greenfield, 1980, p. 163). Greenfield, though arguing for better 'images' of what schools are, held that since schools are made up of different people, these images will be many and varied.

The School Frame and the Curriculum

To examine the effects of decentralization on the curriculum at the school level, schools were grouped according to their administrative style, that is, the extent to which they were loosely or tightly coupled. The results revealed that with regard to the program in practice, the administrative style of schools had a moderate effect on the curriculum structures and teaching practices of the schools visited. Although the small sample size made it difficult to test conclusively for the confounding or interacting effects of state affiliation, tentative analyses suggested that, in most of the areas where significant differences emerged in comparing the two groups of schools, the school effects existed in addition to state effects.

As with the system level analyses, with the exception of teachers' perceptions concerning sources of authority for the curriculum and concerning their freedom over teaching practices, there was greater congruence in the responses at Year 11 than Year 9. Teachers in schools that were classified as loosely coupled attached greater importance to students as a source of authority for the curriculum and less importance to sources outside the school than did their counterparts in the schools defined as tightly coupled. The teachers in these schools attached less importance to all specific emphases except factual knowledge about subjects and at Year 9 more importance to content but less to process and context as broad emphases in the curriculum. Furthermore, there was a tendency for teachers in the more supervised or tightly coupled schools to make greater use of more 'traditional' teaching practices such as whole-class instruction, texts, chalkboard, testing and grading, and providing students with advanced warning of the curriculum content. Teachers in the more autonomous or loosely coupled schools made more use of what might be considered less structured practices such as use of a wide range of materials, individualized instruction, an enquiry approach, negotiation, enrichment, group work, teacher worksheets and diagnostic testing. On the other hand, the profiles for the ideal program, in all curriculum areas examined and at both year levels, were very similar.

The Individual Frame

Smith (1983, 1986) argued that the relative effects of the different frames influencing the curriculum were related to teachers' views of the structure of subjects. In addition, Young (1979, 1981) has commented on the crucial role played by conceptions of knowledge in the process of its social

organization and distribution. He studied teachers' epistemologies
how these related to issues of curriculum organization and assessm
Young found that teachers could be categorized according to their vi
of knowledge:

> Teachers either accepted a logical/empiricist view of the physical
> sciences as an epitome of knowledge, or adopted a view which
> gave epistemic priority to more 'subjective', 'intuitive' or 'per
> sonal' ways of knowing (called here 'hermeneutic'), or in the case
> of a small minority, adopted a dualistic system in which both
> types were recognized, called here the 'forms of knowledge'
> approach because of its resemblance to the view of Hirst (1965).
> (Young, 1981, p. 197)

Young argued that the formal properties of the curriculum codes that
Bernstein (1971) identified were present in particular dominant epistemologies and were supportive of a particular sort of institutional relationship
between schooling and society in general. Bernstein had distinguished
two types of curriculum codes: integrated and collection. In an integrated
code, weak classification (that is, a weak separation between subjects) and
weak framing (that is, weak teacher control over selection, organization
and pacing of knowledge) resulted in the subordination of previously
insulated subjects or courses to some relational idea, whereas in the
collection code, which involved strong classification and framing, there
was a separation of distinct subjects and a high degree of teacher control
over how they were taught.

Although Young acknowledged that a view of knowledge was not
the same as a view of curriculum, he argued that one possible grounding
of curriculum organization was in teachers' views of the way human
knowledge, in general, was organized. Thus he argued that teachers'
epistemologies would be related to curriculum codes because they both
supported forms of encoding which took place and because, in the case of
the most common views, they had wide societal support which conferred
legitimacy on ways of organizing the school curriculum.

The Individual Frame and the Curriculum

There was a significant correlation between scores on the scale measuring
epistemologies and those on the curriculum development scale, which
measured preferences for types of curriculum organization. In addition,
examination of specific items from some of the curriculum questions
suggested that teachers displaying a 'scientistic' epistemology were more

likely to favour the use of tests to grade students, the use of exercises to test what has been learnt and the use of diagnostic testing than were those teachers who displayed a preference for the 'hermeneutic' epistemology. Similarly, teachers who were more likely to display a scientistic episte-mology showed a greater preference for control over students than did other teachers. This could be discerned in the preference that the scientis-tic group had for chalkboard techniques, the use of whole-class instruc-tion, and to a lesser extent the use of textbooks and other written material. It could also be seen in the preference that the hermeneutic group had for encouraging an enquiry approach, encouraging decision-making skills and group work practices.

A consistent pattern in the relationship between epistemologies and the curriculum emerged at both year levels and in both the program in practice and the ideal program. Those with a scientistic epistemology were more likely to support a traditional educational organization and those with a hermeneutic epistemology were more likely to support a less structured educational organization. Further analyses into the association between the curriculum and teacher epistemologies revealed that the relationship was in the main somewhat stronger at Year 11 than at Year 9 and, with the exception of issues related to sources of authority for the programs and teaching freedom within those programs, stronger in the ideal program than in the program in practice.

The Community Frame

Although the review of research indicated that the community had not been a significant influence on curriculum decision-making, it was ack-nowledged that policies and practices were in a state of change and that consequently the community frame was potentially important in relation to decentralization of curriculum decision-making.

The Community Frame and the Curriculum

Although outwardly there appeared to be considerable differences across schools in terms of community influence, on closer examination there were substantial similarities. Parent and community input to curriculum decision-making, no matter what the subject area, was considered by the teachers to be virtually non-existent, although they were generally not opposed to such involvement on an advisory basis. Where schools ex-pressed a desire for greater community influence, this was related more to increasing the support for the school in an informal way than for increasing the direct contribution of parents and the community to curriculum decision-making.

In general, schools were closely attuned to the aspirations of their communities and, without direct input from these communities, curriculum philosophy, more often than not, matched these aspirations. Where it did not, considerable effort was made to 'educate' the community concerning the merits of the school's educational philosophy. Thus, although parents did not consider that they had the authority to influence the curriculum, in the main they did so in a rather subtle and indirect way.

Discussion and Implications

School-based Decision-making

Although the initial theoretical groundings for the research hypothesized that school-based decision-making would be less prevalent in Queensland, it should be noted that teachers in all states argued that it was teachers within the school who were the most important source of authority for the curriculum. In Queensland, however, this was less likely to be individual teachers and more likely to be faculty heads. Thus it was the perception of teachers that school-based curriculum decision-making was the norm — state differences related only to the nature of that autonomy.

The nature of the autonomy was, however, a predictor of the type of curricular and instructional practices that emerged in schools. This was revealed both in the state analyses and in the analyses which compared the responses of teachers in the two groupings of schools: loosely coupled and tightly coupled. In effect, therefore, the evidence suggested that it is not only system level reforms that can affect the curriculum but also school level reforms. Having said this, however, it also transpired from the research that there was a strong relationship between system level and school level policies. No Queensland school was classified as autonomous. It would appear that before substantial school level devolution can occur in that state a system level environment conducive to that policy needs to emerge.

The case study visits included schools where decision-making had virtually been handed over to various school committees and also ones where decision-making was highly centralized. There appeared to be problems associated with each approach: in the former it seemed that decision-making could become time-consuming, frustrating and based on entrenched faculty views; in the latter there was the serious risk of alienating staff forced to operate in ways which may be contrary to their philosophies. Perhaps a middle course would avoid these problems, but it is less easy to advocate a set number of steps that will bring about such a compromise.

Teacher-based Decision-making

While changing the balance of control of decision-making to enable teachers individually to have more freedom would seem likely to produce changes to the curriculum of the schools, the nature of the changes might be related to the epistemological views of teachers.

This relationship might help to explain why teachers do not necessarily fully embrace the curriculum philosophy that is associated with a school ethos, as was evidenced by the fact that in the ideal program, as opposed to the program in practice, there were few differences between the responses of teachers in the two groups of schools analyzed in the school frame. Even in the case of the schools in the study which for different reasons had managed to attract staff more likely to be in agreement with the school philosophy, disputes over that philosophy and how it affected individual teaching styles were common and sometimes intense. Perhaps this is not surprising, for schools are comprised of individuals and, although organizations may shape individual beliefs, there is an intricate and dynamic relationship between the two.

Although such a finding emerged quite clearly in the present study, Ramsden, Martin and Bowden (1987) have argued that intraschool differences in relation to approaches to learning can be very small and that a school ethos can emerge across different teachers and faculties. If that is the case, the question arises as to what it is about those schools which enables individual differences to be subjugated to the school ethos. Is it related to the teacher characteristics of that school or perhaps the leadership style of the principal?

The present study indicated that in any school there would be differences in approach from teacher to teacher, and the initiation of reforms designed to alter the nature of the curriculum could be met with some resistance. When these reforms are also designed to alter the locus of control for decision-making, by, for example, involving parents and the community, the epistemological preferences of teachers have added importance. For example, the hermeneutic group was more likely to support the participation of parents and students in curriculum decision-making whereas the scientistic group viewed only professional opinions on the curriculum as legitimate.

If curriculum reform can be impeded by the epistemological views of teachers, reformers need to know how these views emerge and whether they can be altered. For example, do they emerge as part of university teaching in different disciplines, through teacher training programs or from certain deep-rooted values or beliefs that individuals hold? Perhaps scientists or historians are socialized into membership of their disciplines, and part of this socialization entails the establishment of a particular view of knowledge.

Parent and Community Participation in Decision-making

There was very little evidence from the case study visits that parents and the community had made any direct contributions to the organization of the schools' curricula, even in those states where such contribution was actively encouraged. School councils would appear, in the curriculum area, to be reactive bodies not proactive and, even in their reactive role, discussion followed by legitimation of school-developed policies appeared to be the norm. Only one example was forthcoming of a curriculum policy that emerged in the school council, and the introduction of this program was thwarted by faculty interests.

It is not surprising that teachers do not perceive that decentralization has greatly affected decision-making at council level. In the states where councils existed teachers' attitudes were fairly consistent. While they acknowledged a legitimate advisory role for parents and the community in all areas of the curriculum — academic and affective — they were concerned that council authority could go beyond advice. Even in Queensland, where councils have not been introduced, teachers held the same attitude towards parent and community involvement.

Administrators in states where councils existed, however, perceived the situation with regard to community influence in a different light. The community, through school councils, was regarded as having as much authority over the curriculum as the central and regional offices. Given the conclusions reached from the case study visits and from teacher responses to the questionnaire, this poses an anomaly. Most likely, it would seem that the perceived influence of the school council in Victoria and South Australia relates less to the direct inputs that these bodies are making in the curriculum area and more to the fact that the school administration is obligated to involve them in discussions about the running of the school. Thus an element of accountability may contribute to the perceptions of the administrators.

Moreover, it is possible that the perceptions of the administrative staff, perhaps more so than teachers, were affected by their acknowledgement of the strong indirect influence that the school community has. Schools do in a general way take notice of the values and attitudes of their communities in developing programs. In two of the Victorian schools, although a discussion of the balance of VISE Group 1 and Group 2 subjects had not taken place at council level, the decision by these schools not to introduce or extend Group 2 subjects was justified in terms of the administrators' perceptions of parental attitudes. This indirect influence would probably explain why the community was perceived to be no less an important influence in Queensland as it was in the states where councils existed. Community influence, it is clear, does not have to be focused through councils: it can emerge through political pressure or through a subtle matching of community and school values.

Given the fact that in the states of Victoria and South Australia there is a policy to continue the pursuit of community participation through councils, the effect of such participation on the curriculum perhaps needs closer attention. School communities whether located in the more advantaged or disadvantaged areas are likely to adopt a reasonably conservative and traditional attitude to education. This attitude may or may not meet the expectations of a school administration, and it certainly will not meet the expectations of a large proportion of teachers who are being granted increased responsibilities in the curriculum area, at least in schools of certain administrative style. This conflict of values may be reconcilable when the community influence on the school remains indirect, but when the conflicts have to be faced more directly it may not be so easy. In one school in the study, where just this situation was occurring, rather than alter the school-developed curriculum philosophy, the school spent much time at council meetings trying to explain and justify that philosophy. Even so, concern, if not resentment, about the council's lack of influence, was hidden just below the surface.

If genuine community participation would lead to greater consistency in policy and practices across schools, this would appear to be in conflict with the espoused desire for diversity. On the other hand, a partnership between schools and their communities would have advantages to schools in terms of the support they would receive from those communities, to the Education Department in terms of accountability, and to the communities in terms of providing them with influence in key educational issues, as opposed to peripheral issues of school management.

Decentralization and Curriculum Renewal

The relationship between decentralization and curriculum renewal is not straightforward. Different types of decentralization, for example, might lead to different types of curriculum emphases. Moreover, and perhaps more fundamentally, the research indicated that the similarities in approach from state to state, school to school, and teacher to teacher were as interesting as the differences.

A number of reasons may contribute to this. First, it may be that there are not great differences in Australia in terms of the extent of decentralization or that most of the real decentralization that has occurred took place some time ago and affected all systems. For example, it may be that the limitations placed on the role of external examinations and assessment authorities, which have affected all states, may have been more fundamental influences on curriculum practices in schools than regionalization or community participation or even school administrative style. Second, the nature of schooling and of the preparation of teachers for entry into schools is similar in all systems. Teachers across the country and overseas have common day-to-day problems to face in their interactions with students and, given certain similarities in preparation, it is perhaps not surprising that practices do not substantially vary. The constraints on teachers are not simply constraints of curriculum control imposed by systems, the community or the school. Teachers, for example, have to find their own style with regard to classroom control, and all teachers have to acknowledge that the different objectives of senior school students have to be taken into account. It is not surprising that in the program in practice there were less system and school differences at Year 11 than at Year 9, although analysis of the individual frame suggested that, if anything, the effects of teacher epistemologies were stronger at Year 11.

The three states were chosen to reflect three hypothetical models of governance, and outwardly there might appear to be a consistency in the findings as they relate to the models. Queensland, reflecting the administrative model, revealed a more traditional curriculum; South Australia, reflecting the professional model, revealed the most open style of curriculum; and Victoria, reflecting the participatory model, revealed a mixed pattern. If it were assumed that in Victoria the conservative influence of the community combined with the more progressive influence of the professionals in schools would produce such a mixed pattern, the results could be easily explained. However, the evidence suggested that the community was no greater an influence in Victoria than elsewhere.

The anomaly of the Victorian responses may simply reflect some problems in the sample of schools or teachers in that state. On the other hand, it may reflect a more fundamental difference in the relationship between schools and central offices in South Australia and Victoria, the two states defined as decentralized. Owen (1978), in an examination of the impact on schools of the Australian Science Education Project, indicated certain system level differences that may be important in understanding how decentralization has had an impact on those two states. He commented that a complex set of political and administrative circumstances in Victoria had resulted in a period when contact between teachers in government schools and the inspectorate was limited. Changes in assessment procedures and the relatively sudden and early (for Australia) devolution of decision-making to schools in 1968, he argued, contributed to this situation. Owen further argued that in Victoria no curriculum framework existed upon which science teachers could base decisions regarding the planning and execution of science programs, and no coordinated, centrally organized network existed to introduce and support new methods of science teaching. In contrast, in South Australia the Secondary Science Curriculum Committee had, also at a time when devolution was being advocated in that state, constructed a curriculum guide to aid school-based curriculum development. Furthermore, the widely accepted consultancy service in that state provided support for the implementation of courses.

Changes have occurred since the time that Owen was writing but it may be that during the formative years following devolution in those two states, the system level support that was available in South Australia, but perceived not to be in Victoria, has affected the process of curriculum renewal. In other words, it is not sufficient to introduce policies of decentralization if curriculum change is advocated. These policies need to be linked with satisfactory support structures, otherwise schools will be left in a vacuum and school and teacher responses to devolution will vary greatly. Faced with such a vacuum, it is perhaps not unreasonable that many schools or teachers may have clung to more traditional and recognized practices.

It is a reflection of this issue that one of the facets of reform in the administration of education in Victoria has been in the area of curriculum support structures for schools. However, unlike in South Australia, where the school-centre relationship enabled a partnership to develop which allowed devolution to be tempered by accepted guidelines, in Victoria there has been a history of conflict. If teachers were willing at one time to refuse the entry of inspectors into schools, it is not surprising that the emergence of a structure whereby devolution and central control can each be satisfied has not proved easy.

References

AINLEY, J. (1984) 'Policy Formulation and Coordination in Australian Schools,' *Unicorn*, 10, 1, 16–28.

BERNSTEIN, B. (1971) *Class, Codes and Control: Volume 1 Theoretical Studies towards a Sociology of Language*. London: Routledge and Kegan Paul.

BIDWELL, C.E. (1965) 'The School as a Formal Organization,' in MARCH, J.G. (Ed.), *Handbook of Organizations*, pp. 972–1022. Chicago, Ill.: Rand Mc-Nally.

COHEN, M.D. and MARCH, J.G. (1974) *Leadership and Ambiguity*. New York: McGraw-Hill.

CONNELL, W.F. (1970) 'Myths and Traditions in Australian Education,' *The Australian Journal of Education*, 14, 3, 253–64.

CORWIN, R.G. (1974) 'Models of Educational Organization,' *Review of Research in Education*, 2, 247–95.

DAHLÖFF, V.S. (1969) *Ability Grouping, Content Validity and Curriculum Process Analysis*. Göteborg: University of Göteborg, Institute of Education.

DAVIS, M. and STACKHOUSE, E.A. (1983) 'Anomalies in Elementary Schools: Illustrations of the Garbage Can and Institutional Models Applied to School Organizations,' in BALDRIDGE, J.V. and DEAL, T. (Eds), *The Dynamics of Organizational Change in Education*, pp. 321–31. Berkeley, Calif.: Mc-Cutchan.

FIRESTONE, W.A. (1985) 'The Study of Loose Coupling: Problems, Progress, and Prospects,' in KERCKHOFF, A.C. (Ed.), *Research in Sociology of Education and Socialization*, Vol. 5, pp. 3–30. Greenwich, Conn.: JAI Press.

GREENFIELD, T.B. (1980) 'Theory about Organization: A New Perspective and Its Implications for Schools,' in BUSH, T., GLATTER, R., GOODEY, J. and RICHES, C. (Eds), *Approaches to School Management*, pp. 154–71. London: Harper and Row.

HALL, R.H. (1963) 'The Concept of Bureaucracy: An Empirical Assessment,' *American Journal of Sociology*, 69, 32–40.

HERRIOTT, R.E. and FIRESTONE, W.A. (1984) 'Two Images of Schools as Organizations: A Refinement and Elaboration,' *Educational Administration Quarterly*, 20, 4, 41–57.

HIRST, P. (1965) 'Liberal Education and the Nature of Knowledge,' in ARCHAMBAULT, R.D. (Ed.), *Philosophical Analysis and Education*, pp. 113–38. London: Routledge and Kegan Paul.

INTERIM COMMITTEE OF THE AUSTRALIAN SCHOOLS COMMISSION (1973) *Schools in Australia*. Chairman: P.M. KARMEL. Canberra: Australian Government Publishing Service.

KALLOS, D. and LUNDGREN, V.P. (1976) *An Enquiry Concerning Curriculum: Foundations for Curriculum Change*. Göteborg: University of Göteborg, Institute of Education.

KANDEL, J.L. (1938) *Types of Administration*. Melbourne: ACER.

KATZ, F.E. (1964) 'The School as a Complex Social Organization,' *Harvard Educational Review*, 34, 428–55.

LIJPHART, A. (1975) 'The Comparable-cases Strategy in Comparative Research,' *Comparative Political Studies*, 8, 2, 158–77.

LORTIE, D.C. (1969) 'The Balance of Control and Autonomy in Elementary

School Teaching,' in ETZIONI, A. (Ed.), *The Semi-professionals and Their Organizations: Teachers, Nurses, Social Workers*, pp. 1–53. New York: Free Press.

MARCH, J.G. and OLSEN, J.P. (1976) *Ambiguity and Choice in Organizations.* Bergen: Universitetsforlaget.

MEYER, J.W. and ROWAN, B. (1977) 'Institutional Organizations: Formal Structure as Myth and Ceremony,' *American Journal of Sociology*, 83, 2, 340–63.

MISKEL, C., MCDONALD, D. and BLOOM, S. (1983) 'Structural and Expectancy Linkages within Schools and Organizational Effectiveness,' *Educational Administration Quarterly*, 19, 1, 49–82.

OWEN, J. (1978) *The Impact of the Australian Science Education Project on Schools.* CDC Professional Series. Canberra: Curriculum Development Centre.

RAMSDEN, P., MARTIN, E. and BOWDEN, J. (1987) 'Approaches to Studying in Different School Environments,' Research Working Paper 87.12. Parkville, Vic.: University of Melbourne, Centre for the Study of Higher Education.

RAWLINSON, R. and SPRING, G. (1981) *SBCD: Support Services for Teachers and Schools.* Canberra: Curriculum Development Centre.

SMITH, D. (1983) 'On the Concept of Perceived Curriculum Decision-making Space,' *Curriculum Perspectives*, 3, 1, 21–30.

SMITH, D.L. (1986) 'On the Curriculum Planning Processes of Teachers,' *Curriculum Perspectives*, 6, 2, 1–7.

STACKHOUSE, E.A. (1978) 'Another View of School Structure,' in ABRAMOWITZ, S. and TENENBAUM, E. (Eds), *A Survey of Secondary School Principals*, pp. 39–50. Washington: NIE.

STURMAN, A. (1986) 'The Application of Organizational Models to the Study of Schools,' *Journal of Educational Administration*, 24, 2, 187–212.

WEBER, M. (1952) 'The Essentials of Bureaucratic Organization: An Ideal-type Construction,' in MERTON, R.K., GRAY, A.P., HOCKEY, B. and SELVIN, H.C. (Eds), *Reader in Bureaucracy*, pp. 18–27. Glencoe, Ill.: Free Press.

WEICK, K. (1976) 'Educational Organizations as Loosely Coupled Systems,' *Administrative Science Quarterly*, 21, 1, 1–19.

WEICK, K.E. (1980) 'Loosely Coupled Systems: Relaxed Meanings and Thick Interpretations,' Paper presented at the Annual Meeting of the American Educational Research Association, Boston.

YOUNG, R.E. (1979) A Study of Teacher Epistemologies, PhD thesis, Monash University, Melbourne.

YOUNG, R.E. (1981) 'A Study of Teacher Epistemologies,' *The Australian Journal of Education*, 25, 2, 194–208.

Chapter 15

Horizontal Accountability

Fazal Rizvi

In his book, *Sense and Sensibilia*, the philosopher John Austin once quipped that much of recent philosophy was dominated by 'a worship of tidy-looking dichotomies'. Austin's observation might well apply to recent writings on educational accountability, for here we find a tendency among many educationists to view systems of accountability in a dichotomous way. Thus we find writers either opting for managerial models, which stress the need to make schools accountable to some higher bureaucratic authority, or preferring democratic models, which suggest that schools should be self-governing. The former emphasize economic considerations and the need to ensure efficient use of resources, measured against a well defined set of objectives, while the latter stress more cultural criteria, and the need to promote experimentation and more diverse educational outcomes. But must these two approaches to educational accountability always be viewed in contra-distinction to each other? Is it possible to develop a position that cuts across the dichotomy in terms of which most recent writers have presented the issue of educational accountability?

To consider this issue more fully, we need first to acknowledge that 'what is accountability?', 'what is its purpose?' and 'how might it be achieved in a devolved system of educational governance?' have always been questions that have posed special difficulties for those who are committed to school-based decision-making and management. State schools are part of a wider system of educational provision funded through the public purse to carry out functions that the state considers desirable. How the state should ensure that these functions are carried out within a framework which recognizes teachers' professionalism and schools' local autonomy is an issue that needs to be resolved if we are to claim to have cut across the dichotomy between the managerial and democratic models of accountability.

This is not a straightforward issue, for it requires deliberation over questions about the role of the state in educational decision-making, the nature of the contractual relationship between the state and schools, the purpose and uses of accountability in educational administration and the adequacy of the mechanisms of public accountability. Nor is it the type of issue which admits an abstract universal solution. Ultimately, it is a practical question, one which must be explored in the particular circumstances in which it has relevance. It is the nature of practical questions that they do not admit final answers, applicable to all contexts, proving entirely satisfactory to all interests alike. As Burnheim (1985, p. 186) argues, the process of deliberation over such practical questions 'calls for continual, detailed reflection, speculation, evaluation and struggle.'

The best way to examine the issue of educational accountability might, therefore, be to examine the available data on experiments which have sought to carve out a practical position between the need for public audit for the efficient use of resources and the goal of school-based decision-making. In an attempt to see whether it is possible to resolve the tensions posed by these competing requirements, this chapter seeks to describe the practical politics of a program of reform committed to school-based decision-making. It discusses how the Participation and Equity Program (PEP) in the state of Victoria, Australia, viewed the notion of accountability and constructed a decision-making structure that enabled schools to develop ways of working that suited them best and at the same time ensured that they worked within the framework of certain centrally established guidelines. Drawing upon an extensive overview evaluation of the program (Rizvi and Kemmis, 1987), this chapter evaluates the PEP strategy, analyzing its strengths and weaknesses, and suggests that the requirements of public accountability and school-based decision-making and management are not as irreconcilable as many educational writers have suggested.

Approaches to Accountability in Education

The purpose of a system of accountability in education is to ensure that public funds are used in accordance with the guidelines set down, to improve the quality of educational provision and, where possible, to provide information to show that this is being done. Few would deny that public schools are accountable. However, this is an empy assertion unless' we also state clearly the form, extent and character of their accountability. That is, we ask questions such as to whom are schools accountable, for what, and how are proposals for accountability to be implemented and whether these procedures are consistent with specifically *educational* criteria. Answers to all these questions require that we also examine the issues concerning the nature of public schools and their responsibilities to the state and society.

A review of the literature in this area shows that educationists have adopted two broad approaches in response to these questions. The traditional models of accountability view schools in a hierarchical and instrumental relationship with the bureaucratic centre. Within the framework of 'line authority', teachers are accountable to principals, principals to regional bureaucracies, the regional bureaucracies to the centre and, in the Westminster system of government, the centre to the representatives elected to govern the state. Accountability is in terms of measurable, preferably behavioural, outcomes. Teachers are accountable for the achievement of prespecified performances by students. Although there are variations of this approach to accountability in the management literature, such as management by objectives, program budgeting and performance contracting, its basic thrust involves a unidirectional contractual obligation: that is, the obligation of individuals to report to their superiors, but not the other way round. The teacher is directly accountable to the organization, and only indirectly to the school community. Hugh Sockett (1976, p. 39) has dubbed this model 'utilitarian' not only because of its orientation toward a teleological ethic, but also because it is suggestive of Bentham's mechanistic felicific calculus.

The idea behind management by objectives (MBO) is that educational managers and teachers should agree on the results by which performance is to be judged. Each objective is prespecified and judged individually. The teacher is no longer accountable to pupils, parents or colleagues, but is judged against the criteria of a neutral technology. The supposedly impartial bureaucracy is given the authority to judge performance. The assumption that a neutral accountability technology is possible is also embodied in the idea of program budgeting which requires a structure in which all results related to common objectives are compared for cost and effectiveness. While in MBO each objective is assessed individually, program budgeting involves comparative judgments across the widest network of related objectives. In this way program budgeting is a more flexible tool: it requires that priorities among objectives be established, and that resources be allocated according to the amount that programs contribute to them. But it is also a more difficult mechanism to implement.

Both MBO and program budgeting were developed by US armed forces researchers in the 1950s, but in one form or another they have provided the basis for many of the accountability systems generated by educational bureaucracies over the past thirty years (see Lacey and Lawton, 1981). But are systems applicable to the military, which has rigid authority and penalty structures, applicable to education? Clearly not; because education is a more diffuse and socially complex enterprise. The dynamics of education involve considerable uncertainty: it is not possible to prespecify all the objectives of education, let alone prioritize them. Since good teaching requires making choices continually, having to work from objectives might very well be self-defeating because the objectives might become mechanisms for avoiding rather than making choices. Both MBO and program budgeting rest on the assumption that practical reason can be reduced to technical-instrumental concerns — the application of means to achieve given ends. But as Codd (1988, p. 11) has pointed out, such an assumption is based on the mistaken positivist dichotomy between facts and values, implying that measurement and observation can avoid the problems of value justification.

The managerial models of accountability have other problems. First, they mistakenly assume that pupil performance is a fair and valid way of accounting for a teacher's skills. The teaching-learning process is affected by variables which exist both within and outside the school, beyond the control of teachers. Socio-economic status, ethnicity, language, resources available in the school are just some of the factors which cannot be ignored in accounting for results. Second, the managerial models involve the assumption that all educationally desirable experiences can be stated in terms of measurable objectives: this is to distort and trivialize both the nature of human activities and the process of education. As Pincoff (1973) has argued, educational goals consist in the development of 'excellences', which are not the kind of dispositions that are determinate and can be prespecified. Finally, managerial models have politically unacceptable consequences. They encourage educational consumerism, since their concern is primarily economic rather than cultural and educational. The criteria of efficiency and economy are treated as unproblematic, given priority over all other values. The emphasis is on optimizing the use of resources, rather than creating sites where students get opportunities to develop their needs and interests. The critieria for judging what is worthwhile are thus external to the schooling context, imposed by the state to meet its own requirements.

The managerial models of accountability in education are concerned with one-way accountability: the subordinate in the hierarchy gives an account to a superior for the resources used to achieve certain results. In contrast, the democratic models view accountability as a two-way process: the teacher is accountable to a variety of constituencies, including the pupils. Sockett (1976) has characterized these models in terms of four major characteristics. First, accountability is for the principles of practice rather than for specific results. Second, accountability is rendered to diverse constituencies. Third, the teacher is to be regarded as an autonomous professional, rather than a social technician. Fourth, the purpose of accountability is allied to providing information for constituents. Accountability is thus tied to the emerging needs of the school. The school communicates information to the whole community, so that the contingent outcomes of the teaching-learning process can be widely known and debated. The emphasis here is on process, rather than outcome.

Viewed in this way, schools are seen as self-accounting. That is, they can no longer be labelled simply as good or bad, but are judged in terms of the criteria of excellence that they themselves develop. Accountability means being responsible for actions that are internal to agreed values and beliefs about the evaluation of educational performance. In very general terms this approach is justified against what is thought to be involved in a democratic way of life. MacDonald (1978) has suggested that democratic accountability models seek an incorporation of democratic social values, implying a rejection of the language of control and management. In them, distinctions between facts and values, between means and ends, give way to a concern with empathic understanding, practical deliberation and a commitment to value pluralism.

More specifically, Simon (1981) has suggested that the case for democratic school self-evaluation is based on a number of other claims. First, self-evaluation enables schools to develop a more accurate understanding of teaching-learning processes. Second, cyclical processes of review allow schools to determine the extent to which they are providing the quality of education they espouse, and what areas require attention and remediation. Third, in an effort to develop collective understanding, self-evaluation allows teachers to cut across arbitrary bureaucratic boundries, such as departments. Fourth, it provides more learning opportunities for everyone involved in schools. Finally, teachers get further opportunities 'to develop their professional decision-making skills, enlarge their perspectives and become better informed about the roles, responsibilities and problems of their colleagues' (Simon, 1981, p. 120).

While these arguments have considerable merit, the democratic approaches to accountability in education are not without their own limitations. The most serious of their problems is the assumption of an idealist epistemology. They emphasize the 'subjective meaning' of social action, but ignore the reality of social structure. As Carr and Kemmis (1983, p. 97) point out, such a view 'tends to assume that social conflicts are always the result of different social groups having conflicting *inter-*

pretations of reality rather than contradictions *in that reality* itself.' Such a limitation prevents these approaches from providing an adequate basis for social change. This fact implies that democratic approaches to accountability have conservative political consequences in their relation to existing social order.

In a sustained criticism of MacDonald's views on evaluation, Lakomski (1983) has elaborated upon this point. She has argued that the value pluralism implicit in the democratic approach implies a 'sophisticated relativism': that is, there is an assumption that when groups disagree, there is no way of establishing one of them as correct. Apart from the paradox involved in any attempt to refute this claim, Lakomski (1983, p. 273) contends that this view is located in the framework of a liberal pluralism that is profoundly conservative because it allows the self-justification of its own assumptions; and since it

> ... *takes for granted* the political framework of liberal pluralism so it accepts uncritically the very program it evaluates. More specifically, it does not raise the question of how and why *this* programme came to be conceived and implemented. Worse, it cannot even *raise* the question given its grounding in social phenomenology.... The consequence of the inability to account for the social and educational programmes and to judge their worth leads democratic evaluation implicitly to affirm the *status quo*.

If schools are to be self-evaluating in their own terms, then any outside authority is denied. But this makes the idea of judgments *across* schools a relatively meaningless notion. Without cross-school comparisons, however, we have no way of coherently talking about educational inequalities. Since schools are left to develop their own way of organizing relationships, they are also left free to maintain the status quo within and across schools, even if that status quo means leaving such 'inherently unequal provisions between and among private and public sector schools as exist in Australia effectively intact. Ultimately, the democratic approaches to accountability provide us with no clear way of dealing with the issue of educational inequalities.

For a program like the Participation and Equity Program (PEP), this was a fatal limitation because educational inequality constituted the central idea around which the program was designed. The program designers in the state of Victoria had recognized the limitations of both the managerial and democratic approaches to evaluation and accountability and emphasized that program activities had to be assessed against a set of measurable program-wide public criteria, but they also stressed the importance of school-based decision-making and participatory democratic processes. In this way they had to carve out a position between some of the requirements of managerial and democratic approaches to educational accountability. In what follows, I describe how PEP conceptualized accountability and discuss the main achievements and problems with its strategy.

The Participation and Equity Program in Victoria, Australia

The Participation and Equity Program (PEP) was a program of educational reform initiated by the Australian Labor Government in 1983, in a context of, among other things, high unemployment among young people, their social alienation, and, by OECD standards, their comparatively low retention rates in upper secondary schooling. Some concomitant educational concerns for the national government were to facilitate curriculum change, to seek changes to the organization of secondary schooling and, through these measures, to promote equity. At the organizational level the Australian Commonwealth Schools Commission, given responsibility to devise its philosophical base, saw PEP essentially as a school-based program. In its documents the Commission eschewed centre-periphery conceptions of educational change, rejecting the notion that changes as far-reaching as those proposed by PEP could somehow be imposed 'from the top'.

Within the context of the Australian federal system, while it was the central government that initiated PEP, it was the state governments that had to implement it. In the state of Victoria the central government's understanding, communicated through the Schools Commission's *PEP Guide*, of what needed to be done to achieve school improvement was reinforced by the philosophical orientation of the Victorian Government's ministerial papers, released in 1983. Just as the Commonwealth Schools Commission's *PEP Guide* (1985) stressed an active partnership between home, school and the wider community, and wanted schools to develop 'real processes of genuine accountability, instead of merely reporting to a passive school community the outcome of policies it has had no hand in shaping' (p. 16), so the Victorian ministerial papers also emphasized the principles of genuine devolution of authority and collaborative, participative decision-making processes.

Arguing that the processes of education must be informed by the values of participation and equity, PEP construed the process of reform itself as an educational process. The program's rhetoric emphasized the importance of devising administrative structures that would encapsulate

PEP's democratic aspirations, and so would provide models for the operation of the program at school and classroom levels. Particularly during its first year, the administrators of the program in Victoria repeatedly quoted these sentiments as they struggled to develop a structure that reflected the commitment to collaborative decision-making processes.

How were these democratic sentiments translated into an administrative structure? In attempting this task, those charged with the responsibility for establishing and implementing the program in Victoria had some help from the guidelines provided in the Commission's *PEP Guide*. One senior PEP officer described these guidelines in the following terms:

(a) Talk heavily about people and not resources as being the main item of expenditure.

(b) Ask States to take a non-submission approach.

(c) Suggest large scale funding per school to be intensively directed rather than using the margarine approach i.e. spread a little everywhere.

(d) Have a system of targeting which pre-determines what schools are in the Program. . . .

The Schools Commission had specified that 75 per cent of total program funds be allocated to targeted schools, though at a later stage this requirement was reduced to 55 per cent. The rest of the funds allocated to each state could be spent on other system level initiatives and administrative costs. Target schools were not to exceed or fall below the level of 40 per cent of all government secondary schools in the state. From the Commission's perspective the targeting of schools was to form the backbone of the program: the targeted schools were to be drawn into the program whether they liked it or not. The Schools Commission, however, had little to offer in the way of explicit criteria for the identification of target schools. It expected that states would have available the 'relevant data such as school retention and participation rates and the concentration in particular communities of students from groups on whom the Program is to focus. . .' (*PEP Guide*, p. 26). In Victoria the 1981 version of the Disadvantaged Schools Index (DSI) was used as a measure to identify schools to be targeted. In all, 178 schools were initially targeted, though in later years the list was changed when a more up-to-date DSI became available.

The program also rejected a submissions-based funding system on the grounds of equity: it was believed that that strategy would once again benefit schools with expertise in submission preparation. Targeting particular schools could, on the other hand, help schools which were relatively unskilled, unorganized and unpractised at securing funds through submissions. It was also felt that schools were generally reacting against submission strategy. The program was keen to try another way of generating school reform, to invite schools which had not previously participated in special programs to be part of a program that encouraged them to re-examine their curricula and organizational practices. According to a senior officer of the program, the submissions strategy had become self-defeating: earlier submission-driven programs had inhibited learning or policy development since much attention was given to the politics and administration of funding rather than to the educational activities for which the programs were created in the first place. Program consultants and support staff had come to be perceived as acting in administrative and inspectorial roles rather than as facilitators of learning.

It was argued that while the main reason in the past for the submissions approach was accountability, this had proved inadequate. Schools had simply devised ways of presenting the desired information for yet another year's funding. Program officials had no way of telling whether the accounts presented were accurate (Stephens, 1984, pp. 70–1). In Stephens' view, PEP represented a new way of funding schools and approaching the accountability issue. Schools were targeted on the basis of trust, and a complex support structure was established to help schools develop activities to achieve the program's central objectives.

The targeted schools were each allocated funds to evaluate current curriculum practices and organization in order to determine the extent to which they met, effectively and equitably, the needs of *all* students. Schools were to identify their particular educational needs in collaboration with parents, teachers and students. The information collected was to be used to initiate activities in nine specific areas: curriculum; teacher renewal and support; teacher parent student interaction; assessment, accreditation and credentialling; groups with particular needs; education and the arts; school structure and organization; post-school experience-school links; and public support for education. With such a comprehensive list, target schools were given considerable latitude to devise activities that they considered most important. As far as the program was concerned, schools were in the best position to judge what their priorities are. Both its central requirements — that schools initiate activities which catered to the needs of all students and worked for more equitable outcomes and that decision-making processes of the program include parents, teachers and students — were thus formal ones.

The program's key implementation strategy related to the idea of time-release. The PEP funds allocated to schools could be used to release teachers from timetabled duties to work together in the investigations and actions proposed by their schools. The program officials believed that for perhaps the first time in the history of special programs in Australia the government had recognized the importance of teachers' reflection upon and evaluation of their own practices. Schools were asked 'to set aside time to consider clear goals and educational strategies for achieving them in a collaborative decision-making process involving teachers, parents and students' (*PEP Guide*, p. 16). The program also allowed schools to use funds for the employment of extended or casual emergency teachers, for the employment of school council appointed personnel to work with the school and its community and for other school-based program development activities.

It is important to note that the designers of this strategy had in mind a particular view of how schools change. It was argued that substantial change in schools could not occur unless whole-school communities reflected on their total practice, including curriculum, teaching-learning styles and organization. The emphasis was on processes of negotiation and consensus at local school levels. Radical transformation of education was sought through an emphasis which required a systematic and consciously active approach to learning about how current practices reproduced inequalities, and how access and success in curriculum were only possible when school communities were able to think together and make informed decisions together. This approach to school improvement was thought to imply a view of evaluation as a continuous and participatory process that linked reflection and plans for action. Many in the Victorian program referred to PEP as 'a learning program'. The role of regional and central consultancy was to support school-based initiatives and encourage their development rather than be prescriptive about the nature and pace of changes. The role of administration was to create conditions that enabled schools to proceed with curriculum development without the unnecessary bureaucratic restrictions that had bedeviled earlier reform efforts.

This approach to school change was consistent with the observations of a number of activists in Victorian education. As Hannan (1984, p. 44) argued: 'I have to say that PEP needs a vision of how change happens in school. My own views on this are rather firm. I don't believe in top down change. Change comes through the involvement of practitioners. Practitioners have to be at the centre and in control of schemes for reform. Support from outside — in this case from or through or in the name of PEP — then consists of people to help with fact-finding, theorising, comparison and criticism.' Hannan's view also reflected the principles of the School Improvement Plan (SIP) outlined in *Ministerial Paper 2*.

SIP saw evaluation as a cooperative task for the whole school community involving a process of continuing critical review and renewal. Learning was considered an essential concern of SIP which had, as a primary focus, the aim of improved educational outcomes for all students. In target schools PEP complemented the SIP orientation in giving the idea of school-based decision-making additional rhetorical force.

PEP's strategy of targeting schools and giving them considerable latitude, however, did not receive universal approval among the program's designers. Some believed that the strategy would be too difficult to manage, would be confrontational and might involve very high risks. Schools, they feared, might not use the grant money for the purposes of genuine reform. To allay these fears, the Victorian *PEP Guide* carried a section entitled 'Activities Specifically Discouraged'. This list of proscribed practices also served to define the nature and scope of the program's objectives. The following activities were precluded:

- both top-down centralized control and laissez-faire local approaches, either in the Program as a whole, or at school level, PEP requires cooperative problem solving;
- token participation in decision-making processes;
- development of separate or alternative courses into which students are streamed on the basis of perceived academic potential or performance;
- practices which exclude students on the basis of gender, ethnicity or disability from access to mainstream learning;
- emphasis on competition in learning;
- labelling and testing procedures which discourage continuing participation in education;
- development of programs which lead to the exclusion of some students from the study of traditional intellectual disciplines;
- school organizational arrangements which make it possible to pay attention to individual needs and learning paces. (*PEP Guide*, p. 14)

Even with this statement, the discussion of program goals in the *Guide* and the nomination of the broad areas for action, some members of state PEP committees and program administrators remained uneasy. They argued that there was still no administrative mechanism for ensuring that these guidelines were adhered to. The program had to confront the issue of accountability, but this had to be done within the requirements of a commitment to school-based decision-making.

PEP's Approach to Accountability and Evaluation

Victorian PEP acknowledged that a level of managerial accountability could not be avoided but it sought to view the structure of this accountability in a very general way through which each targeted school was required to provide a statement of its purposes, structure and activities to the program's central managers, and through them the state government and the Commonwealth Schools Commission. Other more specific elements of managerial accountability were rejected because the program designers believed that they were incompatible with the principles of participation and equity. In Victoria PEP was regarded as an open and experimental program, objectives of which could not be stated in behavioural terms. In particular, objectives such as reflecting, evaluating, negotiating and understanding could not be easily translated into measurable terms. Moreover, PEP encouraged a diversity of activities, rendering it impossible to develop a unidimensional scale against which the heterogeneous efforts of all schools could be measured. The designers of the program thought, moreover, that a managerial accountability mechanism, even if such a thing could be devised, would not only not promote learning, but in some circumstances might prove to be a disincentive for some schools to be experimental by engendering defensiveness.

The managerial model of accountability was also thought to be politically unacceptable since many in the program agreed with House (1973) that it embodied control assumptions. Committed to school-based decision-making as the program was, its designers were reluctant to establish a scheme in which education was organized like a corporation which required subordinates to be strictly accountable to the organization and in which the organization was not accountable to the individual. In a program committed to democracy, accountability must be reciprocal, based on the assumption that all members of the school community have direct access to decision-making processes. The program sought a mechanism in which educational values and the idea of public interest were continuously negotiated, rather than agglomerated in some central bureaucratic dictate. It wished to provide school communities with ample opportunities for learning and for disseminating information, including what it called 'practitioner crafted accounts' of curriculum innovations and organizational experiments.

It is within the framework of these principles that PEP developed its notion of peer accountability for schools. The program wished to see accountability as horizontal rather than vertical. The idea of 'horizontal accountability' involved emphasis on accountability to school communities, to parents and students, as well as to other schools, rather than to a central committee or the educational bureaucracy. It was seen as a major step towards devolution. The program's centre gave itself the minimal role of overseeing developments, and ensuring in a very general way that schools did not abuse the guidelines established by the Victorian PEP Committee in order to meet the broader accountability requirements that the Schools Commission, with most of the real powers of decision-making, transferred to schools themselves. The major accountability function was handed over to the Schools Reference Groups (SRGs).

Schools Reference Groups were created to serve the purposes of 'horizontal' accountability. The size of SRGs varied from three to seven grant schools, which normally included both technical and high schools, and from 1986 special schools. The membership of each SRG normally consisted of at least three representatives from each grant school, including at least one teacher, one parent and one student. These representatives were to negotiate their understanding of the broad objectives of the program and moderate each other's plans for curriculum reform. This accountability scheme acknowledged that schools themselves had considerable 'expertise' to develop their own curriculum. But beyond the peer accountability function, SRGs were also established to provide schools with a wider forum to reflect on the planning and implementation of their program activities. In the jargon of action research this process was referred to as 'the sharing of learning through collaborative reflection'. Each SRG was serviced by a regional consultant whose task it was to keep records of meetings and provide information and advice on regional and central issues. SRGs normally met at least three times each term to consider an agenda which they had determined for themselves, and to assist one another in whatever ways they saw fit.

In turn, the work of the SRGs was, at least partially, coordinated by Regional Reference Groups (RRGs), though the relationship between SRGs and RRGs was not considered to be that of a line authority, and not all regions saw the need to create these groups. Program officials insisted that the relationship between the program's central office and SRGs was not of a hierarchical kind. The centre was to provide all kinds of information that it thought the SRGs might find useful. It also made available particular consultancy services, but only when these were requested by the SRGs themselves. In turn, SRGs were requested to submit profiles of school PEP activities and school plans so that these might be collated to obtain state-wide information.

In line with the non-submission-based approach to funding, and in line with ideas from the ministerial papers, a model for accountability within the program was constructed, as shown in Figure 15.1.

Figure 15.1 PEP accountability in Victoria

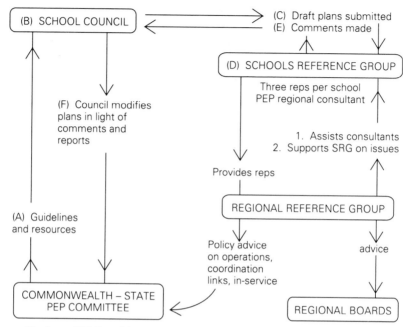

Source: Stephens (1984), p. 74.

While the membership of Schools Reference Groups included representatives endorsed by the school council from each target school including a teacher, a parent and a student, all of whom were directly involved in the school's PEP program, SRGs also had the power to co-opt other members. The formal structure of SRGs was seen as creating conditions necessary for 'horizontal accountability' by allowing peers from participating schools to discuss proposals and to offer criticism and advice. Target schools were expected to submit a formal plan for the use of their PEP funds to the SRG for consideration. On the basis of feedback received they were then expected to amend proposals until they fell within an agreed understanding of the program's guidelines through debate at the SRG level. In this way it was intended that the judgment about the adequacy of plans would not be made by 'outsiders' who did not have a responsive stake in the outcomes of action at the school level, but by people who were directly involved in translating the program's broad guidelines into practice. Some regional consultants in the program referred to this approach as 'responsive accountability' (as opposed to control accountability), since schools were required to be sensitive to the attitudes and values which structured their audience's interaction with them under the particular cultural and political conditions which prevailed in the local contexts.

Of major concern to the program's designers in Victoria was the need to ensure that its approaches to accountability and evaluation complemented each other. Evaluation along broad action research lines was to be a key principle. The first Victorian *PEP Guide* (1984, p. 48) set the tone for this: 'Evaluation is not simply a requirement imposed for the purposes of (hierarchical) accountability. As the Program aims at improvement of the organization and practice of education at the level of systems organization, Program administration and support services, whole-school curriculum and individual approaches to teaching, evaluation becomes a major tool in the achievement of the Program's aims.' Evaluation was seen not so much as a means of finding out the program's effect but as a key strategy in achieving the program's objectives. All schools were expected 'to engage in the cyclical process of evaluation, planning, implementation and ongoing evaluation to improve school organization and curriculum.' The program stressed that 'improvement depends on a capacity to learn, both individually and collectively, to make progressively better decisions by monitoring the outcomes of current action, and plan future action on the basis of the best information possible' (*PEP Guide*, 1986, p. 27) Clearly, school-based evaluation approaches were primarily to serve the needs of the school rather than some outside agency.

In SRGs the requirements of evaluation and accountability merged. While at the school level evaluation represented a starting place for investigation and action, at SRGs participating schools reported accounts of developments to each other with the expectation that their accounts and further plans might be subjected to criticism and advice. SRGs were designed to moderate school-based decisions but also to promote a 'shared approach to school based curriculum development' and encourage 'sharing of resources between schools and the development of broader curriculum options between schools' (*PEP Guide*, 1986, p. 25). Instead of viewing accountability as a one-way process which required schools to report to its SRG, PEP conceived it as a two-way process: participating schools were accountable to each other; the information they collected was essentially for their own use, written in a form that was accessible to school communities, including teachers, students and parents, represented on the SRGs. How did this accountability strategy fare? In the next section, I want to describe some of its successes, and discuss the problems schools encountered in trying to develop effective SRGs.

Schools Reference Groups

The Schools Reference Group strategy represented a major innovation which the program itself did not adequately appreciate. Much of the recent debate over school accountability has been between those who advocate centralized control systems and those who support the notion of democratic accountability. On the one hand, educational bureaucracies have put forward various management approaches such as performance contracting, Michigan State accountability system and national assessment of educational progress, while, on the other hand, educational researchers such as MacDonald (1978) and Elliott (1980) have proposed the ideas of teachers as autonomous accountable professionals and self-accounting schools. The SRG strategy represented a fresh way of looking at the issue, one that cut across the hoary dichotomy between school autonomy and centralized control. It placed school learning at the centre of reform efforts, and developed a mechanism that viewed accountability as a two-way process in which educational criteria played a dominant part.

For some schools, the SRG strategy enabled them to have direct formal contact with their neighbouring schools for the first time. While inter-school sports competitions were common enough between many other schools, they seldom had the opportunities to discuss educational matters together. Such contact led to targeted schools becoming familiar with the plans that other schools had devised for the use of their PEP funds, how the schools saw their educational priorities and what problems they encountered in promoting the goals of participation and equity. Schools learned of a broader range of curriculum options and procedures by drawing on the experiences of other schools. As one teacher pointed out in late 1986: 'As far as I am concerned, even if PEP doesn't achieve anything else, SRGs would have been a major achievement. It has allowed schools to share their experiences, their difficulties and their successes together. I knew nothing about ... High School, now I am better informed. I know now that some of the problems we have had at this school are not unique. I reckon that even when PEP goes, as it no doubt will, SRGs will be an idea well worth keeping in some form....'

However, as might have been expected, the SRG strategy had a slow and confused beginning. Despite schools being saturated with the rhetoric of school-based decision-making contained in the ministerial papers, they had remained highly routinized bureaucratic places, suspicious of programs of reform that promise democracy yet do not deliver resources and support needed to practise it. It was in this context that PEP represented an experiment in developing a non-bureaucratic and non-hierarchical approach to school reform. As an organizational innovation, it sought to bring the needs of accountability and self-evaluation and learning together. These ideas represented a radically new way of working for most targeted schools. Imbued with an understandable level of cynicism, in 1985 most schools seemed unclear about the *real* purposes of the Schools Reference Groups. Lacking a clear understanding of the program's emphasis on schools devising their own ways of working together, many SRGs wanted clear directives from the central office and the PEP committee. Past programs had given schools manuals to guide their work; in contrast, PEP was encouraging schools to develop their own manuals, to become responsible for their own actions. The regional consultants found it difficult to respond to many of the schools' queries about how to conduct SRG meetings, for many of them had not themselves developed a clear model. The SRG strategy was as much of an experiment for them as it was for schools. At a conference of the regional PEP consultants in May 1985 it was clear that there were competing views about the nature and scope of SRGs. Some saw them as decentralized groups which collected information for accountability, as mechanisms for ensuring that central guidelines were adhered to; others saw them as open-ended structures, to be developed into forms that the participating schools desired.

These consultants did not wish to impose any particular view of how schools ought to work together on SRGs. They wished to see schools themselves negotiate the best way of working with each other. Lacking any established pattern for their work, SRG meetings were variously seen as learning exchanges, in-service activities, show-and-tell sessions and administrative committees whose task it was to approve school plans. As one regional consultant argued in late 1985, SRGs had not developed as 'forums for critical debate about curriculum, democratic processes in schools and the specific curriculum of member schools. Only on rare occasions do Schools Reference Groups question the practice of individual schools or identify to what extent member schools are ignoring or addressing the needs of disadvantaged groups within those schools.' Teachers from one school were understandably hesitant to evaluate critically the school plans of another. Some teachers found it difficult to reconcile the notions of school-based development and cross-school critical commentary. In one region in particular, where a 'rationalization' process was under way with the accompanying threat of closures or unfavourable amalgamations, there was a reluctance to be open about the problems schools were facing for fear of political misuse of such information. In such circumstances schools in some SRGs adopted a 'you scratch my back, I will scratch yours' attitude. It was clear that the SRG strategy had to work within a broader bureaucratic structure, the values of which could not be easily reconciled with PEP's approach to evaluation and accountability.

As might be expected, there was considerable variation in the role and function of various SRGs. While all groups, after initial hesitation, facilitated and supported evaluation and the development of school plans, the degree to which they were committed to these tasks varied. At some SRG meetings nothing more than show-and-tell occurred, while at others broader educational issues were taken on immediately and examined systematically before the approval of a plan was granted. Schools were made to justify their plans of action in terms of the goals of participation and equity as had been negotiated earlier.

Throughout 1985 a number of schools perceived SRGs to be inconsequential and ineffective. The morale of participating schools received a severe knock when the Federal Government announced that the PEP budget would effectively be cut in half. PEP was not a very significant part of the overall concerns of the schools anyway; now there appeared even less at stake. Cynicism that had already existed in schools about the commitment of governments to reform programs was intensified. In such a climate even the evaluation tasks that SRGs had to undertake became difficult to arrange and were mostly completed superficially. For some teachers attending SRG meetings became a chore: 'another meeting to attend on top of everything else'. In such cases the regional consultants saw their task in terms of a challenge to raise the level of critical thinking and debate in SRG meetings. For a number of reasons, however, this objective was difficult to achieve.

First, the membership of SRG groups changed often, with new representatives of schools attending meetings when others lost interest. This meant that there was little continuity in the conduct of tasks: the same ground had to be covered repeatedly. Often the same committed few teachers and parents attended the meetings.

Second, considerable distrust existed between schools which had historically regarded themselves in competition with each other, making communication between them difficult to achieve in SRG meetings. A technical school in the western suburbs of Melbourne, for example, refused point blank to work with its neighbouring high school, forcing the regional consultant to mediate in the dispute, which was not easily resolved.

Third, at meetings where principals attended (usually those which dealt with funding matters), they tended to dominate the proceedings, often making students and parents feel redundant and unwelcome. At some SRGs only junior members of staff attended; these teachers were perceived as having little authority to speak on behalf of the whole school, let alone commit their schools to particular plans of action.

Fourth, as already indicated, some schools were reluctant to reveal their problems to other schools in their SRG for fear that information might be misused. This was particularly so in the south-central region where a plan for reorganization and rationalization of schools coincided with the establishment of the SRGs. In a political climate where closures and amalgamations of schools were a real possibility, some schools felt it prudent not to divulge information that could be seized upon and used against their interests. For the SRG strategy to succeed, it was essential that schools trust each other; yet in the context of the rationalization process many teachers and school administrators understandably found it difficult to be frank and open about the problems and issues their schools confronted.

Fifth, some schools found the role of the students on SRGs unclear. Since there had been little precedent for students working on issues of school reform, many teachers found it difficult to discuss openly the organizational and personality issues confronting their schools.

Sixth, since meetings were often held after school, the idea of student involvement gave rise to practical problems. In particular, questions such as how the students were to travel to the school where the SRG meeting was to be held, and under whose guidance, had to be clarified.

Seventh, some SRGS found it difficult to understand the role of the regional consultants. They were often seen as having the requisite information and skills to judge particular plans of action, but other SRGs found regional consultants intrusive and viewed their presence on SRGs suspiciously. The role of regional consultants on SRGs continued to be poorly understood. While in most cases consultants provided a supporting role, in some others they were viewed as the experts. Consequently, directions were sought from them not only on administrative matters but also on matters of educational policy. Developing non-hierarchical ways of working in an educational system still governed by notions of accountability to the centre and line authority was never going to be easy.

Eighth, some SRG members found they did not meet often enough to develop good working relationships, to establish trust between schools. They believed that more time was needed to develop an adequate understanding of the notion of horizontal accountability. As it was, few schools continued to abuse the consultative processes. School plans were approved which did not receive adequate attention or scrutiny. Many of these plans required intervention from the Schools Unit, and had to be rejected because they fell outside the broad guidelines developed by the program. In a few remote cases school-approved accountability processes

317

were ignored cynically; more generally, some schools continued to find it difficult to come to terms with the evaluation and accountability part of their role, not only because they believed that they did not have the appropriate skills but also because the idea of evaluation through action research was poorly understood. Accountability was also seen by some SRG members in narrow, financial terms, and not in the the broader educational context PEP had envisaged.

Finally, there was the problem of deciding exactly whom the teachers, parents and students attending SRG meetings represented (the schools, themselves, or their constituencies) and what authority they carried to commit schools to certain plans of action. The relation between school councils and SRGs remained unclear. Those who attended SRG meetings were not always members of their school council, and they were not sure whether their reports were being adequately discussed by the school council. Many of these participants felt that despite the PEP's rhetoric of mainstreaming, at their school the program activities were considered marginal.

Despite these difficulties, towards the end of 1986 there was some evidence to sustain the view that most SRGs were beginning to come to terms with their roles. While many of the problems remained unresolved, they were being tackled in the belief that the SRG strategy was well worth experimenting with. As a result of considerable trial and error, schools were beginning to define the role and mode of working of SRGs in a way that suited their interests, making SRGs into bodies that were not simply imposed from above but forums that could even survive after the demise of PEP in late 1987. Indeed, many regular participants on SRGs, and the regional consultants in particular, believed that as a new way of conceiving the issue of accountability, the strategy had great potential. Most schools agreed that SRGs had provided important forums for educational discussion and for learning from the experiences of others.

In addition to the specific administration and evaluation tasks they were required to undertake, Schools Reference Groups tackled a range of educational issues and problems, including tertiary access and credentialling; accreditation for student participation on decision-making committees; the nature and scope of PEP task forces; the ministerial papers; the Blackburn Report and the issues of retention, the new VCE and assessment procedures; and the various proposals for school rationalization, where these were applicable. In various SRG meetings schools helped each other by thinking through strategies for improving communication with parents, discussing ideas about the use of PEP funds, exploring strategies for the use of funds provided through PEP's capital grants program and more generally examining, and attempting to resolve, the problems associated with teachers' time release and the availability of emergency teachers. SRGs also provided schools with an opportunity for pooling resources and coordinating activities among member schools, enabling inter-school visits and, in a few notable cases, developing collaborative curriculum projects.

By the end of 1986 most schools conceded that the SRG strategy was at least a useful discussion forum for those who attended. Others were considerably more enthusiastic about its success and saw enormous possibilities in its further development, though they were unclear as to how this might happen. The following remarks by a teacher were typical:

> The SRG has been very useful to this school. Normally five or six of us attend and we have all got a great deal out of being involved. We have discussed the issue of retention rates, the problem of descriptive assessment and student participation on curriculum committees. We also talked about *Ministerial Papers 2* and *6* as well as major curriculum initiatives that have been debated through teacher journals like the Hannan article on 'Towards a Democratic Curriculum' and the key issues raised within the Blackburn Report. Students in particular have gained a great deal from going to SRG meetings. We have also organized visits to other schools to see how they have organized their PEP ... and that has been very useful.... Our program this year is much better because of SRGs than it would have been without it.

Discussion

In the development of the SRG strategy the role of the regional consultants turned out to be crucial. The strategy was based upon an assumption that it was possible to develop collaborative and trusting relationships between schools. The regional consultants were given a major task in enabling SRGs to develop into critical self-reflective communities. However, as a regional consultant noted, 'Consultants had to develop their own role as well as school participants. No one had experience of SRGs and how to operate in them as it was a new way of networking schools. The concept of horizontal accountability and action research evaluation is new to schools and it needs a lot of time to develop an understanding of these concepts and to realize the valuable potential of SRG meetings.' However, the limited time was not the only difficulty the regional consultants faced. Other difficulties were linked to the more general theoretical problems with the program's conception of horizontal accountability and its location within a broader bureaucratic structure that remained largely untouched by the program's ideological thrust.

Regional consultants provided the primary focus of support for program development and a link between schools and the PEP Committee and the regional offices. Their work was crucial in developing the confidence schools needed to implement activities and projects designed to achieve greater participation and equity. Yet their work was not always appreciated by schools which were only too willing to vent their anger over such matters as the announcement of the cuts over which they had no control. The consultants also faced the brunt of schools' wrath over such administrative difficulties as schools had in getting emergency teachers through the Ministry's Human Resource Branch to cover for the time release promised by the program. Since the program was committed to mainstreaming, it was required to rely upon Ministry's existing services. But those employed to provide these services were not always in sympathy with the administrative innovations which the program's distinctive orientation entailed. It was clear to the consultants that until the values embodied in the notion of horizontal accountability were accepted by the Ministry as a whole, they faced an uphill battle in convincing schools that the idea could work.

Schools had differing expectations of the PEP consultants. Some regarded them as having administrative responsibilities only, while others were prepared to view them in ways that the consultants themselves preferred, as change agents, facilitators, general curriculum consultants and educational listening posts. Some regional consultants saw themselves as buffers between the centre and schools. The educative change agent role of the consultants was particularly difficult in schools which showed a lack of interest in the program, at least during its first year, and which refused to make problematic those features of school life which schools themselves refused to open to question, especially in relation to issues of equity.

The consultancy role was bedeviled by a conflict of loyalties. Many consultants were appointed for their skill in supporting school-based activities; at the same time, however, they believed that they were increasingly obliged to perform administrative tasks expected of them by the program's committees and its central and regional administration. Ironically, they found themselves in the classical bind of school inspectors in former years: they wanted to see themselves as educational change agents and servants of schools, yet some schools continued to view them in terms of their administrative responsibilities, as servants of central and/or regional administration.

The regional consultants occupied an ambiguous position in the program's organizational structure. Part of the problem lay in the efforts of the program to regionalize consultancy support on the one hand, and to centralize the decision-making processes about key operational issues on the other. As things turned out, the consultants believed that not everyone involved in PEP's central office was committed to the idea of regionalization. Regional bureaucracies, on the other hand, had little understanding of PEP's goals, and many had no evident commitment to them. Far from receiving support from regional bureaucracies, consultants were confronted with the major task of having to convince regional officers to take the program seriously. In the end the PEP consultancy role became as much servicing the regional office as schools. In an effort to mainstream PEP reforms, consultants faced a fundamental dilemma. They wanted to mainstream PEP into general, regional concerns and yet they were conscious of the need to avoid being subsumed within the culture of the regional bureaucracy. On the one hand, they wanted to be critical of the developments occurring in regional offices that were contrary to the principles of PEP, but on the other hand, they were required to be loyal to the bureaucracies they served.

The time that regional consultants did spend with schools was devoted to ensuring that representative structures were put in place in schools and in SRGs. A great deal of energy was expended in trying to get more parents and students attending task force or SRG meetings regularly. So much so that at some regional offices PEP consultants were often regarded as special program consultants, concerned with establishing participatory processes. This perception highlighted a major theoretical problem with PEP's notion of 'horizontal accountability'.

The 1986 Victorian *PEP Guide* maintained that 'accountability is essentially about the relationship between actors and decision makers working within the framework of policy', and 'to be accountable, all those who initiate decisions must be responsible to those affected as an outcome' (p. 31). However, fearing that this definition was stated at an unacceptable level of generality, the *Guide* went on to state conditions for the needs of accountability that must be met at each level of the program:

- decisions were reasonable and based on available information;
- the decision making processes were based on a democratic and participatory framework;
- adequate steps had been taken to gather information to enable informed decisions;
- decisions taken have fallen within the framework established by Program guidelines and state education policy and related regulations.

These conditions were widely understood to highlight participatory processes. Schools were not accountable for the achievement of specified results; rather, they were asked to explore options and experiment with curriculum and organizational innovations. They were accountable to the various constituencies through their SRGs for adhering to certain principles governing decision-making practices. Schools were to demonstrate to SRGs that they had abided by certain procedural principles.

While this emphasis by Victorian PEP on accountability for the adherence to principles of decision-making and accountability to diverse constituencies rather than to the centralized bureaucracy represents a major advance on the mechanistic hierarchical views of accountability, it does pose a major theoretical problem. It suggests far too fundamental a division between accountability for certain outcomes and accountability in adherence to certain principles of practice and decision-making processes. Arguably, processes and outcomes cannot be so easily dichotomized. This problem is similar to that discussed by White (1986) in relation to PEP's definition of curriculum.

White objects to the Victorian *PEP Guide's* definition of curriculum as the 'sum of all experiences, planned and unplanned, developed by the school community. It includes not only what is taught, and approaches to teaching and learning, but also the way the school is organized' (p. 11). The definition, as White points out, was developed by teacher activists in the 1970s as a useful way of demanding that schools look at what they were really doing. But in the mid-1980s, under PEP, White maintains, the definition became removed from the context of its formation and has become less useful, being taken to mean almost anything that takes place in schools. The definition lacked a value orientation; it made no distinctions in respect of what constitutes quality in schools, except on extraneous grounds.

Given the formalistic nature of this definition of curriculum, Victorian schools struggled with the dilemmas concerning the desirable outcomes of education. Since on this definition everything done in schools is equally curriculum, schools themselves had to determine what was good curriculum and what was not. Schools had to give content to the objectives of participation and equity. Similarly, lacking a detailed analysis of 'participation' and 'equity', the program left SRGs with no clear way of judging the content of the many activities schools proposed. It is true that SRGs were important forums where the program objectives could be and were further explored, but ultimately they could not reject idiosyncratic understandings of the program's objectives, as long as the principles of decision-making processes were adhered to.

In the final analysis it has to be admitted that the Victorian PEP's understanding of accountability and its construction of the SRG strategy represented an important experiment through which the goals of school-based decision-making and public accountability could be expressed. Rejecting the notion of self-monitoring schools, PEP established a mechanism which provided groups of schools with forums in which to discuss issues of mutual concern and at the same time meet the requirements of peer accountability. However, this accountability remained confined to principles of practice and not to outcomes, and even in this limited way it was mostly marginal to the broader concerns of schools. PEP's location within the larger structure of the Education Ministry meant that its success was always going to be dependent on the bureaucracy conceding some of its power and influence. Such was not the case; indeed, if anything, in Victoria the bureaucracy has reasserted itself.

References

BURNHEIM, J. (1985) *Is Democracy Possible?* Cambridge: Polity Press.

CARR, W. and KEMMIS, S., (1983) *Becoming Critical: Knowing through Action Research*. Geelong: Deakin University Press.

CODD, J. (1988) *Knowledge and Control in the Evaluation of Educational Organizations*. Geelong: Deakin University Press.

COMMONWEALTH SCHOOLS COMMISSION (1983) *Participation and Equity in Australian Schools: The Goal of Full Secondary Education*. Canberra: Australian Government Publishing Service.

ELLIOTT, J. (1980) 'Who Should Monitor School Performance in Schools,' in SOCKETT, H. (Ed.), *Accountability in the English School System*. London: Hodder and Stoughton.

HANNAN, W. (1984) 'Participation and Equity,' in *Proceedings of the National Conference on the Participation and Equity Program*, Canberra.

HOUSE, E. (1973) *School Evaluation: The Politics and the Process*. Berkeley, Calif.: McCutchan.

HOUSE, E. (1979) 'The Objectivity, Fairness, and Justice of Federal Policy as Reflected in the Follow-through Evaluation,' *Educational Evaluation and Policy*, 1, 1, 28–42.

LACEY, C. and LAWTON, D. (Eds) (1981) *Issues in Evaluation and Accountability*. London: Methuen.

LAKOMSKI, G. (1983) 'Ways of Knowing and Ways of Evaluating: or, How Democratic Is "Democratic Evaluation"?' *Journal of Curriculum Studies*, 15, 3, 265–76.

MACDONALD, B. (1978) 'Accountability, Standards and the Process of Schooling,' Mimeo, University of East Anglia.

MINISTER OF EDUCATION (1983) *Ministerial Paper Number 1: Decision Making in Victorian Education*. Melbourne: Department of Education.

MINISTER OF EDUCATION (1983) *Ministerial Paper Number 2: The School Improvement Plan*. Melbourne: Department of Education.

Participation and Equity Program Regional Consultants (1986) *A Regional Perspective in PEP*, A Report Prepared by Regional Consultants in Victorian PEP, Victorian Participation and Equity Program, Melbourne.

Pincoff, E. (1973) 'Educational Accountability,' *Studies in Philosophy and Education*, 8, 2, 71–82.

Rizvi, F. and Kemmis, S. (1987) *Dilemmas of Reform: An Overview of PEP in Victorian Schools*. Geelong: Deakin Institute for Studies in Education.

Simon, H. (1981) 'Process Evaluation in Schools' in Lacey, C. and Lawton, D. (Eds), *Issues in Evaluation and Accountability*. London: Methuen.

Sockett, H. (1976) 'Teacher Accountability,' *Proceedings of the Philosophy of Education Society of Great Britain*, 10, 34–57.

Stephens, A. (1984) 'Non-Submission Based Approaches to Funding,' *Proceedings of the National Conference on the Participation and Equity Program*, Canberra.

Victorian Participation and Equity Program (1984 and 1986) *PEP Guide*, Melbourne: Victorian PEP.

White, D. (1986) *Education and the State: Federal Involvement in Educational Policy Development*. Geelong: Deakin University Press.

Part 5

Summation

Chapter 16

School-based Decision-making and Management: Retrospect and Prospect

Patrick A. Duignan

A Developing Rationale for School-based Decision-making

The move toward school-based decision-making reflects a change in thinking from more rational, normative and prescriptive approaches in educational decision-making to a recognition of the complex context of decision-making in our educational systems and organizations. Life in organizations is a good deal more uncertain and complex than many educational bureaucrats appreciate. Many educational organizations, including schools, have unclear goals, uncertain technology and fluid participation (Cohen and March, 1974). Connections between goals and activities are difficult to establish and cause and effect relationships are tentative at best. Schön (1983, p. 16) argues that the situations of practice in today's organizations are inherently unstable, and traditionally accepted management and administrative techniques and procedures are inadequate when dealing with the increasingly critical task of 'managing complexity'. Policy- and decision-makers are confronted with dynamic situations that 'consist of complex systems of changing problems that interact with each other'. Most managers or administrators find themselves 'embroiled in conflicts of values, goals, purposes and interests' (p. 17). The complexity, uncertainty, instability, uniqueness and value conflict inherent in organizational practice of the 1980s have made it necessary for policy- and decision-makers to develop new ways of thinking and acting in order to be effective (Duignan, 1987a, p. 7). They must be able first to appreciate this complexity and uncertainty and respond by applying multiple theories, perspectives and frames to their decisions (Bolman and Deal, pp. 4–7). It is more likely that such multiple perspectives and frames will be applied to decision-making in education if different groups, especially those with a direct interest in education, are involved in the making of these decisions.

Estler (1988), in her insightful analysis of different decision frames, supports this point of view. She argues that the specific mix of problems, choices and participants related to a decision situation will greatly influence the nature of the decision made. She concludes that a consideration of the specific circumstances — the setting — related to a decision does not 'fit easily into any of the rational perspectives on decision making' (Estler, 1988, p. 311). Consistent with a post-rational, organized-anarchy view of decision-making (March, 1982; Weick, 1982), she argues for 'a conceptual leap from the assumption that decision-making is a process for achieving goals [an assumption central to rational approaches to decision-making] to one in which decision-making is often a process only loosely connected to organizational outcomes or individual intention' (p. 312). These ideas, Estler points out, form the background for a contextual model of choice to describe decision-making under conditions of ambiguity in goals, technology and participation — labelled a 'garbage-can model' by Cohen, March and Olsen (1972). The challenge to the traditional, rational, top-down model in which most important decisions were made by central bureaucrats has helped promote a more participatory, democratic approach to educational decision-making.

A second major argument in the developing rationale for school-based decision-making, derived from 'arguments from theory of knowledge, control theory and economics' (Evers, 1990), stresses the 'fallibility' of decisions of hierarchical, centralized decision structures. Evers (1990) argues that there are good grounds for preferring less hierarchical and more decentralized decision structures in education. He believes that a top-down, hierarchical view of decision-making places too great a premium on the initial correctness of decisions. Such a one-way approach to decision-making can, he suggests, be seriously affected by error. Evers promotes an adaptive view of organizational learning, with the provision of feedback loops for at least a sampling of those affected or likely to be most affected by decisions, and for the correction of errors of knowledge and judgment in decision situations.

Evers argues that where knowledge is reckoned as fallible (and most natural learning systems are based on this premise), 'there is nothing out of the ordinary in a design which confers, at its strongest, de facto veto over the outputs of centralized decision-making.' In supporting a move toward more decentralized school-based decision-making, Evers suggests that 'organizations which instantiate in their structure a basic learning design would, over time, become more efficient decision makers.'

There is an extensive literature which supports the notion of greater involvement in educational decision-making at school and community levels. Few, if any, in education argue against such a common-sense idea.

Yet a number of problems, tensions and constraints are evident in the practice of school-based decision-making. These are the focus of the discussion in the next section of this chapter.

Problems, Tensions, Constraints in the Practice of School-based Decision-making

Implicit in most views of participatory democracy seems to be a claim that such an approach to decision-making is in some way superior to centralized approaches. What evidence exists for such claims? Estler (1988, p. 309), in her review of research on participatory decision-making, concludes that 'reviews of research related specifically to the relationship between participation and decision outcomes consistently note ambiguity and non-support for related hypotheses.' She points out that the 'weakness of positive results when found and of methodological questions related to much of the research leave many questions related to the effects of participation still very much in need of further research.' Her main conclusion, however, is that the benefits of participation may derive not from 'direct effects on decision outcomes but in indirect effects associated with morale and satisfaction.'

Evers (1990) concludes that on current evidence the justification of internal participation in schools (teacher and students) 'is modest at best'. Reviewing the work of Locke and Schweiger (1979), who drew their conclusions from research in mostly non-educational organizations, Evers reports one of their major findings: 'there is no evidence that participation in decision-making is superior to more directive methods in increasing productivity.'

A key factor in the decision process is the knowledge possessed by participants. Processes that lead to a reduction in knowledge error should improve the quality of decisions. Evers (1990) concurs with Chapman's (1990) conclusion from her review of literature that 'in the long term, at least, there may be a direct positive relationship between increased school-based decision-making and improvements in educational outcomes.' Based on her analysis of research findings, Chapman argues that through participation 'increased information, knowledge and creativity [are] brought to bear on decision-making', as well as 'increased feelings of trust, an increased sense of control [by participants] and greater commitment' by those who have to implement the decision.

Most research to date has focused on the effects of internal (teacher and student) participation in decision-making at school level. There is a need for more research which focuses as well on the external participation by community representatives in educational decision-making.

While the direct positive benefits of school-based decision-making are difficult to discern, some negative effects have been reported. Chapman (1990) reports that even teachers who are not satisfied with the quality of decisions in their school perceive the costs of involvement to be too great and, as a consequence, consciously opt out of the decision processes. Usually, teachers will not involve themselves in the decision procedures of their school if such involvement detracts from their teaching. Chapman (1990) concludes that an immediate cost of teacher involvement is time. Teachers have to balance their time commitments among administration, teaching and personal life, and the increased time demand of involvement in decision-making 'has contributed to increased tiredness and stress which in turn has affected classroom practice and attendance.' Estler (1988, p. 309), in her analysis of the findings of Firestone's (1977) study, argues that the unique distribution of time and skills between administrators and teachers is a barrier to teacher participation in decision-making.

Blackmore (1990) sees a more sinister outcome for teachers of present practices of democratic participation which she perceives as having been appropriated for centralist and corporate purposes. She argues that the trend towards the increased representation of teachers, students and parents 'in the name of the democratic process' has, in certain instances, worked against the collective interests of teachers because it commits them to a decision-making process, and the outcome of that process, 'which appears to be participative and democratic, but which often produces unfavourable and undemocratic outcomes, as in the case of many school closures and amalgamations.'

Teachers for various reasons, especially those related to benefits for teaching and time costs, may find it difficult to participate fully in school-based decision-making. The school community may also be confronted with barriers to participation.

Seddon *et al.* (1990) argue that the politics of participation in school-based decision-making are influenced by relationships in the broader society. While parents form a constituency with direct concern for their children's education, there are some parents who, for various reasons, fail to take a political stance and are excluded from participation. The representative nature of participation in school-based decision-making assumes common interests and aspirations among parents of a school. According to Seddon *et al.* this 'homogenized view' of a school community's needs and interests presents a view of parents and community which overlooks major social and cultural differences, even antagonisms. Such representative democracy is not likely to serve the intention of broad participation in educational policy and decision-making. Rizvi (1987, p. 26) agrees:

> The problem with the Victorian experiment [with decentralization of decision-making in education] is that not only have powers given to the school councils been restricted by numerous sets of central guidelines but also the participation on the so called 'representative' councils has been confined to the same few, who happen to be mostly male and anglo-celtic.

This view was supported by the Deakin University study (1984) of attempts at devolution in Victoria up to 1984. The Deakin study (1984) also highlights other forces that tend to operate against participatory democracy at the local level. A finding in the study is that participation is costly in terms of community members' time and energy. As well, principals are often regarded by parents as reluctant to share power. Teachers and teacher unions also often attempt to oppose increased participation by parents.

The weaknesses of representative democracy and possible alternatives are discussed at length by Walker (1990). His discussion of a pragmatic theory of interests and of the desirability of direct involvement by a representative sample of those whose legitimate interests are affected by decisions (a system of statistical democracy) within a functionally decentralized system of schooling offers an alternative approach to participation which will be discussed later in this chapter.

School-based decision-making faces a number of obstacles before it can be regarded as fully democratic. One of its greatest tests, however, is the way in which the ideas and discourse of participative democracy are being appropriated by centralists and corporate managerialists (Blackmore, 1990; Duignan, 1987a).

A Return to Centralist Structural and Administrative Arrangements

Blackmore (1990) argues that the divergent discourses and conceptualizations of corporate management and school-based decision-making of the 1970s have tended to converge in the 1980s. She suggests that 'participation is now invoked as a managerialist procedure to obtain greater accountability, e.g., program budgeting.' Emphasis on school-based decision-making is 'thereby connected to managerialist objectives of efficiency and effectiveness at the system level.' Blackmore suggests that in the 1980s the rhetoric of participatory democracy, as it relates to school-based decision-making, has been appropriated by 'corporate logic'.

The tension between centralizing and decentralizing tendencies in educational decision-making has been the subject of much discussion in the literature (Olson, 1970; Bates, 1985; Duignan, 1987a; Caldwell, 1990). Duignan (1987a, p. 15) argues that while the rhetoric of devolution and participation is prevalent in most Australian states, there are counter-balancing forces for, and evidence of, the development of centralist, corporate structures for decision-making (e.g. the establishment of corporate management groups in Victoria and Western Australia). Olson (1970, p. 233) referred to this phenomenon as the 'seeming paradox of simultaneous power centralization and decentralization.'

Bates (1985) also discusses this paradox. He recognizes two 'dominant metaphors' in the debate that accompanied the early attempts at reforming the Victorian education system (prior to 1982). On the one hand, the rhetoric was for increased community participation and control and, on the other hand, for corporate management. He argues (1985, p. 289) that this situation constituted a 'confusion of incompatible political myths', a type of 'ideological schizophrenia' (Duignan, 1987a, p. 18). In pointing to the inherent conflict in ideologies, Bates (1985, p. 298) states:

> The related modes of political authority are clear: on the one hand notions of participatory democracy, and on the other hand of representative democracy. The forms of administration are clear: on the one hand a devolved system of decision making, and on the other a decentralized system of control. The interests to be served by either model are clear: on the one hand those of the local community, and on the other those of a dominant oligarchy.

Why then, despite a strong push for the democratization of decision-making in educational systems such as Australia, are there emerging even more powerful counter-balancing forces?

The first reason is that devolution is often conceived of in centralist terms. The terms 'decentralization' and 'devolution' are often used synonymously. Beare (1986, p. 22) points out that within the frameworks of educational bureaucracies both terms are confused and are operationalized through the 'formal handing over of power from a superior office or officer to one lower down in the hierarchy.' In practice devolution is usually conceived of in bureaucratic, hierarchical terms: tiers of authority, status, hierarchy, rules and regulations. Even in the Victorian restructuring experiment, which attempted to promote devolution, collaboration and participation, there appear to be strong centralist counter-forces at work to provide a 'better' balance of power distribution. Also, even where policy devolution occurs, for example, curriculum policy responsibility was devolved to school councils in Victoria, administrative frameworks and structures continue to exert centralizing influences. Much of the rationale for such recentralization is based on arguments to do with the locus of responsibility and accountability in a Westminster system and with the need for a ministry of education policy review and evaluation 'with a strong capacity for policy development, policy review and evaluation, and a capacity to implement policy decisions quickly' (The Government Decision on the Report of the Ministry Structures Project Team, 1986).

Second, Bates (1985, pp. 283–4) points out that reform 'can have a distinctly conservative impulse and be directed simply towards a more effective maintenance of the status quo rather than towards significant alternations in the direction and practices of the system under review.' Frazer (1985, p. 253), in his analysis of organizational change in Victorian education, argued, similarly, that 'old behaviour patterns and organizational loyalties can cloud the objectivity and inhibit the creativity of even the most committed agency member.' In attempting to explain why such a 'conservative impulse' reappeared in the context of educational change in Sweden, Wallin (1987, p. 5) places the blame on what he calls the 'lingering rule system'.

Wallin examines what happened when the centralized Swedish education system attempted to devolve decision-making on resource allocation closer to the schools. He observes that when the central rules on resource allocation were abolished, they were not replaced by 'uniform and unambiguous, centrally-determined principles for decision-making at different levels.' Soon there was a call from the local level for direction, stability and 'order'. He likens the decision-making process of allocation to a 'low-pressure area in which air flows in from surrounding high pressure areas' until the pressure gradient is levelled out. One such 'high pressure area' is the old rule system. He concludes that:

> ... remnants of the old steering system survive in the form of structural elements in the organization of work. Old rules, that have been discarded, linger on because they are cornerstones in complex and demanding situations.... The reality of this co-existing, lingering rule system pushes reforms in a conservative direction. In fact, these rules serve to guarantee that no system changes will come about. (Wallin, 1987, p. 4)

Seddon *et al.* (1990) note a 'conservative trajectory' in the restructuring of Victorian education. They note that in the latest restructuring participation 'is to be reduced in scope and "encouraged" only within tighter central guidelines.' They label the restructuring as 'dynamically conservative' rather than 'reformist', and argue that devolution and school-based decision-making is, primarily, 'a policy delivered from the centre to be implemented in a bureaucratically efficient and politically neutral manner.' Seddon *et al.* offer an explanation for this conservative trend. They argue that participation in educational decision-making continued to occur, even after the restructuring, within a historical understanding of 'the nature of education and educational administration, and the roles of education participants.' There was, in fact, little or no change in the goals and values of the underlying school and school system organizations. Bureaucratic structures and bureaucratic rationality continued 'to shape and channel participation in relatively safe directions, practices and arrangements.'

Estler (1988) argues along similar lines. She states that a conservative, bureaucratic rationality persists in educational systems because it serves a largely symbolic function. It provides 'a kind of legitimation' by giving the appearance of rationality to processes necessarily surrounded by ambiguity; it lends meaning to the lives of participants who live in a world valuing rationality; and it provides a sense of order to participants in an environment that is often disorderly.

Estler argued that in many cases it is not the reality of participation that is important but the appearance of participation. Seddon *et al.* (1990) concur when they argue that the apparently neutral and legitimate bureaucratic authority structures within which participation occurs can present a universal discourse, 'speaking for all participants'. This universal discourse constitutes a conservative force 'because it has led to a concern with appropriate consultative processes as much as with the substance of, and the values inherent in, policy.'

Perhaps a more realistic appraisal of the apparently conservative trends is that the rhetoric of devolution and local participation, and the excitement of potential participants over new structures, clouded the reality that nothing much had changed, except structural frameworks. In effect, we are not witnessing a return to conservatism but merely a continuation of it. Broadfoot (1985, p. 108) is convinced that if all that is delivered in a restructuring is administrative devolution, rather than a real transfer of power to make policy decisions, the result could well be more, rather than less, central control, as the location of control may be less important than the strength of control. In other words, decentralized control need not mean weaker control. So-called decentralized systems do not necessarily allow more grass roots autonomy. Through administrative devolution, 'the administrative function becomes more efficient at the local level.' Taking recent educational examples of decentralization in France, Broadfoot (1985, p. 117) argues that these attempts at decentralization have been 'more than compensated for by the increased efficiency of the local administration of the education service through widespread use of centrally-provided computer packages which both collect detailed data on individual schools and help in the various administrative tasks of finance, staffing and schooling organizations.' Such detailed local information provides central bureaucrats with a clearer picture than ever before of the whole education system.

The conservatism of educational systems may also reflect the strengthening in our society of a technicist administrative ideology which finds its expression in corporate management techniques (Broadfoot, 1985; Blackmore, 1990). Common political, social and economic problems in most industrialized Western countries — e.g. financial stringency, structural unemployment, low productivity, breakdown in traditional values and relationships — are prompting similar educational arrangements in all these countries, such as 'the provision of a more technocratic and vocationally-oriented, bureaucratically efficient education system' (Broadfoot, 1985, p. 115). Such technocratic ideology is being championed by centralist bureaucrats who find it more comforting to legitimate policy decisions in terms of objective, rational decision-making processes. Devolution, in such a context, is an illusion.

It would appear, therefore, that there are powerful forces working against a fuller realization in practice of school-based decision-making and management. What, then, is the likely future of school-based decision-making and management? What can be done to help realize greater democratic participation in, and more local control of, educational decision-making?

School-based Decision-making and Management: Suggestions for a Brighter Future

The suggestions and recommendations in this section are derived from (1) ideas presented by authors in this book, (2) discussions conducted at the Conference on School-based Decision-making and Management held in Victoria, Australia which inspired this book, and (3) the author's own research and experience in educational systems. The recommendations constitute a set of interrelated propositions which should be regarded as an overall framework for enhancing the effectiveness of educational decision-making at the school level.

A New Epistemology of Practice Is Required

The dominant epistemology of practice — technical rationality based on a positivistic philosophy — must be challenged and replaced if effective school-based decision-making is to become a reality. This epistemology assumes a world that is relatively certain and substantially rational and linear in which ends are given; needs can be identified; goals provide direction; effectiveness can be measured; power can be understood and used to achieve established goals; decisions are made by choosing the best alternative; people and groups behave rationally in attempting to further their own self-interests; and hierarchical structures and linear management techniques (e.g. management by objectives, programmed budgeting) are the most efficient ways of controlling and coordinating the behaviour of people in organizations (Bolman and Deal, 1985, pp. 148–9).

In a world that departs significantly from the traditional notions of technical rationality — a world of complexity, uncertainty, instability and uniqueness — there is a need for a more coherent and holistic epistemology or 'frame' that is based on a different set of assumptions about the nature of organizations and organizational behaviour. A cultural or symbolic frame copes better with the dynamics of such complexity and uncertainty in organizational life. Bolman and Deal (1984, p. 150) make this point rather forcefully:

> The symbolic frame is most applicable in organizations with unclear goals and uncertain technologies. In such organizations, ambiguity is everywhere. Who has power? What is success? Was a decision made? What are the goals? The answers to such questions are often veiled in a fog of uncertainty. . . . The symbolic frame sees the rush of organizational life as more fluid than linear. Organizations function like complex, constantly changing, elastic pinball machines. Decisions, actors, plans, and issues continuously carom through a labyrinth of cushions, barriers, and traps. Managers who turn to Peter Drucker's *The Effective Executive* for guidance might do better to study Lewis Carroll's *Through the Looking-Glass.*

The cultural frame helps focus attention on the subjective and interpretive aspects of organizational life (Jekinek *et al.*, 1983). It provides a clearer understanding of the process of decision-making in a context of ambiguity, and competing values and interests. Various participants representing different interests within a school community will bargain for their particular position. The decision process becomes sharply interactive

(Cohen *et al.*, 1972). The cultural frame better accommodates the complex contextual reality of decision processes than the traditional rational bureaucratic frame. It also fits better with the assumptions underlying the remaining recommendations in this section. In fact, it provides a partial conceptual framework for them.

Organizations as Learning Systems

The organization's learning system — the way knowledge is generated and cumulatively built up in the organization — can also either promote or inhibit growth and development within an organization. Kolb (1974, p. 41) argues that 'the most effective learning systems are those that can tolerate differences in perspective' among organizational members. Some organizations have a culture in which criticism, reflection, assessment and negotiation of different value positions are encouraged and cultivated. Other organizations have norms that inhibit such actions. Schön (1983) sums up very well the potential positive and negative characteristics of an organizational learning system:

> ... managers live in an organizational system which may promote or inhibit reflection-in-action. Organizational structures are more or less adaptable to new findings, more or less resistant to new tasks. The behavioral world of the organization, the characteristic pattern of interpersonal relations, is more or less open to reciprocal reflection-in-action — to the surfacing of negative information, the working out of conflicting views, and the public airing of organizational dilemmas. Insofar as organizational structure and behavioral world condition organizational inquiry, they make up what I will call the 'learning system' of the organization. The source and direction of a manager's reflection-in-action are strongly influenced, and may be severely limited, by the learning system of the organization. (Schön, 1983, p. 242)

Effective school-based decision-making requires organizational learning systems that encourage reflection, criticism, assessment and negotiation. Educational leaders must help to create the conditions within which such processes can occur. They must become 'agents of organizational learning' (Schön, 1983, p. 165). They must try to build a culture in which all organizational members can appreciate the possibilities for change and contribute their talents in bringing about desirable change.

As stated earlier, Evers (1990) also argues for education systems and institutions to become adaptive learning systems with 'double loop learning' features, because top-down learning and decision structures can be seriously affected by errors in knowledge. In double-loop learning conditions, 'goals, aims, objectives, values, in fact all knowledge that figures in the making of a decision [as well as judgments], is subject to revision through error elimination.' A participative approach, where participants in the decision process test their knowledge and judgments in an open learning environment using adaptive learning strategies, is likely to promote more efficient decision-making.

A Need for Educative Leadership

Consistent with the view of a school or school system as a learning system is a notion of educational leadership which is primarily 'educative' in intent and outcome. Duignan and Macpherson (1987) argue that, by using a cultural and value-based paradigm, leadership can be viewed as essentially educative in nature and process. They envisage an educative leader as one who challenges others to participate in the visionary activity of identifying what is worthwhile, what is worth doing and preferred ways of doing and acting in education. Such leaders encourage others to commit themselves to educational and professional practices that are, by their nature, educative. Duignan and Macpherson believe, as Fay (1975) has argued, that theory can change practice through an educative role. Fay argues that through an educative process theory can help broaden the horizons of practitioners by increasing their self-consciousness of the conditions in which they find themselves. It is an 'enlightening' process which helps people to see the opportunities for change and to break the bonds imposed by habitual ways of knowing and doing (e.g. rational bureaucratic thinking). It can empower people.

Foster (1986, p. 21) holds a similar view of leadership. He argues that leadership involves being critically educative. In his view critical education involves 'the notion of power, but not "power over" but "power to".' He argues that 'the leader ... must have intellectual power-to-analyse and power-to-criticise, and dialogic power to present. The educative use of power is realized in the empowerment of followers, which provides the actors themselves with insight and reflection into the conditions of their existence and into the possibilities for change.' Enabling the possibilities for change is at the heart of any leadership activity. Through critical analysis, negotiation and compromise, the dialectic of leadership can become 'educative', thereby making all organizational members aware of the possibilities in organizational life.

Leadership is 'educative' in another sense as well. Evers (1987) argues that an educative leader is one who creates, promotes and applies knowledge. The leader is also learning (Northfield, 1987); through reflection, experimentation and feedback leaders learn about what will and will not work in specific situations. In this way they develop their professional artistry and become adept at dealing with 'messy' and uncertain situations.

Educative leaders help re-create the structures and conditions in which others can learn, grow and develop a sense of their own importance. Such leadership should help everybody within an organization to be 'somebody'. It should help reduce feelings of anonymity and impotence and help develop a sense of the possible. It should allow organizational members 'to dream the impossible dream'; to see opportunities and potential in the routine and mundane; to cultivate the art-of-the-possible (Duignan, 1987b).

Educative leaders help promote adaptive learning strategies and positive organizational learning systems. They regard situations of value and interest conflict as 'normal'. Above all they encourage participation, believing that it is their obligation to draw out the talents of all those who are part of the school community. They help build a positive school culture within which such participation is valued (Duignan, 1987c).

A Need for New Approaches to Representative Democracy

As stated earlier, there are constraints on full participation by a school's community in the decision processes of its school. A major constraint in most school contexts is the narrow representative nature of participation, with limited or no opportunities for some community members, including parents, to take part in the process.

If, as Evers (1990) suggests, it is desirable that knowledge claims and judgments should be tested and corrected through the use of feedback loops from those most affected or likely to be affected by decisions, then Walker's (1990) ideas of 'statistical democracy' and a 'theory of interests' are to be commended. He argues:

> (1) that everyone with a legitimate interest in a decision has a right to representation in respect of that decision, ... (2) that only those with a legitimate interest in a decision have a right to representation in respect of that decision ... [and] (3) that those with legitimate direct interests in a decision should have majority representation with respect to the decision.

Those with legitimate direct interests are students, to be represented, perhaps, by their parents. Accepting that parents have a legitimate interest in decisions affecting their children, how can these interests be most effectively represented? Within existing democratic structures 'representatives' may not be representative of all legitimate interests, or, as Walker (1990) points out, they may 'develop their own particular interests.' Walker (1990), drawing on the ideas of Burnheim (1985), proposes a solution to the weaknesses of present practice in representative democracy. Under a system of what he calls 'statistical democracy', decision-makers would constitute 'a representative sample of those whose legitimate interests are affected by their decisions.' He proposes (p. 9) that using this system:

> All individuals with legitimate interests would have an equal opportunity for nominating and being selected as a representative. Individuals selected at random from the nominees, and given strictly limited tenure of office, would have little incentive to do other than to promote the interests they represent. They would be more likely than career politicians to be in tune with the needs and views of those of whom they are statistically representative.

Walker also argues that such a system of representation would be most effective in a functionally decentralized educational system where those with a direct legitimate interest in an educational function (e.g. educating the disadvantaged) would have an equal opportunity to represent these interests at a state level (not just in a geographical area). Walker's ideas are both appealing and practical for those who are disillusioned with many of the shortcomings of school-based decision-making which have been discussed earlier in this chapter and in some previous chapters.

Need for a Reappraisal of Accountability

Accountability procedures in education have traditionally followed a top-down, rational, bureaucratic model. Rizvi (1990) reports that the designers of the Participation and Equity Program (PEP) in the state of Victoria questioned, from the outset, 'how a hierarchical accountability mechanism, even if such a thing could be devised, could ever promote learning and be an instrument of improving educational quality.' The designers of PEP rejected the notion of direct hierarchical accountability and decided to search for an accountability system that was sensitive to local priorities and circumstances while at the same time adhering to the framework of a set of centrally established broad guidelines (the program was required to provide a statement of its purposes, structure and activities to the state government and the Commonwealth Schools Commission). The solution that was adopted, despite its shortcomings, deserves careful consideration by those who are searching for viable alternatives to hierarchical (vertical) accountability mechanisms.

Rizvi (1990) reports that it was argued by the program designers that because PEP was committed to all members of a school's community having direct access to the decision-making processes, they should create accountability mechanisms that would allow discussion, negotiation and feedback at the local level. Program designers decided to adopt a horizontal rather than a vertical approach to accountability. This was a type of peer accountability which emphasized accountability 'to school communities, to parents and students, rather than to central committee or an educational bureaucracy.'

The program designers created Schools Reference Groups (SRGs) within a geographical area made up of representatives from three to seven school communities. The structure of SRGs created 'conditions necessary for "horizontal accountability" by allowing peers from participating schools to discuss proposals and to offer criticism and advice.' Through a process of what Rizvi refers to as 'the sharing of learning through collaborative reflection' a type of 'responsible accountability' was achieved. Rizvi eloquently sums up the major strength of the SRGs and the notion of horizontal accountability when he states that:

> The SRG strategy represented a fresh way of looking at the issue, one that cut across the hoary dichotomy between school autonomy and centralized control. It placed school learning at the centre of reform efforts and developed a mechanism that viewed accountability as a two-way process in which educational criteria played a dominant part.

It would appear that Rizvi's idea of horizontal accountability is compatible with, and complements, the idea of schools as learning systems, educative leadership, statistical democracy and theory of interest discussed earlier.

Need for School-based Decision-making to Be Curriculum- and Client-Driven

Some authors in this book have argued that school-based decision-making and management should be curriculum- and client-driven (e.g.

Caldwell, Spinks, Sturman, Walker). Walker justifies his student-focused, school-based decision-making with his theory of interest which identifies students and parents as having a legitimate direct interest in the decisions that affect them. Sturman (1990) argues that 'the ultimate value of administrative change should be measured in its effects upon the education that students receive'; therefore, 'a study of curriculum decision-making and the effects are of prime importance.' However, Spinks offers the strongest argument for a curriculum, client-based approach. He argues that 'the effectiveness of any organization or institution is not only a product of its knowledge and expertise but also its skill in delivering that knowledge and expertise to the client and to the benefit of the client.' A school-based approach to curriculum decision-making, according to Spinks, enables schools to change more quickly to meet the emerging needs of the students. A requirement for such local curriculum control is the need for the school to control vital resources. The focus of school-based decision-making should be learning and teaching with resources seen as a key support. Spinks argues that for such a responsive approach to learning and curriculum to operate efficiently 'there must be local control and responsibility for resources.' Only with such control can schools match resource use to curriculum priorities for the benefit of students.

If central bureaucracies are to 'hand over' such resources to schools, then a new epistemology of practice, with new ways of thinking about participation, accountability and educational leadership, is required. Otherwise, as Broadfoot has argued (1985, pp. 107–8), only the location of bureaucratic control will change. There will be an administrative change but no real shift of power to the school and community.

There is need for a changed conception of educational leadership at the school level to promote curriculum- and client-driven decision-making. Spinks advocates an educational leadership role for the school principal who is primarily responsible for 'effectively delivering learning programs to students through the best use of resources available.' He points out that many of the problems that arise in our education systems and schools result from viewing educational leadership and resource management as distinctly different roles. This point of view is strongly supported by Duignan (1988, p. 3), who argues that 'the maintenance of a distinction between leadership and management functions at the conceptual and/or practical level is counterproductive to our search for a practical theory of educational leadership.' Like Spinks, he advocates an educative leadership role for the effective school principal.

Conclusion

Education systems in many countries have moved, in varying degrees, from the highly centralized systems of the past. Yet there is still a long way to go before a truly decentralized and developed system is achieved. The desire for participative democracy in educational decision-making is strong in many countries, but there are still obstacles and frustrations for those wishing to be involved. Indeed, there is evidence that we are in a period when the forces for centralism are again mobilizing. What is to be done? Perhaps the final statement should come from a poet.

> The last word on how we may live or die
> Rests today with such quiet
> Men, working too hard in rooms that are too big
> Reducing to figures
> What is the matter, what is to be done.

> (W.H. Auden, 'The Managers')

References

BATES, R.J. (1985) 'The Socio-political Context of Administrative Change,' in FRAZER, M., DUNSTAN, J. and CREED, P. (Eds), *Perspectives on Organizational Change*. Melbourne: Longman Cheshire.

BEARE, H. (1986) 'Conflicts in School Goverance,' Paper presented at the Jubilee Conference in Educational Administration, Armidale, New South Wales.

BOLMAN, L.G. and DEAL, T.E. (1984) *Modern Approaches to Understanding and Managing Organizations*. San Francisco, Calif.: Jossey Bass.

BLACKMORE, J. (1990) 'School-based Decision-making and Teacher Unions: The Appropriation of a Discourse,' in CHAPMAN, J.D. (Ed.), *School-based Decision-making and Management*. Lewes: Falmer Press.

BROADFOOT, P. (1985) 'Towards Conformity: Educational Control and the Growth of Corporate Management in England and France,' in LAUGLO, J. and McLEAN, M. (Eds), *The Control of Education*. London: Heinemann.

BUTTS, R.F. (1955) *Assumptions Underlying Australian Education*. Melbourne: Australian Council for Educational Research.

CALDWELL, B. (1990) 'School-based Decision-making and Management: International Developments,' in CHAPMAN, J.D. (Ed.), *School-based Decision-making and Management*. Lewes: Falmer Press.

CHAPMAN, J. (1988) 'Decentralization, Devolution and the Teacher,' *Journal of Educational Administration*.

CHAPMAN, J. (1990) 'School-based Decision-making and Management: Implications for School Personnel,' in CHAPMAN, J.D. (Ed.), *School-based Decision-making and Management*. Lewes: Falmer Press.

COHEN, M.D. and MARCH, J.G. (1974) *Leadership and Ambiguity*. New York: McGraw-Hill.

COHEN, M.D., MARCH, J.G. and OLSEN, J.P. (1972) 'A Garbage Can Model of Organizational Choice,' *Administrative Science Quarterly*, 17, 1–25.

DEAKIN INSTITUTE FOR STUDIES IN EDUCATION (1984) *Restructuring Victorian Education: Current Issues*. Geelong: Deakin University.

DUIGNAN, P. (1987a) 'The Politicisation of Administrative Reform in Australia,' Paper presented at the British Educational Management and Administration Society Annual Conference, Southampton, 11–13 September.

DUIGNAN, P. (1987b) 'The Challenge of Leadership: Empowering Self and Others,' *The Educational Administrator*, 29, 3–16.

DUIGNAN, P. (1987c) 'Leaders as Culture Builders,' *Unicorn*, 13, 4, 208–13.

DUIGNAN, P. (1988) 'Reflective Management: The Key to Quality Leadership,' *International Journal of Educational Management*, 2, 2, 3–12.

DUIGNAN, P. and MACPHERSON, R.J.S. (1987) 'The Educative Leadership Project,' *Educational Administration and Management*, 15, 49–62.

ESTLER, S. (1988) 'Decision Making,' in BOYAN, N.J. (Ed.), *Handbook of Research on Educational Administration* pp. 305–19. New York: Longman.

EVERS, C.W. (1987) 'Ethics and Ethical Theory in Educative Leadership,' in EVERS, C.W. (Ed.), *Moral Theory for Educative Leadership*. Melbourne: Ministry of Education.

EVERS, C.W. (1990) 'Schooling, Organizational Learning and Efficiency in the Growth of Knowledge,' in CHAPMAN, J.D. (Ed.), *School-Based Decision-making and Management*. Lewes: Falmer Press.

FAY, B. (1975) *Social Theory and Political Practice*. London: Allen and Unwin.

FIRESTONE, W.A. (1977) 'Participation and Influence in the Planning of Educational Change,' *Journal of Applied Behavioral Science*, 13, 2, 167–87.

FOSTER, W. (1986) *The Reconstruction of Leadership*. Geelong: Deakin University Press.

FRAZER, M. (1985) 'Designing Detailed Organizational Change,' in FRAZER, M., DUNSTAN, J., and CREED, P. (Eds), *Perspectives on Organizational Change*. Melbourne: Longman Cheshire.

GARMS, W.I., GUTHRIE, J.W. and PIERCE, L.C. (1978) *School Finance: The Economics and Politics of Public Education*. Englewood Cliffs, N.J.: Prentice-Hall.

Government Decision on the Report of the Ministry Structures Project Team (1986). Melbourne: Ministry of Education.

JELLINEK, M.L., SMIRCICH, L. and HIRCH, P. (1983) 'Introduction: A Code of Many Colours,' *Administrative Science Quarterly*, 28, 331–8.

KALLOS, D. and LUNDGREN, U. (1979) 'The Study of Curriculum as a Pedagogical Problem,' in *Curriculum as a Pedagogical Problem*. Stockholm: GWK Gleerup.

KARMEL REPORT (1973) *Schools in Australia*. Canberra.

KIRNER, J. (1985) 'Organizational Change in Education: The Parent Line,' in FRAZER, M., DUNSTAN, J. and CREED, P. (Eds), *Perspectives on Organizational Change*. Melbourne: Longman Cheshire.

KOLB, D.A. (1974) 'Learning and Problem Solving,' in KOLB, D.A., RUBIN, I.A. and McINTYRE, J.M. (Eds), *Organizational Psychology*, 2nd ed. London: Prentice-Hall.

LOCKE, E. and SCHWEIGER, O. (1979) 'Participation in Decision-Making: One More Look,' *Research in Organizational Behavior*, 1, 265–339.

MARCH, J.G. (1982) 'Emerging Developments in the Study of Organizations,' *Review of Higher Education*, 6, 1, 1–18.

NEW SOUTH WALES, DEPARTMENT OF EDUCATION (1987) *A Statement of Corporate Purposes and Goals*. Sydney: Department of Education.

NORTHFIELD, J., et al. (1987) 'Leadership to Promote Quality in Learning,' in NORTHFIELD, J., DUIGNAN, P.A. and MACPHERSON, R.J.S. (Eds), *Leadership for Quality Teaching*. Educative Leadership Monograph Series No. 1. Sydney: Department of Education.

OLSON, M.E. (1970) *Power in Societies*. New York: Macmillan.

QUEENSLAND. DEPARTMENT OF EDUCATION (1985) *Education 2000: Issues and Options for the Future of Education in Queensland*. Brisbane: Department of Education.

RIZVI, F. (1987) 'Multi-culturalism and Educative Leadership,' in F. RIZVI (Ed.), *Educative Leadership in a Multicultural Community*. Sydney: Department of Education.

RIZVI, F. (1990) 'Horizontal Accountability,' in CHAPMAN, J.D. (Ed.), *School-based Decision-making and Management*. Lewes: Falmer Press.

SCHÖN, D. (1983) *The Reflective Practitioner*. New York: Basic Books.

SEDDON, T., ANGUS, L. and POOLE, M. (1990) 'Pressures on the Move to School-based Decision-making and Management,' in CHAPMAN, J.D. (Ed.), *School-based Decision-making and Management*. Lewes: Falmer Press.

SELLECK, R.J.W. (1985) 'The Restructuring: Some Historical Reflections,' in FRAZER, M., DUNSTAN, J. and CREED, P. (Eds), *Perspectives on Organizational Change*. Melbourne: Longman Cheshire.

SPINKS, J.M. (1990) 'Collaborative Decision-making at the School Level,' in CHAPMAN, J.D. (Ed.), *School-based Decision-making and Management*. Lewes: Falmer Press.

STURMAN, A. (1990) 'Curriculum Decision-making at the School Level,' in CHAPMAN, J.D. (Ed.), *School-based Decision-making and Management*. Lewes: Falmer Press.

TASMANIA. EDUCATION DEPARTMENT (1987) *Secondary Education: The Future*. Hobart: Education Department.

WALKER, J.C. (1990) 'Functional Decentralization and Democratic Control,' in CHAPMAN, J.D. (Ed.) *School-based Decision-making and Management*. Lewes: Falmer Press.

WALLIN, E. (1987) 'A Political and Pedagogical Analysis of the Swedish School Reform,' *AERA Division B Newsletter*, No. 7, April, 1–7.

WEICK, K.E. (1982) 'Administering Education in Loosely Coupled Systems,' *Phi Delta Kappan*, 63, 10, 673–6.

WESTERN AUSTRALIA. MINISTRY OF EDUCATION (1987) *Better Schools for Western Australia: A Program for Improvement*. Perth: Ministry of Education.

Notes on Contributors

Lawrence Angus has worked as Lecturer in Education at Monash University since 1986. Prior to that he taught in state and private schools in South Australia, Victoria and England before joining the Social and Administrative Studies Group at Deakin University in 1983. Dr Angus has a major interest in critical approaches to educational administration and has since 1983 conducted research into educational restructuring in Victoria, Australia.

Jill Blackmore has been Lecturer in Social and Administrative Studies at Deakin University since 1987, following two years of teaching at Monash University. While teaching mathematics, history and general studies for fifteen years in the Victorian state secondary school system, she earned a master's degree in educational studies at Monash University in the history of education, and later an MA in administration and policy analysis and a PhD in history and sociology at Stanford University. Her teaching experience has influenced her current academic research interests in gender relations, teacher unions, school-based decision-making and administration, school-to-work transition, organizational evaluation and the history of education.

Brian Caldwell is Reader in Education and Dean of the Centre for Education at the University of Tasmania. He holds the degrees of BSc and BEd (University of Melbourne) and MEd and PhD (University of Alberta). He has served as a teacher and school administrator in Victoria, Australia, and Alberta, Canada. He is co-author of *The Self-Managing School* (with Jim Spinks) and *Creating an Excellent School* (with Hedley Beare and Ross Millikan). His interest in efforts to restructure schools and school systems spans more than a decade, with research and consultancies in Australia, Canada, New Zealand and Britain. He is currently

Chief Investigator of the Exemplary Schools Study Project under a research grant of the Australian Research Council.

Judith D. Chapman is Director of the School Decision Making and Management Centre within the Faculty of Education, Monash University. After beginning her career teaching in secondary schools in Australia and Europe, she undertook postgraduate study in the United States of America. Since her return to Australia she has undertaken projects on behalf of national and international authorities. She has completed two projects of national significance on educational leadership on behalf of the Australian Commonwealth Government and recently completed work on institutional management in Asia and the Pacific on behalf of UNESCO and decentralization and school improvement on behalf of OECD.

Patrick A. Duignan graduated with a BA and HDipEd from University College Dublin before going to Canada where he started his professional career as a secondary school teacher, later becoming a deputy principal and principal. In Canada he completed BEd, MEd Admin and PhD degrees specializing in educational administration. He was also an Assistant Professor in Educational Administration at Memorial University in Newfoundland, Canada, for two years. In 1979 Dr Duignan took up a position in the Department of Educational Administration, University of New England. In 1988 he took leave from there to establish a postgraduate program in educational management at the New Universiti of Brunei Darussalam. Dr Duignan has a distinguished research and publication record in the area of educational administration. He has focused his research efforts on the role and professional development needs of school principals and on effective leadership in educational institutions.

Colin W. Evers is Senior Lecturer in Education at Monash University, with research and teaching interests in three areas of educational studies: philosophy of education, educational research methodology, and educational administration. He holds BA and LittB degrees in philosophy and mathematics, and a PhD from the University of Sydney in philosophy of education. He is co-author of *Knowing Educational Administration* (with G. Lakomski).

John Hattie is Professor of Education and Head of the Department of Education at the University of Western Australia. His main research interests are measurement, statistical analysis, latent trait theory, factor analysis, cognitive processes and self-concept. He has undertaken research projects on performance indicators, assessing school effectiveness and measuring educational outcomes.

Lawrence Ingvarson is Senior Lecturer with the Faculty of Education, Monash University. He has done extensive work in the area of teacher education, including most recently a report to the Commonwealth Schools Commission, Canberra, on 'Professional Development and the Improvement of Schooling: Roles and Responsibilities'.

Gabriele Lakomski is Senior Lecturer in the School of Education at the University of Melbourne where she teaches educational administration and policy studies. Her research interests include theory developments in educational administration, decision-making, policy analysis, epistemology and social and critical theory.

Phillip N. McKenzie is Senior Research Officer at the Australian Council for Educational Research in Melbourne. His major research interest lies in the economics of education, particularly the study of resource allocation in government school systems. Between 1984 and 1989 he was Editor of the *Australian Education Review* series.

Colin J. Marsh is Associate Professor at Murdoch University, Western Australia. He has written extensively about curriculum development and especially school-based decision-making. Recent books include *Spotlight on School Improvement* and *Reconceptualising School-Based Curriculum Development*. He is editor of the journal *Curriculum Perspectives*.

Millicent E. Poole is Professor and Head of the Social, Administrative, Comparative and Policy Studies Group in the Faculty of Education at Monash University. Culture and life possibilities comprise her main areas of interest, especially in relation to adolescent and youth life choices associated with gender, social class and ethnicity. However, she is increasingly concerned with social and economic policy and how this affects education. She is editor of *Australian Journal of Education*, Vice-President of the Australian Council for Educational Research, and a former president of the Australian Association for Research in Education.

Fazal Rizvi is Senior Lecturer in Social and Administrative Studies of Education at Deakin University, Victoria. Before completing his PhD in Philosophy of Education at King's College, University of London, he taught in primary and secondary schools. His research interests include the politics of multiculturalism, problems of democratic reform in educational administration, and social justice and education. He has published widely in these areas, and was the major author of *Dilemmas of Reform: An Overview of the Participation and Equity Program in Victorian Schools.*

Terri Seddon is currently lecturing in sociology at the Faculty of Education, Monash University. Her work includes teaching in the Masters in Educational Policy and Administration program. She is researching educational restructuring in Australia, with particular reference to New South Wales and Victoria. This research builds on, and brings up to date, earlier work which examined educational restructuring between 1900 and the 1930s. She is currently completing a monograph, co-edited with Christine Deer, on post-compulsory curriculum in Australia.

Brian J. Spicer joined the Faculty of Education at Monash University in 1970 after a distinguished career as secondary teacher and college lecturer. Initially appointed as lecturer-in-charge of geographical education, his major interests today lie in the field of educational administration, specifically in the area of curriculum, finance and resource management. He has been involved in numerous research projects since 1972; his most recent study of the 'Changing Assumptions of Australian Education and Their Implications for the Administration of Schools' will be published as a monograph in 1990.

Jim M. Spinks has worked for the Education Department of Tasmania for twenty-six years and for the past sixteen years as a principal. Over the past twelve years he has been involved in developing an approach to school management which is referred to as Collaborative School Management or more recently as School Self-Management. Since 1984 Jim has been working as a consultant in the educational management field throughout Australia and particularly in Victoria where over 1000 schools have adopted the school self-management approach. In 1985, with Brian Caldwell, he co-authored the book, *Policy Making and Planning for School Effectiveness: A Guide to Collaborative School Management*; they have since co-authored a second book, *The Self-Managing School.*

Andrew Sturman was educated at London University. He worked for seven years at the Home Office criminological research unit during which time his research and publications focused on vandalism and community development. Andrew Sturman settled in Australia in 1978 and until 1989 was employed at the Australian Council for Educational Research, where his interests and publications have been in the areas of school organization, transition from school to work, multiculturalism and curriculum decision-making. In July 1989 he took up a position at the Victorian State Board of Education as a policy analyst.

James C. Walker is Senior Lecturer in Social and Policy Studies and Associate Dean of the Faculty of Education at the University of Sydney, where he teaches courses in philosophy of education, educational policy analysis and educational administration. He has published numerous articles on philosophical aspects of educational theory, research and policy, and has conducted empirical research on the subcultures of young people and teachers in relation to secondary schooling and the transition from school to employment, unemployment and tertiary education, reported in his book *Louts and Legends: Male Youth Culture in an Inner City School.*

Index